The Birth of Israel, 1945–1949

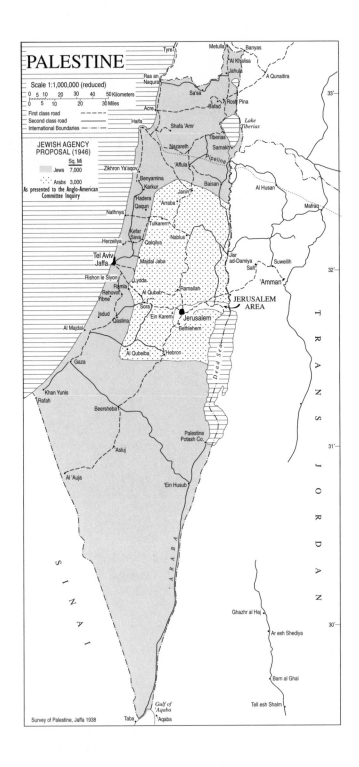

The Birth of Israel, 1945–1949

Ben-Gurion and His Critics

Joseph Heller

University Press of Florida
Gainesville/Tallahassee/Tampa/Boca Raton
Pensacola/Orlando/Miami/Jacksonville

Copyright 2000 by the Board of Regents of the State of Florida
Printed in the United States of America on acid-free paper ∞

All rights reserved

05 04 03 02 01 00   6 5 4 3 2 1

Library of Congress Cataloging-in-Publication Data

Heller, Joseph, 1937–
The birth of Israel, 1945–1949: Ben-Gurion and his critics / Joseph Heller
p. cm.
Includes bibliographical references and index.
ISBN 0-8130-1732-7 (c: alk. paper)
1. Zionism—Palestine—History. 2. Palestine—Politics and government—
1917–1948. 3. Israel-Arab War, 1948–1949—Causes. 4. Ben-Gurion, David,
1886–1973. I. Title.
DS126.4.H44 2000
320.54'095694—dc21   99-24293

Map reproduced by permission of Frank Cass & Co. Ltd. from *Zionism and
Arabism in Palestine and Israel*, edited by E. Kedouri and S. G. Haim.

The University Press of Florida is the scholarly publishing agency for the
State University System of Florida, comprising Florida A&M University,
Florida Atlantic University, Florida International University, Florida State
University, University of Central Florida, University of Florida, Univer-
sity of North Florida, University of South Florida, and University of West
Florida.

University Press of Florida
15 Northwest 15th Street
Gainesville, FL 32611–2079
http://www.upf.com

Contents

Here is also a basic fault in our political life. Any nation can draw a parallel between its external policy and its internal policy. What representatives say for the outside world is meant for the outside world, and is not supposed to become a negotiable commodity in internal life. For us this distinction is almost completely blurred. The external and the internal are in fact one sphere, and what you say for external need has an impact internally. Above all, internally.

Pinchas Lubianiker [Lavon], 15 May 1947, "Clarifying Our Political Situation," *Hapoel Hatza'ir* 19, no. 36 (4 June 1947): 6

Preface

This is the first comprehensive book on the internal decision-making process of the Zionist leadership in Jerusalem in the crucial period of 1945–49. I analyze the policies and methods pursued by the Yishuv leadership in order to achieve a Zionist solution in Palestine. The book covers the period from the end of the Second World War to the armistice agreements that followed Israel's War of Independence. I am not concerned with non-Zionist parties, such as the ultra-Orthodox Agudat Israel and the PKP (Palestine Communist Party), or with Zionist parties in the Diaspora. My basic assumption is that Zionist decision making took place in the Jewish Agency Executive in Jerusalem; in other words, the Yishuv—the pre-1948 Jewish community in Palestine—was the center of policy formulation. Rarely did members of the Executive based in Britain and America question decisions made in Jerusalem.

The alleged failure of world Jewry to rescue European Jewry during the Holocaust gave a psychological and political boost to the Yishuv leadership's claim to represent Jews everywhere as it strove for the establishment of a Jewish state. Yet in this sense the Holocaust was only a catalyst. The thrust for a Jewish state preceded the Holocaust. The Jewish state came into being as a result of the Yishuv's accumulation of power and its exploitation of diplomatic windows of opportunity between 1945 and 1949.

Previously, the subject of this book has been treated from the perspective of diplomatic history, as a function of British-Zionist diplomacy (e.g., M. J. Cohen, *Palestine and the Great Powers 1945–1948*). The innovative aspect here lies in shifting the balance from *Aussenpolitik* to *Innenpolitik;* that is, in viewing the crux of the struggle for the Jewish state not from the more usual external, diplomatic dimension but from the perspective of the domestic political-ideological debate conducted by the Zionist parties in the Yishuv over means and ends. An example of this shift from the external to the internal is Uri Bialer's *Between East and West: Israel's Foreign Policy Orientation 1948–1956.*

By 1945, David Ben-Gurion, the preeminent leader of the Yishuv and the Zionist movement, had become aware that a Jewish state could not emerge without a diplomatic and/or military breakthrough—if the Arabs refused to accept the great powers' decision in favor of a Jewish state. True, Ben-Gurion had already foreseen such a scenario in 1937. Since then, however, the Zionist consensus in the Yishuv had collapsed due to the emergence of an independent radical right and an independent radical left; the revival of activities by a moderate statesman possessing great stature, Chaim Weizmann; and the reappearance on the public stage of binationalist intellectuals headed by Martin Buber and Judah L. Magnes, together with the newly established new immigrants' party, Aliyah Hadashah. It was no accident that since the idea of a Jewish state had become a practical proposition in 1937, Ben-Gurion was fearful about the possibility of civil war in the Yishuv.

The crucial need to unify the polarized Yishuv as a sine qua non prior to a successful political campaign with the British and a military showdown with the Arabs constituted the crucial test case of Ben-Gurion's leadership. Yet, the new consensus could emerge only by convincing old allies, the General Zionists and the national religious parties—this much was a relatively straightforward task—and, more problematic, by reviving old alliances with the radical left and even, albeit temporarily, with the radical right.

Once such a consensus had been achieved at home, a successful *Aussenpolitik* (with the exception of the underground radical right organizations IZL and Lehi in 1946–47 on the British front) could be achieved by inducing the United States, if not actively to support Zionism, at least to refrain from opposing it; and by not alienating the Soviet Union. Only *Innenpolitik* based on controlled activism and resting on a foundation of Jewish immigration and settlement, combined with a policy advocating a Palestine partitioned between Jews and Arabs, could appeal to the great powers. Unlike Benny Morris (*The Birth of the Palestinian Refugee Problem, 1947–1949*), I maintain that the idea of forcibly "transferring" the Palestine Arabs was marginal to the Zionist leadership's doctrinal approach. The main task at hand was to convince the great powers that the only way to address the Arab problem was by the peaceful partition of Palestine, not by a population transfer. Nevertheless, if the approach to the great powers should fail, only war remained as a viable option.

The first Israeli provisional government represented a sweeping consensus. But once the war emergency ended, a permanent government was established that lacked a broad consensus, relying on the National Religious Party and various splinter groups. Still, *Innenpolitik* remained a prime consideration of most Israeli governments both left and right. As Henry Kissinger is reported to have said, Israel has no foreign policy, only domestic policy.

The idea of a Jewish state, the drama unleashed by historical events and processes beginning with the First Aliyah in 1882, and the Balfour Declaration in 1917, had received a tremendous boost by 1945 in view of the universal need to shape a new world order. The Zionists' desperate will, Britain's lack of will to govern, Arab negative policy, and the Great Powers' readiness to accept a Jewish state all played their part in this unique history. The interaction between these diverse schools of thought and the internal and external factors impinging on the Jewish community in Palestine during this brief but crucially formative period is the principal theme of this book.

The General Zionists and the national-religious parties, Mapai's (Mifleget Poale Eretz Israel) partners in the Jewish Agency Executive and in the provisional government, are excluded from this study. The General Zionists lacked a coherent ideological program and were represented in the Jewish Agency by both "hawks" and "doves," as we would say today, though both wings, with the exception of Moshe Sneh, ultimately supported Ben-Gurion. Second, virtually no archival material exists, other than for the marginal group of Ha'oved Hatsioni; the daily *Haboker* did not really represent the General Zionists' opinion, being heavily infiltrated by Revisionist writers.

As for the national-religious groups, Mizrachi and Hapoel Hamizrachi, they espoused a cogent ideology but unfailingly supported Ben-Gurion, perhaps because of their leader Rabbi Fishman's admiration for him. Conceptually, however, they had little to add to the public debate. In other words, the national-religious groups were to all intents and purposes pragmatic, though their daily, *Hatsofeh,* gave substantial place to articles based on a religious-fundamentalist viewpoint. Similarly, the leader of Hapoel Hamizrachi, M. Shapira, was the most loyal adherent of Ben-Gurion's cautious activism on the Jewish Agency Executive (JAE). A symbol of moderation, Shapira was an integrative force in the Executive. Archival material is also scarce for the national-religious parties. On the radical right, I have deliberately omitted Lehi, having published a separate book on that subject.

For the present study I have relied heavily on primary sources taken from a large range of archives, first and foremost the rich Central Zionist Archives (CZA) in Jerusalem, especially the political department series, the Jewish Agency Executive protocols, and the highly interesting private archives. Second in importance were Mapai's archives (or the Labor Party archives), which contain minutes of the sessions of its political committee, its secretariat, councils, and conferences. Mapai's crucial role as the key party in the Zionist struggle makes this archive indispensable for our subject matter. Third, the radical left archives are of great importance (supplemented by its press). Unfortunately, the radical right archives are devoid of any significance, making its press, both the legal and illegal, the only available source. Of the smaller archives, the Weizmann archives are of special value. Translations from these sources are by the author.

Finally, I would like to express my thanks to two institutions at the Hebrew University of Jerusalem, the Davis Institute of International Relations and its current and former directors, Amnon Sela and Sasson Sofer, respectively, and the Eshkol Institute for Research on Israeli Society, the Shein Center and Jacob Metzer, the dean of the Social Sciences Faculty, for generously financing editorial expenses. I owe a special debt of gratitude to my colleagues at the Hebrew University: Professors Jonathan Frankel, Yehoshua Porath, Gideon Shimoni and Avraham Greenbaum. They encouraged me and read all or part of the manuscript, though of course responsibility for the contents is entirely mine. Last, I would like to thank Barry Davis and Ralph Mandel for their exceptional dedication to the editorial aspect of the book. My son Danny deserves special gratitude for his computer expertise. Without him this book would not have been written.

Last but not least, I would like to thank Judy Goffman for her extremely efficient editorial work at the University Press of Florida.

Chronology

2 November 1917	Britain issues the Balfour Declaration supporting a Jewish "national home."
1922	The League of Nations approves the British Mandate for Palestine.
7 July 1937	Royal (Peel) Commission on Palestine recommends partition and the establishment of a Jewish state on one-fifth of the country's territory.
17 May 1939	The British government issues a White Paper limiting Jewish immigration and settlement.
May–November 1942	"Biltmore plan" for a Jewish state approved by a Zionist convention in New York and by the Jewish Agency Executive in Jerusalem.

1945

8 May	End of World War II.
22 May	British Labour Party conference at Blackpool decides on pro-Zionist policy.
31 August	President Truman asks the British government to permit 100,000 Jewish war refugees to enter Palestine.
15 September	The British press reports that the 1939 White Paper policy will continue.
1 October	Ben-Gurion orders the establishment of the United Resistance Movement.
6 October	First clash with the British military.
10 October	Palmach frees 200 illegal immigrants from British transit camp.
31 October–1 November	Resistance Movement sabotages the Palestine railway system.

13 November	British Foreign Minister Bevin announces continuation of White Paper policy and establishment of the Anglo-American Committee on Palestine and Jewish refugees.
23 November	First illegal ship with Jewish survivors captured by British authorities.
25 November	Clashes between Jewish settlers and British military leave eight dead.
27 December	IZL attacks British police stations in Jerusalem and Jaffa.

1946

21 February	Palmach attacks radar stations at Haifa.
February	Anglo-American Committee visits camps of Displaced Persons in Europe.
25 February	IZL and Lehi attack British military airfields.
6 March	Anglo-American Committee arrives in Palestine.
27 March	Clashes between police and Haganah as illegal ship tries to run British blockade.
7 April	Illegal immigrants on hunger strike in Italy, followed by Yishuv leaders' hunger strike.
1 May	Publication of the Report of the Anglo-American Committee of Inquiry.
13 May	Beginning of illegal immigration from Soviet-controlled Romania.
12 June	Bevin repudiates Anglo-American Committee Report.
13 June	Arab League conference in Bludan decides on military assistance to Palestine Arabs.
17 June	Palmach dynamites bridges linking Palestine with neighboring countries.
29 June	"Black Sabbath": British on massive arms search; Yishuv leadership and many Haganah activists arrested.
4 July	Pogrom at Kielce, in Poland, triggers "flight" movement from Poland to the American Zone in Germany.
22 July	91 killed as IZL blows up King David Hotel, headquarters of British administration.
30 July	Publication of Morrison-Grady plan on provincial autonomy in Palestine under British rule and possibility of partition after five years.

5 August	Meeting of Jewish Agency Executive in Paris endorses partition.
12 August	British declare that illegal immigrants will be expelled to Cyprus.
9 September	Opening of London Conference on Palestine with the Arab League states.
4 October	Truman's Yom Kippur declaration on the need for compromise between Zionist and British views on Palestine's future.
6 October	Haganah sponsors overnight establishment of eleven settlements in northern Negev.
5 November	Jewish leaders and activists released from detention by British authorities.
9 December	22nd Zionist Congress opens in Basel.

1947

27 January	Informal talks between British government and Jewish Agency.
31 January	British civilians evacuated from Palestine; security zones established for British military and police.
18 February	Bevin announces referral of Palestine problem to UN following failure of the London Conference.
1 March	IZL bombs British officers' club in Jerusalem, killing twelve people.
31 March	Lehi bombs oil refineries in Haifa.
16 April	British hang four IZL men; two condemned IZL and Lehi members commit suicide.
4 May	Acre prison break-in by IZL to free detained com rades.
14 May	Soviet UN delegate Gromyko declares support for binational state or partition, followed by appointment of special commission on Palestine (UNSCOP).
20 July	Expulsion of *Exodus* with 4,500 refugees on board.
29 July	British hang three IZL members.
1 August	Two British sergeants hanged by IZL.
31 August	UNSCOP Report calls for partition into two states; minority wants federal state.
8 September	*Exodus* disembarks its illegal immigrants in Hamburg, Germany.
26 September	British declare they will withdraw from Palestine on 15 May 1948.

29 November	UN General Assembly passes partition resolution for two states in Palestine.
30 November	Arab attack on Jewish vehicles triggers Israel's War of Independence.

1948

14 January	First arms deal between Haganah and Soviet-controlled Czech government.
10 March	Approval of Haganah plan to occupy Arab-held areas in Palestine.
31 March	Jerusalem under siege by Arab irregular forces.
1 April	First Czech arms shipment arrives; Haganah operation to open the road to Jerusalem.
9 April	IZL and Lehi perpetrate massacre at Arab village of Deir Yasin on outskirts of Jerusalem.
12 April	Greater Zionist Actions Committee sets up People's Administration (Minhelet Ha'am).
13 April	Arab irregulars perpetrate massacre of convoy on its way to Hadassah Hospital on Mount Scopus in Jerusalem.
22 April	Haganah occupies Haifa.
28 April	IZL fails in attempt to capture Jaffa.
13 May	Etzion Bloc falls to Jordan's Arab Legion; Haganah occupies Jaffa.
14 May	Jewish state proclaimed; Ben-Gurion heads provisional government; United States recognizes Israel de facto; Count Bernadotte appointed UN mediator in Palestine.
17 May	Soviet Union recognizes Israel de jure.
30 May	Jewish Quarter in Old City of Jerusalem surrenders to Arab Legion.
31 May	Haganah becomes Israel Defense Forces (IDF).
11 June–9 July	First truce.
22 June	IZL arms ship *Altalena* sunk by IDF, killing eighteen.
28 June	First Bernadotte plan.
17 September	Second truce; Bernadotte assassinated by Lehi.
26 September	Israeli cabinet rejects Ben-Gurion's plan to occupy road to Ramallah and Jericho.
15 October	Israeli counterattack on Egyptian Army leads to IDF's conquest of northern Negev.

1949

7 January	Cease-fire on the southern front.
25 January	Elections to the First Knesset.
24 February	Armistice agreement with Egypt.
8 March	Ben-Gurion's first government excludes both left and right radicals.
23 March	Armistice agreement with Lebanon.
3 April	Armistice agreement with Jordan.
20 July	Armistice agreement with Syria.

Abbreviations

BGA	Moreshet Ben-Gurion Archives, Sde Boker
CAHJP	Central Archives of the History of the Jewish People, Jerusalem
CZA	Central Zionist Archives, Jerusalem
DPFI	Documents on the Foreign Policy of Israel
FRUS	*Foreign Relations of the United States*
HA	Haganah Archives, Tel Aviv
Hatsohar	The Revisionist Zionist Alliance
HHA	Hashomer Hatza'ir Archives, Givat Haviva
Hish	Field Force (Heil Sade)
IDF	Israel Defense Forces
ISA	Israel State Archives, Jerusalem
IZL	Irgun Zvai Leumi (National Military Organization)
JAE	Jewish Agency Executive
JIA	Jabotinsky Institute Archives, Tel Aviv
KMA	Hakibbutz Hameuchad Archives, Efal
Lehi	Lohamei Herut Israel (Israel Freedom Fighters, or Stern Gang)
LIA	Lavon Institute Archives, Tel Aviv
LPA	Labor Party Archives, Bet Berl
Maki	Miflaga Komunistit Israelit (Communist Party of Israel)
Mapai	Mifleget Poale Eretz Israel (Labor Party of the Land of Israel)
Mapam	Mifleget Hapoalim Hameuchedet (United Labor Party)
NZO	New Zionist Organization (The Revisionist Movement)
Palmach	Haganah shock troops (Plugot Mahatz)
TJFF	Transjordan Frontier Force
PDD	Political and Diplomatic Documents
PKP	Palestine Communist Party
UNSCOP	United Nations Special Commission on Palestine
WA	Weizmann Archives, Rehovot
WZO	World Zionist Organization

Introduction

In this book I examine the decision-making process in the struggle for independence waged, on the one hand, by the national institutions of the Zionist movement—the Jewish Agency Executive, the Small Zionist Actions Committee, and the Zionist Congress—and, on the other, by the Yishuv's political parties, such as the Mapai Center. The external aspect is considered first: their attitude toward the great powers—the United States and the Soviet Union—and toward the Arab question. This leads to an extensive discussion of the internal ideological debate over the most effective, or, alternatively, the least harmful, methods by which to obtain independence from Britain: Was a political struggle sufficient, or did it have to be combined with, or supplanted by, violence? Moreover, what political solution should Zionism adopt: a partitioned state within borders economically and strategically viable, within a regional federation, or borders reflecting historical and ideological propensities? Or was a binational state preferable—and if so, what would be the most compatible political regime: a federation of national autonomies or functional rather than territorial binationalism?

These questions had to be answered if the Zionist movement was to survive. More often than not, its interests had benefited from cooperation with the British. But after 1945, the onset of the Cold War and the preponderant weight of the Arabs in the Middle East pushed them apart. Zionism now had to integrate itself into the interests of other powers, and such interests certainly existed. Now, in the immediate aftermath of the Holocaust, there was no alternative to a Jewish state, certainly not when the broad range of Zionist forces had become convinced that the existence of a Jewish state before the war could have prevented the Holocaust. In retrospect, many felt that the deliberations over the establishment of a Jewish state in 1937–38 had been a historic opportunity missed. In this postwar period, the leadership was scattered across three continents in three centers: Jerusalem, London, and

New York. Decisions, however, were made exclusively in Jerusalem. Thus the disagreements that arose in discussions held by the leadership in London or New York are not considered here, since the participants there were only the adjuncts of the Jerusalem leadership under Ben-Gurion. Personalities such as Chaim Weizmann and Abba Hillel Silver had to accept decisions even if they objected to them. Within a short span of time, and particularly after the proclamation of the state, the concentration of the decision-making process in the hands of one personality, a kind of charismatic mediator, became critical because of the weight of the decisions involved and the impossibility of deferring them; hence the dramatic character of the struggle for independence.

The idea of a Jewish state had its origins during the waning years of the Ottoman period, antedating the First World War. However, the prospects of obtaining a colonization charter were poor, despite Herzl's endeavors with the Turkish sultan and the German emperor, since the sultan viewed Zionism as one more European attempt to subvert the Ottoman Empire. An initiative by the British government to grant the Zionist movement a colonization charter also failed, due to internal discord within the Zionist movement and London's withdrawal of the plan. The possibility of Jewish settlement under international auspices appeared on the international agenda only within the framework of the postwar new world order that emerged following the collapse of the Ottoman Empire and the redistribution of its territories at the peace conferences of Sèvres and Lausanne. In the meantime, the seeds of the new order, and England's plight in the war, had engendered the Balfour Declaration, which received legal validation when the League of Nations made Britain the Mandatory for Palestine in 1922. The Mandate, which was temporary, charged the British government with the task of preparing the local inhabitants for self-rule.

More specifically, the Mandate's pro-Zionist articles ensured clear-cut British support for the creation of a Jewish "National Home" by encouraging immigration and dense settlement. Until its termination in 1948, then, the Mandate was of crucial importance, as it constituted a kind of promissory note enabling the Zionist movement to accumulate power toward the creation of a state, even though in 1917 the Arabs of Palestine outnumbered the Jews by nearly ten to one. Such, in any event, was the situation at the level of principle; in practice, of course, the Mandate was subject to the vagaries of international developments, which could affect England's ability to realize its commitments not only in Palestine but globally. The upshot was that British policy was caught between the government's undertaking to assist the

Jewish national home and its obligation to encourage the entire population of Palestine, made up largely of Arabs, to advance toward self-rule. Britain's decision in the direction of gradual decolonization enabled the national home to be built at an accelerated pace until the late 1930s, when the pressures of Arab nationalism, exerted against the background of the rise of Italian fascism and Hitler's accession to power, reduced England's ability to pursue its de facto Palestine policy. Still, the narrow crack that remained after the onset of accelerated decolonization (1939) enabled Zionism to go on accumulating power, albeit less intensively, and generated struggles that led Zionism to solicit support from alternative power centers—though these, in the form of the Soviet Union and the United States, would become accessible only after the Second World War.

The process of accumulating and consolidating power—in the form of demographic growth, economic infrastructure, security, and settlement—became the Zionist code of action, to provide the basic infrastructure for a state. The test of the entire Zionist leadership lay in its ability to advance this process in the knowledge that time was running out and that it was essential to exploit to the maximum England's readiness to accept the emergence of the "state-in-the-making" as a process that would promote Palestine's economic independence. However, even though the Zionist movement invested prodigious efforts to raise funds, step up immigration, purchase land, and build a progressive Jewish society based on Western democratic criteria, Weizmann, the architect of the Balfour Declaration and the Mandate, was prevented by a dearth of resources, especially manpower and financing, from bringing into being a substantive infrastructure that would reach the level of critical mass in the first decade of the Mandate. Paradoxically, this missed opportunity served to slow down national resistance by the Arabs and delayed the more severe British restrictions on the Jews. Faced with the bloody events of 1921 and the accompanying political resistance by the Arabs, London still favored a pro-Zionist Mandate, since basically the Arabs were isolated and weak in terms of political power. The Jews, in contrast, were considered entrepreneurs with future potential for the region. The events of 1921 brought about the White Paper of 1922, which referred to a national home in Palestine, rather than to Palestine as the national home, and also severed Transjordan from the Mandate's applicability.

The second decade was more conducive to Zionism, in the wake of Jewish distress in Eastern and Central Europe. However, from the beginning (1929) strong Arab resistance flared up, marked by massacres of Jews in Safed and Hebron. That the Yishuv had good reason to fear the political repercussions of these events and their consequences for the government's interpretation of the Mandate became evident in the White Paper of 1930. However, the threat to immigration and settlement posed by that document (authored by Lord Passfield, the colonial secretary) proved to be only temporary: Zionist pressure and its own weakness led the British government to retract the new policy in the "MacDonald Letter"—but not the pledge to grant self-rule to Palestine's inhabitants. Prime Minister MacDonald's letter was a blow to the Arabs (who referred to it as the "black letter"). Arab terrorism mounted until it reached its peak in the sweeping revolt of 1936.

At the same time, the Zionist leadership was increasingly apprehensive that its ability to accumulate sufficient power to build the national home would be jeopardized. True, between 1922 and 1931 the Jewish population grew from 83,790, or 11 percent of the total population, to 174,606, or 18 percent. However, this increase was not meaningful in terms of creating an economic and political infrastructure. Chaim Arlosoroff, the director of the Jewish Agency's Political Department, gave expression to the mounting concern. As the second decade of the Mandate opened, Arlosoroff was extremely skeptical about Zionism's prospects of building a state by evolutionary means. Regional and international pressures, he argued, would dissuade Britain from continuing to help the Jews build up their strength. Following the granting of independence to Iraq, which was a mandate of the same class as Palestine, Arlosoroff believed the entire mandate system was doomed. He feared moves toward unity in the Arab world, the eruption of a world war against the Soviet Union, and the disintegration of the Zionist idea. It is instructive that Arlosoroff thought that the weakness of the Jewish settlement movement ruled out partition as a viable solution to the conflict between the two peoples. Thus the realization of Zionism, he concluded, required, as a sine qua non, a transition period during which the Jewish minority would rule with an "organized revolutionary government"; he could envisage no other way by which the Jews could achieve a majority or even strike a balance with the Arabs.[1]

History proved Arlosoroff unduly pessimistic (from the Jewish point of view, that is). In practice, Zionism enjoyed three more years in which it could continue to accumulate power to build the national home and achieve an irreversible critical mass. The population leaped from 192,137 at the end of 1932 to 355,157 three years later (the Jewish Agency has slightly higher figures: from 199,600 to 375,400). The turning point was the eruption of the Arab Revolt in 1936, which radically disrupted

Zionism's plans and sharply altered the development of the Palestine question. The government was forced to choose between Jews and Arabs. Until then, the British had deliberately deferred a decision and not given in to the Arabs' demand for self-rule, as this would have sparked a conflict with the Jews. The British Parliament's defeat of the motion to establish a Legislative Council in Palestine was the straw that broke the camel's back where the Arabs were concerned, for it ruled out the possibility that they could veto the development of the national home. More important than this defeat was the Arabs' fear that they would become a minority under the impact of Jewish immigration. As British and French prestige in the region declined, due to Italian aggression in Ethiopia (nearly a quarter of a million Italian soldiers passed through the Suez Canal without interference) and the advance of Syria and Lebanon toward independence, the Palestine Arabs' pent-up national frustration erupted into a general strike and a full-scale revolt against British rule in the country.

How did the Zionist leadership react to this extreme turn of events? Although in practice they were working toward a state, tactical reasons grounded in a sense of caution kept their official policy from raising that demand publicly: such a Zionist initiative would be rejected by the Arabs and would fail to get a sympathetic hearing from the government. Official Zionist policy, then, advocated "parity" between Jews and Arabs in governance and in the meantime enabled the continued accumulation of power. Obviously, parity was not a viable long-term policy, since it implied the creation of a binational state.[2]

Although parity did not receive government legitimization, in the short term Zionism secured government support because the Arab Revolt was directed primarily against British rule. The result was the emergence of an ad hoc partnership, temporary and pragmatic, between Zionism and the government, although already looming on the horizon was the possibility that the British authorities would restrict *aliyah* (Jewish immigration to Palestine/Israel) and would prevent Jews from purchasing Arab land.

The government's support did not affect the shaping of Zionist policy. However, the parity formula was inadequate in the face of the Arab Revolt. A long-term solution was now called for, without resort to tactics of various sorts. Unexpectedly, the situation was saved, from the Zionists' point of view, by the appointment of the Peel Royal Commission. In its historically important report, the commission maintained that the mandate had failed and that Palestine should be divided into a Jewish state and an Arab state, the latter to be linked to Transjordan.

In the event that partition were to be rejected, the commission adduced an alternative proposal: a political maximum for Jewish immigration. Unlike the partition idea, the alternative portended the White Paper of 1939.

Virtually overnight, the policy of the top Zionist leadership did a turnabout: from a tactical advocacy of parity in government between Jews and Arabs to overt support for partition, which had its genesis in the initiative of the Peel Commission. Ben-Gurion, the central figure in the Jewish Agency Executive, the major decision-making body in the Zionist movement, immediately sat down to draft a partition plan of his own, comprising 10.9 million *dunams* (4 dunams = 1 acre) for the Jews, 12.5 million dunams for the Arabs, and 1.9 million dunams set aside for an autonomous Arab area that would also be open to Jewish settlement (the Acre and Gaza districts). Never losing sight of the need to secure international support, Ben-Gurion thought it would be possible to call on the United States and France in this connection—the latter, indeed, had created an ostensible precedent by severing the Alexandretta District from Syria and annexing it to Turkey.[3]

However, what threatened the integrity of the Zionist movement was not Ben-Gurion's plan, which would make do with about half of western Palestine, without Jerusalem, but the Peel Commission's partition plan, which allocated the Jewish state about a fifth of the area. The leadership was inclined to accept the plan, with certain modifications, such as the addition of the New City of Jerusalem, the potash and electricity plants, the Jordan Valley, and perhaps also the Negev as far as Eilat. The acerbic ideological debate that ensued in the Yishuv was not necessarily conducted between right and left; it cut across parties and generated the "Greater Israel" dispute, which rages to this day. A split in the movement was averted thanks to a compromise put forward by Berl Katzenelson and approved by the 22nd Zionist Congress by a vote of 299–160. It empowered the Jewish Agency Executive to conduct negotiations on the establishment of a Jewish state while rejecting the concrete proposal of the Peel Commission.

The debate over partition ended when the British government withdrew its support for that solution at the end of 1937 as the Arab Revolt flared up anew. The crucial lesson that had been learned, by Ben-Gurion especially, was to avoid the emergence of a dispute that bore the potential to split the movement and perhaps even to spark civil war. Ensuring the broadest possible consensus was a major factor in the success of the Zionist movement. In fact, an ideological schism was averted twice: in 1931, when the General Zionists and Hamizrachi made a decision against entering into an alliance with Ze'ev Jabotinsky at the 17th Zionist Congress; and in 1935, with the secession of the Revisionists—who in the past had threatened to drag in their wake the conservative faction of the right-wing General Zionists and Hamizrachi—a historic decision that effectively placed control of the Zionist movement and the Yishuv in the hands of Mapai under Ben-Gurion.

Already in 1933 Mapai had become the largest party in the world Zionist movement, with 44 percent support of the overall Zionist vote, while the weight of the General Zionists declined steadily. Mapai was created in 1930 in a merger between two parties, Achdut Ha'avodah, which defined itself as moderate socialist, and the nonsocialist Hapoel Hatza'ir. Mapai did not suffer a significant decrease in support until 1946, when it fell to 37.5 percent due to the separate appearance of two labor parties that had broken with it: the Le'achdut Ha'avodah movement and Hashomer Hatza'ir. The former advocated Zionist maximalism and political activism, the latter displaying political moderation vis-à-vis the Arabs and a Soviet and Communist orientation externally; both drew their support primarily from kibbutz movements: Hakibbutz Hameuchad and Hakibbutz Ha'artzi, respectively. Nevertheless, already in 1935 Ben-Gurion had formed his coalition in the Jewish Agency with his permanent partners: the General Zionists, who declined from 36.3 percent in 1937 to 31.9 percent in 1946, and Hamizrachi, which maintained a constant strength of about 12 percent. The social and political ideology of these two parties was more amenable to shaping a pragmatic foreign policy. No domestic opposition seriously threatened the massive majority Ben-Gurion enjoyed thanks to this coalition. Mapai could not prevent the departure of labor's radical wing, but that would occur only toward the end of the Second World War.

The lesson of the 1937 partition controversy was that a strong Zionist consensus was necessary, whatever the cost. Hence the use of the state slogan without an attempt to demarcate its borders, at least for public consumption. This was accepted by the coalition parties—moderate left, conservative right, and nonideological religious center—whose partnership enabled the accumulation of power to continue in the difficult period following the termination of the partnership between Zionism and Britain, which until 1936 had been based on the Yishuv's economic ability to absorb Jewish immigration. With the collapse of the Peel plan, the British government adopted the commission's alternative scheme: the ability to absorb immigration according to political criteria. Within three years, that policy, which critically slowed the growth of the national home, was formally grounded in the 1939 White Paper. The new policy might have impelled Zionism to launch a revolt against the government, albeit not while the war on Nazism was being fought, but that scenario was averted in any event because the government permitted the immigration of another 75,000 Jews during the next five years and because the military exploited Zionism's support in the war, which Zionists believed helped to consolidate their power. Between 1939 and 1945 the Jewish population in Palestine increased from 474,000 to 525,000, the number of Jewish settlements rose from 218 to 262, and 40,433 new immigrants arrived, the majority legally, as part of the White Paper quota.

The Arab Revolt made it perfectly clear to the Zionist leadership that the time available for accumulating power was rapidly running out. Ben-Gurion warned his confidants that the Yishuv faced the danger of annihilation—not only disturbances by the Palestine Arabs but a future war involving Arab states such as Iraq and Saudi Arabia.[4]

The conclusion was that the accumulation of power was the critical test for military capability. True, on the eve of the world war the Haganah—the unofficial army of the Yishuv under the command of the Jewish Agency—had expanded from a local to a national force, but it was hardly a modern army. A General Staff had been created, and by the end of the war the Haganah numbered 25,000 men and women, but only 4,609 belonged to the Field Force (acronym Hish) and another 1,488 to the Palmach (acronym for shock troops), forces which were basically paramilitary in character. A larger force, of about 30,000, was assured through enlistment by Yishuv residents in the British Army, and it was the existence of that force, not the Haganah, that persuaded Ben-Gurion that the Yishuv had military potential. In any event, the Haganah had still not become a modern army by the time the Second World War ended; only Israel's War of Independence, in 1948, would bring about the emergence of a true army, with the absorption of the Yishuv's British Army veterans.

The situation was compounded by the fact that the Haganah's strategic planning was based wholly on static defense and, until September 1945, on cooperation with the British authorities. Indeed, until June 1946 the adoption of an active defense against enemy attacks was not even contemplated.

One of the central questions addressed in this book involves the internal political polarization and its interaction with the Yishuv's external policy. The rift itself had begun to appear in the second half of the 1920s, with Ze'ev Jabotinsky's creation of the Revisionist Movement, which was blatantly hostile to labor. The Revisionist Movement evolved into a radical-right political party after failing to incorporate the conservative and religious right within its ranks, and being unable to jettison the maximalist right, which pushed it toward extremism. In its first years, the new party leaned toward the middle class and displayed more of a British orientation than any other party. Its program meant that Britain was to be entrusted with the creation of the Jewish national home. Hence another of its catch phrases, the "Iron Wall," meaning that Arab resistance was accepted as self-evident but that it must be crushed by a Jewish defense force under British command. Throughout the mandatory period, the Revisionists ignored the decolonization processes that had begun to play a part in British policy toward Zionism—they were under the sway of a conceptual dogmatism holding that the Balfour Declaration and the Mandate constituted a sacred and unbreakable moral-legal and political contract.

Jabotinsky's expectation that Britain would bring into being the Jewish state at any price, and on both sides of the Jordan, if only Zionism would demand this by means of unrelenting pressure, naturally caused great dismay in the Zionist movement, since in practice this was not a realistic option, as Weizmann and Ben-Gurion realized. The upshot was an upheaval within the Revisionist Movement itself, when three maximalist intellectuals joined forces: Uri Zvi Greenberg, Abba Achimeir, and Yehoshua H. Yeivin. Influenced by the rise of fascism in Europe, a development with which the latter two, in particular, identified, they led Revisionism in an anti-British direction and counter to the Zionist establishment, which in their eyes was betraying the Zionist idea. Their rift with Jabotinsky, who was seeking a third way between democracy and fascism, reached its crescendo on the eve of Arlosoroff's murder. Only the murder prevented a schism within Revisionism, as it was condemned en bloc by the labor movement for the assassination. Internal and external pressure forced Jabotinsky to resign from the World Zionist Organization. A situation of possible civil war was averted only by an agreement between Ben-Gurion and Jabotinsky that put an end to the mutual political violence and addressed the issues of compulsory arbitration in labor disputes and *aliyah*. The agreement failed to win the necessary endorsements, but it made the two leaders acutely aware that internecine hatred and violence constituted a danger to the very existence of the national home and that deterioration must be prevented even without a formal agreement.

In practice, the scope of the right vs. left confrontation was reduced to a conflict between the Haganah and the Irgun Zvai Leumi (IZL, or Irgun), the National Military Organization; the latter was founded in 1931 as a nonpolitical underground organization by Avraham Tehomi, who accused the Haganah of having failed to protect the Yishuv against the Arab rioters in 1929. In 1937, the Irgun itself underwent a split, some members returning to the Haganah and the remainder forming a Revisionist underground movement under the command of Jabotinsky himself. However, a crisis ensued because of Jabotinsky's refusal to adopt a policy of indiscriminate reprisal against Arabs, a policy which assumed an anti-British character and brought about a split in the Irgun and the establishment of the Lohamei Herut Israel (Lehi), the Israel Freedom Fighters or "Stern Gang." Stern tried to lead his splinter group into an alliance with Italy and Nazi Germany, in the mistaken belief that an anti-British front could be established with the enemies of the Jewish people. Despite his failure, the organization continued to exist as an anti-British underground which resorted to terrorist activities. Indeed, it was revivified on the basis of a new, Soviet orientation and a futile attempt to link up with the Le'Achdut Ha'avodah movement in the Yishuv.[5]

The split in the Irgun paralyzed the organization for four years, until it was reestablished by Menachem Begin in 1944, this time as an anti-British underground determined to fight the White Paper regime that prevented—deliberately, in the Irgun's view—the rescue of Jews from Hitler's clutches. The Irgun's reorganization and its declaration of a "revolt" again nearly ignited a civil war in the Yishuv. Ben-Gurion and the leadership declared war on the Irgun. Their fear was that Begin, by proclaiming a revolt against the British in the midst of the Second World War, was jeopardizing the process of accumulating power, which would soon reach a successful conclusion upon the war's termination, as Churchill had promised Weizmann. The internal conflict was aggravated after Lehi activists assassinated the British Minister Resident in the Middle East, Lord Moyne. Lehi, though, was not the target—it agreed to call off its anti-British terror—but rather the Irgun, the larger underground group. The decision to hand over Irgun personnel to the British Police (the so-called "hunting season") caused a temporary rift within the leadership: the representatives of the General Zionists and Hamizrachi resigned in protest. However, the impact of Ben-Gurion's charismatic personality, against the background of the Holocaust, ruled out any other leadership alternative. The rhetoric of the Irgun, the sole rival for the leadership, lacked a solid foundation.

No potential alternative coalition existed that was ready to take over from the elected official leadership. Certainly there was no alternative program, apart from the Biltmore Plan (addressed later), that called for the establishment of a Jewish state in western Palestine. The Revisionist Movement tacitly admitted its failure by rejoining the World Zionist Organization after the war, though neither it nor its offshoots, the Irgun and Lehi, abandoned their uncompromising demand for a Jewish state on both sides of the Jordan.

The threat from the right was offset by the radical left's readiness to support Ben-Gurion's efforts to eradicate the Irgun politically, in part (Hashomer Hatza'ir) by cooperating with the British, and in part (Le'achdut Ha'avodah movement) by taking independent action. Ben-Gurion would not forgive the Irgun its secession, which jeopardized the drive to accumulate power, until the organization's absolute suppression in the wake of the *Altalena* incident (see chapter 12).

Mapai disagreed deeply with the radical left over the Yishuv's external orientation and the solution to the Palestine question, but these disputes surfaced only at the height of the Second World War, and in any event the radical left represented a minority view. Since 1927, Hashomer Hatza'ir had embraced the Marxist worldview and supported the Soviet Revolution, though rejecting Communism's negative attitude toward Zionism. Mapai's suspicions regarding Hashomer Hatza'ir intensified during the 1930s following Stalin's "great purges" and his ambivalent approach in the period of the Ribbentrop-Molotov accord. That mistrust would metamorphose into a principled dispute with Hashomer Hatza'ir (from 1948 a constituent part of the new Mapam movement—Mifleget Hapoalim Hameuchedet) during the Cold War. Hashomer Hatza'ir's binationalism elicited less suspicion than its pro-Communism, since it was geared toward the indeterminate future and advocated a Jewish majority; the idea was that a binational regime would come into being only after the Arabs forsook feudalism and adopted a progressive approach.

The Le'achdut Ha'avodah movement, on the other hand, did not develop a binational theory; on the contrary, its slogan was a socialist state in the undivided Land of Israel. Opposed to partition, the movement rejected the idea of establishing a state immediately in favor of international supervision over the Mandate. The Le'achdut Ha'avodah movement also displayed considerable sympathy for the Soviet Union and Communism, although not taking this as far as did Hashomer Hatza'ir. However, these differences with the leadership did not generate a total confrontation with the Jewish Agency coalition led by Ben-

Gurion, such as existed with the radical right. The reason was that the moderate left and the radical left were partners in the process of consolidating power, as was most evident in the Histadrut Federation of Labor, the Haganah, and the Va'ad Leumi (the Yishuv's supreme body for internal affairs). In the final analysis, the very existence of the left would have been impossible without the absolute dependence of its kibbutz movements, Hakibbutz Ha'artzi and Hakibbutz Hameuchad, on the budgets of the Yishuv and the Zionist establishment. The fact that its base of support was in the kibbutz movements only underscored that dependence. Resources to meet existential needs—capital, labor, settlement, and *aliyah*—were allocated only in return for "national discipline."[6]

Thus, the national consensus was strengthened by a dual process: the left's dependence on the national institutions—that is, the Jewish Agency Executive, the Va'ad Leumi, and the Histadrut; and the ongoing enfeeblement of the right, which was deprived of crucial resources. Nor was it only the radical right—the Revisionist Movement, the Irgun, and Lehi—that was weakened but the conservative right as well: the General Zionists split between 1931 and 1946 into a moderate faction, the Association of General Zionists, espousing views close to Weizmann's, and a more rightist faction, the Alliance of General Zionists, led by Emil Schmorak and Peretz Bernstein, which opposed Weizmann and Yitzhak Gruenbaum, claiming Gruenbaum was not subject to party discipline. Similarly, the absence of a strong liberal center, apart from Aliyah Hadashah, whose leaders were Felix Rosenblueth and Georg Landauer, also helped produce a potent national consensus. The historic alliance between the conservative right and the labor movement, which had its genesis in the period of Weizmann's dominance in the leadership (1921–31), was accepted even more emphatically in the period of Ben-Gurion's dominance. It was Ben-Gurion who coined the phrase "from a class to a nation" (*mima'amad le'am*), setting it forth as the primary operative code to temper the conflict between "class" and "nation" by affirming that an objective identity of interests, bearing a constructive goal, existed between their needs: building the land by the working class.[7] This policy obligated controlled activism in all spheres—diplomacy, security, settlement, immigration—by means of a constant quest for a balance between prospects and risks.

However, polarization at home and the need to dull its edge as much as possible was only one aspect of the thrust to accumulate power at any price. The second aspect was Zionism's international struggle. At the outset of the war, Zionism exploited the window of opportunity of extensive enlistment by Yishuv residents in the British Army, but it also had to contend with the White Paper, particularly where *aliyah* was concerned. The clashes with the authorities over this issue threatened to torpedo the intelligence and military cooperation with the government. The confrontations reached a dangerous head following the promulgation of the land laws, which prohibited the purchase of land by Jews in most of Palestine; the searches for illegal weapons in the Yishuv's possession; and in particular the scuttling of the *Patria* with its 256 illegal immigrants toward the end of 1940, the expulsion of 1,645 survivors, and the sinking of the *Struma* in early 1942, which claimed the lives of 769 illegal immigrants. Only the cessation of the illegal immigration campaign, because of constraints caused by the war, averted a dangerous escalation between England and the Zionist movement.

The growing difficulties faced by Zionism in its efforts to establish the national home in the wake of the White Paper—before reports of the Holocaust reached the Yishuv—induced the Zionist leadership under Ben-Gurion to try to unite the Jewish people at the height of the war around the Biltmore Plan as the opening move in an international struggle for a state. The Biltmore Plan was three-tiered: opening the gates of Palestine to Jewish immigration; placing control of immigration and settlement in the hands of the Jewish Agency during the transition period; and establishing a Jewish state in Palestine. The only objectors to this plan were the radical left and Ichud, an association of nonparty intellectuals founded by J. L. Magnes, the president of the Hebrew University (the forerunner of Ichud, Brit Shalom, which espoused binationalism, had disbanded in 1933). The left demanded a binational regime and the immigration of two million in a ten-year period, in the formulation of Hashomer Hatza'ir, whereas Ichud called for a binational regime with numerical parity. In fact, there was another objector as well: Chaim Weizmann, who saw Biltmore as a foundation for renewed cooperation with Britain, in contrast to Ben-Gurion, who had despaired of Britain and considered Biltmore a point of departure for cooperation with the United States. The dispute between the two was not ideological but practical: how to conduct the external political game. Ben-Gurion remained faithful to his messianic notion of a one-time transfer operation after the war, in which millions of Jews would be brought to Palestine and would fundamentally alter the demographic balance between Jews and Arabs in the country. Weizmann, though, advocated a slower influx of Jews, based on his pro-British orientation, which would be rendered irrelevant if Ben-Gurion's revolutionary ideas were implemented.[8] This was effectively a theoretical dispute, since the question of orientations could not be decided while the war raged. At another level, though, the dispute was over the optimal method in the anti-British struggle; Weizmann, in contrast to Ben-Gurion, took a dim view of the mounting, Haganah-inspired activism in the Yishuv.

In Ben-Gurion's eyes, the disagreement over Zionist tactics boiled down to the question of the leadership. Already at the time of the presentation of evidence to the Peel Commission, Ben-Gurion said that it would be best if Weizmann were kept away from the political negotiations, as he was liable to begin with a plan for a state but conclude by obtaining land reserves.[9] To Ben-Gurion, Weizmann's willingness to put a temporary stop to *aliyah* even before the arrival of the Peel Commission could mean only one thing: the "utter ruin" of Weizmann's standing in the Zionist movement.[10] Weizmann was not the only one who was distanced from the decision-making center in the late 1930s; the same fate befell the "Group of Five" led by Dr. Magnes, who opposed unlimited aliyah and a partitioned state for fear that it would result in unceasing bloodshed because of the irredentist impulses of both sides in the conflict. The Magnes group's alternative was a Jewish minority of 40 percent. Ichud was formed in 1942, in response to the Biltmore Plan, after the bloody disturbances of 1936–39 had seemed to refute the ideas of its predecessor, Brit Shalom. Besides trying to inculcate the idea of a binational regime within a federative regional framework, Ichud also objected to the anti-British activism being manifested by the opposition parties and by others as well. Regional federation convinced Magnes to agree to numerical parity. This federation would alleviate Arab fears of Jewish domination. If in the late 1930s this group was considered a threat to the idea of a Jewish state, in the 1940s its support for immigration (though only of half a million) and settlement neutralized its opposition to a state. In retrospect, the harm it did to the Zionist consensus was minuscule, as emerges from its denunciation by Albert Hourani, the representative of the Arab national movement, before the Anglo-American Committee (1946) and from the United Nations Special Commission on Palestine (UNSCOP) decision on partition.

Also in the camp of Ichud was Aliyah Hadashah, the party of the German immigrants. They took an anti-activist stance as well, but the question of the constitutional solution to the Palestine question split them into advocates of three viewpoints: binationalism, a cantonal federation, and partition. In short, not only the radical right, out of absolute opposition, and the radical left, out of partial opposition, but also

Weizmann, Ichud, and Aliyah Hadashah sought to challenge Ben-Gurion's conception of controlled activism and partition by supporting Britain and decrying violent activism. Their weakness derived from the impracticability of a British orientation in the light of the decolonization processes.

At the end of the war, as the decisive campaign for the establishment of a state loomed, and following the death of Berl Katzenelson and Eliahu Golomb (the unofficial leader of Haganah), only Moshe Shertok and Moshe Sneh remained at Ben-Gurion's side. Shertok would not be neutralized by Ben-Gurion until the 1950s but in any event represented no more than a corrective to Ben-Gurion's policy, while Sneh neutralized himself by September 1946. Decision making in the period under discussion was thus Ben-Gurion's exclusive prerogative. He should not be thought of as a solitary or isolated statesman but as a charismatic leader who, even before the time for decision arrived, demonstrated to his colleagues in Mapai, the Jewish Agency Executive, and the Histadrut that there was only one decision maker who took calculated risks and reaped successes, based on a belief in Zionist realpolitik and the accumulation of power.

Treatment of the Arab question was another test for the leadership's ability to coordinate between internal and external factors without affecting the consolidation of power. Here, caution had to be exercised in order not to escalate relations with Britain prematurely by agitating the Arabs. A decision on the Arab question was tantamount to a decision on the political solution—which would only be possible after the war, in the context of a new world order. The Palestinians were still licking the wounds they had sustained in the Arab Revolt, while the Arab states were preoccupied with the question of Arab unity. Hence the conviction that there was no need for an initiative on the Arab front, apart from propaganda. In any event, the total conflict between the Jews and Arabs shifted Zionist diplomatic energy toward the Western powers, the United States in particular (and later the Soviet Union as well). Nor was there any point in repeating the well-known slogans about full cooperation and equality of rights or a friendship pact with the Arab states. These would be voiced after the war, and for propaganda purposes only. Dealing with the Arab question, propaganda, and the collection of information was left in the hands of the bureaucracy. This was not a manifestation of realpolitik but a systemic paralysis, owing to the fact that Jewish-Arab relations bore the status of a zero-sum game at both the regional and local levels.

Zionist realpolitik was the product of the intersection of the internal debate in the Yishuv over partition and the use of force with the external pressures to which the Yishuv was subjected. At its core were the following rules of the game: the constant accumulation of power in terms of creating the infrastructure for a state; avoiding the use of non-essential force against the British or the Arabs; and unrelenting efforts to persuade the great powers of the positive contribution of a future Jewish state to regional and international stability, together with the moral argument of Zionism's ultimate justification following the Holocaust. This fusion of restraint, demographic growth, and diplomacy proved its effectiveness, if not toward Britain then toward the United States and the Soviet Union, in the critical years between 1945 and 1949. Its concrete expressions were immigration, settlement, agricultural and industrial expansion, Haganah restraint in the face of Arab terrorism, diplomacy that emphasized the necessity of a Jewish state to effect an international solution of the Jewish problem, and the state's expected contribution to developing and raising the living standard of the region's Arab population. True, Britain no longer supported the idea of the national home, but the Yishuv core that had been created by 1945 was for the most part ready to struggle for a state despite the opposition of the Mandatory power if a diplomatic solution were not forthcoming. The question was whether it would have the strength to fight alone. Leaders of the Zionist movement never thought it could triumph without external support, still less in the event of hostile intervention by the Arab states.

As World War II ended, such intervention did not appear realistic in light of the assumption—which was mistaken—that the powers, and especially the United States, would assist in the state's establishment in the wake of an international decision. The transition from the stage of naïveté as to the prospects of a political decision to the stage of armed struggle was sharp and unexpected in part, but it was the only realistic option in the conditions of the war's end. The Yishuv, the Holocaust survivors, and American Jewry were ready to bear the necessary risks, but as I later show, the support of the two great powers in place of England was vital. Zionism had a double problem: Would there be enough external windows of opportunity to enable the establishment of a Jewish state in part of Palestine within the framework of a the new world order? And would the Zionist movement, under Ben-Gurion's leadership, be able to prevent internal polarization and forge the same broad consensus as it had in the past? On the plane of external politics, the prospects were unknown. As for domestic politics, the experience of the recent past seemed to promise success, but obstacles still had to be overcome and opponents isolated in three circles: within the Jewish Agency coalition, within the radical left, and within the radical right. The ideal was to engineer the maximum mobilization and combination of internal and external factors without conceding the principle of a sovereign Jewish state in those areas of the country not densely populated by Arabs.

I

The International Arena

The International Policy of the Jewish Agency and Mapai

1

Rise of the American Orientation

From Humanitarian Aid to Political Recognition

From the time the Balfour Declaration was issued, Zionist leaders understood that the movement's viability would depend on their ability to muster international support. British backing was guaranteed from 1917, but the active United States support, which was needed beginning in 1939, was not fully assured until seven years later. Before December 1941, American isolationism stood in the way.

The Yishuv had looked to Washington with mounting expectations particularly after the publication of the White Paper by Britain, in May 1939, which limited Jewish immigration to Palestine to 75,000 over five years and confined the Yishuv's area of settlement to 5 percent (as of February 1940) of the country's territory. Indeed, the White Paper threatened to destroy Zionist aspirations altogether by bringing about the establishment of an independent Palestinian state in which the Jews would remain a permanent minority.

American Jewry, with its ability to influence the administration, had a crucial role to play in the struggle for a Jewish state. Grasping this, David Ben-Gurion, the chairman of the Jewish Agency and leader of the ruling Mapai party, and the dominant personality in this narrative, spared no effort to mobilize American Jews in support of the Zionist vision. Turning to both Zionists and non-Zionists in the Jewish community, he appealed to them not in the name of ideology (which generated controversy over what constituted the essence of the Jewish people) but pragmatically, on the basis of the Biltmore plan of May 1942. The idea was to establish a "Jewish Commonwealth" in Palestine within the framework of what was envisaged as the new, postwar democratic world order. In 1943, the American Zionist Emergency Council, the major coordinating body of the Zionist struggle in the United States, was created. Headed by Dr. Abba Hillel Silver and Dr. Stephen Wise, the AZEC cast its net across the country and kept up relentless pressure on both houses of Congress.

Although this lobbying produced pro-Zionist resolutions in both the Senate and the House of Representatives, it could claim no concrete results until the advent of the Truman administration. Truman had already adopted a pro-Zionist policy, albeit only at the humanitarian level, in the summer of 1945, when he announced his support for the immigration to Palestine of 100,000 displaced persons (DPs) from Europe. A year later, he advocated the establishment of a Jewish state in part of Palestine, though that position did not acquire operative force until the fall of 1947, when it gained the support of a United Nations committee of inquiry (UNSCOP).

The president's pro-Zionist tilt was sharply criticized by officials in the State Department, who saw it as conflicting with the true strategic interests of the United States, which lay in the Arab states and in Saudi Arabia especially, where American oil companies had concessions.

Of all the international issues that arose after the onset of the Cold War, only Zionism caused a major disagreement, not to say a rift, between the White House and the State Department.[1] Whereas the former had to take into account electoral considerations, and in 1947 favored a Jewish state in part of Palestine, the latter argued in favor of strict national interest and took into account the emerging Arab national claims.

State Department pressure led, in December 1947, to the imposition of an American arms embargo on both sides in Palestine after the eruption of hostilities. Still more serious, in March 1948, again at the State Department's initiative (and without the president's knowledge), the U.S. representative to the United Nations announced that his country was withdrawing its agreement (which had been a White House initiative) to the partition of Palestine in favor of a "trusteeship" regime.

Although the trusteeship idea never reached fruition because of Soviet opposition and British reluctance, Washington did not give Israel—which was fighting for its life—the kind of active support it received from the Soviet Union. On the other hand, despite the Czech arms that were delivered to Israel (with Soviet permission) and the diplomatic support of the Eastern bloc for the nascent state, the Middle East did not (before 1967) become a contentious arena in the Cold War like Germany and China. The United States accepted Israel as a fait accompli after it had proven itself on the field of battle. However, the defeat of the Arab states and the emergence of the Arab refugee problem threatened to generate a new rift between the United States and Israel because of Washington's desire to place its relations with Israel in the context of its own (and, to a degree, British) interests in the region. In fact, neither Israel nor the Arab states succeeded in generating deeper American involvement even though the conditions for this seemed ripe. Paradoxically, Israel benefited from Washington's marginal political-strategic involvement in the region, as the British were not able to recruit the Americans for their anti-Israeli approach.

Clearly, then, no American orientation was forced on Israel, just as it was not coerced into adopting a Soviet orientation, and Israel pursued a pro-Western line of neutrality.

Historical hindsight suggests that the Zionist movement and Israel had no choice but to rely on the Western powers because of their shared democratic and liberal values and because of the British government's benevolent policy toward Zionism until the spring of 1939. British policy changed radically, however, with the publication that May of the White Paper initiated by Colonial Secretary Malcolm MacDonald. Thus the Zionists never really needed the support of the United States before 1939. A year earlier Ben-Gurion had addressed the question of Zionism's potential allies. Zionism, he said then, was never more in need of allies. But it was a political fact that it had only one ally: Britain. Even if Britain's support was hardly enthusiastic and was even, at times, contemptuous, in this critical period Zionism had no choice but to garner support wherever it could. Ben-Gurion accepted that America was isolationist, but "there might be events which could force America, morally or politically, to abandon the policy of isolation and become an active factor in the international political arena. . . . For the moment the majority of the American people follow an isolationist line persistently and zealously . . . as long as [this is so] the strength of American Jewry does not contribute its full weight in the political balance of the Jewish people."[2]

After the Munich conference in which the West sacrificed Czechoslovakia to Hitler, Ben-Gurion no longer put his faith in Britain's capacity or goodwill toward Zionism. When it became clear earlier, at the Evian conference on refugees held in July 1938, before Munich, that America was willing, at least in theory, to assist refugees, Ben-Gurion wondered: "America did not stand up for the Czechs, will it stand up for us? Will it quarrel with England because of us? As far as we know,

Roosevelt does not believe in Palestine as a haven for Jewish immigration."[3] Nonetheless, Britain's appeasement policy seemed to make his American option stronger.[4] Certainly once the war erupted he believed that the Yishuv could survive only with the Allies' help, that of America in particular. Clearly such aid would be needed to establish a Jewish legion to assist the Allies. True, the Jews and the Zionists in America were afraid that they would be accused of disloyalty. But Ben-Gurion saw no cause for despair, remembering the Irish model of assisting their brethren in the homeland.[5]

Ben-Gurion became even more optimistic about American Jewry's ability to come to the Yishuv's rescue shortly before Pearl Harbor, when it seemed clear to him that America would "most probably" enter the war. Zionism, he now believed, must concentrate its activity in America. Moreover, the United States would play a vital role in shaping the postwar world, as it would presumably emerge as the least exhausted power. Europe would be dependent on America for its survival. For Zionism, the American stand would be crucial. America more than Britain might countenance a fundamental solution of the Jewish problem.

The State Department was influenced by Arab-Muslim dominance in the Middle East, but its consuls in the region, with their pro-Arab orientation, wielded far less influence than their British counterparts. Prophetically, Ben-Gurion stated that the United States had fewer interests and fewer prejudices and was more objective. In October 1941, just back from the United States, he was highly optimistic that the majority of American Jews would become actively involved in building Jewish Palestine. He was confident about the readiness of a great democracy like America to adopt courageous and all-embracing solutions, such as Zionism, for the world's troubles. "The moment we succeed in convincing America to support the Zionist solution of the Jewish question, all our problems today—the real and the imagined—will be diminished." Never had any Zionist leader of Ben-Gurion's stature stated, as he thus did, that "American support for a Jewish state in Palestine is the key to our success."[6]

Not surprisingly, given this approach, the most important Zionist conference during the war took place in the United States. In May 1942, at the Biltmore Hotel in New York, a meeting of Zionist leaders issued a public call for the establishment of a "Jewish Commonwealth" in Palestine after the war. America's entry into the war was a precondition for the emergence of a strong Zionist movement. In his grand plan for the war's aftermath, Ben-Gurion linked the significant role America would play in feeding Europe and transferring populations with his plan to move two million Jews to Palestine at one stroke. This was no dream, he insisted. The models existed: Heinrich Kaiser's plan to move half a million soldiers overnight, or the transfer of one and a half million Greeks from Asia Minor by the Turks in the early 1920s. Walter Lowdermilk, an American soil conservation expert, who was preparing a book on the potentialities of Palestine, spoke of a "Jordan Valley Authority," which Ben-Gurion envisaged as a Middle Eastern Tennessee Valley Authority. The project would enable five million Jews to settle in Palestine. In the United States no one was frightened by the idea of spending vast sums for such purposes. As to security, ten million American soldiers would suffice to keep the world at peace. The only condition for success was a strong Zionist movement in America.[7] Equally prophetic was Ben-Gurion's assessment of the postwar situation for Jewish refugees; Palestine, he said, would be their only choice, for America's gates would not be opened after the war: "America will pour in millions and billions to assist Europe, but will not bring in millions of Czechs and Slovaks, Hungarians and Poles who were expelled from one place to another . . . and no exception will be made for the Jews. America's gates will not to be opened, and there are no other gates." Ben-Gurion was convinced that America, which had spent $60 billion on the war by 1942, would not be deterred, after the war, by the smaller sums that would be needed to develop both sides of the Jordan River to settle Jewish refugees.[8]

Chaim Weizmann, the president of the Jewish Agency, similarly thought that the Jewish potential in America had not been exploited to the full in favor of Zionism. American Jewry was in a position to exercise far greater influence on the Palestine question, thanks to its place at the "nerve center" of American life: in politics, commerce, intellectual pursuits, the press, theater, radio, and public opinion. Roosevelt was sympathetic to the Jews' suffering but did not believe that Palestine was the solution: "He considers the Zionist enterprise a small affair . . . and he wonders why this ancient and clever people decided to take root in this small piece of land. . . . Look here, at the enormous wasteland of southern California, where Jewish settlers could do wonders."[9]

The successful struggle by Zionist activists to get both houses of Congress to adopt pro-Zionist resolutions on the eve of the presidential elections in 1944 was not considered by the Yishuv leadership a turning point in relations with America. Moshe Shertok, the head of the Jewish Agency's Political Department, noted that the Zionist lobbyists were inclined to value such pronouncements as a goal rather than a means. The resolutions remained ineffectual because they did not become a lever to pressure England to change its Palestine policy. "Instead, they [American Zionists] continue frantically to obtain resolutions, declarations, thus making it seem that only they are of importance to us."[10] Shertok was disappointed at Roosevelt's failure to offer even "interim" help on Jewish immigration to Palestine. Ben-Gurion believed that "the very fact that five million Jews and more are concentrated in key positions in America, and their full mobilization in support of the Zionist claim, could be a crucial factor, or a vital element in American policy."[11]

Roosevelt's policy on Zionism did not improve as far as the Yishuv was concerned. On the contrary, it worsened after his meetings with Stalin and with King Ibn Saud of Saudi Arabia in February 1945, two months before his death. The president warned the American Zionist leader Dr. Stephen Wise that Zionist propaganda might ignite a third world war and foment a *jihad* (holy war) against the Yishuv.[12] Nonetheless, Ben-Gurion was "in great despair" when he learned of Roosevelt's death, even though the Zionists did not place their long-term hopes in any particular president.[13] Shertok, however, was worried that the great powers might decide on the establishment of a Palestinian Arab state.[14]

On the eve of the San Francisco conference, which laid the foundations of the United Nations immediately after the war, the Zionist leadership was gloomy about the prospects of preserving the pro-Zionist articles of the British Mandate, given the possible change in Palestine's status from mandate to trusteeship. Trusteeship would probably not include the vital mandatory articles on *aliyah* (Jewish immigration to Palestine) and settlement, as formulated in 1922 in an entirely different world order. Shertok understood that, despite congressional resolutions, U.S. policy was not certain.[15]

With the new presidency, Zionism had never been more central to the worldview of the average American Jew. This was the message given to the Small Zionist Actions Committee, the Zionist parliamentary body meeting in Jerusalem, by Rabbi Dr. James Heller, of the United Palestine Appeal (UPA).[16] The basic assumption of the Zionist leadership was that a concerted effort on behalf of Zionism both in Palestine and in America would produce results, particularly in view of the prevailing opinion that the new president was "an honest man: if he makes a promise he will keep it."[17]

However, Truman's first statement on Palestine, delivered on 15

August 1945 (that he would not send half a million American soldiers to help establish a Jewish state), jolted Zionist circles. Two weeks later Truman "redeemed himself," from a Zionist point of view, by recommending to newly elected Prime Minister Clement Attlee that his country permit the immigration of 100,000 Jews to Palestine. After this, the Zionist leadership would look to Washington to pressure the British government to revise its policy. First, Zionist pressure should be used to threaten suspension of a pending American loan to Britain.[18] Despite the conflicting perceptions of Truman's policy, the Zionists increasingly concluded that his support for the entry of 100,000 Jews into Palestine was basically humanitarian. Moreover, if America supported the Jews, Russia might counter by appearing as the protector of the Arabs.[19] The active pro-Americans in Mapai, such as Eliezer Liebenstein (Livneh), said the Zionists should take advantage of the ostensible "religious renaissance" in America and should also turn for help to the American labor movement.[20]

Ben-Gurion also looked elsewhere. The Jewish DPs who were languishing in camps in Germany might be a potential boon for the Zionist campaign to win independence in Palestine. After visiting the camps in October 1945, he met with General Walter Bedell-Smith, General Eisenhower's chief of staff. He urged Bedell-Smith to grant the DPs various rights, including self-rule, permission to reside in both rural and urban areas in Occupied Germany, professional education, voluntary physical training, a weekly military air transport of mail, books, and emissaries from the Yishuv. On 29 October Ben-Gurion met with Eisenhower himself, who accepted his plan for the refugees' professional education and spiritual rehabilitation.[21]

Ben-Gurion had achieved far more than American consent to an autonomous cultural area in Germany. In effect the Americans agreed to create a Jewish refuge for East European Jews fleeing renewed pogroms. The Anglo-American Committee (discussed later)—which in February 1946 investigated the conditions of the DPs as part of its mandate to examine the entire Palestine question—noted in its report in April that these Jews, whose number by July stood at 85,000 in the American Zone and 120,000 in all of Germany, aspired to go to Palestine. This concentration of Jews was thus successful from the Zionist viewpoint due to the methodical work of Yishuv emissaries.[22]

From the outset Ben-Gurion assigned the Holocaust survivors a central role: "The Zionist role is not to rescue the survivors in Europe, but to rescue Eretz Israel [Land of Israel] for the Jewish people. And the Yishuv, American Jews and the European refugees have a special mission in this rescue."[23] No one in the Yishuv, the "breakaways" (*Porshim* in Hebrew) included, questioned this. Thus, the survivors also played a role in cementing the Yishuv consensus. The issue was how to transform them into a political instrument. This was a blatant leadership challenge, which Ben-Gurion took on to meet as a short-term goal.

The establishment in October 1945, at British initiative, of the Anglo-American Committee of Inquiry on the future of Palestine and the Jewish refugees did not dislodge the Zionists' misconception that America, too, had betrayed them by supporting British policy. Nothing was known of Truman's insistence that the committee should investigate not only the Palestine question, as the British demanded, but also the conditions of the European refugees. Ernest Bevin's anti-Zionist statement of policy in Parliament on 13 November 1945 convinced the Zionist leadership that Anglo-American "collusion" was intensifying, apart from the feeling of "great despair" at this "betrayal" by a socialist government.[24]

Yet Ben-Gurion still believed that the British Labour Party, as distinct from the Cabinet, was loyal to Zionism: "It would be an unjust mistake to despair of the Labour party. It has integrity." This turn of events led him to warn against the possibility that Zionism in America might be identified with "reactionary" forces, by which he meant Rabbi Dr. Abba Hillel Silver, the most prominent American Jewish leader and the chairman of the main Zionist lobby group. In Ben-Gurion's view, Zionist success in America was conditional on Silver's removal from the leadership in favor of such personalities as N. Goldmann, R. Szold, J. Heller, and S. Wise. Poale Zion (socialist Zionists) should be an independent force, not Silver's lackeys.[25]

Ben-Gurion set the tone of the Zionist line toward America. It was his recent visit to the DP camps in Germany that had persuaded him of American readiness to let the Jewish refugees settle in Palestine. "America is destined to play a very great role," he asserted.[26] Unlike most of his colleagues he grasped the significance of Truman's announcement immediately after Bevin's 13 November statement, in which the president consented only to the appointment of the committee and to its terms of reference—not to the rest of the foreign secretary's words, which attacked the Zionists. Truman's (late August) letter to Attlee on the immigration of 100,000 Jews was still on the committee's agenda.[27] Ben-Gurion also reminded the Elected Assembly of the Yishuv that President Woodrow Wilson had committed the American government to the establishment of a "Jewish Commonwealth." And the two great parties in America had also pledged to assist in creating a Jewish state.[28] Ben-Gurion, back from lengthy visits to America and Britain, grasped postwar realities. Hence, "the most important thing I saw in the Diaspora . . . [is that] there are pioneer and struggling forces which would support the Yishuv if it were to take action."[29] Not everyone in the Mapai Center, however, was as certain as Ben-Gurion and Shertok about America's positive role on the committee.

The view among some senior figures in the Yishuv, such as S. Meirov, P. Lubianiker (Lavon), and Shertok's deputy in the Agency's political department, B. Joseph, was that the British were more cunning than the Americans, and "would deceive them." David Remez, the chairman of the Va'ad Leumi (National Committee, the Yishuv's supreme body in internal affairs), pointed to the view of James G. McDonald (a member of the Anglo-American Committee and afterward first American ambassador to Israel) that the DPs should settle only in Palestine. Joseph thought that McDonald supported Magnes's binationalism (as discussed later). Y. Ben-Zvi, the president of the Va'ad Leumi, reminded his colleagues that Britain was not a totalitarian state like the Soviet Union, where the government could arrange everything in advance. He believed a wedge could be driven between the two Anglo-Saxon powers. Shertok warned that boycotting the committee (because of its alleged anti-Zionist bias) could lead to the Zionists' boycotting of the UN when it discussed replacing the mandate with a trusteeship. Giving evidence, Shertok explained, did not necessarily mean agreement with the committee's conclusions. Believing in the "Labour Party's conscience," he warned that refusal by Yishuv leaders to appear before the committee would mean that "we release those pro-Zionist Labour politicians, such as Barbara Gould and Jim Middleton, from their commitments."[30] On 10 December 1945 the Mapai Center voted 16-2 in favor of cooperating with the Anglo-American Committee; two days later the Small Zionist Actions Committee followed suit with a vote of 16 to 11.[31]

Despite all their earlier fears, the Zionist leadership saw the publication of the Report of the Anglo-American Committee of Inquiry (late April 1946) as a positive turning point. Even if the report did not recommend the establishment of a Jewish state, it dealt two serious blows to the 1939 White Paper: the committee supported the immediate admittance of 100,000 Jewish refugees to Palestine and urged the repeal of the Palestine land laws (promulgated in February 1940, although new laws to protect the Arab tenants were to be enacted).[32] But Ben-Gurion found little cause for elation in the report.[33] He tried to persuade Washington to take responsibility for three points: accelerating the immigration of the 100,000; opening the American Zone in Germany to Jewish refugees; and a $250 million loan for the development of Palestine. On these questions he could report to his colleagues with considerable optimism.[34]

Nonetheless, Mapai's Political Committee did not share Ben-Gurion's optimism about America. Its source of information was the American consul in Jerusalem, who stated officially that his government emphasized the advisory character of the committee's report. Nothing in the official statement seemed to justify Ben-Gurion's upbeat report from New York, where he was on a visit after the report's publication. It spoke only of an American "interest" in Palestine based on sympathy for the victims of fascism and a willingness to assist them, the fact that American citizens had given substantial aid to the national home, and the deep interest the American government had in facilitating harmonious relations with the peoples of the Middle East. Y. Sprinzak, secretary-general of the Histadrut Federation of Labor, accepted this at face value, unlike Golda Meyerson (Meir) and Bernard Joseph; the latter was "deeply distressed," as he was certain that Anglo-American collusion was involved.[35]

In fact, Mapai in Palestine had far less information than Ben-Gurion, hence its pessimism. Ben-Gurion's ability to read the pulse of Washington firsthand and his contacts with Ben Cohen, adviser to Secretary of State James F. Byrnes, and with General John H. Hilldring, assistant secretary of state in charge of the refugees, and indirectly with Treasury Secretary Fred Vinson convinced him that only "great and permanent pressure" from America might change British policy. He was aware of the fact that these American officials were willing to take seriously Zionist claims that the survivors would be transferred to Palestine. Ben-Gurion was optimistic that the United States could be induced to pressure Britain.[36]

The growing American involvement in the Palestine question led to the establishment by both Britain and America of a special cabinet committee consisting of the secretaries of state, treasury, and war and their British equivalents. They in turn appointed representatives to a new Anglo-American committee of experts headed by the State Department's Henry F. Grady and by Sir Norman Brook, secretary of the British cabinet. This body was maneuvered by its British members into taking an anti-Zionist stance. This took the form of a new plan, named after its two architects, Morrison and Grady, which made the immigration of the 100,000 conditional on a political solution involving a federal autonomy regime—a situation which, if implemented, would be a serious setback to Zionist strategy. Salvation for the Zionists came via Undersecretary of State Dean Acheson, who informed the British that the president could not accept the Morrison-Grady report (Home Secretary Herbert Morrison read out the plan in Parliament). The intervention of pro-Zionists like James G. McDonald, Senators James Mead and Robert Wagner, the president's adviser David Niles, and Ben Cohen all played a part in dissociating America from Britain's Palestine policy.[37]

How did this latest change in Truman's policy on Zionism, which was brought about by direct pressure of the Zionist lobby, affect Zionist decision making? After all, Truman himself said only that he supported the entry to Palestine of the 100,000 and nothing else. The Yishuv leadership was now under two-pronged pressure to define more precisely its desired political solution. First of all, there was American Zionist pressure, not least from Silver. On top of this, in Palestine itself the British sweep on the "Black Sabbath" (29 June 1946), in which they exposed the Yishuv's structural weakness by arresting some 2,700 Zionist activists, was followed by the blowing up of the King David Hotel in Jerusalem (22 July) by the Irgun Zvai Leumi (IZL). In a crucial special meeting of the enlarged Jewish Agency Executive, held that August in Paris, three possible solutions were debated. The basic assumption was that nothing could be done to improve the Zionist political position by appealing to the British; only an approach to the Americans was viable. It was clear that an alternative solution must be presented to the president if Morrison-Grady were to be rejected. The first suggestion was a modified Morrison-Grady plan, calling for the extension of the area allotted to the Jewish province, which included less than a fifth of the country; an expansion of Jewish autonomy; and greater authority for the Jewish Agency on immigration. The second suggestion was to focus on the concrete demands that Truman was ready to accept, namely the entry of 100,000 refugees and the repeal of the land laws. The third suggestion, which won majority support from the beginning, favored partition. The inner consensus was that this was the only way to bring about Jewish independence. As to the timing, the pressure of the survivors in Europe was such as to rule out further delay, and Truman must be convinced that a final political solution was essential.

The drama in Paris reached a climax when Rabbi Yehuda L. Fishman, the Mizrachi leader, became an active supporter of partition. In a speech Eliahu Dobkin, a member of the Jewish Agency Executive, called "terribly shocking," Rabbi Fishman reminded the conference of his previous strenuous objections to partition because it was "heresy, since according to the Jewish faith the whole Land of Israel belongs to the Jewish people. But after seeing the situation in the Diaspora, I reached the conclusion that we could not rescue the survivors without Jewish independence even in part of Palestine." Weeping passionately, he declared: "If you, God, leave us without Jews, then I give up the Land of Israel and the Messiah. I know that this is heresy and that I am a heretic."[38]

Similarly, Wise also withdrew his earlier objection to partition, as Silver had already done in America. By a vote of 22 to 1 the Paris conference decided to support the partition of Palestine. Goldmann was sent to America, where he succeeded in persuading both Acheson and the American Zionist leadership to accept this stand. On 12 August Acheson recommended to the British government that the Zionist plan, which he described as an improvement on the Morrison-Grady plan, be included in the forthcoming London Conference on the future of Palestine, convened by Bevin in September 1946 and attended until January 1947 solely by the Arab states.

Eliezer Kaplan, the leading moderate leader in Mapai, who wanted an improved Morrison-Grady plan, reminded his colleagues, who were still unreconciled to partition, that the greatest danger in Paris had been Truman's possible retraction of his readiness to go on fighting for the 100,000 and for repeal of the land laws, which would have been a tremendous setback for Zionism.[39] The partition formula, euphemistically called in Paris a "viable state" (because of the prevailing Greater Israel mood), was approved by the Mapai Political Committee by 14 to 1 with 3 abstentions.[40] The second phase of Washington's shift toward greater support for Zionism was initiated by Truman's announcement on Yom Kippur (4 October 1946) that he favored a compromise solution between the Morrison-Grady and the Jewish Agency plans. Until Truman's historic statement, the atmosphere in Mapai was still pessimistic about American policy.[41]

The Yom Kippur announcement was a great victory for the anti-Soviet, pro-American faction in Mapai, led by E. Liebenstein. It created a "new situation" that demanded the renewal of the campaign for the immigration of the 100,000 DPs instead of the drive for a state.[42]

Meyerson, who had replaced Shertok (imprisoned since the Black Sabbath) in the Political Department of the Jewish Agency, claimed that for the first time there was no discord on Palestine or Zionism between the president and the State Department, though Kaplan was more skeptical.[43] The British high commissioner, Sir Alan Cunningham, told Shertok that the Arabs believed the Zionists wielded immense power in the international arena. Five million Jews were entirely on their side, and so was the rest of America. Shertok replied that this was "very important, but it is not [America] that will implement policy. You [Britain] are the policy-makers, not America."[44]

Though there was as yet no promise by Washington to support the Zionist program of a "viable state" (i.e., partition) the American Zionist leadership triumphantly claimed at the 22nd Zionist Congress, held in Basel in December 1946, that America stood behind Zionism. This was the conclusion of Silver, the most powerful leader in American Zionism, who attributed the Yom Kippur announcement to the "immense" pressure of public opinion. While emphasizing that in 1944 Roosevelt had promised more than Truman had, he acknowledged that Truman, unlike his predecessor in office, had rejected a protest by King Ibn Saud on immigration. Silver claimed that this change in U.S. policy was a success of American Jewry.[45]

By February 1947, the London Conference split into separate meetings, now held in parallel with each side. Both the Anglo-Arab and Anglo-Zionist conferences failed to reach agreement, and the British government announced its decision to transfer the Palestine problem to the United Nations. In this situation, the Zionist leadership hoped that Bevin's recent brutal attacks on America "might perhaps push it to take a strong stand." In addition, encouraging news was reported: General George Marshall, upon assuming the role of secretary of state in January 1947, had directed the American consuls in the Middle East to support a "viable Jewish state," in addition to pressing for the entry of the 100,000 Jews into Palestine and the abolition of the White Paper land laws.[46]

Liebenstein, with his entrenched pro-American stance, complained that in America (and England) the Yishuv was perceived to be pro-Soviet, "and who knows the price we have already paid for [our] pro-Russian sentimental expressions and the continuance of League 'V' [a pro-Soviet body established by Zionist socialist parties in 1942 to assist the USSR] after the war"; he warned against "any expression on our part about being dependent on Russia."[47] There was U.S. hostility to any possible Soviet involvement.[48]

In the light of Bevin's recent announcement, in the wake of the failure of the London Conference, that Britain was transferring the Palestine problem to the UN (18 February), some in Mapai saw as a serious option the possibility that the recent American takeover from Britain in Greece might be followed by a similar takeover in Palestine. Shertok admitted that the fate of partition depended on whether the United

States would consider it a viable solution and would be prepared to act as the initiator.[49]

A special effort indeed had to be made to enlist America's support. As the strongest power in the UN, it could influence the twenty-one Latin American states. The chances were better than with any other state. But Shertok warned the Jewish Agency that pressure must be restrained. The 200,000 DPs in the American Zone were a heavy burden on the U.S. budget; they could not be abandoned because America was a democracy and public opinion there was pro-Zionist. Yet, he admitted that there was a clash between American political interests and its humanitarian reasons for support ("the bride [i.e., the Zionist cause] was too beautiful"), and therefore Zionist policy in America, so far, was a failure. Yet, there was wide room for maneuver. The fact that the United States had recently become more deeply involved in the region via its aid to Greece and Turkey enabled it to pressure England's weakening position on Palestine. Western containment of the USSR should be applicable everywhere.[50] Ben-Gurion was less sanguine. There was little possibility of applying sufficient pressure on the United States. The Jewish people could never comply with anti-American policy. Certainly American Jewry could not. Apart from "certain circles" in America, he said, "we do not have any real friend."[51]

Less than a month before the appointment of the United Nations Special Committee on Palestine (UNSCOP), the Yishuv leadership was in complete darkness as to the future attitude of the administration toward the Palestine question. The Soviet volte-face in mid-May 1947 (announced by Gromyko) was to have a momentous impact on the shaping of American policy, but not before UNSCOP published its report. The Zionist lobby in America did what it could. E. Epstein (Elath), the Jewish Agency representative in Washington, claimed that now the Western powers could be sympathetic to Zionism, now that there was less fear of "driving the Arabs into the arms of Russia." This point was stressed by Shertok in a meeting with Acheson. If the Americans feared that the Jews were now in the Russian camp, following the Gromyko declaration, it should be stressed that "Palestine Jewry and the Zionist movement are wholeheartedly and irrevocably democratic. . . . The economic structure of Palestine Jewish community is based on free enterprise. . . . Jewish communities abroad . . . realize that communism would obliterate their very identity and their freedom."[52]

Fearing that only Russia would support Zionism, because America was veering again toward the anti-Zionist line of Britain, Ben-Gurion assumed that America was going hand in glove with England.[53] Uncertain about what Zionist long-term policy should be, and in face of protest and Shertok's fear that the Yishuv might be "pulverized" between the "two millstones" of the United States and the USSR, he stuck to the convenient stand of no commitment to either East or West but "ourselves and the UN." In an attempt to avoid needless internal debate in intrigue-ridden Mapai, he deliberately played down the world schism, which he thought exaggerated, largely artificial, and the product of maneuvering by statesmen.[54]

In the UNSCOP report in late August 1947, the majority favored partition, but Meyerson was worried that the Silver–(Emanuel) Neumann leadership had made vehement speeches under pressure from their more passionate followers, and that this might influence the U.S. government against partition.[55]

To Zionist relief, on 11 October 1947, Marshall publicly supported the UNSCOP majority recommendation for partition. The two-thirds majority that voted for the majority report on 29 November 1947 in the UN General Assembly, including the United States and the Soviet Union, resolved the Zionist dilemma between East and West, at least for the time being. Ben-Gurion in particular was delighted, as the vote showed that there was no "necessary antagonism" between East and West. This "international orientation" of Ben-Gurion was particularly welcome to Zionism since it promised "maximum unity" for the Yishuv's labor movement, so far deeply divided on this issue (see chapters 8 and 9).[56] But this vaunted internationalism proved useless in the face of bloody events in Palestine. Nonetheless his main goal was realized: to prevent great power rivalry over Palestine.

Less than two months after the UN vote, on 19 January 1948, George F. Kennan, head of policy planning in the State Department, came out forcefully, in a secret circular, against any support for Zionism in view of American interests in the Middle East. A little later this shift was given public expression by the American envoy to the UN, Warren Austin.[57] The Mapai leadership was immediately alert to this threat. The fear was of a third world war involving the Near East, with the Americans possibly categorizing the Yishuv as communist (an old British ploy to show the Zionists as disloyal to the West), rather than perceiving the Arab threat to their interests.[58] Warren Austin's "coup" against Truman—on 19 March 1948 he announced that his country no longer supported partition but a trusteeship in Palestine—generated the most serious crisis yet in the Zionists' unrelenting attempt to influence American politics. Again, it was Liebenstein, the most pro-American of the Mapai political elite, who assured his colleagues that not all was lost. "States," he said, "are established not in the councils of the UN but by force of arms and by revolution." Zionism must not appear to be anti-American, he warned, because America would become the decisive factor in the region. Ultimately, however, salvation would not come from the Gentiles. Zionism would succeed by adopting a three-part program: an effective military initiative; constructive administrative activity; and an intelligent diplomatic line.[59] In the meantime Ben-Gurion issued a public statement that the Jewish Agency would never agree to a trusteeship, no matter for how brief a period.[60] Particularly worrying from the Zionist point of view was the attempt, initiated by Secretary of Defense James Forrestal, to bring about a bipartisan position on the Palestine question, thus rendering the Zionist lobby ineffectual.[61]

Epstein attributed the about-face on partition to a decision by the National Security Council. More precisely, the recent input of the American military in the formulation of policy, with fears rising of a third world war, had an adverse effect on the Zionist position. A major consideration of the armed forces was the need to keep Middle Eastern oil flowing, as this was a sine qua non for the success of the Marshall Plan to rebuild Europe in the face of the Soviet threat. "It is not important," he warned ominously, "whether the Yishuv is communist or not, it is enough that it has a pro-Soviet orientation. . . . Serious dangers face American Jewry and Zionism, which some might see as a fifth column, operating against the interests of the American nation and state."[62]

Ben-Gurion refused to be deterred by the American retreat from partition. He did not believe that the 19 March change was more than temporary. Nor did he think that an American declaration could in itself prevent or create the Jewish state. Since he believed that the military campaign, now more than four months old, was about to be decided in favor of the Yishuv following the success of Operation Nachshon, which opened the way to Jerusalem in early April, he was even more adamant in his refusal to decide between East and West, even though the crucial Czech arms had begun to arrive.[63]

But it was Shertok who had a more incisive view of the reasons for the American retreat from partition. He offered a four-part explanation: (1) the lack of vigilance in the White House on the Palestine issue, though this was no longer the case in view of the coming presidential election and the weight of the Jewish vote; (2) the waning of the influence of the delegation to the UN and the reassertion of State Department predominance; (3) the apparent military weakness of the Yishuv, which was exploited by opponents of Zionism to promote trusteeship;

and (4) most important, the international crisis, specifically the soviet-ization of Czechoslovakia in February, which inflicted on America a "war psychosis." The trusteeship plan was not credible to many UN members, and the Jewish Agency also knew that its implementation would be very problematic.

Within a few weeks Shertok could declare that trusteeship was a failure and that a Jewish state was again viable. Explaining, he noted the strong opposition to the plan by the Jewish Agency; the Agency's success in convincing "Lake Success circles" that the Jewish state was a living reality; and, the key element, the Yishuv's military victories. Yet the State Department did not give up its attempt to torpedo the partition resolution. American policy was guided by regional and global interests. The main obstacle was Soviet support for the Jewish state. According to Shertok, the trusteeship plan would have aimed at excluding Russia from the region. But the plan had collapsed, as it lacked support in the UN. Instead, the State Department had conceived the idea of an armistice agreement, which Shertok believed was politically motivated. The idea, he thought, was to delay Jewish independence. How was this conspiracy concocted? Two states, according to Shertok, Jewish and Arab, would soon be established in Palestine, and would fight a war without the control of either the United Nations or the United States. It would be a harbinger of the third world war, and a political decision could prevent it. Moreover, the Jewish side could not count on American dollars, for to Washington such a conflict would be a "disaster" and deeply contrary to its interests. Far worse: the Arabs had the oil, but not five million sensitive (i.e., Jewish) "hostages." Today there was a united Jewish front, apart from the tiny anti-Zionist American Council for Judaism. But what would central figures in American public life, like Henry Morgenthau, Herbert Lehman, and Joseph Proskauer say to an armistice of the kind envisaged by the administration? Shertok told Secretary of State Marshall that the Jewish state needed victories in order to survive, for "you do not buy friend-ship at the price of suicide!" Shertok did not conceal from his Mapai colleagues Marshall's warning: "You are strong now, but beware of relying on first victories! I myself am a military man, I warn you not to heed your military advisers too much. . . . Your war has just begun, what will be the outcome?" Was Marshall implying that America would take revenge if its advice went unheeded? Shertok was not deterred: public opinion and an election year were solid counterweights to American skepticism.[64]

On 14 May the United States recognized Israel, immediately after its declaration of statehood, rushing to do so before the Soviet Union, and as part of the East-West competition on the emerging new Middle East. The new state was, however, deeply perturbed by the fact that the American recognition was not de jure but only de facto, involving the appointment of a special plenipotentiary instead of an ambassador. De jure recognition was not yet feasible, the State Department said, because the question of borders was not settled. Washington was upset by the Israeli bombing of Amman on 1 June 1948 (retaliation for Jordan's siege of Jerusalem). The State Department also made it clear that Israel must decide which camp had the upper hand: those who supported the West or those who favored the Soviet bloc: "Until then we will not be quick to recognize you and we will not commit ourselves on anything."[65] On top of this, Shertok said, General Albert C. Wedemeyer, chief of plans and operations on the Army General Staff, had noted with dismay that a severe blow delivered by Israel against the Arabs could destroy the Arab regimes that formed a buffer against the Soviet Union.[66]

Here was a real danger for the nascent state: the possibility that the interests of the West and the Arabs would converge. A case in point was the Negev. The Arab states were anxious to prevent its domination by Israel, as this would drive a wedge between them. Britain, too, was interested in the large desert as an alternative to its bases in Egypt. Here was another opening for cooperation between Britain and America against the background of Cold War escalation. Israel's position, Shertok argued, was unambiguous: "We will stand fast in the Negev not because we are making an a priori alliance with another force in the world [i.e., the Soviet Union] which does not want the Negev to serve as a British base. We [also] have no interest in the Negev being a British base." Indeed, the empty Negev was integral to the Zionist vision of settling millions of immigrants in Israel. Shertok explained that although Israel greatly valued the Soviet Union's support, it could not become involved in the global conflict. "If we wish to establish the State of Israel and to rescue the Jewish people, we can not cut ourselves off from the force which is called in Europe the 'West,' a term which first and foremost includes the United States."[67]

Count Bernadotte was the UN mediator appointed on 14 May to find a solution to the Palestine problem. His first plan urged a "union" between Israel and Jordan under King Abdullah, with Jerusalem as the capital, and cut off the Negev from Israel—a step with Cold War ramifications, since the Negev was perceived in the West as a strategic base against the Caucasus. Shertok was adamant that Israel's "basic" policy was grounded exclusively in the UN. But here was a "contradiction between the United States as a political-national-imperialistic factor . . . and the United States as one of the foundation-stones of the international system."[68] Nevertheless, he was confident that despite the grave difficulty of retaining the Negev for Israel, the situation would eventually be resolved through the UN.

The final verdict on Israel's predicament was given by Ben-Gurion, who declared that "No UN resolutions . . . will help us, if our forces do not resolve the situation." The first Bernadotte plan should not be identified with American policy but with Britain, stated Ben-Gurion, who called the mediator "Bevin's agent."[69] Policy making in Washington was still regarded by Israel as being divided between the "traditionally" pro-Zionist White House and the State Department, said to be fundamentally anti-Zionist. Hence the pressure for a cease-fire, since the State Department feared that continued fighting would force America to grant Israel increasing assistance. In addition, U.S. elections loomed and this had brought dividends in the form of recognition initiated by the White House, said Shertok. James G. McDonald's appointment as a special emissary was Truman's personal choice and contrary to the wish of the State Department.

Continuation of the war, according to Israeli officials, would probably sway public opinion to force the White House to lift the arms embargo against Israel and facilitate negotiations for a first American loan. Such steps would identify the United States with a fighting Israel, against its interests in the Arab world. At the same time, there was the danger to Israel of American military intervention if the State Department, which probably had information on Israel's arms sources, prevailed. Again, only a cease-fire could prevent intervention. Shertok argued that American realism would not take seriously the so-called imminent danger of Israel's occupation of Nablus, Jenin, the Galilee, and perhaps Amman: "Either they would have to approve these occupations, thus embroiling themselves very deeply with the Arab world, or they would have to demand that we give up these conquests, thus fomenting an unnecessary quarrel with the Jewish world." Israeli policy makers, then, did not believe that American policy, perceived to be neutralized by the conflicting approaches of the White House and the State Department, could play a decisive role in the Arab-Israeli war.

On another front, continuation of the fighting might aggravate U.S.-British relations, because the former did not wish to take sides. Already Britain's participation in the Marshall Plan and its request for an additional loan had soured Anglo-American relations. Britain after all had given the Arabs military assistance. Moreover, concern was still rife that a third world war could be triggered by American entanglement in some corner of the world. With this reading of the situation, Israel's leaders, although they could easily have gained more territory, decided nevertheless to support the cease-fire proposed by the United States in the UN on 17 May, in order to avoid serious friction with Washington, from which support was still needed. Indeed, a concerted effort was needed to obtain the West's recognition for Israel's newly conquered territories beyond the partition borders established by the UN—not because Israel had a "general orientation" toward the West but because it already had recognition from the East.[70] Moreover, there was a danger, Epstein feared, that the heightened U.S.-Soviet tension over the Berlin crisis might induce Bevin to "facilitate" joint Anglo-American action in Germany, by "seeking" concessions at Israel's expense.[71]

In fact, American policy toward Israel was a mixture of White House and State Department policy considerations. Thus, there was little danger that Bevin could have influenced America's Palestine policy as he had wished since 1945. The danger to Israel that American policy would again fluctuate between the White House's pro-Jewish tendencies and the State Department's pro-Arab inclinations resurfaced after McDonald's arrival in Israel. According to Ben-Gurion, the pro-Jewish American special representative told him of his "deep anxiety that in America things are going to be decided that seem justified and sensible, but that we [Israel] might not accept, such as a demand to return the refugees. We should not delude ourselves that because of elections in America they will not impose sanctions against us."[72] Within days the American attitude had changed. Ben-Gurion noted that McDonald had received a cable from Washington expressing the hope that Israel would be "a great constructive force within its borders and an influence for good throughout the region. The administration wishes to assist in every legitimate and constructive way." First and foremost, America wanted to clarify whether any Arab states were interested in starting peace negotiations. But Washington was also keen to know how Israel would react to three options: annexation of Western Galilee to Israel in exchange for the Negev becoming part of Transjordan; internationalization of Jerusalem, or any other arrangement acceptable to Israel and the Arab states, on condition of free access to the holy places; and Israel's finding a constructive means to ease the suffering of the Arab refugees. However, Israel's interests barred its acceptance of all these points. Thus Ben-Gurion was astonished at the American intention, as presented by McDonald, to mediate between Bernadotte, the British, and Israel; mediation, he believed, was needed only between Israel and the Arabs. He added, also, in a rare disclosure of his principled attitude on the Arab question: "As I see it, we deserve the whole of western Palestine, and such a Jewish state hardly diminishes anything from the enormous Arab area. But I would have chosen, if the choice had been mine, a much smaller area together with a Jewish-Arab agreement, rather than the whole area without the Arabs' agreement." Ben-Gurion was opposed to severing Jerusalem from the Jewish state and did not believe that the return of the refugees was feasible without a stable, permanent peace.[73]

Bernadotte, by the time of his assassination (17 September 1948), had modified his original plan considerably by doing away with the Israel-Transjordan union. Israel, however, rejected the second version as well, since it still chopped off the Negev, reducing the state to an area of five million square kilometers, and called for the return of Arab refugees and an international regime for Jerusalem. At the opening of the third UN General Assembly session in Paris on 21 September, Marshall stated that Bernadotte's second plan was "a fair basis" for resolving the Palestine question, and "strongly" encouraged both sides to accept it in its entirety as the "best" of all plans. Shertok admitted that the plan had more chance of succeeding with the moral force of the "martyr" than if he were alive.[74] In any case, Ben-Gurion tellingly drew a distinction "between the positions of the governments and statesmen on the Palestine question and their readiness and ability to harness their forces in support of such an attitude." For example, Marshall had warned Shertok not to establish a Jewish state, but American forces were not used to prevent its founding. ("Had they been used, the state would have been wiped out immediately.") On the contrary: Washington gave it de facto recognition.[75]

This distinction between the political and military dimensions was of particular relevance one day earlier, when Ben-Gurion suffered a defeat in the cabinet on his proposal to attack Latrun, a vital junction on the Tel Aviv–Jerusalem road. His opponents (including three Mapai ministers) feared possible UN intervention.[76]

Was Ben-Gurion tempted to occupy a major part of the West Bank because he was certain that no great power military intervention was likely, or was he thinking in terms of a future alliance with Jordan's King Abdullah? Newly available Israeli cabinet records suggest the latter, and a limited attack on Latrun.[77] Indeed, the building of the "Burma Road," which circumvented Latrun, reduced that sector's strategic importance.

In the meantime, relations with the United States were still far from stable, and not only because Washington backed the Bernadotte plan. Two problems hindered friendly relations between Israel and America: continued Soviet aid and the border issue, the Negev in particular. Truman and Marshall expressed their anxiety at the Czech arms shipments to Israel. Shertok was quick to reply that Israel's first preference was for American weaponry.[78] As to the borders, Epstein hardly calmed the Israeli government with his interpretation that Marshall, in his statement of 21 September on the Bernadotte plan as a "basis" for negotiations, meant to improve the borders. The official Israeli explanation given to McDonald was that the Negev in Israeli hands would be good for the Arabs because settling the area would preoccupy Israel for many years and would be a guarantee against its expansion into the neighboring states.[79] Shertok was convinced that if Israel had given up the Negev a crisis would have been created with the Soviet Union, because the West had earmarked the area as an anti-Soviet base.[80] He was relieved when a key member of the American delegation to the UN, John Foster Dulles, later secretary of state, told him that he (Dulles) was not bound by Marshall's commitment to the Bernadotte plan.[81]

But the real test of Israeli-American relations arrived when Israeli forces wiped out the Egyptian army in the northern Negev (15–22 October 1948). Abba Eban, first Israeli representative to the UN, reported that the military successes had diminished U.S. support for the Bernadotte plan. But on 24 October Truman stated that he still supported the plan as the basis for a new effort to end hostilities. A day later the Americans pointed out that a decision on a "final settlement" of the border issue would be made only after the presidential elections. Tension reached new heights since at this juncture Israel discovered that the Bernadotte plan was the product of Anglo-American collusion.[82] Israel faced the possibility of Security Council sanctions if it refused to comply with the demand to withdraw from the northern Negev. American support was needed for passage of the Anglo-Chinese motion (26 October) to impose sanctions. Shertok made it clear to Marshall that a withdrawal would be "suicide" for Israel. Simultaneously Israel's friends in Washington pressured Truman, who immediately intervened to block a possible American stand in favor of sanctions; Truman was incensed at the State Department for making him a "fool" in British eyes. Sanctions might enable the Egyptians to beef up their forces and renew their offensive.[83] Truman remained faithful to Israel after the elections, although contradictory information (reflecting the old division between the White House and the State Department) claimed that the United States still supported the British strategic concept of creating a bridge from the Persian Gulf to the southern Negev via Jordan. The Americans also changed their view on Jerusalem: they now favored a plan to divide the city between Israel and Jordan in a trusteeship.[84]

Israel's trials and tribulations over American policy grew more acute following new difficulties in view of the Security Council decisions on 4 and 6 November 1948 demanding withdrawal from the northern Negev. The problem was not the White House, where self-confidence reigned after Truman's election victory, but the State Department. Shertok had to reassure Marshall that Israel's policy was one of equilibrium: an anti-Soviet policy was ruled out mainly because of the large number of Jewish potential immigrants who were being held as hostages by the Eastern bloc. Israel would not grant military bases to either the East or the West, Shertok said, while reminding his interlocutor that his country had been the first to declare an arms embargo. Marshall expressed admiration for Israel's military accomplishments, but admitted that there was some anxiety in Washington that Israel might be tempted to solve all its political problems by force. Israel, at any rate, preferred not to lose territory even at the price of not being recognized by the UN. At the same time, Shertok refused to rely on the Soviet veto "which represents us as being identified with the Soviet bloc. . . . We obligate ourselves to them to a degree that I do not know whether we can defray." Marshall, according to Shertok, claimed that Israel was using American Jewry to pressure the government, something that "could not be tolerated" in interstate relations.[85] Israel remained wary, realizing that the State Department would not change its basic views. Neither was the White House able to go into the daily details of policy, thus enabling the State Department to maintain "considerable room for maneuver without coming into clear conflict with the generalizations of a presidential directive."[86] Robert Lovett, the undersecretary of state, who shortly before had been reproached by Truman for supporting the British point of view, now stated that de jure recognition would not be granted before the general elections in Israel, and then only if neither the Communists nor Menachem Begin, the leader of the right-wing Herut, achieved power.[87] To his own intimate party circle Ben-Gurion did admit that it was in large measure owing to American diplomatic assistance that Israel had succeeded in rebuffing the UN demand for its withdrawal from the territory it had taken in the Negev.[88]

British policy, which by late 1948 was still opposed to a viable Jewish state, could not be counterbalanced by American support alone. Israel definitely needed Soviet backing as well. Ben-Gurion's and Sharett's (formerly Shertok) policy was to maneuver carefully between the conflicting positions of the three powers. Israel's vital need was to expand its borders, not because of any lust for expansion but as a strategic necessity. But this consideration clashed with the danger of annexing a large number of Arabs in the West Bank. So did the risk of a confrontation with the UN for rebuffing the 29 November 1947 boundaries.

A few days before the first general elections to the Israeli parliament (25 January 1949), the American Export-Import Bank approved a $100 million loan to Israel, and even Secretary of Defense Forrestal, Israel's strongest opponent in the administration, expressed "great admiration" (according to Epstein) for the military victories that reflected Israel's desire for independence. The abstention on the loan issue by Mapam—the Marxist-Zionist party—did not affect the government's massive majority of 85 to 3 (17 March 1949).[89]

Nonetheless, Israel's lobby in the United States utilized key officials in the president's close circle to go on playing off the White House against the State Department, although reportedly the contradictions between the two were being resolved under the new secretary of state, Dean Acheson, who took office in January 1949. Both continued to uphold the view that Israel should not be permitted to annex territories beyond the 29 November borders unless it exchanged them for territories already in its possession.[90] Israel had to walk a fine line to ensure that American policy would interpret its adamant attitude on the border question not as a pro-Soviet line but as a strategic necessity.

It was urgent to inform both the Americans and the Soviets that Israel was neutral in the Cold War. Israel explained to Soviet bloc representatives, following queries by Moscow, that its emissaries to America were on a mission to American Jewry, not to America as such. Ben-Gurion told an internal meeting at the Israeli Foreign Ministry that objectively, Israel could not by any criterion join either bloc.[91] Nonetheless, relations with the Soviet Union deteriorated. Although Moscow helped torpedo the Bernadotte plan, it rejected Israel's basic conception on immigration.[92] From this point of view the fact that Mapam was excluded from the coalition was considered a "serious symptom" by I. Barzilai, Mapam member and Israeli minister in Poland.[93] Nor were relations with the United States much better. The "indignation" of Truman and Acheson over Israel's reluctance to return Arab refugees, Israel's refusal to accept a give-and-take principle on the borders question, and the controversy over Jerusalem's internationalization were "affecting badly" Israel-U.S. relations.[94]

The American evaluation of Israel's future fate between the two global rivals was summarized to the Israelis by the CIA agent Sam Klaus. Besides being skeptical as to the ability of either the Arab states or Israel to develop the Middle East, he complained about Soviet influence in the Israeli army and about the presence of Soviet spies in the country. But the real communist danger, in his view, emanated not from Maki (the Communist Party of Israel) but from Mapam, which had great influence in the army and was openly pro-Soviet (see chapter 10). In a talk with Ben-Gurion himself, Klaus said he was impressed with Israel's neutrality; even Mapam, he thought, would yield to pragmatic considerations (to ensure American assistance for the absorption of mass immigration) and accept neutrality. Unconsciously, he said, Mapam was directly helping the communist interest, not because of its socialist worldview but by its insistence on maintaining friendship with the Soviet Union. Israel's dependence on arms from the Soviet Union would be reduced if it could buy military equipment in America, Klaus told his Israeli interlocutors.[95] Klaus's visit should be seen in the context of the shaky character of Israel-U.S. relations, due to the overall American strategy in the Cold War. Those relations were not resolved by the results of the Knesset elections of January 1949, notwithstanding Mapam's mediocre showing and the fact that it joined the opposition.

Analyzing Israel's position in the Acheson era, Sharett proudly divulged that he had told both American Jews and the secretary of state himself that "the time had passed when he needed the assistance of American Jews. . . . We deal with the administration as equals in a qualitative sense. Diaspora Jews are not responsible for our foreign policy and they do not have to give an opinion. . . . We are responsible for them, but they are not responsible for us. . . . But we always remember that the world will judge them in terms of our [national] standards."[96]

Nonetheless, while the Soviet Union supported Israel's territorial claims, Washington demanded an exchange of territories. Suppose Israel reached an agreement with the Arabs, Sharett noted; the State Department might disagree on the ground that it was unjust. Similarly, a settlement with Jordan might appear as "collusion" in Soviet eyes: "How would we appear in the eyes of the Soviet Union?"[97] Indeed, by late May 1949, the State Department had convinced Truman that Israel should be reproached for its attitude toward the return of Arab refugees and for its insistence on getting "territorial compensation" beyond the 29 November borders. Ben-Gurion's reply to McDonald was terse and unequivocal: "America has the right to voice its opinion on the Palestine conflict, but . . . the state did not originate as a result of the UN resolution . . . America did not lift a finger in our rescue, and also declared an embargo, and had we been annihilated we would not have been resuscitated. . . . Will we ask for America's mercy to send us an army to defend us? America is enormous—we are a small people and helpless. We cannot stand up to American force, but our survival takes precedence over accepting its view. The language of defiance and threats is intolerable."[98]

Sharett gave public expression to Ben-Gurion's anger. Less emotional than the prime minister, he stated that in the first place the UN resolution of 11 December 1948, concerning the establishment of the Palestine Conciliation Commission (initiated on 25 November for the settlement of the Arab-Israeli conflict), did not mention the principle of territorial exchange; second, the territories occupied by Israel beyond the 29 November borders were "absolutely vital" for its security and survival. Israeli soldiers did not sacrifice their lives for nothing. Their leaders would not renounce this "holy and blood-saturated territory."[99] Eban predicted a "far-reaching rift" with the United States if no compromise could be found on the Arab refugee issue. Another diplomat was pessimistic about Israel's ability to persuade world (i.e., American) public opinion. In the American perception, he said, Israel was not sensitive to a great humanitarian problem. Israel was granted aid to solve the Jewish refugee problem but had created a greater (Arab) refugee problem.[100]

Analyzing Israel's position on the eve of the meeting of the Conciliation Commission at Lausanne, Sharett estimated that the USSR could afford to ignore Arab views and adopt a pro-Israeli attitude; conversely, America could not allow a one-sided orientation. Hence its effort to diminish Israel's territory. Since the Negev was empty, it could be detached from the Jewish state. Washington was keen to demonstrate to the Arab states that it was making efforts on their behalf. Sharett believed, however, that if the Americans reached the conclusion that their goal was unfeasible, they would not insist on Israeli territorial concessions. Nor would they insist on the return of the refugees, a problem which needed an urgent solution, but one which, as Israel thought, should be humanitarian and financial. In the United States, Israel should take the line that it was not in "America's pocket." "Our internal situation is still unresolved and therefore we have to initiate a careful policy, so that we are not driven into the hands of the [Communist] East."[101]

Fortunately for Israel, by summer 1949 the armistice agreements with the surrounding Arab states were signed, neutralizing the Americans' inimical attitude in the Conciliation Commission. Yet, the armistice agreements were military in nature, not political. Sharett did not believe America would support an obsessive British attempt to cut off the Negev, the armistice agreements notwithstanding, since it would be difficult to obtain a UN majority for this. It was urgent to revive the Lausanne Conference (where the Conciliation Commission was in session) in order to reduce the tension with Washington, especially over the refugees: "The focal point of the refugee question, from the point of view of the UN and the United States, lies not in the moral realm but in the practical sphere."[102] On the principle of territorial exchange, in the Negev, Western Galilee, and Lydda-Ramleh, the State Department was adamant: "For giving up territory [below latitude 31] Israel would get peace and security guaranteed by America and financial assistance for its development. The world interest requires immediate peace in the region, and a just peace means concessions." But Sharett instructed Eliahu Sasson and Reuven Shiloah at Lausanne not to take fright.[103]

Israel's diplomatic efforts were ultimately successful. Initially, even Truman himself was not helpful vis-à-vis the State Department. He recalled to Eliahu Elath (formerly Epstein) that his initial assistance for Jewish refugees had been motivated by humanitarian considerations, and only Bevin had turned it into a political issue. Israel's refusal to allow Arab refugees to return, it was explained to Truman, was due to the difficulties the new state faced in absorbing hundreds of thousands of Jewish refugees. The president was convinced by the security implications of the Arab refugees' return. He himself, it was recalled, had a development plan for the Euphrates and the Tigris region in which Arab refugees could become efficient citizens in a democratic, progressive environment. Truman was also moved by the Israeli project to turn the Jewish people into a healthy nation by settling on the land. Again he was asked to send a military expert to help organize the Israeli army on lines appropriate for a democracy similar to the American armed forces.[104]

In view of the deteriorating international situation, the United States could not afford to remain indifferent to the situation in the Middle East as Truman stated: "[America] is afraid it might miss the bus. It will wake up one day and find that the [Middle] East has turned communist. The lesson should be learned from the situation in the Far East. America cannot delay the planning and implementation of its economic and strategic plans in the Near East because of the repugnant policy of this or that side."[105]

The Cold War was on the threshold of the Middle East. America's regional policy called for the material, military, and political consolidation of the Arab regimes, which had been shaken by their defeat in the war with Israel. Territorial compensation in the southern Negev would be the best way to soften the débâcle. The State Department feared that Arab refugees from Palestine, whose social and educational level was higher than that in the neighboring countries to which they had fled (or been expelled), might become a destabilizing factor. In short, a quick settlement of the Arab-Israeli conflict required Israel to make territorial concessions and show a greater willingness to permit refugees to return.[106]

An attempt to counterbalance the dominance of the State Department was made by Elath in an appeal to Clark Clifford, a presidential aide and a well-known supporter of Israel. Two arguments were adduced: first, the negative effect on Israel of territorial losses would be comparable to the United States being called upon to give up territory to Japan or to "compensate" Germany; second, the recent armistice agreements could be modified only by *"mutual* consent."[107] The State Department warned Israeli leaders not to delude themselves, claiming that on this issue it was in complete agreement with the White House. Any attempt to recruit American Jewry to pressure the White House would only increase anti-Semitism in America and make the State Department even more hostile.[108]

In this state of affairs the Israeli mission to Washington offered a pessimistic evaluation of American strategy during the transition period from the Marshall Plan to NATO (July 1947–April 1949); Elath wrote to Sharett:

> I have good reason to believe that in a military exigency the administration might try to force us to abandon our neutral position and stand completely on its side. . . . They have probably concluded here that there is no escape from a [world] war. And if so, the situation is that "anybody who is not with us is against us." However, there is no assurance that such a change in our policy and our abandoning of neutrality in favor of a total American orientation will bring about *immediately and automatically* a change of heart on their part. One might think that America's interests in the Middle East, mainly relating to oil and [military] bases, would have prevented Washington from moderating its attitude to a degree that might have damaged its image in Arab

eyes. Forsaking neutrality might help us in certain influential circles, Jewish and non-Jewish in America, and strengthen our position amongst certain personalities, but it will not bring about a revolution in our relations with the United States.[109]

Elath concluded that there was good cause for anxiety, but that the situation did not warrant a radical change in Israel's policy.

Eventually, Israel's policy makers concluded, through trial and error, that it was necessary to negotiate with the State Department itself, without White House intervention. A case in point was the "suspension" of the loan from the Export-Import Bank, which was saved only by Israel's consent to the return of 100,000 Arab refugees. The lesson was that relations with the official who had initiated the loan's "suspension," George N. McGhee, assistant undersecretary of state, should be improved. In short, "no method [involving] conceit and arrogance should be adopted toward the State Department."[110] Overall, though, there was no place for pessimism, since the National Security Council had no wish to alienate Israel; in its assessment an Israeli orientation toward the West was a clear necessity. The management of the Arab-Israeli conflict would be dictated by this assumption.[111] By summer 1949 the Israeli leadership realized that, notwithstanding the crucial assistance received from the Soviet Union, sustained—and sustaining—support must come from the United States. With the benefit of hindsight, it is clear that since 1945 Zionism seems to have been highly successful in enlisting American support for the establishment of a Jewish political entity. Yet, Washington's need to reconcile its strategic posture with its interests in the Arab world, against the background of the Cold War, held out the prospect of failures as well as achievements for Israeli policy makers. Hence their appeal to France. America would take a staunchly pro-Israeli stance only in the 1960s, especially after the Six-Day War.

2

Relationship with the Soviet Union

From Antagonism to Vital Aid

Were Zionist-Soviet relations inherently inimical? This question implies another: was the Zionist orientation toward the USSR foredoomed, or was its failure the result of an inner struggle in Mapai? Given the Soviet and communist enmity to Zionism, the answer seems obvious. Yet the labor movement in Palestine was initially enthusiastic about the October Revolution and its aftermath: the Western orientation was perhaps not as inevitable as it may seem in hindsight. The Balfour Declaration in support of a Jewish national home in Palestine, issued by the British foreign secretary in 1917, and the Palestine Mandate awarded to Britain by the international community after World War I seemed to signify the victory of a Western orientation within Zionism. But Britain's backtracking from its commitments to Zionism in the 1939 White Paper put this in doubt. Yet, was Soviet Russia an alternative at this stage? Hardly, since unlike Britain before 1939, it was not regarded as a world-class power. Although Ben-Gurion saluted Lenin in 1923 for his methods of seizing power in Russia, he was never sympathetic to the Stalinist regime. He drew no distinction between his social democratic outlook and his considerations as a Zionist decision maker. During the Arab Revolt of 1936–39 he expressed his antipathy both for the Comintern and for Soviet Russia because of their support of Arab terrorism. He rejected the left-wing Hashomer Hatza'ir's differentiation between the Comintern's (ideological) "diversion" from "revolutionary socialism" and the Soviet Union's political attitude as a state. He did not rule out, however, the possibility of future Soviet support. First, he did not believe that the Soviets would always remain allied with the reactionary Mufti of Jerusalem and the landowning effendi; and he also thought Moscow might have a change of heart about Zionism. "Not socialist ideology but political interests determine the Soviet attitude toward foreign affairs. Our real 'sin' is our weakness."[1]

Ben-Gurion had a positive opinion of some aspects of the Soviet regime, such as its "attitude toward the national question [sic], the emancipation of women, and the Red Army."[2] Of course, he would have been delighted if the Soviet Union had not opposed the Zionist enterprise, but there were no grounds for thinking, like Hashomer Hatza'ir, that the two shared some sort of common fate. Moreover, he pointed out, in 1938—even though anti-Semitism was a criminal offense in Russia—the Soviets had declared "war on the Jewish people's hopes in its homeland."[3]

However, during the period between the German invasion of the Soviet Union in June 1941 and the German defeat at Stalingrad in February 1943, Ben-Gurion predicted that after the war Russia's global influence was bound to grow. The Zionist movement could not ignore this fact, not least because the largest Jewish community in Europe resided in the Soviet Union. Again, he was convinced that the Soviet attitude toward Zionism was "not a question of principle but of political tactics. It is part of their war against British imperialism, and Zionism is perceived as a tool of imperialism. It is . . . impossible not to believe that after the war, in an entirely different situation, Soviet Russia will not be able to change its approach to Zionism." Probably the Soviets would reject the idea of Jewish immigration from Russia and bar Zionist activity within their borders; communist principles, however, would preclude them from opposing Jewish immigration to Palestine from other countries or the establishment of a Jewish state in Palestine as the "most realistic solution to the problem of non-Russian Jews. For a time, Soviet Russia supported the establishment of a Jewish state within its borders. . . . There is no reason why Russian communism should reject a similar solution for Jews outside Russia."[4] Moreover, the Russian-British-American alliance was a historic opportunity for Zionism to induce the Soviets to reconsider their relationship to Zionism, still totally negative. Ben-Gurion, however, refused to accept the idea espoused by left-wing Zionism that the movement should be oriented toward the Soviet Union because it represented "the forces of tomorrow." Although agreeing that every opportunity should be seized to effect a breakthrough in relations, he said that the Zionists themselves should act to ensure "that we ourselves will be the forces of tomorrow."[5] This was the message of Zionist representatives who met with the Soviet ambassadors in London and Washington, respectively, Maxim Litvinov and Ivan Maisky, during the early 1940s.[6]

However, this policy was unproductive. Liebenstein spoke for many of his colleagues in the Mapai Center when he rejected the concept of the radical left that socialist Zionism and the Soviet regime shared a common ideology. Such an approach, he warned, missed the true function of foreign policy, namely to ensure "mutual concrete national interests."[7] Liebenstein saw the possibility of a trade-off, since Zionism could mobilize Jewish public opinion in America to achieve greater sympathy for the Soviet Union, and help to derail the Arab "federation" then being considered. The Soviet Union feared a cordon sanitaire of independent states—Arab and non-Arab—along its western border. On the other hand, Liebenstein foresaw an aggravation of anti-Semitism in the Soviet Union, where the Jews were concentrated mainly in elite professions.[8]

Until the Yalta Conference in February 1945, Ben-Gurion discerned no shift in the Soviet attitude toward Zionism. (The Jewish Agency was deluded for few months into believing that the Big Three had decided in Zionism's favor.) In the meantime, he was perturbed at Hashomer Hatza'ir's attempts to exploit the public debate on foreign policy for its own purposes. Most scandalously, on the day of the Histadrut elections, in the summer of 1944, the movement's paper published a telegram to *Davar* (the Histadrut's daily, under dominant Mapai influence) from the Soviet-Jewish News Agency stating that it would no longer transmit material to *Davar* because of the latter's "hypocritical" attitude toward Russia. Publication of the cable poisoned relations between Mapai and Hashomer Hatza'ir for a long time.[9]

Zionist opinion, at both the public and policy-making levels, yearned for a positive change in Soviet policy. Those who could not understand why apparent similarities of worldview did not obligate a more sympathetic approach by Moscow had to be reminded that foreign policy was almost always divorced from ideology. Thus, a reconciliation by the Soviet Union "will come neither as a result of kibbutz settlement, nor as a consequence of Marxism espoused by this or that opposition party, nor by translating Lenin or Stalin into Hebrew."[10]

In 1944, Eduard Beneš, the Czech statesman, told Dr. Goldmann about a "positive move" by the Soviets on Zionism: if the Americans and the British were to support a Jewish state, the Soviets would not stand in the way.[11] In February 1945 the Soviet representative to the World Conference of Trade Unions held in London backed the idea of a Jewish national home. Such developments gave the Zionist leadership hope that a real change was in the offing. But at Yalta itself Stalin, in an informal discussion with Roosevelt, disparaged Zionism. He dubbed the Jews "middlemen, profiteers and parasites."[12] Stalin's calumnies did not reach Zionist ears. But even so, Zionist experts on the USSR, although cautiously optimistic about its attitude, were under no illusions that a modification in the totalitarian character of the Soviet regime was imminent and might bring about a change in Moscow's policy on Zion.[13]

This analysis remained basically unchanged in the immediate aftermath of the war. A case in point was Dr. Moshe Sneh, the chief of the Haganah National Command and head of the defense section of the Va'ad Leumi. Sneh, soon to join the major decision-making body of the Yishuv and the Zionist movement, the Jewish Agency Executive, was perturbed at the still pro-British line of the Zionist movement. At that time a member of the General Zionist party, which had a basically Western orientation (though he would conclude his career in the Communist Party of Israel), Sneh rejected the basic division in Zionism between those who supported the pro-British line, following Weizmann, and those on the left who turned to the Soviet Union. Terming this a "superfluous debate," Sneh said that the future of Zionism depended upon cooperation among the Big Three (Britain, America, and the Soviet Union). Shertok said that the Jewish Agency would continue to push for a state irrespective of whether there was an agreement among the powers.[14] At this time Zionist policy makers needed Soviet assistance primarily to facilitate immigration from Hungary and Romania. If this could not be done legally, the Jewish Agency might be forced to step up illegal immigration even in countries under Soviet control.[15]

The need to secure Soviet support explains why Mapai was troubled by the V League, a radical propaganda body, not entirely Zionist in its viewpoint, which had been established (May 1942) by the Histadrut after the Nazi invasion of Russia. The idea behind it was officially to grant aid to the Soviet Union and get it to revise its attitude toward the Yishuv. Mapai's concern was that the league might fall under the control of anti-Mapai forces. Liebenstein said there was no place for the league's existence, since in the coming years the Yishuv's fate would be bound up with the British Empire "for good and ill, and such propaganda might well endanger external relations."[16] Liebenstein's view, however, remained a minority opinion. Shertok argued that it would facilitate the evacuating of Jews from Eastern Europe.[17] In a meeting with the Soviet chargé d'affaires in London, V League chairman S. Kaplansky (one of the founders and leaders of Poale Zion and the head of the settlement department of the Jewish Agency in the 1920s) and D. Remez did not hesitate to present Zionist demands and to inquire about possible contact with Soviet Jewry. At the same time, the Soviet diplomat assured his interlocutors that there was no doubt in "Soviet circles" that the Yishuv was "progressive" in character.[18]

Although few expected a radical shift by Moscow in its attitude toward Zionism (especially after the bitter disappointment at Yalta became known in June), the Jewish Agency Executive permitted Sneh to express optimism publicly about the possibility of a transformation in Soviet policy. During the war Moscow had become convinced that in the Middle East only the Yishuv had fought fascism. After the abolition of the Comintern, the world communist movement, Jewish communists adapted themselves to the slogans of *aliyah* (immigration) and statehood. For the Zionists, Sneh said, Soviet sympathy was essential because of Moscow's "enormous" influence in the UN, the Soviet Union's geographical proximity to the Middle East, and its direct and indirect influence in Eastern Europe, where large numbers of Jewish refugees awaited the opportunity to get to Palestine.[19] Sneh's opinions are of special importance in view of his being, together with Ben-Gurion and Shertok, one of the triumvirate of Zionist decision makers. Similarly, Liebenstein was the main spokesman for activist policy in Mapai.[20] When the Anglo-American Committee of Inquiry was established in late 1945 with the aim of finding a solution to the Palestine problem and to the plight of the Jewish refugees, only the left-wing Zionists regretted that the Soviet Union was unrepresented on the body. Both Ben-Gurion and Shertok thought it was pro-Arab. According to the latter, the Soviet argument was that the way to solve the Jewish problem was by eradicating fascism and anti-Semitism, not by immigration to Palestine. In early 1946 Shertok revised his analysis. Previously the Jews were a tool in the reactionary and imperialistic British hands against the progressive Arab forces. Now, the Soviet formulation was: no Jewish problem exists in Russia; if there is a Jewish problem outside Russia, it is the "headache" of the Western powers; and if the latter were to accept a Zionist solution for the Jews outside Russia, Moscow would not object.[21]

One consequence of the debate in Mapai over the approach to be taken toward the Soviet Union was that cooperation with Hashomer Hatza'ir was perceived to be counterproductive. Ben-Gurion ruled out a union with Hashomer Hatza'ir, stating that in its eyes "the fate of the Russian empire and the binational state outweighs all else."[22] Not surprisingly, Ben-Gurion did not fail to mention to the Jewish Agency Executive the Soviet Union's negative attitude as noted in *Novoya Vremya*, an official Soviet organ: "They [the Soviets] are happy that Jews are fighting England, but will not give them the satisfaction due Jews who fight, and therefore they write 'inhabitants'."[23] Yet Dobkin, who was in charge of immigration on the Jewish Agency Executive, had spoken with "highly placed" Soviet Jews (in the NKVD) who had begun to grasp that the Yishuv was not an imperialistic instrument and that the Jews needed a territorial center.[24]

The publication of the Anglo-American Committee Report did not change the Zionist perception of the nature of Soviet involvement in the Palestine question (in view of the Soviet refusal to collaborate with the committee). Y. Sprinzak, the secretary-general of the Histadrut, was particularly skeptical: Russia, he was certain, would block UN approval of the committee's recommendations.[25] Some senior Mapai members called for public criticism of the USSR, but there was division within the party.[26] In any event, Ben-Gurion (supported by Goldmann), in the historic convention of the Jewish Agency Executive in Paris in August 1946 (which decided on partition), declared his despair of a pro-Soviet orientation.[27]

In that same summer of 1946, a number of anti-Zionist pamphlets were published in the USSR that displayed the "consolidation of a new official Soviet line inimical toward Zionism," according to Arye Levavi, the Jewish Agency expert on Soviet affairs. A thorough survey of the Soviet press (prepared by Dr. Jacob Robinson, the legal adviser of the Jewish Agency in America) turned up not a single word of sympathy for the Zionist cause. The Balfour Declaration was represented as a British betrayal of the Arabs, and Zionism was nothing but a British tool.[28]

The exacerbation of Soviet anti-Zionism had reverberations in Mapai's internal discussions—and, as such, on the Yishuv's policy. Zalman Ahronovich (Aranne, later minister of education) said, "If, God forbid, there had been a Soviet presence in Palestine, the consequences would have been the same [as in Russia itself]: liquidation of Zionism with the addition of one element—Yiddish."[29] Liebenstein pointed out that Stalin had not uttered a word in favor of Zionism.[30] The yearning for Soviet recognition of Zionism was great. Golda Meyerson said that although the way had not yet been found "to make the great sphinx speak," there was no cause for despair.[31] The estrangement from Russian Jewry was especially painful.

Sneh's attempts to bring about a gradual shift toward the Soviet bloc were strongly opposed by Goldmann and Kaplan, who said that alienating Britain would play into Moscow's hands. Ben-Gurion, too, said he was "absolutely" against such a policy shift, because this would "present us as the enemies of the Western Bloc and as an integral part of the Soviet Bloc." Yitzhak Ben-Aharon of the Le'achdut Ha'avodah movement supported Ben-Gurion, leaving Sneh isolated.[32]

By early 1947, with Bevin's historic announcement (transferring the Palestine question to the UN), even a staunch pro-American and unabashed anticommunist like Liebenstein was longing for Soviet support. He urged that meetings be held with Russian officials wherever possible.[33] Shertok said he had been thwarted at every turn in trying to hold serious talks with the Russians. Although Moscow wanted the British to leave Palestine, he said, this should not be construed to mean that the USSR supported the establishment of a Zionist state in Palestine.[34] This anxiety, particularly as displayed by Mapai's senior figures, reflected the confusion of the Yishuv public in general and of the dominant party in particular. It was indeed the most difficult period the Yishuv had faced for some time: Britain had transferred the Palestine question to the UN, but the Soviet Union still had not shifted its policy. Given America's silence, Zionist expectations from the Soviet Union grew significantly, especially in view of the Eastern bloc's influence in the UN. The concrete impact of these reflections in Mapai was that although temporary despair was discernible, cautious pragmatism remained the order of the day owing to the Mapai leadership's determination to exploit the UN arena to the full.

Ben-Gurion could only reflect pessimistically about future Soviet maneuvering. Undoubtedly Moscow would be supportive of the Yishuv's campaign against England, he said, "but this does not mean we will get anything in return." Because the Jewish people were so widely dispersed, Zionism must take a position of "nonalignment," a point reiterated even after Gromyko's declaration of 14 May 1947.[35]

What grounds did Ben-Gurion, or even Shertok, have for their guarded optimism as to the stand of the Soviets? Some information came from Goldmann, who met with Loy Henderson, the head of the Near Eastern section in the State Department, and with Andrei Gromyko, the Soviet representative to the UN. Russia, according to Henderson, would accept neither the independence recently granted unilaterally by Britain to Transjordan nor an exclusive British presence in Palestine. Speaking frankly to Gromyko, Goldmann complained bitterly to the Soviet diplomat that the Jewish Agency had been trying to arrange talks with the Kremlin for several years, but in vain. During the war the Russians had said they were occupied with more urgent matters—but had nevertheless found time to receive Arab representatives.[36]

In February 1947, in the midst of the private and informal Anglo-

Zionist talks, which represented a last-ditch effort to salvage a good relationship between the sides, Ben-Gurion, in a final effort to persuade Bevin that the future Jewish state would be loyal to Britain and the West, made an unambiguous anti-Soviet declaration: "He [Ben-Gurion] hoped there would not be another world war, but if there was, then they would have no choice, but must be on the side of England, as in the last war. It was true that many of the Jews of Palestine, including himself and Dr. Weizmann had come from Russia, but the Jewish people as a whole could not survive under a totalitarian regime, whether friendly or not to the Jews. He knew that many Russian Jews would leave Russia if it were possible. Spiritual matters played a great part in the life of the Jews; they belonged to the liberal world of Britain, even more to the world of labour Britain, and they regarded with great anxiety any weakening of Britain's position in the world in general and in the Middle East in particular."[37]

On the eve of Gromyko's pro-Zionist declaration, none of the experts foresaw the revolutionary change planned by Stalin with regard to Palestine.[38]

Gromyko's declaration of 14 May 1947, made in the General Assembly of the UN, though first pointing to the semi-military police state of British rule in Palestine, mentioned Jewish suffering during the Nazi Holocaust and the fact that survivors were without a homeland. Gromyko went on to justify the Zionist claim: "The fact that no single Western European state proved capable of ensuring the defense of the elementary rights of the Jewish people, and of protecting it against violence on the part of the Fascist hangmen, provides an explanation of the Jewish aspiration to create their own state." Furthermore, he recognized for the first time the connection between a "considerable part" of the Jewish people and the Palestine question and its future government. Neither an Arab state nor a Jewish state would bring "a just solution," he said. Hence "the legitimate interests" of both peoples could be "properly protected only by the creation of one dual independent democratic Arab-Jewish state . . . based on equal rights." Partition should be considered as a second alternative, only if it proved impossible for the two peoples to coexist within one state.[39]

How did the Zionist policy makers and bureaucrats react to Gromyko's statement, which fell like a "bombshell" on the Yishuv's leadership? Unlike the situation in America, Soviet policy was not affected by a Zionist lobby. The Yishuv was regarded by the Kremlin as a powerful entity that could be exploited in the Cold War. Levavi offered several possible reasons for Moscow's turnaround, such as disappointment with the Arabs, who were unable to wage an anti-imperialist war; an effort to win the sympathy of American Jewry; a wish get the Mandate abolished, which could be accomplished only by supporting the Jews; possible stabilization of Eastern Europe by means of a mass Jewish exodus to Palestine; and the idealistic interpretation, according to which the Soviets recognized the progressive character of Zionism.[40]

As for Ben-Gurion, he warned the Elected Assembly of the Yishuv against exaggerating the value of pro-Zionist declarations made by world leaders. To a closed session of the Jewish Agency Executive, however, he stated that the center of gravity was in Washington but that it was essential to persuade the Soviets to abandon the idea of a unified Jewish-Arab state.[41] Tactically Ben-Gurion withdrew his support for partition, in favor of Jewish immigration and development throughout the entire country, based on the wartime plan prepared by American experts for the immigration of 1,250,000 Jews in one decade, which could not be implemented in only part of Palestine. Gromyko, however, ruled out the possibility of a Jewish state in all of Mandatory Palestine, calling it an impractical solution that would not get the necessary two-thirds majority in the UN. Ben-Gurion tried to get Gromyko to permit a Zionist delegation to visit the USSR. But the Russians, not for the first time, were evasive.[42]

Ben-Gurion was motivated by realpolitik free of any ideology when he consolidated his Soviet policy after the war. In the background was a growing need to rely on America, which would be actively involved in the resolution of the Palestine question. Although he called Gromyko's declaration "an important moral-political document," he was sharply critical of the Soviet-prone circles in the Yishuv who saw it as salvation: "They are inclined to forget that it contains much that is negative, namely, that part which comes out against British policy, and demands the evacuation of Britain from Palestine. Second, and this is the most significant argument, it should not be forgotten that the *Russians are not the owners*." Ben-Gurion went on to say that it was virtually certain that the Middle East would be dominated for "the next decade" by the "Anglo-Saxon bloc," and anyone who "makes a Jewish reckoning will not declare a life-and-death war on the Anglo-Saxon world, as many in our opposition do."[43]

Meanwhile, the Jewish Agency sought to clarify the implications of Gromyko's declaration for the future of the national home in Palestine. M. S. Vavilov, the first secretary of the Soviet embassy in Washington, explained to Epstein (Elath) that the Soviet decision—to support either binationalism or partition—had been made only after a "careful and comprehensive" analysis of the Yishuv enterprise, which was capitalistic, according to Vavilov, and had nothing to do with Marxism. Epstein reported also that Vavilov refused to commit himself either to binationalism or to partition: "Priority will be given to that solution which appears to be the most realistic and constructive."[44] He had displayed great interest, however, in the impact of the Gromyko declaration on the Jewish public and its organizations in America.[45] Whether the Russians wanted to create a split in the Anglo-American anti-Soviet front remains a mystery to be solved only by the opening of the Soviet archives. UNSCOP's historic recommendation, in late August 1947, to divide Palestine and create two states, one Arab and one Jewish, had an immediate impact on Zionist policy. In another meeting, Elath reassured Vavilov on generalities and mentioned the aforesaid V League as proof of friendship to the USSR, but he did not conceal the Yishuv's attachment to "Western democracy."[46]

It was not until 13 October that the Soviet delegate to the UN, Semion Tsarapkin, publicly announced his country's support for a two-state solution in Palestine. Moscow indeed would prove a staunch supporter, providing diplomatic and military assistance, during the 1948 war. Following the UN General Assembly vote of 29 November adopting UNSCOP's partition plan, Ben-Gurion nonetheless reiterated that in foreign affairs the Jewish state would remain nonaligned. Besides the Jewish state's commitment to "world peace and the unity of mankind," the fact that two-thirds of world Jewry was dispersed in the West, and the remainder in the East, meant that identifying with one of the rival sides "ignores the command of Jewish history," namely "peace between nations."[47] Ben-Gurion adhered to this commitment to pragmatic neutrality even after Washington's retreat from the UN partition resolution in March 1948. To the demand of Moshe Sneh, now a senior figure in Mapam, that the Yishuv shift its orientation to the USSR, Ben-Gurion reaffirmed that Zionist policy must be based on world unity and on the hope of Russian-American cooperation.[48]

After the Soviet Union recognized Israel de jure on 17 May 1948, three days after the Jewish state had formally come into being, Ben-Gurion made it clear to Mapam that its "a priori assumption" that Russia "belonged" to that party was wrong: "The ambassador to Russia cannot be a member of Mapam, because he must be one hundred percent an ambassador . . . of Israel."[49] "The Jewish people cannot be neutral," he asserted, "we are not 'neutral'. Neutral is someone who does not care. We care very much whether it will be a world of peace, freedom, equality and justice; or a world of wickedness, malice, rearmament, international hatred, wars. In such a world we will not survive. We really and truly wish for global peace."[50]

Compounding its turnabout, the USSR rejected the Bernadotte plan, initiated on 27 June 1948 and making Israel a diminutive partner in a union headed by Abdullah. Addressing the Security Council, Gromyko accused the mediator of adding fuel to the flames instead of promoting peace. His proposal to create a union of Israel and Transjordan, cutting off the Negev from Israel, and to make Jerusalem an Arab city contradicted the partition resolution of 29 November 1947, Gromyko said.[51] By offering this vital diplomatic aid on top of the crucial military aid, the Soviet Union became Israel's major supporter at this stage among the great powers. Indeed, it would not be going too far to suggest that without the Soviets' unambiguous aid, whatever their motives, Israel's establishment would have been far more difficult, and the state might even have been stillborn.

It was not until late August 1948 that an Israeli diplomatic delegation left for Moscow. Levavi spoke for those who were optimistic about future Israel-Soviet relations. He claimed to "see signs" that Eastern bloc assistance might be forthcoming in areas of major importance for the nascent state. He was particularly optimistic about economics, Jewish immigration, and the "cultural-social" affinity between the majority of Israelis and Russian Jewry. The new government should also work to moderate the "potential tension between the United States and the Soviet Union over the Palestine problem."[52] Abba Eban, Israel's representative to the UN, was also hopeful: "It is clear that while the USSR has a great deal of subjective sympathy for our cause, its attitude rests on the still more stable foundation of enlightened self-interest."[53]

On 7 September 1948, Golda Meyerson (later Meir), the first Israeli representative to the USSR, was received by V. Molotov, the Soviet foreign minister. To her expression of gratitude for Soviet assistance, Molotov noted that there was nothing unusual in this, since the USSR gave its support to all nations fighting for independence. In the immediate future Russia's assistance against Bernadotte's plans to infringe upon Israeli sovereignty was assured since Bernadotte was identified as "Bevin's agent," according to Ben-Gurion.[54] Soon enough, however, the Soviets clarified the limits of their pro-Israeli line, hinting that no interference in the affairs of Soviet Jewry could be countenanced. V. Zorin, Molotov's deputy, explained to Meyerson and her deputy M. Namir that the Jewish problem existed only in countries not progressing toward socialism. He supported Israel's position on the borders questions, particularly in the Negev, as well as on the refugee issue and on Jerusalem.[55]

A first disquieting indication that the Soviet Union was not about to fulfill Zionist hopes for free emigration, however, was an article published by the writer Ilya Ehrenburg in *Pravda* on 21 September 1948. Ehrenburg wrote that Jewish emigration from the Soviet Union and the Eastern bloc to Israel was out of the question, defined Israel as a capitalistic state, and condemned Zionism.[56] Shertok immediately cabled Golda Meyerson to express his anxiety.[57] Her reply played down the article's pejorative tone, describing it as pro-Israel but anti-immigration. She attributed more weight to the friendly tone of Soviet official declarations in support of Israel's struggle against the Bernadotte plan than to the reservations harbored by Ehrenburg or others concerning emigration and Israel's capitalist regime.[58] In fact, relations with the USSR remained friendly. On the eve of Israel's final victories in the Negev in October 1948, the Israeli military attaché in Moscow, Yohanan Ratner, submitted to the Soviet military authorities a lengthy list of equipment sought by Israel, including 70 tanks, 680 heavy and light artillery pieces, and, for the air force, 50 fighters and 24 light bombers. Meir and Ratner suggested to General Antonov, the deputy chief of staff, that Britain was arming the other side and that Israel expected the war to heat up. Israel, they said, could not rely on UN decisions alone; much would depend on its own military capability. The Soviets were thought to be highly sensitive to the future of the Negev, which could become an anti-Soviet base if annexed by Jordan or Egypt. Shertok, for his part, feared that the Soviets might initiate a crisis with Israel if the latter made concessions to the Arabs. And the head of the Middle East Department in the Soviet Foreign Ministry was concerned lest American officers join their British counterparts who were advising the Arab armies.[59]

At the same time, however, Jewish immigration to Israel from Russia's allies encountered considerable resistance from those countries, at least from Jewish communists. Communist doctrine could never agree to Jewish emigration because this negated its basic ideology, namely, that there was no Jewish problem, certainly no anti-Semitism, in the Soviet Union. Assimilation was therefore the communist prescription for the Jewish question. Zionism and communism were incompatible. A deterioration in Israeli-USSR relations was only a matter of time, especially because Soviet diplomatic and military aid stemmed originally from indirect motives, such as the wish to undermine British imperialism.

Shertok tried to break the deadlock on the delicate question in a meeting with A. Vishinsky, the Soviet deputy foreign minister. Israel, he explained, could not survive without immigration from Eastern Europe. Moroccan Jews could not build the country as could Russian Jewry ("the salt of the earth"). It was no accident, Shertok pointed out, that the majority of the Israeli cabinet consisted of Russian-born Jews. Nevertheless, he was not asking for immigration from Russia but from countries like Romania. Shertok disagreed that the departure of 100,000 Jews from Romania would harm that country's revolutionary or class future. He added that although Soviet assistance was vital to Israel, so was the support of American Jewry, and by now Russia must have abandoned the hope that American Jewry would become a pro-Soviet bastion. On the contrary, Vishinsky expressed the fear that they might become, consciously or unconsciously, an instrument in the hands of the American government, and Shertok promised that Israel would struggle against such tendencies. Finally, Vishinsky remained noncommittal both about emigration from the Soviet bloc and about Moscow's attitude toward American Jewry, whose financial assistance for immigration and development was vital, Shertok explained. The immigration question was becoming increasingly contentious both in the USSR itself and throughout Eastern Europe.[60] Soviet fears were clear: Israel, with the aid of American Jewry, might turn out to be an American asset manipulated against the Soviet Union. The situation was compounded by the grant of a $100 million loan to Israel (19 January 1949) from the American Export-Import Bank, a government institution.

Little wonder that the situation soon began to deteriorate. On 1 February 1949, the head of the East European department in the Israeli Foreign Ministry, Shmuel Friedman (later Eliashiv), complained to the Soviet minister in Israel, Pavel Yershov, about the increasing frequency of anti-Israeli writing in the Soviet Union, which claimed that the Jewish state was drawing closer to the United States. Friedman denied that Mapai bore a bourgeois character, describing it as a labor party, and said he detected the fingerprints of S. Mikunis, the leader of Maki (the Communist Party of Israel) in the Soviet publications. Yershov dismissed the anti-Israeli pamphlets as unofficial and therefore of no importance.[61] Within a week, however, Zorin told Golda Meyerson and the minister-designate, Mordechai Namir, that the Israeli diplomatic mission to the USSR was now forbidden to send letters to Soviet citizens of Jewish origin encouraging them to leave their homeland for Israel and promising them visas; this was illegal and must be stopped. Nor could the mission continue to publish a bulletin for public distribution in Russian without the permission of the Soviet Foreign Ministry. Meir denied that the diplomatic mission was encouraging Jews to emigrate, apart from isolated cases, but promised to stop both activities. Although only thirty to forty applications from relatives of Soviet citizens in Israel had been received to enable family members to leave, and only one bulletin had been published, the acerbic tone of the Soviet order left the Israeli delegation "bitterly surprised."[62] Two days later the Soviet ambassador to Washington expressed concern lest Israel become part of the Marshall Plan, Elath reported. The USSR, stated the ambassador, would not demand that Israel join the Soviet bloc, since the majority of Israelis were not communists, but it ought to remain absolutely independent of foreign control.[63] An aggressive alliance against the USSR had been formed, *Izvestia* reported, an offshoot of NATO in the Mediterranean that included Israel.[64]

The deterioration in Soviet-Israeli relations seemed to be unavoidable, given the double pressure for emigration exerted both by Israel and by the Jewish population in Eastern Europe. Relations reached their lowest point in Romania, where Zionist activists were arrested and the Israeli minister, R. Rubin, offered Romanian Foreign Minister A. Pauker $400,000 as a bribe to facilitate immigration.[65] On the surface, however, Soviet-Israeli relations seemed smooth enough. Zorin appeared sanguine when he summed up the situation to Namir: Israel had solved its major problems, having expelled the British, attained independence, defeated the Arabs, and "forced" them to agree to a "peace treaty (*sic*)." Namir replied that this was too optimistic a picture. More difficulties were to be expected, and moral, economic, and political support from friends would be needed.[66] In practical terms, however, nothing encouraging had come from Moscow; there had been no response to a loan request, according to Eliashiv and Namir.[67] Eastern bloc leaders also tried to intervene in Israeli internal affairs: the Hungarian communist leader and Stalin's confidant M. Rákosi complained about Maki's exclusion from Knesset committees. He was assured by E. Avriel, the Israeli minister, that Israel's internal policy was dictated neither by tactical needs nor at the intervention of foreign countries.[68] Namir, formerly one of the formulators of Mapai's Soviet policy, was unhappy about the contentious role of the V League (the pro-Soviet lobby) in Israeli-Soviet relations. The league spread virulent opinions against Israel, believing that this was the way to muster Soviet support for the Israel of "tomorrow." In contrast to his off-the-record pessimism, Namir recommended that Israel should show appreciation and friendship for the USSR and cultivate extensive cultural and social relations with it, notwithstanding the spread of anti-Zionism in the Soviet bloc. These were a necessary counterweight to pro-American leanings in Israel.[69] The fact is that Israel was never in a position to play off the Soviets and the Americans against each other. Levavi, now Namir's deputy in Moscow, stressed that friendly relations with the USSR were an Israeli interest for several reasons: to ensure continued immigration from the Eastern bloc; for support in the UN; to pressure the West to take into account Israel's needs; and in the event of another world war the Soviets might conquer the Middle East. Indeed, as the Cold War intensified, so did its potential impact on Soviet-Israeli friendship. The crucial question was whether Israel could pursue its "neutral" line and expect the West to pressure the Arabs to make peace in accordance with its interests. Levavi warned that the vicissitudes of the Cold War could lead either of the two global blocs to turn against Israel.[70]

Clearly, though, all the options that had been available in May 1947, when the Soviet-Zionist honeymoon had begun with Gromyko's statement, were still viable two years later. Vishinsky, now foreign minister, continued to applaud Israel's settlement of the Negev because if left empty it might whet the appetite of foreign powers. At the same time, Namir's frequent requests for loans were consistently evaded by the Kremlin.[71] Sharett was not deterred by these meager results. He found the overall record satisfactory: the Soviets had helped drive out the British; their diplomatic mission in Israel showed that they held the country in higher regard than they held any Arab state; and "the Russians know that we are not their satellite. They wish us to stay independent and not be used as a base for England and America."[72]

The USSR began to suspect, however, that Israel was edging closer to the Americans: Israel had granted concessions to Standard Oil and Ford, according to Tsarapkin.[73] The Soviets, moreover, were concerned that the Israeli army was adopting the American military model. Sharett said this was "inconceivable," while noting that Israel wished to "benefit from the experience of veteran, advanced armies." He asked Namir to remind the Soviets that the Israel Defense Forces (IDF) had asked to send officers to study the organization of the Soviet Army. Stories such as the one in Kol Ha'am, the Maki daily, that an American general controlled IDF General Headquarters, were simply ludicrous.[74]

A far more serious cause of the deterioration in Soviet-Israeli relations was Moscow's campaign against Jewish writers and scientists, which was triggered by a general Jewish national awakening in the Soviet Union. Sharett was "shocked." Israel had no part in the Jewish cultural revival, though the new state's appearance on the international stage and the enthusiasm over the opening of the Israeli embassy in

Moscow had certainly contributed. As Golda Meyerson reported to the cabinet, the awakening of Soviet Jewry following the embassy's opening in Moscow had damaged their position to some extent. Still, Namir was not deterred, although foreseeing that the aggravation of the Cold War might implicate Israel and exacerbate the situation of Soviet Jewry. But he consoled himself with the "Zionization" of Soviet Jewry.[75] Namir thought the danger of a "hot war" might cause the Kremlin to be more suspicious toward certain ethnic groups and to isolate them from the outside world. Soviet Jewry was obviously first on the agenda in this sense. Consequently, contrary to Sharett, he did not think this was the time to demand Jewish emigration, as Ehrenburg had warned him.[76] Given the volatility of Soviet-Israeli relations, did Israel have a policy or did it only react to unfolding events? In fact, Israel definitely had a policy, resting largely on Zionist ideology. However, it wanted to remain neutral as long as possible, although the multiplying difficulties made both the policy makers and the diplomats skeptical about how long this could continue before the final rift. Differences between the two countries over Jewish immigration could not be swept away as merely tactical. Soviet Jews themselves did not let this happen, governmental persecutions notwithstanding.

Hence no alternative policy was formulated, because pragmatic neutrality could not be divorced from the Zionist approach to Jewish immigration. Sharett thought it important to reassure the Soviets particularly on neutrality. Israel, he said, opposed the defense treaty of Arab states being contemplated by the West, which would be directed against the USSR.[77]

Summing up the balance of Israeli maneuvering between East and West, Sharett was not very optimistic, but his analysis was grounded in the kind of realpolitik that was crucial for a small, fragile, newly established state. His conclusion was that no deviation should be made from the present line of neutrality. First, it would be counterproductive to identify with the West because of the immigration potential from the Eastern bloc. A shift away from the "principle of nonalignment" would be interpreted by East European Jews as their "complete abandonment." Soviet Jews in particular might regard such a step as the "severance" of the emotional bond between them and Israel. Moreover, this would be "terrible ingratitude" on Israel's part after the vital assistance the Eastern bloc had given Israel in a crucial period. Such a policy shift would also cause *"a serious internal shock."* Indeed, since Gromyko's statement of May 1947, linkage between the foreign and internal policies of Israel was crucial.

Sharett warned that "the permanent rift between the present coalition and the leftist opposition would be as nothing compared to the 'hell' which would prevail in the internal life of the state and the labor movement if such a turn [away from nonalignment] were to occur." It would be little short of disastrous, he maintained, in this formative period of the state, to "generate shock-waves which might fan the hatred between the rival camps and sow confusion among the public."[78] Israel was, however, unquestionably a "Western democracy" and "ideologically . . . an anti-communist entity."[79]

There was then no alternative to the policy of nonalignment but if the democracies were attacked by the USSR, Israel could not remain "neutral in the fateful choice between the freedom of man's spirit and its enslavement." There was absolutely no comparison to be made between Israel and the Arab states in terms of resistance to communism. Theirs "is due to the natural fear of a certain elite that Soviet domination in the Middle East will mean their extermination. Only in Israel does such resistance have deep roots in the nation at large."[80]

Sharett's nightmare was that Israel, by pursuing a hyperaggressive policy, might find itself in opposition to the whole world. Three enormous blocs—Soviet, Catholic, and Arab-Muslim—posed a potential danger to Israel. So alarmed was he by the possibility, envisaged by Ben-Gurion, that the Soviet Union might force Israel to agree to the internationalization of Jerusalem and retreat to the 29 November borders that he submitted his resignation, which Ben-Gurion rejected.[81] Sharett was in fact caught between the Scylla of the USSR and the Charybdis of America. The latter suspected that Israel was leaning toward the East: "Its [Israel's] present policy," said Sharett, "was not taken as a guarantee for the future, because the present government could collapse, and there was a strong enough opposition which did not conceal its sympathy for the Soviet Union." But the "best guarantee" against Israel's joining the Eastern bloc would be a strengthening of the ties between American Jewry and Israel, which was perfectly consistent with American policy to guarantee Israel's international status. A major step in this direction would be an announcement by the secretary of state that the administration viewed favorably American Jewish investments in Israel and closer connections between American Jews and Israel.[82]

Sharett's fear, in the summer of 1949, of the disastrous effect that a change in Israel's foreign orientation might have on internal politics, particularly on the leftist opposition, must be examined within the context of Mapai's key decision-making bodies, the Center and the Secretariat. Two subjects can illuminate the stand of Israel's dominant party regarding the state's foreign policy orientation: the future of the V League, the pro-Soviet lobby established during World War II, and the question of Mapam's joining the coalition headed by Ben-Gurion.

Mapai was of two minds about the future of the V League. One possibility was to leave it solely in the hands of Mapam and Maki, which were already exploiting it for their benefit. The second was to retain control and direct it more effectively to the needs of the state's relations with the USSR. The pragmatic trend in Mapai, spearheaded by Moshe Baram (later minister of labor), called for the party to turn the incessant controversies between Mapam and Maki, on the issue of which was the true communist party, to its own advantage in order to enhance the current line of friendly neutrality toward the USSR and not to leave the impression that it identified with Sneh. According to Baram, the league—which he thought was superfluous but should not be abolished for fear of damaging relations with the USSR—should promote the "friendly relationship" between the USSR and Israel and "encourage Soviet understanding for the national and social liberation foundations of the Zionist enterprise."[83]

A second trend, represented by M. Neustadt (Noy), urged official reciprocity. Strange as it may sound today, the following analogy was suggested: if Russia wished to commemorate the Nazi aggression of 22 June 1941, a major event in Soviet history, the V League should demand the celebration of the twenty-fifth anniversary of the founding of the Histadrut, a key Zionist event. Some, notably Grabovsky, took the stand that the league was "a communist-Mapam agency for . . . slander against Zionism and Israel. . . . It is an insult to Mapai that it has continued the league's distorted and camouflaged existence." Finally it was Baram's viewpoint that prevailed, owing to the importance of maintaining friendly ties with the Soviet Union, assuring "a minimum of" affinity with Russian Jewry, and preventing the domination of the league by Mapam and Maki. Israel's fragile link with the USSR, dictated by the convenient line of neutrality, and Israel's immigration needs, required that the league continue to function as one more link in the weakening Israeli-Soviet relationship.

More serious was the question of whether Mapam, Israel's second largest party, which was in an advanced stage of sovietization, should be invited to join the coalition. Sharett saw two difficulties if Mapam were to join in view of its clear pro-Soviet line (see chapter 10): within the cabinet and at the international level. As regards the first, it had already been shown that the government could rule successfully without Mapam (which participated in the provisional coalition government until 10 March 1949, when Ben-Gurion presented Israel's first democratically elected government). Sharett in fact supported Mapam's co-option but was aware of the "grave" difficulty this would create from a foreign policy viewpoint, although he did not mention America explicitly. Notwithstanding Mapam's so-called plan to seize power in Israel, if a revolutionary situation developed, Sharett concluded that Mapam's inclusion in the government was an internal necessity in order to prevent a complete schism in the Israeli labor movement.[84]

Ben-Gurion's view was that Mapam could be brought into the government only together with the General Zionists, in order to maintain a balance between left and right. More than Sharett, he felt that Mapam's inclusion would "aggravate our international position on one side [America] without correcting it on the other side [USSR]." Moreover, Ben-Gurion thought Mapam lacked the Jewish "backbone" of Mapai: "They are in the thrall of a blind and stupid faith, adhering to formulas they have not examined," he said.[85]

Israel's delicate international position no doubt reinforced Ben-Gurion's decision to exclude Mapam from the government. By the time the Korean War brought about Israel's de facto abandonment of its neutrality, Mapam had completed the first phase of its sovietization. In retrospect, Ben-Gurion's rejection of Mapam, even with the General Zionists as a counterweight, was vindicated. From both short- and long-term considerations Israel could benefit infinitely more—materially, politically, and culturally—from America than from the USSR. Conversely, America could do Israel far more harm, even passively, than could the USSR. But in the period under discussion Ben-Gurion could not commit himself officially to either West or East, especially not during the War of Independence (which ended on 10 March 1949), when Mapam was a member of the Provisional Government. Ben-Gurion gave what was perhaps the best explanation of this noncommittal line to the writer Arthur Koestler: "Being a Jew is not only a biological fact but, consciously or unconsciously, a moral, ethical [dimension]. We have a special Jewish content, which should be the world's legacy. . . . Government by compulsion without freedom of election or freedom of conscience, thought and speech, cannot be reconciled with socialism, but we are not compelled because of this to identify ourselves with the 'West'. I wish our future to be built on prophetic ethics . . . on supremacy of science and of advanced technology."[86]

The fact that the Zionist ethos was founded on the values of Western civilization, including social democracy, signaled a probable Western diplomatic orientation. In 1948, even Mapam understood this. But by 1949, it was clear to Ben-Gurion that the evolving Western orientation must leave the Marxist-Zionists out, if Israel wished to retain its credibility as an independent democracy.

II

———

The Regional Arena

The Arab Question

3

Consolidation of Official Policy

This discussion of the Zionist attitude toward the Arab question refers primarily to the Arab states, less so to the Palestine Arabs. To begin with, the basic Zionist conception was that the Arabs were one nation. Second, since the Palestine Arabs had shown absolute opposition to Zionism they were written off as a partner. The Arab states, however, were thought to espouse a more moderate policy because of the Faisal-Weizmann agreement (1919), which had envisaged an independent Arab kingdom in Iraq and Syria and a vaguely defined Jewish Palestine. This was adopted by the Zionist leadership as a possible future scenario for Jewish-Arab coexistence. The development of Zionist policy toward the Arabs can be divided into three main periods. The first was the decade of illusion and naïveté, beginning in 1919, when the Faisal-Weizmann agreement created the delusion within the Zionist movement that the Palestine Arabs could be ignored and that the Arab world was a monolithic entity. The fundamental Zionist conception was that the Palestine Arabs must pay the price for the Jews' return to their homeland and must find compensation through the satisfaction of Arab national ambitions in neighboring countries. The second was the period of realpolitik (1929–37), in which Zionist decision makers came to realize that an armed conflict with the Arabs was probably unavoidable and that consequently, in the limited time available, it was essential to attain a maximum of power through land acquisition, immigration, economic growth, and self-defense. The third was the period of nation building in part of Palestine (1937–47) in order to achieve the agreement of the great powers and of the Hashemite dynasty in Transjordan to a Jewish state.

In the first period, reliance on Britain's colonial vigor, on the weakness of the Arabs, who were still under colonial rule, and especially on the Palestine Arabs' internecine strife enabled the Zionist leadership to discount Arab national ambitions in Palestine. The second period was marked by growing realization in the Zionist movement that ominous events lay ahead, but also, to the Yishuv's fortune, by Britain's continued belief that the consolidation of the Jewish presence in Palestine through immigration and settlement should be actively assisted, in order to help the Palestine economy stand on its own feet. Britain's strongly pro-Zionist policy enabled the Yishuv to realize the first phase of its crystallization of power by increasing its population from 156,481 in 1929 to 386,084 in 1937 (out of a total population then officially estimated at 1,383,320). Even during this period of realpolitik, Zionist leaders attempted to reach an agreement with the Arab leadership both in Palestine and in the neighboring states (Iraq achieving independence in 1932 and Egypt in 1936). Ben-Gurion in particular, in a series of meetings with Arab leaders, tried to obtain their consent to a Jewish state (to include Transjordan) in return for Jewish agreement to an independent Arab federation throughout the Middle East. This utopian design converged with the Zionists' successful attempts to foil the British plans to establish a legislative council in the hope of placating Palestine Arab national feelings. The Yishuv did not succeed in achieving Arab acceptance of its political ambitions, while the British failed to moderate Arab bitterness. This situation of stalemate finally led the British to despair of continued rule in view of the irreconcilable national goals of both sides and to propose partition (in the Peel Commission report of 1937). The Zionists accepted this policy in principle but did their best, during the decade that followed, to increase the area allotted to them by the Peel Commission and to accumulate more power.[1]

The success (or failure) of the Jewish Agency's Arab policy must be assessed by five criteria: (1) whether Zionism made good on its promise of full rights for the Arab minority; (2) whether the size of the territory claimed by the agency proved realistic; (3) whether the degree of sovereignty sought was commensurate with the situation on the ground; (4) how much support the "transfer" idea received in the Zionist movement; and (5) the attitude that was taken toward the emerging Arab states as distinct from the Palestine Arabs. Most Zionist parties were ready to grant minority rights to the Palestine Arabs, although the left opted for a binational solution.[2]

In 1937, a Zionist majority was willing to be satisfied with only part of Palestine, meaning the Peel proposal with vital additions such as Jerusalem and part of the Negev. Ben-Gurion wanted the Jews to get 10.3 million dunams (4 dunams = 1 acre), more than twice the Peel

Commission's recommendation (4.9 million dunams).[3] The assumption, though, was that the rest of the country would go to King Abdullah of Jordan, not to the Palestine Arabs. Following the Holocaust, the majority in favor of partition increased, in order to hasten the establishment of a state (see later discussion). In addition, to offset the Peel proposal limitations on Jewish territory, the Yishuv demanded full sovereignty in its area, to be preceded by a transition period in which the Jewish Agency would have full authority to implement immigration and settlement.[4] As for the transfer idea, which was officially raised for the first time by the Peel Commission, it received a short-lived but enthusiastic reception among the Zionist parties, with the exception of the left. Ben-Gurion offered a corrective to the Peel proposal: "The Hebrew state will negotiate with the neighboring Arab states the voluntary transfer of Arab tenants, workers and *fellaheen* from the Jewish state to the neighboring countries."[5] A special committee, established by the Jewish Agency to examine the transfer problem, considered the transfer of no more than 87,000 Arabs out of the 290,000 who were to be included in the Jewish state. The Jewish Agency's expert on settlement, Yosef Weitz, said that the transfer should be to Transjordan mainly (and Syria), and that it should be voluntary and include mainly those without land.[6] The volatility of the "transfer" issue, however, soon became apparent; it fueled the Arabs' frustration and resulted in violence (as demonstrated by the second phase of the Arab Revolt, in September 1937). Finally, as noted, Zionist thinkers and policy makers rarely distinguished between Palestinian Arabs and other Arabs. The basic assumption was that they were one nation and one people, and therefore peace and cooperation could be offered only to sovereign Arab states.[7] But only Transjordan and the Maronite Church in Lebanon lived up to this expectation, the former because of Hashemite pragmatism, itself the result of weakness and isolation in the Arab world, and the latter because of fear of Islam.

If transfer was again on the Zionist agenda in 1944, it was not by Zionist initiative. It was the British Labour party that at its conference of May 1944 adopted a radical resolution on this issue, as it did on the borders question, demanding expansion in favor of a Jewish state. Ben-Gurion's reaction was that this might be "problematic." If asked about the Zionist program he would not have mentioned transfer because it might be harmful to Zionism on two scores: it could cause damage in world public opinion by creating the impression that there was no space in Palestine for the Jews unless the Arabs were excluded; and it would heighten Arab vigilance.[8]

The marginal role the Arab question played in Jewish Agency considerations was exemplified earlier in its decision, by a vote of 6 to 2, not to include Arab Articles in the Biltmore program. (The articles would have promised equality to the Arabs as a minority in the Jewish state.) That the the Arabs would yield to a fait accompli was reinforced by Eliahu Sasson, the Jewish Agency's senior Arab expert: "The Arab by his nature submits to force . . . so the Palestine Arabs could not oppose a solution of the Palestine problem which would be implemented by force."[9] Shertok, whilst demonstrating some empathy with the Arab arguments, endorsed the message: "The focal point of the conflict is the issue of aliyah, but an Arab-Jewish agreement is feasible only with very limited aliyah."[10]

When Ben-Gurion finally brought his version of the Arab Articles before the executive and the parliamentary body of the Zionist movement, in March 1945, he emphasized that they had no "ideological meaning, nor were the articles a final aim of the Zionist movement or a constitution for the forthcoming Jewish state." They were only a political instrument in the Zionist struggle. Ben-Gurion's formula contained two articles:

(1) The Jewish state will be established with full equal rights of all its inhabitants—irrespective of religion and race—in the political, civil, religious and national spheres, without domination and subjugation. Every community will enjoy full autonomy in running its religious, educational, cultural, and social institutions. The Arab language and Arab schools will enjoy all state rights. In all the [Arab] towns and villages municipal self-rule will be established. The state will endeavor to equalize the standard of living of all the citizens of the Land of Israel. (2) The Jewish people will strive for cooperation with the Palestine Arabs for maximal development of the country for the benefit of all its inhabitants and for a friendly alliance between the Hebrew state and the Arab peoples in the neighboring countries on the basis of mutual action and mutual assistance for the progress and peace of all the countries in the Middle East.

Nonetheless, Ben-Gurion admitted that all this would be relevant only after the arrival of 700,000 more Jews, "which will solve the question of formal democracy."[11] Two veteran members of the Jewish Agency Executive, Rabbi Fishman of the Mizrachi national religious party, and Y. Gruenbaum of the General Zionists, both in the final analysis Ben-Gurion's admirers, opposed the mooted Arab Articles. The former was

afraid that they amounted to a binational state and demanded a declaration on the rule of the Torah in the Jewish state. Gruenbaum conceded the need to define the status of the Arab minority but objected
to the vague formulation.

Shertok, who admitted the Arab Articles were "very crude, very
hasty," strongly denied that there was a shred of binationalism in them:
"No mention was made of equal rights for two national bodies . . . it is
clear that the reference is to personal equal rights, of individuals, but
they too have rights which are political rights." Ben-Gurion's formulation won a majority of 3 to 1 in the executive (Gruenbaum abstained),
and 12 to 2 in the Small Zionist Action Committee (6 abstentions).[12]

Ultimately, the Arab question was dealt with after May 1945 as a
problem that unavoidably had to be resolved by force alone. The high
commissioner, however, had categorically warned the Yishuv leaders
that he would not tolerate private armies. Only legal defense would be
tolerated: the auxiliary police (*notrim*, the Jewish Settlement Police),
perhaps the transfer of the Jewish Brigade (which was established as a
British army unit in 1944 and managed to fight in Italy) to Palestine (as
a counterbalance to the Arab Legion and the Transjordan Frontier
Force—TJFF) or, alternatively, increasing the number of Jews in the
general police force. The authorities were well aware of the threat the
Arab rulers posed to the Yishuv. E. Golomb, the Haganah eminence
grise, said Arab sources claimed that the Arab Legion numbered 17,000,
but in fact it was only half that size. Because it included Bedouins, the
Haganah considered it not well-organized, but the legion was trained
and controlled by the British and had a mobile force of more than 2,000
men. Surprisingly, the TJFF, although it numbered only 3,500, was taken
more seriously because it had a "few tanks" and force members had
received good training. All in all, Golomb took into account two and
half Iraqi divisions in addition to 11,500 Arab Legion and TJFF troops.
From the Zionist point of view it was "quite a serious force . . . we
know that the Arabs are undaunted and audacious in their threats."
There were 1,900 Arab policemen and only (due to poor salary) 700
Jewish police. (The British police numbered 3,000 to 4,000). As for the
auxiliary police, their total number was 4,400 Jews and 4,000 Arabs.
This was about to change in favor of the Arabs. What was required,
said Golomb, was "an independent Jewish force which can act against
any danger, even if others defend us."[13]

Members of the Mapai Center like Y. Kossoy, co-secretary of Mapai
(with Z. Feinstein), referring to Bevin's anti-Zionist speech of 13 November 1945, found it "astonishing" that a socialist minister could not

see the real difference between the "socialist" Jews and the "feudal" Arabs, whose Muslim governments "would support any effort after the war to submerge the world in a sea of fascism, a sea of racial hatred."[14] Discussions on Arab policy were now limited mainly to considerations of defense, and force remained the main arbiter of Zionist politics until the armistice agreements in 1949 and beyond. Shertok was now worried about the orderly armies of the Arab League rather than local and foreign gangs.[15]

Meanwhile, the Haganah was preparing for a worst-case scenario. Its new strategic plan ("B Plan") took into account that there would be a "war of extermination against the Yishuv . . . in order to frighten it and to break its will to resist, and to prove to the authorities and the world that there will be no peace and order without an anti-Zionist solution." B Plan was defined as "offensive-defensive" and as such signaled a strategic change, the idea being to "annihilate the foe's armed force before it can achieve its goal to attack." All in all, the Haganah's assessment was that the Arab League's army would not be able to launch effectively a large regular force but would only be able to assist in a guerrilla war.[16] The Haganah, however, was not in a position to implement its program because of its meager resources.

Following the elections in Britain in the summer of 1945, Ben-Gurion and Sneh cautioned against reliance on the recent pro-Zionist promises of the victorious Labour party, which included not only a Jewish state but a transfer of the Arabs.[17] After it became clear to the Jewish Agency in mid-September 1945 that the Labour government had decided to continue the 1939 White Paper, they tried to effect a change.[18] Bevin's rejection of Zionist policy did not, however, affect the Yishuv's long-term ideological line of establishing a Jewish state at all costs. In the meantime ominous reports were received about Arab preparations in Damascus to organize "gangs" for action in Palestine. Iraq's Nuri Said warned of a Soviet danger if the West did not strengthen the Arabs. Like Abdullah, he urged a solution based on the "Greater Syria" idea, involving local autonomy for the Jews or the partition of Palestine but with limited immigration and without an independent Jewish state.

The Missed Opportunities of Eliahu Sasson

Believing that Nuri was about to convince the British government to implement his plan, Sasson recommended to his superior, Shertok, what amounted to a compromise with Nuri.[19] To an extent, he told Shertok, anti-Zionist feeling was fanned by Britain, who was using Arab opposition to Zionism as cement to achieve Arab unity.[20] Sasson's fears were realized on 2 November 1945, when a Cairo mob attacked Jews and Jewish property in the city, destroying synagogues. In neighboring Libya 120 Jews were killed in the capital, Tripoli, during four days of anti-Jewish rioting (4–7 November). While these pogroms "confirmed" Zionist assumptions as to the fate that awaited Jews under Arab rule, Bevin delivered the coup de grâce to Anglo-Zionist relations in his speech of 13 November 1945. Ben-Gurion retorted by saying that Bevin had apparently not heard about the "enormous difference" between the standard of living of the *fellah* and the Arab worker in Palestine compared to that in the neighboring countries. That difference was the result of the constructive Jewish enterprise.[21]

By this time the Yishuv had launched limited guerrilla activities against the British, now coordinated with underground "breakaway" organizations, the IZL and the Stern Gang (forming, together with the Haganah, the United Hebrew Resistance Movement). The Arab League, in contrast, expressed satisfaction over the principles of British policy, and particularly Bevin's distinction between the Zionist question and the Jewish question.[22]

Surprisingly, just when Ben-Gurion, Shertok, and Sneh had decided on active resistance to Bevin's policy, Sasson, who usually said what his superiors wanted to hear, advised Shertok to renounce the main Zionist tenet: the establishment of a Jewish state as a short-term target. What this devoted, well-connected expert on Arab affairs had in mind was no less than submission to Nuri Said and the Syrian premier, Jamil Mardam (the president of the Arab League), who claimed that Britain and the Arab states were on the verge of agreeing on a plan that would sacrifice the Jews to a new Anglo-Arab honeymoon. Yet agreement with the Arab world entailing one of several alternatives was possible: a binational state in Palestine in its present borders with numerical equality; partition, with Jewish Palestine to become a Crown colony, or the annexation of Palestine to Transjordan and the establishment of a combined state, under Abdullah. Besides guarding British interests in the region, each of these options would also enable hundreds of thousands of Jews to immigrate and would "pave the way, if not for us, then for our children to achieve political independence one day."[23]

Sasson was not proposing to abandon the long-term idea of a Jewish state, although he rejected it as a short-term policy. Shertok did not reply in writing, but there is no doubt that he flatly rejected this as a heresy against the Zionist creed.[24] Undoubtedly, no one in the Political

Department of the Jewish Agency supported Sasson's radical views, nor did he ever raise them again.[25]

In any event, no change was called for in the basic assumptions of the Zionist leadership (that partition was inevitable) as a result of Bevin's 13 November declaration. Since the adoption of the Biltmore resolutions in 1942, however, Ben-Gurion had carefully managed to avoid any discussion of partition, knowing that this explosive issue would almost certainly cause internal turmoil. Sasson predicted confidently—and accurately—that the testimony by Arab representatives during the hearings of the Anglo-American Committee of Inquiry would hold out no hope for an Arab-Jewish compromise. The Arabs objected to additional Jewish immigration beyond the 1939 White Paper limits and claimed that the region would never know peace if a Jewish state were established. They favored the creation of a Palestinian state based on the status quo and would affirm their readiness to give all the necessary guarantees for Jewish security. The Jewish DPs could be resettled in the West, and the Arab states would contribute generously toward that goal.[26]

Significantly, the Zionist leadership paid little attention to Sasson's analysis. Indeed, the leadership placed little trust in the "Arabists," not because of questioning their competence, but because of skepticism over the options they adduced for solving so complex a problem. Ben-Gurion, in his appearance before the Anglo-American Committee, was concerned to dampen down fears about a Jewish state. In this state, Arab citizens would have "absolute equality, as though they were Jews." At the same time, "every effort" would be made to let them preserve their own way of life. Contrary to his secret statements, he foresaw an optimistic immediate future of cooperation between Jews and Arabs.[27] Shertok's main argument was that economic and social cooperation between Jews and Arabs proceeded, despite political differences. Jews could offer much to the Middle East economically and could contribute to its range of "ethnic elements" and an array of "religious and political alignments."[28]

No internal Zionist debate took place in the political parties, or in other bodies, to determine the policy line that should be presented to the committee on the Arab question. The decision was made solely by the Jewish Agency leadership, which had little difficulty consolidating its policy in view of the Arabs' total negation of Zionism. To this the Jewish Agency could respond only with pragmatism that reflected the primacy of *Innenpolitik* by clinging to the idea of a Jewish state idea in two-thirds of western Palestine. In any event, only the fringe elements of Zionism expressed a different opinion (discussed later). The other Zionist parties accepted Ben-Gurion's tactics as a necessary approach for the time being, as long as the Western powers were the only hope for realizing the idea of the Jewish state and were well aware that he was the head of the main Jewish security organization (the Haganah).[29]

Given the capacity of this organization compared to that of the Palestine Arabs, the leadership of the Yishuv did not believe that independent Arab states would take up arms against a Zionist solution; they would fear jeopardizing their interests through a Palestine adventure. Egypt was busy demanding the evacuation of the British and attention was focused on Sudan and Libya, not on Palestine. Iraq was engaged with the insurgent Kurds, who were incited by the USSR, and was so completely dependent on Britain that Baghdad would not send troops to Palestine without British agreement. Syria and Lebanon hardly had armies, only a gendarmerie for internal needs. Saudi Arabia had no common border with Palestine and was in conflict with Transjordan, and it was inconceivable that Ibn Saud would send troops to Palestine. At most only some small "gangs" would infiltrate, as in the past, and the Jews could easily deal with them. Far from needing half a million soldiers to defend the Jewish state (as Truman thought), a few air squadrons to control the frontiers would be sufficient. Never before had Arab dependence on Britain been so great, and therefore the Arabs would accept the Jewish state as a fait accompli, provided the great powers took the initiative in its establishment.[30] This was the very opposite of the point made by Auni Abd al-Hadi, the leader of the Pan-Arab Istiklal party and a member of the Arab Higher Committee, who had insisted to Sasson that the Palestine Arabs would not be isolated; they would get the full support of the Arab states.[31]

No serious discussion took place regarding the military might of the Arab states. This does not mean that people were not doing their jobs or that decisions were made in a vacuum. The only response to the potential Arab threat could be the continued consolidation of power in terms of people, namely immigration, the development of the economy, and military preparations by the Haganah. The subject had not been deliberated by the Yishuv's political bodies since the summer of 1945. The general tone was publicly expressed by the Mapai activist Liebenstein, who believed that the Arab forces were at the mercy of British decision makers and who scoffed that the purported "enormous Arab forces" amounted to nothing but Arab "fairy tales."[32]

True, the Yishuv exhibited itself as the weaker side, in order not to prejudice the committee of inquiry and Western public opinion against the establishment a Jewish state that might be engulfed in permanent war. Still, the leadership was careful not to create the impression that the Yishuv was impotent, as this might reinforce the fears of Truman and others that foreign military intervention was needed.[33]

Ben-Gurion was alarmed at the prospect of a UN trusteeship, which would not allow the Jews to offset the dangers of an increasing Arab population. The establishment of Transjordan (January 1946) as an independent state encouraged him. If a state could be established for 300,000 Bedouins, what about 600,000 Jews with millions behind them?[34] At a meeting held at Weizmann's home on 10 March 1946, Shertok, with Ben-Gurion's prior consent, discussed with R. Crossman and B. Crum, both pro-Zionist members of the Anglo-American Committee, the establishment of a Jewish state in a partitioned Palestine. The heavily populated Arab area should be annexed to Transjordan, Crossman suggested, but no equivalent area was drawn as compensation.[35]

The partition plan was not made known to the Jewish Agency Executive, other than Ben-Gurion and Shertok, because official policy was for the whole of western Palestine, as envisaged in Biltmore, and to preclude a fierce internal debate the plan was kept top secret. It was, however, by no means revolutionary. It was certainly not the result of collusion of any kind on the part of the either Jewish Agency or the newly established Kingdom of Jordan. It was simply an extension of the Peel Commission's proposals. The one significant difference was the size of the territory to be allotted to each side. The Zionists now wanted about two-thirds of western Palestine, whereas the Peel report had offered them about a fifth of the country (see map). Considering that since the publication of the Peel Commission report the Holocaust had created the need for more area in order to settle survivors, the enlarged Zionist claim did not seem wildly out of place to the two committee members, Crossman and Crum. (Ultimately, the committee did not recommend partition, which could hardly have been achieved peacefully.) Both Zionists and Arabs finally concluded, each group for their own reasons, that only the use of force would resolve the problem. In addition, a Jewish state covering two-thirds of the country would be broadly acceptable to the Zionist movement and the Yishuv public. The limited territory allocated to the Jewish state by the Peel Commission was one of the strongest arguments mounted against it in 1937 and afterward. But partition was the only feasible solution in view of the hostile and dense Arab population in the "Triangle" (i.e., the

West Bank area of Jenin, Nablus, and Hebron) and the lack of support in the West for a solution giving the Jews all of western Palestine.

Ben-Gurion and Shertok did not doubt for a moment that Abdullah would eventually agree to the partition of western Palestine, which would enable him to annex the Triangle, including Lydda and Ramleh, but deluded themselves that he would concede the Negev. They had first, however, to get the consent of official circles of the leading Arab state, Egypt. Sasson was therefore sent to Egypt in the spring of 1946. He reported that, with the exception of Saudi Arabia, there was a virtually unanimous consensus on partition, "particularly if Britain and America give it their support and carry it out at once, that is to say, within two or three months." This also dovetailed with the Jewish Agency's conception that Zionism should be implemented by the great powers. Since the pro-Zionist members of the Anglo-American Committee accepted the idea, it remained only to persuade Bevin, who was really the inspiration for the anti-Zionist members of the committee, not to mention the Americans, whom the Zionists thought were in Bevin's pocket. Sasson therefore proposed a union of the Jewish state with Transjordan under Abdullah in order to stabilize the area with the consent of the surrounding Arab states, Iraq, Transjordan, Syria, and Egypt.

This wishful thinking by Sasson suited his superiors, as at least diplomatic options would be seen to be considered before force was resorted to. It might also have some influence on Bevin.[36] The flimsy attempt (the British government had its own intelligence information on the nature of Arab agreement to partition) to persuade the British government and the Anglo-American Committee to adopt the Zionist point of view that partition was a feasible solution, however, failed.[37] Ben-Gurion's assessment that Arab reaction to the committee's report must be negative, because it abolished the 1939 White Paper and denied the Arabs' right to self-rule, was correct. One minor crumb of comfort for them was in the report's recommendation that the development plans for irrigation would need to take into account the advice of the neighboring Arab countries.[38]

In other words, the committee's recommendation that the 100,000 refugees should be permitted to immigrate to Palestine was taken by the Jewish Agency as signaling the end of the lengthy period of inaction and as a portent of disturbances from the Arabs. For them, even the remote possibility of large immigration was a casus belli, as it was tantamount to the establishment of a Jewish state.

In the meantime, Dov Joseph could offer the Jewish Agency Executive some comfort in the form of a Zionist-Maronite alliance.[39] This supposed potential of the Middle Eastern minorities was also the subject of public discussion. "The historical disaster of all these nations [Kurds, Assyrians, Maronites, and Zionists] is that they do not act in concert. . . . The time has come for the Zionist movement to take the initiative and lead the Middle Eastern national minorities' war for survival."[40] Although the possible affiliation with a minorities policy along these lines was discussed in the executive, mainly because it was favored by leaders like Gruenbaum, the concept had no effect on long-term policy making because of the minorities' inherent weakness. Its status as a sideshow notwithstanding, the idea was considered a propaganda tool that should not be forsaken while Zionism was confronting inquiry committees and Western public opinion.

The turning point came in the Arab League conference at Bludan, in Lebanon, in June 1946, at which the Palestine question received greater prominence than ever before. The Palestinian delegate Jamal Husseini suggested the recruitment of an army of 100,000 men to conquer Palestine and the establishment of a Palestinian "government in exile" with a budget of ten million British pounds. The high command should consist of the Arab ministers of defense. This plan was, however, held in abeyance; the Arab League still hoped that political pressure would be enough. Meanwhile, a special Palestine committee would be established to organize the Arabs' needs for their "war" in Palestine.

When the details of Bludan became known to the Jewish Agency, Sasson said that the only way to obstruct Jamal's plan was to press for the implementation of the Anglo-American Committee's recommendations.[41] But the Jewish Agency was not impressed. Although the regular armies of the six independent Arab states were estimated to number about 100,000 troops, they were "poorly organized, ill-trained and badly equipped, and generally weak from a military point of view." Furthermore, the likelihood of combined action was "extremely remote." Only the Transjordanian army resembled a serious fighting force, in the form of the British-trained Arab Legion, but it was small (now estimated at 8,000 troops without the TJFF; see chapter 2). The major armies in size were those of Egypt (45,000), which despite its "many serious shortcomings" was the "most modern" of all Arab forces, and of Iraq (31,000), which was undergoing "intensive reorganization" by the British but had made recently a "poor showing" against the Kurds. Overall, Arab strength did not seem to constitute a genuine threat: "Unless a great foreign power directs the resistance of the Arab armies, it is unlikely that they will be capable of joining in any united action. In view of the rigid control which the British exercise over the Egyptian, Transjordanian, and Iraqi armies, it is unlikely that any military action can be taken without the consent or encouragement of the British."[42]

Indeed, the Jewish Agency was wedded to the British orientation until the summer of 1946 when Britain tried to break the backbone of the Yishuv in Operation Agatha (the "Black Sabbath," 29 June 1946; see chapter 4) and initiated the plan for provincial autonomy ("Morrison-Grady"; see chapter 1). These developments, however, afforded the government another opportunity to compromise with the idea of a Jewish state at the London Conference (September 1946–February 1947)—the last British attempt to reconcile Arab-Jewish claims. The British connection was vital to Zionism if the Jewish Agency's partition plan were to be implemented. Soviet involvement now loomed larger than ever before; if Britain could not resolve the Palestine issue it would have to refer the problem to the UN, where the USSR could intervene formally. Soviet intervention should deter Britain from supporting the Arab case. The Soviet attitude, Sasson argued, could well "be friendly; not out of love for us or hate for the Arabs, but out of political considerations regarding England."[43]

In July Ben-Gurion developed his plan to establish a neutral territory on both sides of the Jordan.[44] It was probably intended merely as a tactical move against opponents of partition inside the Zionist movement (as he suggested to the 22nd Zionist Congress), apart from demonstrating the will to be liberated from Britain, as his maneuvering in the convention of the executive in Paris that summer suggests.

Sasson was thus free to discuss partition with both Abdullah and Ismail Sidky, the Egyptian prime minister, in order to obtain their support for a Jewish state within that framework. Much discussed in the literature, these talks were as insignificant in Middle Eastern history as the Faisal-Weizmann agreement. In neither case was there a breakthrough to moderate the escalating conflict. Sasson had evaluated wrongly what Sidky told him that summer about the necessity for a breakthrough first of all in the Anglo-Egyptian talks. Similarly, the talks with Abdullah showed that the king had limited power; indeed, he supported the Morrison-Grady plan, in order to please his British superiors. But if the Jewish Agency could obtain the consent of England, America, and the UN for partition, Abdullah would also support it. In other words, Morrison-Grady was a short-term plan, and partition was a long-term solution.[45]

Ben-Gurion sounded an encouraging note at Mapai's Sixth Convention in September 1946, calling, from his temporary exile in Paris, for negotiations "with our Arab neighbors."[46] Significantly, however, Ben-Gurion excluded any chance of agreement with the Palestine Arabs, because of their implacable anti-Zionism. On the same day Auni Abd al-Hadi again clarified the position of the Palestine Arab leadership: "I can see no other outcome but war. Either you will win or we will win. . . . History will judge the Jewish leaders as criminals."[47] As for Sasson, within less than a month he was forced to admit that his talks with Ismail Sidky were nothing but trial balloons.[48]

At the London Conference, it became obvious that neither the Arab states nor the Palestine Arabs were ready to recognize the Jews and sit down with them. Nonetheless, the Arab states, unlike the Palestine Arabs, agreed to the establishment of Palestine as a democratic Arab state; all Jews actually residing in Palestine should be recognized as citizens and receive minority guarantees, but there must be an immediate halt to Jewish immigration, although relatives might be allowed in. Finally, the Arabs made it plain that they would consider "no form of partition whatsoever."[49] Musa al-Alami, the Palestine Arabs' chief representative at the London Conference, was distraught at the Arab states' more flexible position. Finally, he succeeded in persuading most of them to support the Palestine Arabs' stand. Only Egypt and Azzam Pasha, the secretary-general of the Arab League, remained adamant about giving the Jewish minority democratic rights.[50]

Zionist circles still talked of a partition solution, with Britain able to safeguard its vital strategic and economic interests in the region through alliances with both sides.[51] For his part, Sasson felt he had not been insistent enough in pursuing an Arab policy. The Christians of Lebanon could be recruited against the Arab "ocean" and Abdullah could be encouraged in annexation plans against Syria. Hence, three new states—Jewish, Maronite, and Syrian (ruled by Abdullah), would be allied to Britain, and the Palestine question and the Arab-Jewish conflict could be resolved to the satisfaction of the United States, the Arab world, and the USSR. Egyptian neutrality in Arab affairs would be encouraged, and Tunisia, Algeria, and Morocco would be discouraged from joining the Arab League.[52]

Of course, none of Sasson's plans materialized and the Husseinis were more successful in persuading Arab states to support their plans for armed resistance against any attempt to establish a Jewish state. In historical perspective Sasson must be perceived as a prisoner of his own dreams and utopian plans. Sasson's failure became a pattern, but his fiasco was not considered a personal one. Rather, it was the inevitable failure of Zionism's general policy on the Arab question, which since 1936, if not earlier, had been perceived as a zero-sum-game conflict: what was a gain to one side was a loss to the other. Rather than an initiator of policy, Sasson was more of an adviser on Arab affairs, and hardly a creative one in view of the primacy of *Innenpolitik* in Arab affairs. Still, persistent failure, instead of generating a change in ideology or policy—impossible in view of the need for a Zionist consensus on the Arab issue—brought instead a mounting conviction that diplomacy should give way to a military solution. As Sasson saw it, the fault lay not with the Arabs, and still less with the Jews, but chiefly with Britain. Thus, the Arab section of the Jewish Agency continued to build up its connections with Abdullah and his supporters in Palestine and Syria.[53] But within a week of putting forward his plan, Sasson, utilizing his special connections and those of Yolande Harmer, the Jewish Agency's special agent in Cairo, heard that Jamal Husseini had persuaded the Arab League Council to prepared for armed resistance against the Jews.[54]

Countdown to War

The fact that the British refused to budge from the Morrison-Grady plan did not shake the Jewish leadership from adhering to its official minimal program of a "viable" (i.e., partitioned) Jewish state. At the 22nd Zionist Congress, Ben-Gurion reiterated the Yishuv's commitment to full political, national, and religious equality for the Palestine Arabs, while rejecting outright the Morrison-Grady plan. Asserting that it constituted a retreat from the recommendations of the Anglo-American Committee of Inquiry, and more closely resembled the hated White Paper of 1939, Ben-Gurion likened it to the Jewish "Pale of Settlement" in Tsarist Russia. The fact that the British high commissioner, still the source of power, would be able to intervene in the affairs of the district provincial governments, Ben-Gurion said scornfully, suited the plan better to self-government for primitive tribes in Central Africa, not the Yishuv. His basic fear was that Morrison-Grady would make the Jews a permanent minority under a spurious "federal unity" that would actually be Arab rule in disguise.[55]

Small wonder that the Morrison-Grady plan was unanimously rejected by the congress. But the congress's Political Committee got a very different reception when it put to the vote the additional Biltmore Arab articles confirmed in May 1945 (discussed earlier). As expected, only the first of them, referring to full equality for the Arabs in the future Jewish state, was adopted unanimously. In the voting on the second article, dealing with cooperation and alliance, 53 abstained (out of 385 congress delegates); both the radical left and the radical right put forward their own minority resolutions.[56] The coup de grâce to the policy of a peaceful solution was, however, delivered by Ben-Gurion himself in a secret session of the Political Committee (18 December 1946). Noting that until recently the question had been how to defend the Yishuv against the Palestine Arabs, he warned that now "an entirely new situation" had arisen. The point was that Palestine was surrounded by independent Arab states and, even if "politically, culturally and economically this independence is fictitious," they had acquired "the right to purchase and manufacture arms, to create armies and to train them." Although their military potential was at present "nil," to rely on their continuing weakness "would be a fatal mistake." Aggression by the Palestine Arabs posed no danger to the Yishuv, Ben-Gurion said, but an attack by Arab armies at some future stage would be an altogether different matter. In short, "we stand before changes and transformations, and we must not wait until the danger ripens. We must prepare immediately with our utmost technical and financial capability." No mention was made of the vaunted "Hashemite orientation."[57] The immediate implication was that military preparations should be accelerated.

On 7 February 1947, the eve of Britain's submission of its final plan for cantonization (the Bevin-Beeley plan, addressed later) to the Jewish Agency, the last, futile round of the London Conference Anglo-Zionist discussions took place. It turned out to be irrelevant to the British government's final position as articulated the next day. British representatives noted the Arabs' fears about their rights in a future Jewish state, while Ben-Gurion countered that Jews could not live securely in any Arab country.[58]

London's final proposal by Bevin and Harold Beeley (Bevin's adviser on Middle Eastern affairs) was, from the Zionists' viewpoint, an even worse plan than Morrison-Grady. While the former envisaged possible partition, though in a small Jewish area, the Bevin-Beeley plan jettisoned partition and recommended an independent Arab state. The Anglo-Zionist discussions lasting from 27 January until 6 February were a dialogue of the deaf.[59] Later on, Ben-Gurion stated that he had entertained no illusions when he went to the London talks. Meyerson admitted afterward that although she was hopeful that there were "Arab circles" who objected to being ruled by the Mufti and were ready to support a "constructive" Jewish plan, they were "neither strong nor prepared."[60]

On 18 February 1947 Bevin announced the referral of the Palestine problem to the UN. Ben-Gurion reacted by saying that the Jewish Agency had hitherto wished to continue building the Zionist enterprise with Britain but would now proceed in a different direction. He told the Va'ad Leumi on 1 April 1947 that the "two cornerstones of contemporary Zionist policy" were, first, the establishment of the Jewish state, to be followed by a "Jewish-Arab alliance." The alliance, he said, would be based on mutual "equality and independence, as two equal partners for peace and social progress and economic development in the Semitic lands of the Middle East." This was not a remote vision "but actual policy," and it would be implemented in the years to come.[61] Certainly this optimism was for public consumption, both at home and abroad, but it reflected also his belief that in the final analysis, even if preceded by war, peace must prevail between Jew and Arab. He would frequently display this approach during the War of Independence.

The Palestine question was now the UN's responsibility, though Britain continued to rule the country for another full year. Shertok, in a statement to UNSCOP in July, sounded a different note. The idea of Arab-Jewish coexistence in one state was a fallacy, he admitted. Although binational or multinational states do exist, he said, "sovereignty in the ultimate resort is vested in the majority of the population or the majority of some elected assembly. In the last resort the majority prevails, and nowhere do you find two equally balanced communities set against each other. . . . But if you assign equality to both statics and dynamics, then the statics will have the advantage. Equality of veto will mean Jewish defeat."[62]

In the same vein was the testimony of Ezra Danin, a veteran Arab affairs expert, to UNSCOP. Danin's appearance was memorable and deserves to be quoted in some detail:

Judge Sandström (chairman): Well, are you going to be massacred?
Danin: No. We are not sheep. We will not be slaughtered.
Sandström: But they—the Arabs—say that their strength is great!
Danin: Yes, I know that, but our strength is also great.

Unlike the Jews, Danin said, who were ready to sacrifice themselves for an idea, the Arabs interpreted the term *patriotism* differently. Here, self-preservation was predominant: "Confronting death itself, the Arab will be the first to retreat, since he has an alternative, while we Jews stand with our back to the sea." World War II, he summed up, had proven that the essential ingredient for military success was not "cannon-fodder" but combat capability and a readiness to fight.[63] Here was the epitome of the Zionist attitude on the Arab question, clearly reflecting the view of the average Jew in the Yishuv.[64]

By August 1947 the Zionist leadership knew, thanks to constant leaks by the pro-Zionist members of UNSCOP to the Jewish Agency delegation in Switzerland, where the commission held its final sessions, that the two extreme solutions—an Arab state or a Jewish state in the whole of Palestine—would be rejected by UNSCOP. The idea that only part of Palestine would be allotted to the Jewish state had been long accepted by the Zionist official leadership. The only question was how large an area the commission would give each side.[65]

On 18 June, the eve of UNSCOP's visit to Palestine, Ben-Gurion, in order to clarify the stand of the Jewish Agency Executive, again put to the vote the "viable state" formula of the previous summer and won by a majority of one (8 to 7). All three coalition parties—Mapai, the General Zionists, and the Mizrachi group—were split down the middle between realists and messianics.[66] The vote reflected the need to avoid what Ben-Gurion considered a damaging debate over partition; the UNSCOP decision on the issue would, ultimately, cement the Yishuv consensus, as is discussed later.

By now Ben-Gurion was taking a keen interest in the military strength of the Arab states. The main forces were those of Egypt (35,000 troops) and Iraq (about 30,000) though other than Transjordan's Arab Legion, the Arab armies were poorly trained and equipped. Still, they could put a combined total of some 150,000 men into the field.[67] Not all these armies were about to arrive in Palestine, but some might certainly be dispatched. It was clear that Britain would not defend the Yishuv. On the contrary, the British would incite the Arabs.[68]

Partition, as already noted, had been accepted by the Jewish Agency at its Paris convention the previous summer, but that was an ideological decision; the operative moment was about to arrive with UNSCOP. In order to cushion the decision, especially for the activists in Mapai, Ben-Gurion declared to the Jewish Agency Executive that the Zionist movement had the right to the whole of western Palestine. This was an old ploy to comfort those who found it hard to agree to partition.[69]

To UNSCOP Ben-Gurion urged partition for the first time publicly (a "viable state" following the borders proposed by the agency to the Anglo-American Committee). Even if the Arabs of Palestine remained a minority, they would still constitute part and parcel of the great Arab majority in the Middle East. The Arabs of western Palestine were only 1 percent of the region's total Arab population. The existence of independent Arab states in the north, east, and south was "an automatic guarantee not only of the civil, religious, and political rights of the Palestine Arabs, but also of their national needs."[70]

Aware that his testimony to UNSCOP would not alter the inevitability of war, Ben-Gurion had on 18 June 1947 ordered the Haganah to prepare for war with Egypt, Iraq, Lebanon, Syria, and Transjordan. Notwithstanding the tireless attempts to reach an agreement with Abdullah, Ben-Gurion still took into account the potency of the Arab Legion.[71] By summer 1947 Ben-Gurion was convinced that as the UN decision approached, "an Arab force will be recruited in order to exterminate the Yishuv." After the British withdrawal, he warned, "we will face the Arabs. Which means not only Arab gangs but an Arab army." Even if it was not a first-class force, it still had destructive potential.[72]

Fawzi al-Kaukji, soon to be appointed commander of the Army of Deliverance, consisting of volunteers from Arab states to help the Palestine Arabs in their fight against the Jews, had stated that the only solution was the complete annihilation of the Jews. Thus, Ben-Gurion contended, he continued the chain of twentieth-century Muslim genocide, Ottomans against Armenians, Arabs against Christian Assyrians in Iraq.[73] Azzam Pasha, the secretary-general of the Arab League, whom Ben-Gurion regarded as the "most honest and humane among Arab leaders," had warned the Zionists that "as we fought against the Crusaders so we will fight against you, we will erase you from the earth."[74]

The operative turning point occurred in mid-September when the Political Committee of the Arab League convened in Sofar, Lebanon. The Palestine Arabs were promised concrete financial and military aid by the majority of the Arab states, though with reservations as to immediate implementation. In addition, diplomatic and economic and financial measures would be implemented in favor of the Palestinian Arabs.[75]

Following a further series of meetings held by the Arab League Council, the Arab governments declared that "should it become necessary, they would sacrifice all the political and economic interests of the Arab world, in order to save Arab Palestine." For the first time the military chiefs of the Arab states participated in a meeting of the League's Council. Orders were issued to some Syrian and Lebanese units to take up positions along the borders of Palestine. The Mufti was promised funds and freedom of movement for his men and assured of immediate action.[76]

All this was reported with no delay to the Jewish Agency by its agent in Cairo, Yolande Harmer. Ben-Gurion, however, saw no need for panic. To his closest colleagues he still insisted on the need for a declaration by the Elected Assembly that the Yishuv was ready for a Jewish-Arab treaty on the basis of "national equality." In the Political Department Golda Meyerson—having replaced Shertok, who was now at the UN—expressed the fear that in the event of Arab-fomented disturbances, the British would support the Arabs. If Arab states intervened, she said, the Jewish state would be justified in recruiting abroad. Ben-Gurion warned against panic but was well aware that his persistent call for a Jewish-Arab "alliance" had only propagandist significance in the face of Arab militancy.[77]

Typically, Ben-Gurion clarified to his inner circle that he would respect the UN resolution but that if the Arabs did not do so, he would not consider himself bound by the UNSCOP Report, meaning the recommended borders of the Jewish state.[78] The immediate threat was Abdullah, even though publicly he called for peace. Ben-Gurion again asserted that "there is no basis for panic, but there is reason for serious concern."[79]

Within days news reached the Jewish Agency that in a meeting at Aley, a military committee of the Arab League had decided that Palestine would be overrun by forces of the Arab states as soon as the British withdrew. (The previous decision had been to intervene only if the Jews should attack the Palestine Arabs.) Syria and Lebanon would occupy the north of the country as far as Acre-Safed; the rest was to be conquered by the Arab Legion and the Iraqi Army. Some 41,000 troops would take part, including 7,000 Egyptians, who however would not enter Palestine because of a cholera epidemic in Egypt.[80] Abdullah, for the time being, definitely dissociated himself from the Aley decisions.

For the first time, Ben-Gurion stated in public that Abdullah, unlike his fellow Arab leaders, was the only voice of peace.[81] On the eve of the famous Abdullah-Meyerson meeting, which would later acquire almost mythological status, Ben-Gurion expressed anxiety over a possible "secret coalition" between Azzam Pasha and Bevin, which might turn the country into a battlefield. And in spite of his public sympathy for Abdullah, he regarded the Arab Legion as "quite a potential enemy."[82] These conflicting developments convinced Ben-Gurion that Abdullah's pro-Zionist declarations must be taken with a pinch of salt. Not surprisingly, he did not hail the Meyerson-Abdullah meeting of

17 November 1947. Its inconclusive character did little to dissipate the fear that Transjordan might yet join in the Arab states' invasion. The king's ambivalent attitude as to the status of the Jewish state—whether it would be an "independent republic" within the Hashemite kingdom or a full-fledged Jewish state within the UN partition borders—was the most striking feature of the meeting.[83]

Ben-Gurion had to admit, on the eve of the UN's 29 November vote on the partition resolution, that his short-term Arab policy, relating to the Arab states' intervention, had failed. Not so his long-term one— not with regard to the Palestine Arabs, of whom he had despaired altogether, but vis-à-vis the Arab states, whose future line must surely be realistic: once the Jewish state was established they would accept it as a fait accompli, even if war would have to precede peace. This delicate balance between short-term and long-term policies enabled him to maintain unequivocal leadership on the Arab question. Consolidation of this question was a by-product of realpolitik, Ben-Gurion's policy since 1933 when he had begun to head the Jewish Agency's Political Department together with Shertok, supported by an overwhelming consensus in the Yishuv. Although differences with his colleagues in the executive, especially with Fishman and Gruenbaum, were sometimes more than tactical, the final decision lay with him. His futile attempt to distinguish between the Arab states and the Palestine Arabs did not imply a failure in terms of military preparations. Here he relied neither on the Shai (Haganah intelligence) nor on the Arabists but on his own judgment (see later discussion).

Phase One: War with the Palestine Arabs

The outbreak of hostilities on the day after the UN's 29 November resolution caused no change in the basic approach or the operative ideology of the Zionist decision-making elite regarding the Arab issue. Ben-Gurion made clear to his closest colleagues in the Mapai Center four days after the war began that a Jewish state of 600,000, with 40 percent of the population non-Jews, would not be very viable. There was no mention of a possible "transfer" of the Arab population, but the immigration of a million and a half Jews would establish the state. At the same time, he promised "full and absolute" equality to the Arab citizens; there would be no discrimination other than in immigration. Agricultural development would be made available to the Arabs too, and their social services would be raised to the Jewish level. The country's Arabs would receive "national-cultural autonomy," and af-

ter achieving economic, social, and cultural parity, they would constitute a "bridge for the Jewish-Arab Semitic alliance in the Near East."
In a memorable passage of unique importance, Ben-Gurion revealed
his conceptual approach regarding the future relationship between the
Jewish state and its Arab neighbors:

> Every pupil knows that there is no final settlement in history. . . .
> History like nature is full of changes and metamorphoses; the
> only permanent thing is perhaps change itself. . . . Anybody who
> examines his life and any nation searching its history will imme-
> diately discover this simple and elementary truth. But in interna-
> tional life settlements and reforms are fixed, and as long as they
> exist it is necessary to respect them and remain loyal to them, if
> basically they are desirable and lead to progress. The decision of
> the UN for a Jewish state is one of the most important resolutions
> of our time. And the basic commandment to ensure the state's
> peace, its security and prosperity, is the formulation of foreign
> policy for friendly relations and an alliance with the Arab world.
> . . . Any foolish talk of irredentism, of the capture of Jerusalem
> and forcible expansion, of wars of conquest, and the like might
> poison our external relations and the internal atmosphere. Nei-
> ther provocation nor competition but agreement with our neigh-
> bors—this must be the cornerstone of our foreign policy.[84]

Such sentiments might be considered no more than high-sounding
rhetoric, but Ben-Gurion was sincere, though he realized that there was
a gap between such a vision and the grim reality of war. Undoubtedly,
the frequent mention, throughout the war, of an alliance with the Arabs was meant to calm the Yishuv. Ben-Gurion, however, was aware
also of the danger that the UN or the great powers might regret their
support for a Jewish state. Optimism, he thought, was the best political instrument for both domestic and external consumption.

But the situation on the ground spoke a different language. The Arab
League had secretly decided to set up in Syria a military committee
that would organize training camps, arsenals, medical supplies, and
funds. Military operations and guerrilla activities in Palestine would
begin as soon as the British withdrew. If the Arab volunteers should
prove unable to overcome the Jews, then "a large part of the Arab regular forces will . . . join the ranks of the volunteers."[85]

With little hope, all efforts were now directed toward averting an
Arab invasion and toward Transjordan in particular. Hence the readiness to let Abdullah occupy the Arab part of Palestine. Sasson tried

again to persuade the king, who was willing to grant the Jews no more than autonomy along the coast between Tel Aviv and Atlit, to agree to a Jewish state.[86] After the eruption of local hostilities, Ben-Gurion once more had to calm down his colleagues by underrating the Arabs' potential military strength.[87] Meanwhile, the Arab section in the Jewish Agency's Political Department oscillated between optimism and pessimism, saying Sasson "believes in the king" (Abdullah) but that the king's "power is limited, and one should not reckon on him."[88] The leading Zionist expert on Arab affairs now (early February 1948) recommended aggressive military action against the Palestine Arabs.[89] Abdullah, however, was not yet given up. For a while Sasson advocated cooperation with the "sane" Palestinian Arabs, the anti-Husseini opposition, which could set up a republican-democratic Arab state in Palestine.[90]

The capture by the Haganah, in early April, of key points on the Tel Aviv–Jerusalem road, seemed to be a military turning point. Despite the enemy's "nearly unlimited reserves" and the overwhelming numerical disparity between the Yishuv and the Arabs (45 to 1 in the latter's favor), Ben-Gurion was confident of victory. Still, a demographic realignment was essential. The consolidation of victory, he explained, would depend "on a basic change . . . in the composition of the Jewish population and its distribution in the different parts of the country." Moreover, "the war will also bring about a great change in the distribution of the Arab population. . . . We will not be able to win certain parts of the country if we do not populate them with Jews."[91] This conceptual approach, together with the concrete execution of the Haganah's strategic "Plan D" since early March, makes it clear that, although no programmatic policy existed, the dynamics of war themselves triggered the "transfer" of the Palestine Arabs, even though only the first wave of refugees was about to be created.[92] Alternatively, the fact that he was involved in a "total war" probably convinced Ben-Gurion that the Arab population, which was basically hostile, should be reduced in size by expulsion.

On 6 April Ben-Gurion expounded to the Greater Zionist Actions Committee his ideas on the future: "The road to Jewish-Arab understanding will be paved by three means: with force, with independence, with goodwill."[93] Ben-Gurion's conception was that "force" and "goodwill" were reconcilable. Force meant victory, and goodwill meant fair play in peace negotiations.

Sasson tried twice in April to dissuade Abdullah from joining the Arab invasion. Following the Deir Yasin massacre on 9 April, when

IZL and Lehi killed 254 Arabs (see chapter 11), and the fall of Tiberias (18 April) and Haifa (22 April) to the Jewish forces, the king saw no other solution but Jewish autonomy under his rule, a result of inter-Arab pressure on him.[94] The press report on 27 April that Abdullah had "declared war" on the Zionists, and the Arab Legion's attack on Kibbutz Gesher that same day, confirmed Ben-Gurion's longtime conviction that whether there was an official declaration of war or not, the Yishuv should expect either an air bombardment by the Egyptians or an attack by the Arab Legion.[95]

And yet Ben-Gurion gave Abdullah a last opportunity. This was the famous meeting, already mentioned, on the night between 10 and 11 May, in which Abdullah told Golda Meyerson that he would join the war but reiterated his willingness to grant the Jews autonomy within his monarchy, "which would be a wonderful thing for the Jews." Hearing this, Ben-Gurion immediately rushed to Haganah headquarters and ordered his military aides (Yigael Yadin, Yohanan Ratner, and Israel Galili) to prepare for a mobile campaign and to make plans to repulse a full-scale Arab invasion.[96] Ben-Gurion was by no means deterred by the prospect of an Arab invasion, although the sheer numbers gave pause: up to 10,000 troops from Egypt, some 8,000 Iraqis, 5,000 from Transjordan, and 3,000 each from Syria and Lebanon.[97] The number of Arab forces mentioned now was far less than in the assessment of late 1947—29,000 instead of 150,000—but even so the Haganah had no experience of fighting regular armies.

War with the Arab States—Phase Two

The Yishuv's military victories before the Arab invasion of 15 May 1948 had irrevocably sealed the fate of the Palestine Arabs. As to their future, Ben-Gurion turned for advice to Yosef Weitz, the head of the department of development of land and forestry in the Jewish National Fund. Weitz suggested a "post factum transfer" of the 335,000 refugees who had already left—in other words, not letting them return. He wanted to discuss with the Arab states possible assistance for the refugees' resettlement within their borders. This was no new policy, for sporadic suggestions of this kind had been popular in the 1930s, though never supported by any Arab country. Ben-Gurion, however, thought that this idea was "too early and badly timed," although he was for settling Jews in the abandoned Arab villages.[98] The refugee question, however, was a side issue at this stage, since the war itself was not yet decided one way or the other. The first truce enabled a rethinking of the chances for Arab-Jewish negotiations toward a peace agreement. The problem, as Shertok said, was that "our net of connections with the Arab states has been virtually demolished." At the same time, Jewish-Arab relations were carefully watched by Washington, which had been convinced by the British that an Arab defeat might lead to the fall of the present Arab regimes, which were "a bulwark against Bolshevism." But both Shertok and Ben-Gurion understood that "a regime of political bargaining" was necessary.[99]

The Israeli provisional government held its first serious discussion of the Arab question on 16 June 1948. Shertok enumerated the four foundations for a peace settlement, which were still wedded to the 29 November resolution and remained tactical as long as the war continued: a Jewish state; a separate Arab state, neither part of Transjordan nor of Syria; an internationalized Jerusalem; and the economic unity of the Arab and Israeli states and Jerusalem. The idea of an exchange of territory, raised by the UN mediator, was endangering Israeli domination in the southern Negev. Above all, though, Shertok's great "surprise" was the "emptying" of the country's Arab community. This, he said, was "one of those revolutionary changes following which history does not revert to the status quo ante, as there has been no return to the former status for Czechoslovakia and other countries after the war." Shertok was ready to compensate the refugees only for their land and property. Ben-Gurion, taking it for granted that the Arab refugees would not be allowed to return (tacitly agreed to by the cabinet), preferred to discuss his much repeated vision for a Jewish-Arab alliance, once the survival of the Jewish state had been assured.[100]

Was Ben-Gurion afraid that without an alliance the State of Israel would not survive in the long run? Or was he perhaps referring to his long-held perception that such an alliance required a Zionist military victory as a prior condition? Possibly both: "If the Arabs are willing to negotiate, we should not stipulate territorial preconditions that would make it impossible for them to do so."[101] Ben-Gurion considered that winning the military campaign was first and foremost on the agenda.[102]

Meanwhile Count Bernadotte, the first UN mediator for Palestine, whose mission would prove futile, suggested an Arab-Israeli "union" on both sides of the Jordan River, to be headed by Abdullah, but with the Jewish entity to be deprived of the entire Negev and with Jerusalem to be Arab. Ben-Gurion did not object to an alliance with the Arabs provided Israel retained control of immigration: "We can join a federation, but only as a completely independent state." Other ministers— Rosenblueth (justice), Bentov (labor and construction), and Shapira (immigration and health)—were in favor of negotiations on the Bernadotte plan.[103] But Ben-Gurion was outraged by it and wanted to exploit the period between the two truces (9–19 July) to defeat the Arab Legion and the Egyptians at Latrun and in Jerusalem.[104]

Although he was more confident after the territorial gains of the Ten Days' campaign (9–19 July) that the IDF had the capability to succeed, Ben-Gurion was adamant that eventual cooperation between "the two Semitic peoples, Jews and Arabs" was "an historical necessity."[105]

Ironically, however, the greater the Israeli victory, the less probable was a peace agreement with the Arabs. In any event, at this stage the only way to communicate with the Arabs was through Bernadotte. Shertok suggested a resettlement of the estimated 300,000 Arab refugees in the "Arab world," financed by Arab property in Palestine and international aid.[106] M. Assaf, a veteran expert on Arab affairs, reflected policy making when he noted that the recent "exchange" of populations in India and Pakistan, while brutal in character, had received almost universal acquiescence because it was the least of all evils. The best course would be to "exchange" Oriental Jewry for the Palestine refugees, Assaf said.[107]

The issue did not spark a public controversy, since forcible transfer—that is, expulsion—was not supported openly by the official leadership. But secretly, in the cabinet session of 28 July, Shertok said that if returned, the refugees would become a "volatile" fifth column. Both he and Ben-Gurion were unimpressed by Bernadotte's emphasis on the humanitarian aspect, and the cabinet voted (9-2) that as long as the war continued, except for special cases, there could be no return of refugees.[108]

The government saw eye to eye with the public and commanded a solid consensus on this life-and-death issue. Liebenstein argued that the refugee problem had become an international issue only because the Arab states had manipulated world public opinion to believe that the only solution was the refugees' return to their homes. He reflected official thinking when he claimed that the refugees' settlement among their brethren would be "cheaper and more purposeful" than their resettlement in Israel. Moreover, the refugees constituted no more than 1 percent of the population of the Arab League states, and it is customary for each state to solve such minor problems by its own means.[109] International concern about the refugees' return contributed little, if at all, to the consolidation of Israel's policy on this issue, which was regarded as essential to its very survival.

By the summer of 1948, Ben-Gurion was aware that Israel needed more gains, for so far "the victories were not crucial either militarily or politically."[110] Less hawkish opinions were voiced in the cabinet by Shapira and Remez.[111] Sasson was eager to start peace negotiations with the Arab states.[112]

On 26 September the prime minister tried to persuade the cabinet to launch an offensive against the Arab Legion from Latrun to Ramallah, this in order to guarantee access to Jewish Jerusalem, though he assumed he would have to compromise with the Arabs over rule in the city. He also had in mind not only the expulsion of the Egyptians from the Negev but a coup de grâce in the Triangle, meaning the Jenin-Nablus-Hebron region. However his proposal was rejected by a vote of 7-5. Ben-Gurion's setback came as the final Bernadotte plan was gathering more support in the wake of the mediator's murder by Lehi on 17 September and the anti-Israel feelings it generated. Ben-Gurion did concede that to maintain an army of 100,000 would vitiate both the country's economy and its youth.[113]

Bernadotte's final plan (16 September) seemed to leave Israel worse off politically than militarily. It reduced the Jewish state from the 14 million dunams (3.5 million acres) prescribed in the 29 November 1947 resolution to 5 million (mainly by excluding the entire Negev). Israel's aim was to defeat this plan in the General Assembly but also to avoid a return to the borders stipulated by the UN on 29 November. Finally, Shertok once more resisted Bernadotte's plan for the return of Arab refugees. This time, after again citing the Sudeten example, he explained that it was not simply a humanitarian issue of individuals, given that the new state had not been accepted by its neighbors.[114]

Meanwhile, events on the ground took a radically new turn. On 6 October, ten days after losing the cabinet vote on the offensive around Jerusalem and in the Negev, Ben-Gurion persuaded the same body (in a vote of 8-2) that there was no alternative but to launch an offensive against the Egyptians (though not in the Triangle unless the Arabs should attack there).[115] Egyptian cease-fire violations played into Israel's hands and its case could be easily defended; Shertok could now tell the cabinet that the IDF's victories (15–22 October) had made an "enormous impression" at the UN.[116] The barely populated Negev presented less of a problem to the cabinet than the part of Palestine occupied by Transjordan.[117] Israel's declared official line was to prefer an "independent" Arab state in western Palestine. But two factors led to a decision in favor of the Arab area's annexation to Transjordan: the "political weakness" of that entity; and the danger embodied by the Mufti.[118] Abdullah himself was ready to end the war but the British objected because of their strategic interest in the Negev in the event of the Cold War reaching the Middle East.[119]

While Shertok did not dare to question what he considered Ben-Gurion's excessive reliance on military force, Sasson displayed courage when he objected to the Israeli invasion of Lebanon (31 October 1948), after a successful attack on the Lebanese forces in Upper Galilee. Sasson argued that no Christian opposition group could seize power in Lebanon even with Israeli military assistance. Sasson was adamant that the war must be terminated "as soon as possible, even if we have to pay a certain price: territorial, private and international guarantees, and a minor return of refugees." He favored peace with the whole Arab world rather than peace with one Arab state, believing that such a peace would be more durable.[120]

Israel's Peace Initiative

In the wake of its victories, Israel was able to offer Egypt peace publicly. Without specifying the terms, Ben-Gurion told the Provisional State Council on 28 October 1948 that Israel sought "good neighborly relations" with Egypt, "not only because of past memories but also for future needs."[121] In a more down-to-earth vein, Ben-Gurion for the first time spoke his mind to senior IDF officers. He wondered rhetorically whether the Arab peoples would ever forget that 700,000 had defeated 30 million. "Will they forget this insult? Surely they have a sense of honor." Even if "we won not because our army is a miracle-maker but because the Arab army is rotten," this situation would not necessarily last. An "Arab Mustafa Kemal" might emerge, and the entire world situation was volatile.[122]

Ben-Gurion was nonetheless encouraged by Sasson, after the latter talked to Riad as-Sulh, the Lebanese prime minister, an old friend of Zionism and a secret collaborator with Zionism dating back to the 1920s, who admitted that his country would have liked to end the war but could not do it alone.[123] To Sasson the main danger was that a continued belligerent policy by Israel might drive the Arabs into the arms of others, namely the British and the Soviets (in Iraq). Israel, he said, had two choices: withdraw into itself and sever all contact with the Arab states, or forge a network of ties and cooperation with the Arab world. Logic favored the second course, because only this could prevent the subjection of the Arab countries to external powers. The key was Transjordan. Israel should encourage the annexation of the Arab parts of Palestine to Transjordan. This would divert Abdullah from his plans to gain control of Syria and would pave the way for refugee settlement in his dominion. Simultaneously, discussions should begin with the other Arab states.

All in all, despite his frequently changing assessments in the past, caused by the war's fluctuations, Sasson, by late December 1948, had a clear vision of Israel's move toward peaceful relations with the Arabs. This reflected the growing realism and the waning of the general euphoria. Sasson now received support from David Horowitz, the influential director-general of the treasury. He emphasized that future relations could be built on the relationship between an economically progressive Israel and its backward Arab neighbors.

Ben-Gurion was reluctant to allow the Arab parts of Palestine to be annexed to Jordan; his preference was for autonomy in the Arab areas but under Israeli control. The primary consideration of the chief of military operations, Yadin, was a border that would put Israel on the ridge line along the Umm el Fahem–Tul Karem–Kalkilyah line. Sasson feared that such a territorial demand might destroy his basic conception of drawing in Abdullah, as it would leave the king with a small area.[124] Israeli pragmatism and the Arabs' acknowledgment of their defeat led both sides to negotiate successful armistice agreements in Rhodes, with Ralph Bunche, the UN mediator, as the crucial go-between.

Before the start of the armistice negotiations with the Arab states, the Israeli provisional government had to obtain parliamentary approval at a closed session of the Provisional State Council. Ben-Gurion's opinion was that the cabinet should not commit itself in advance to a specific peace plan, but that it would also be wrong to adopt an ultimatum as a policy. The attitude toward Jordan was particularly inconsistent, due to the inherent difficulty of weighing the pros and cons of crucial territorial decisions. Shertok supported the annexation of Gaza to Egypt rather than to Transjordan: "Why should we quarrel with Egypt because of Abdullah and grant him a road in the Negev [between Jordan and Gaza]—which means introducing Bevin's plan?" He explained to the Provisional State Council the motives behind the decision to enter armistice negotiations. He cited the "tremendous" gains in the war as beyond all expectations, the enormous burden of the war's cost, and the need to divert "all our economic and organizational strength to absorb the immigrants."[125]

Although by January 1949 the IDF had advanced into Sinai, the cabinet had little alternative but to order its withdrawal from the peninsula. Shertok claimed that various reasons had induced Egypt to sue for peace—not least its losses in territory, men, and equipment; the IDF's ability to penetrate deep into Egypt (only fear of England had kept the Israeli forces from pushing to Suez); and American pressure on Cairo. Shertok's conclusion was that Egypt's move toward an armistice, far from being coordinated with Britain, was undertaken contrary to London's wishes. The other Arab states had already agreed to hold talks.[126]

The Rhodes talks that commenced on 13 January 1949 with Arab delegations on armistice agreements were welcomed by Israeli decision makers as the beginning of a new era.[127] For Ben-Gurion, peace was "vital but not at any cost." The aim of the war must be an "independent and viable state and a Jewish-Arab alliance."[128] Sharett stressed the agreement's political importance: "Egypt's factual recognition of Israel," as Sharett said, and "an opening for general peace."[129] Despite Israel's sweeping victory, Ben-Gurion was still haunted by the possibility that an Arab Ataturk might emerge, a fear he was to reiterate in April.[130] In late January 1949, he took note of the appearance among Palestinian Arabs of a party (the Ba'ath) espousing the unity of the Arab nation. "The unity of the Arab fatherland does not permit the establishment of a Zionist state within its borders," he said. Israel must seize the time available to it before Arab unity could be forged in order to grow, fortify itself, and consolidate its international standing. In time, the professional Middle Eastern experts of the Israeli Foreign Ministry hoped that "the facts will force the Arab leaders to change their policy." It was crucial to terminate the war as soon as possible.[131]

Typically, the refugee question was not debated; it was regarded at this stage as the least worrying issue. As early as November 1948, the Transfer Committee (established on 30 May) had recommended to the cabinet to insist that the refugees be settled in the Arab countries.[132] Again, no public debate followed, not only because the issue was kept secret but because, as already mentioned, there was a consensus for the transfer (i.e., "flight") idea among the public, except for the radical left (see discussion following). For example, on the eve of the armistice negotiations, the influential commentator Michael Assaf hailed an article that appeared in the Syrian newspaper *Al Qabas*, favoring resettlement not only of 100,000 refugees but also of five million Arabs in Syria's large, uninhabited territories.[133] What would later become a serious issue—the Palestine Arab refugees as a spearhead for national revival and guerrilla warfare—was considered insignificant by Israeli policy makers.

The main issue was the armistice negotiations at Rhodes. According to the Egyptian delegates, their country's aim was not only "military peace" but "political peace," namely a comprehensive peace that included political, military, and economic cooperation. The armistice agreement would obviously be a great contribution to this.[134]

It was Sasson who at the last moment broke the deadlock at Rhodes by holding private talks between the Egyptian and Israeli delegations without UN participation.[135] Egypt adamantly opposed the annexation of the Arab part of Palestine to Jordan, preferring an independent Arab state led by neither the Husseinis nor the pro-Hashemites. Cairo also insisted that Israel permit the return of the refugees. Sasson was optimistic that Egypt might agree to their settlement in the Arab countries and to autonomy for Gaza.[136] Neither he nor any other Israeli diplomat or policy maker opposed what now appeared to be an Israeli official policy: the settlement of the Arab refugees in the Arab countries. This was explained to the American ambassador as the only feasible policy when he was presented with the conclusions of the Transfer Committee (23 February 1949). Far from being a possible time bomb, he was told by Danin—a member of the committee (together with Weitz and Z. Lifshitz)—that transfer was in fact a legitimate historical phenomenon which had successful precedents in the cases of Greece and Turkey, Czechoslovakia and Germany, and India and Pakistan. Looking for "vast land reserves" where the refugees could be settled, the Transfer Committee pointed to an address delivered by the Iraqi minister for development and public works in 1944 on the subject of development possibilities in his country, where only 10 percent of the arable land was under cultivation. Syria and Jordan were also recommended for refugee resettlement, as was Lebanon for Christian refugees. Permitting the refugees' return to Israel was out of the question for several reasons, according to the committee: it would be more costly than resettling them elsewhere; the Arab economy in Palestine was completely ruined; similar resettlement attempts in Europe had failed, and therefore "from a humanitarian point of view" it was inadvisable to bring them back; there was a danger of their becoming a fifth column in view of the continued "provocative and belligerent" statements made by the Arab states; and immigrants to Israel from Arab states, "embittered by their past experience, would not make it easy for the once hostile Arab population to come back here."[137]

In fact, it would have been impossible for Israel to have adopted a more conciliatory policy, for the considerations noted were not excuses but represented the survival mentality of the Israeli policy-making elites in view of the Holocaust legacy and having just emerged from a war of their own. The Conciliation Commission on Palestine, which was established by the UN on 11 December 1948 in order to work out an Arab-Israeli peace, was also presented with the transfer conclusion as the product of rational policy. Not only was it economically unthinkable to bring the refugees back in view of "the gigantic [Jewish] immigration program," but it was also undesirable politically: "Under the happiest of circumstances, a complex and uncertain situation has been created where a single state must be shared by two or more peoples who differ in race, religion, language and culture." Recent history was "replete" with examples of such migrations. Population transfers had been advocated by the Peel Royal Commission and by personalities as diverse as Walter C. Lowdermilk (1938), Sir Norman Angel (1941), Herbert Hoover (1945), and the British Labour party (1944–45). Three specific irrigation projects had been recommended by Israel as resettlement areas: Habaniah in Iraq, where 300,000 could be absorbed into a rural population; the Jezireh in Syria, designed for agricultural settlement of 400,000–500,000 persons; and Jordan, which could support a farming population of 250,000, almost the entire number of farmers among the Arab refugees. All in all, Iraq should absorb 230,000 refugees, Syria 120,000, Jordan 63,000, and Lebanon 62,500. The neighboring states' need for fresh manpower and the necessity to relieve a "human problem" converged in the Israeli mind as a policy certain of success and that could greatly contribute to a stable relationship between Israel and the Arab countries.[138] Indeed, the Conciliation Commission had regarded the Arab refugees issue as the key to the solution of the Arab-Israel conflict. The commission proved a failure, however, as is discussed later, unlike the armistice negotiations, which ended successfully. The first was the Israel-Egypt agreement, signed on 24 February 1949. The entire Negev, the Gaza Strip excluded, was left in Israeli hands, and the Auja area was demilitarized.

Ben-Gurion considered the Egypt-Israeli armistice agreement the third great event of a "year of great achievements," after the establishment of the state and victory in the war.[139] To Sharett it was "a tremendous achievement" which "will open a new era in the consolidation of the state, the development of its foreign relations with its surroundings and in the life of the whole Middle East."[140]

Serious negotiations with Jordan, which had formally begun on 13 January, were deliberately delayed until the signing of the Egyptian-Israeli armistice agreement, because for tactical reasons the government wanted first to assure its "right flank" with Egypt. Consequently it was necessary to drag on the negotiations with Jordan; in any event, Abdullah was still insisting on "impossible" conditions from Israel's viewpoint, such as obtaining the southern Negev. Sasson suggested that Israel make the retention of this area a sine qua non for the opening of talks. Abdullah was informed that if he objected, the conflict might continue for a long time, a situation which neither side desired.[141] To strengthen its position in the negotiations, Israel occupied the southern Negev as far as Eilat, on the northern tip of the Red Sea (10 March 1949), an area which in fact was supposed to be part of the Jewish state according to the 29 November 1947 partition resolution. On 20 March, Abdullah gave in on the question of the first ridge in the West Bank, which would go to Israel (except for the towns of Kalkilyah and Tul-Karem). Sasson saw this as a turning point. It proved that Israeli "toughness" in negotiations with Jordan paid off. With Iraq having empowered Jordan to negotiate in its name and the Syrian prime minister anxious to normalize the situation in his country and start military and political negotiations as soon as possible, Sasson concluded that once the armistice agreement with Jordan was an accomplished fact, "we can safely predict that within five or six weeks, we will have concluded armistice agreements with all our neighbors. We will thus have brought the war to an end and covered the first stage on the road to peace itself."[142] On 23 March the armistice agreement with Lebanon was signed, as was a draft agreement with Jordan, with the final signing on 3 April.

It was the UN Conciliation Commission that took the initiative in advancing Arab-Israeli relations toward a more stable peace than the armistice negotiations could provide. In response to the commission's insistence on the settlement of the refugees and on the internationalization of Jerusalem, Ben-Gurion rejected the 11 December 1948 resolution of the UN General Assembly, which allowed refugees the choice between return or compensation: "Why should we believe that the returning Arabs are motivated by peace? They declared war on us. . . . We are interested in solving the refugee question only in the context of peace." Furthermore, since the Arab states declared war on Israel they must bear the responsibility; in other words, they themselves should absorb the refugees.[143] Basically there was nothing new in his Arab policy: "For peace with the Arabs it is necessary for them to feel that we are strong. This would influence them to enter into a peaceful relationship with us." He called upon the Arab states not to rely only on the Conciliation Commission but to make direct contact with Israel, each Arab country separately, if possible without the knowledge of the others. In fact, this had been the procedure of the armistice negotiations, which had made it easier for Israel to maneuver than if facing a solid Arab front.[144]

Gaza was obviously an issue between Egypt and Israel; if it were annexed to Israel, this would be acceptable and there would be no expulsion of the population. Sharett, however, compared the refugees to the Sudeten Germans, who had acted as a bridgehead for the neighboring motherland.[145] Even the president, Chaim Weizmann, was recruited to convince Truman that the "transfer" of refugees to Iraq represented a "massive opportunity for the general development of the Middle East."[146]

Tension flared up at the end of April, when Syria's refusal to withdraw to the international border, as it had undertaken in the armistice agreement to do, led to the brink of war. Only Israel's fear of the renewal of the war with the rest of the Arab states and the threat of American intervention enabled a more sober attitude.[147] The armistice with Syria was signed on 20 July 1949.[148] Most dramatically, the major problems left unsolved by the Lausanne Conference, involving basic issues such as borders and refugees, led Sharett to conclude that "a formal peace with the Arab states is not a vital necessity for us."[149]

Within twenty-four hours of his initial assessment on 31 May 1949, Sasson changed his mind about Arab readiness for peace. Less than four months after the signing of the armistice with Egypt, he discovered that Cairo was not only refusing to accept even the 29 November 1947 borders but was also demanding Gaza and the southern Negev. In other words, Egypt wanted to revive the Bernadotte plan.[150] These cardinal problems finally led Sharett to advocate the annexation of the Arab part of Palestine to Abdullah, since this would be another nail in the coffin of the 29 November borders.[151]

Speaking in the Knesset on 15 June, he echoed Ben-Gurion on the basic Israeli interest in a "comprehensive and speedy peace" but made it abundantly clear that for security reasons, Israel would not agree to the 29 November borders (because they were strategically nonviable) or to the return of the refugees. The present, postwar borders were "an absolute necessity" for the state's very survival, while the refugees could "explode the state from within." If the large Arab minority (45 percent of the total population) envisaged in the partition plan had remained, "this would have had a strong effect on the governance of the state. But since these masses have been uprooted, other processes have emerged and changed the face of the country." Israel understood the human misery involved and was prepared to compensate the refugees for their lands.[152] Sharett was very conscious of mounting international pressure on Israel to resolve the refugee problem. The only partially resolved Arab question forced Israel to maneuver carefully between national interests and international pressures; and how to avoid setbacks to the former without succumbing to the latter has been a perennial problem for Israel ever since.

To alleviate American pressure, Sharett and the majority of the cabinet were prepared to permit the return of 100,000 refugees. However, Ben-Gurion and Dov Joseph were vehemently opposed, claiming that neither America nor the Arabs would be satisfied with this number, and that security would suffer.[153] Sasson did not press for immediate peace treaties, since for the next three to four years there was no fear that the Arabs would go to war against Israel even without formal treaties. Nor did the refugee problem bother him, since the refugees, he thought, would press the Arab governments to make peace in order to solve their problem. But no Arab state wanted to be the first to take the plunge.[154] Basically Ben-Gurion was in no hurry; his advisers, such as Eban, pointed out that "there is no need to run after peace—the Arabs will demand a price—borders or refugees or both. Let's wait a few years."[155] The Lausanne Conference, however, did in fact present Israeli decision makers with an immediate challenge: should they be satisfied with the armistice agreements as a substitute for peace or should they strive for a more comprehensive arrangement?

Sharett conceded on 25 July, five days after the signing of the armistice agreement with Syria, that the armistice regime apparently exempted Israel from "the compelling need for formal peace treaties with its neighbors, with the armistice agreements substituting for such treaties in two major respects: stabilization of the boundaries and a guarantee against renewed aggression. It is therefore Israel's duty, even for tactical reasons vis-à-vis the Arabs, to refrain from the demonstration of anxiety over the lack of peace. . . . On the other hand, it would be a delusion to imagine that a state of armistice is in itself sufficient. . . . Israel's duty [is] to persist in her efforts for an early attainment of peace both as a goal in its own right and as a tactical dictate of political wisdom."[156]

How should one assess Israeli (and Zionist) official policy toward the Arab question since the end of World War II? That policy was, in the first instance, a self-fulfilling prophecy in the sense that it was thought that agreements with the Arabs would be possible only after an Arab defeat, preferably political rather than military. The Yishuv, however, prepared itself for the latter eventuality should the political-diplomatic effort fail. The constant message to Western governments and public opinion was that Arab opposition to Zionism should not be taken seriously on two grounds: Zionism brought social and economic benefits to the Arabs; and as soon as the Yishuv accumulated enough "power," the Arabs were bound to accept it. Later on, the meaning of power was defined more accurately: the establishment of a Jewish state. In other words, the conflict could be solved either by political-diplomatic means, relying on Britain and America, or by military means, with the assistance of Diaspora Jewry. The incipient Cold War of 1947–49 gave Zionism a vital boost from an unexpected source: the Soviet Union, which at that time ignored the Arab claim for statehood in Palestine and exploited the Anglo-Zionist rift for its own long-term interests.

But Israel had a different agenda than the great powers. By 1949, official Israeli policy was guided by the assumption that the demographic issue was the most acute problem, overriding even the Arab issue. The quest for peace was thus treated as secondary in importance, especially since it entailed territorial concessions that might have long-term strategic implications. The vital need was to absorb Jewish immigration, thereby demonstrating Ben-Gurion's emphasis on the ingathering of the exiles into the Jewish state as the raison d'être of Zionism. Transfer as an official long-term policy must be seen in this context. Strategy and Zionist vision inevitably converged. The armistice lines, whatever their defects, were grasped as the acceptable minimum, and the settlement of Jewish immigrants in former Arab villages was taken to be an ideal fusion of strategy and vision. The failure of the Lausanne Conciliation Commission to obtain a permanent peace was not interpreted either by the decision-making elite or by Israeli opinion as a long-term fiasco but rather as a miracle because of the heavy price such a peace would have required, in terms of border concessions and the return of refugees. Moreover, though the armistice agreements were considered a relative success, they were taken, particularly by Ben-Gurion, as a stopgap that would enable Israel to fill the demographic vacuum.

But the Israeli leadership learned, through trial and error, that neither in external nor in internal politics can the national agenda be dictated by one side to the conflict. What happened in practice was that the Arab states did not allow Israel to give nation building priority over its relations with the Arab states. Both issues were imposed upon Israel at the top of the agenda. And since Ben-Gurion was unable to give up either immigration or settlement, he felt unable to make significant concessions on peace, which was interwoven with the former issues. It was only logical, then, that the infiltrators of the 1950s were seen as a threat to the consolidation of the state and therefore to be dealt with violently. To Ben-Gurion, the return of the refugees was purely a matter of realpolitik, not a moral problem: he thought only in terms of the potential danger they would pose to the nascent, still-fragile state.

In the interplay among the various elements that constituted the Arab question in the Zionists' eyes—the Hashemite orientation, recognition of Palestine Arab minority rights in the coming Jewish state, territorial compromise (i.e., partition), and the transfer of the Palestine Arab population, and not least the military preparations—each had to be given proper weight. The importance of these questions, however, fluctuated in accordance with the dynamics of the political development of the Palestine issue in the regional and international context. While the goal of a partitioned Jewish state, to be achieved through either political or military initiatives, appears as the more permanent component in Zionism's Arab policy, Ben-Gurion's strategic realpolitik led the Jewish Agency to perceive the other aspects—transfer, the Hashemite orientation, and minority rights—as less important elements of the Arab question. Transfer was so because it was regarded as a damaging policy that could have serious repercussions for Zionism's good name in the West and could trigger Arab violence at any time; the Hashemite orientation because Abdullah joined the Arab attack on the Yishuv; and minority rights because they were seen largely through a propaganda prism. Nonetheless, all three were given serious weight after the War of Independence as potentially important, though expectations proved too high. First, the life-and-death struggle legitimized transfer in Zionist eyes, notwithstanding its morally negative implications. Second, it was considered by the victorious government, and to a lesser degree by leftist and intellectual circles (discussed in chapters 6, 8, and 9) as a stabilizing contribution to the Arab-Jewish conflict. The refugees' return could be reconsidered only in peacetime. A marginal political ideology before 29 November 1947, transfer became a pivotal policy after Israel's establishment. Similarly, the minor weight ascribed by the decision-making leadership to the Hashemite policy, contrary to Sasson's recommendation, gave way to a very different course once Abdullah entered the war and seized military control of the West Bank, spurring a renewal of peace efforts.

As long-term policies, however, both of these lines of strategy failed. This was due to a basic flaw in Jewish Agency policy, which consistently ignored the existence of a Palestinian entity. Battered by the Arab states' systematic intervention in Palestine affairs, and by the Palestine Arabs' zero-sum policy toward Zionism, the Yishuv and the Zionist movement responded in kind: by trying to make peace with Abdullah, or the Syrian dictator Husni al-Zaim, and by turning these moves into strategic linchpins of Israeli policy. Ben-Gurion, however, aware of the infirmity of the Jordanian link, refused to sacrifice territory for it, yet he believed that the transfer of Palestinians in their hundreds of thousands was bound to be accepted as a fait accompli. Implementation of the long-promised minority rights for the Arabs in Israel was a poor substitute.

In the final analysis, Ben-Gurion was not sure about his ability to distinguish between long-term and short-term goals. In reality he wavered between a vision of peace with the neighboring states, on the Turko-Greek model, and the fear of a vengeful new Arab ruler who could pull Palestine back to war. Underrating the long-term potential damage of the refugee question (namely, the transfer to the neighboring countries) stood in contradiction to the fear of the potential emergence of a dangerous Arab ruler, on the lines of Ataturk. But this fear was neutralized by his conviction (going back to 1936) that Israel's Arab policy should be focused on survival (a zero-sum game): "We alive and the Arabs dead, or vice versa." Once the idea of a "second round" and the mounting infiltration dominated the national scene, Ben-Gurion adopted a pessimistic approach. Realpolitik was no longer characterized, as it had been before 1949, by an apotheosis of peace in the wake of a war strategy but by the mounting influence of military thinking, which transcended other short- and long-term calculations. This development spawned two different schools on Arab policy, the more forceful one propounded by Ben-Gurion and Dayan, as against the Sharett-Eban school, which relied more on diplomacy. But that debate is beyond the scope of this book.

III

—◆—

The Internal Background of Zionist Foreign Policy

4

David Ben-Gurion, Mapai, and the Victory of Pragmatic Activism

The Aftermath of World War II

On the day Churchill declared victory over Germany, Ben-Gurion wrote woefully in his diary: "Rejoice not, O Israel, unto exultation, like the peoples" (Hosea 9:1).[1] Now he foresaw a possible armed conflict between the Yishuv and the British Mandatory government.[2]

Ben-Gurion spoke of the need for a new mentality and a new approach suited to the times.[3] Quoting the American philosopher C. S. Peirce, the father of pragmatist theory, David Horowitz defined the approach as political pragmatism.[4] The leadership's perception was that the paramilitary Haganah should not be used against the British authorities, who would eventually leave, but should be prepared for the long-term military confrontation with the Arab states. At a meeting on 1 July 1945 in the home of Rudolf Sonneborn in New York, Ben-Gurion sought the advice of nineteen Jewish business tycoons on the creation of a Jewish military industry. After eight hours of discussion those present agreed enthusiastically to supply the necessary funds.[5] It was clear that the small Jewish community in Palestine (550,000) must be augmented by mass immigration from the world's ten million or so Jews, but with the three million in Eastern Europe unable to leave, the greatest hope lay in Oriental Jewry (Jews living in Arab countries in the Middle East and North Africa), numbering some 855,000. Immediate statehood could save the situation.[6]

At the first Zionist convention after the war, held in London from 1–13 August 1945, Ben-Gurion elaborated on his activist conception of Jewish history. The rise of etatism, he said, posed a threat to Jewish survival in the West. Massive state intervention would put an end to traditional Jewish autonomous existence: more power to the state meant less independence for the Jewish community. The only solution was a Jewish state. In the Holocaust, Jews had been exterminated because they did not fight back. If a Jewish state were not established, there would be "a rebellion against the brutal, illegal rule."[7]

Meanwhile, the Mapai Secretariat had firmly backed Ben-Gurion's plan for the first million immigrants, with no hesitation; Mapai supported Ben-Gurion's battle against Weizmann's "minimalism" (see next chapter).[8] At the London convention, the vote on the establishment of a Jewish state in the Biltmore spirit (which did not mention partition) reaffirmed Ben-Gurion's leadership (57 to 15 in favor). Weizmann too cast his vote in favor, although he did not advocate armed resistance (*wiederstand*) to the British as did Shertok and Sneh.[9] Sneh in fact emerged from the London convention as a powerful force and was elected to the Jewish Agency Executive. He still emphasized that Zionist hopes did not clash with British interests in the Middle East, but he also warned that if the gates of immigration remained closed, the Yishuv would have no choice but to resort to force.[10] The main motive behind Ben-Gurion's cautious activism, however, was not to restrain Sneh but to ensure the support of Mapai.[11]

After two meetings with the British colonial secretary, Ben-Gurion clearly foresaw a collision with Britain over the immigration issue.[12] In such a serious crisis, when moderates such as Lubianiker and activists like Tabenkin spoke in one voice, Ben-Gurion could be certain that any activist policy he broached would be accepted.[13] Still, in order to avoid superfluous debate and leaks, he decided not to bring the decision to establish the United Hebrew Resistance Movement (Haganah, IZL and Stern Gang [Lehi]) before an official forum. Ben-Gurion felt he was entitled to take this step by the force of his leadership—which he had taken care to institutionalize since 1935 (when he became chairman of the Jewish Agency Executive), and he instructed Sneh to establish the United Resistance Movement (directed by the X Committee) on 1 October 1945, after the new Labour government in Britain had decided to continue the 1939 White Paper policy on Jewish immigration. This decision pushed the Jewish Agency, which had anticipated a favorable official resolution on large-scale Jewish immigration, to unprecedented extremism, collaborating in guerrilla actions (though doing its utmost to prevent the killing of British policemen and soldiers, a reservation which the IZL and Lehi had accepted). The initiative to establish the United Resistance Movement was not democratically decided by the

Zionist movement's parliamentary institution, the Small Zionist Actions Committee, or by the decision-making body, the Jewish Agency Executive, but by the triumvirate of Ben-Gurion, Shertok, and Sneh, due to its clandestine nature and the anticipated objections.[14]

Ben-Gurion now recommended closing the London office of the Jewish Agency and directing the Zionist movement exclusively from Palestine.[15] Ben-Gurion's grand strategy was to formulate a policy that would win the support of all Zionists, including the radical right and left. The former were more important from this point of view since they could cause great damage if not under official control; hence his orders to the Haganah to cooperate with the breakaways on the basis of the united resistance.

Matters took an unexpected turn, however. On 6 October a bloody incident occurred at Kfar Giladi, a northern kibbutz. The Transjordan Frontier Force (TJFF) opened fire on Jewish settlers who were protecting illegal immigrants, wounding six of the settlers. This, Sneh explained, showed the importance of demonstrating the power of the Haganah.[16]

Hence, on 9 October, the Haganah released some 200 illegal immigrants from the "clearance camp" at Atlit, near Haifa, an operation in which a British policeman was killed. The leadership explained to an enraged high commissioner (who pointed out that the immigrants were about to be released anyway) that according to rumors they were about to be deported.[17] Sneh reiterated his view that there was no contradiction between massive immigration, a Jewish state, and strong British bases in the country—as long as "they are not turned against us."[18] Weizmann and Sprinzak urged caution, while Shertok was trying to avert a rift between Weizmann and Ben-Gurion.[19]

Meanwhile Ben-Gurion turned his attention to the Holocaust survivors. Visiting Germany to see for himself the situation of the Jewish DPs, he also met with General Bedell-Smith and General Eisenhower, to persuade them to concentrate the Jewish DPs in one area. He urged that they be given self-government and professional training. Far from the problems of Yishuv resistance, he immersed himself in the rehabilitation of the refugees in order to prepare them for immigration. He even recruited the wealthy American-Jewish philanthropic organization, the Joint Distribution Committee, long suspected of being anti-Zionist, to underwrite half the cost of illegal immigration.[20] Organizing the illegal immigrant operation was his major preoccupation during a subsequent visit to Paris. Even by early November, there were not yet enough candidates for the first ship bought in America.[21]

Ultimately, though, events were to be decided in Palestine. On the night of 31 October/1 November 1945, the United Resistance Movement struck at 153 sites, mainly connected with the Palestinian transport system (the so-called Night of the Railways). By this time, the Haganah—readying itself to fight the Arabs, not the British—had formulated an "offensive-defensive" plan, which for the first time stated that the aim was the "annihilation" of the armed forces of the (Arab) enemy.[22]

The political leadership was riven by internal disputes between activists and moderates and between supporters and opponents of the United Resistance Movement. Upon his return, Ben-Gurion found even Mapai divided against itself.[23]

The United Resistance Movement was formally established on 23–24 October in a meeting of Sneh, I. Galili, M. Begin, and N. Friedman-Yelin (the last, a Lehi leader, had acted as an intermediary between the Haganah and the IZL, having earlier accepted the Haganah's demand for an end to Lehi terrorism). Sneh and Galili insisted, to no avail, that the IZL and Lehi disband because their very existence was negated by the official Yishuv and the Zionist movement. The Mapai Center was in near pandemonium following the Night of the Railways. Kaplan, who was apparently surprised by the action, threatened that in the event of another such operation he would resign both as acting chairman of the Jewish Agency Executive and as treasurer. He protested strongly that the party institutions had been ignored. S. Meirov, who though not a member of the executive had been a member of the Haganah Central Command since the 1930s, and as such closer to Ben-Gurion than was Kaplan, admitted that the issue was very grave and promised that future operations would be executed with "the maximum of care and calculation. We are interested as far as possible not to irritate the Arabs."[24]

Opinion was divided over the creation of the United Resistance Movement and over the decision-making process that had brought it into being. Meirov claimed that the *ha'apalah* (illegal immigration) was a more effective weapon, within the framework of the Resistance Movement, than establishing new settlements, which might provoke clashes with the Arabs. Yitzhak Ben-Zvi (later president of Israel) supported the opposition line led by Kaplan, protesting also that he had not been consulted (as president of the Va'ad Leumi). The Night of the Railways had only weakened the Yishuv position, Ben-Zvi argued: in any future British search for arms, the Yishuv would not be able to claim that the weapons were needed for defense only. Both he and Lubianiker were against the "coordination" with the IZL and Lehi. Ben-Gurion himself realized that the party was divided between the former members of Achdut Ha'avodah (including Golda Meyerson) and Hapoel Hatza'ir.[25]

But a possible split in the Yishuv leadership was averted by Bevin's declaration in the House of Commons on 13 November (see also "The Missed Opportunities of Eliahu Sasson" in chapter 3), in which he ignored the existence of the Jewish people (referring instead to "the Jewish community in Europe" or just "Jews,") and regretted the Balfour Declaration, claiming it lacked moral validity. Only the representative of the small Poale Agudat Israel, Dr. Yitzhak Breuer, could see a glimmer of hope in the speech, whilst the entire Yishuv leadership condemned Bevin's declaration in the harshest terms.[26]

Reactions were at least as extreme in the Jewish Agency Executive. Both Rabbi Fishman and Moshe Sneh interpreted Bevin's speech as an attempt to "eliminate the Jewish race."[27] The leadership of the Yishuv was now divided between the activists, like Ben-Gurion and Sneh, who supported a nonstop struggle (ma'avak ratsuf) against the British, and the moderates, who favored a struggle linked only to clashes with the authorities on immigration and settlement (ma'avak tsamud). Meyerson and Ahronovich had to play the same game in the Histadrut, trying to find a compromise solution between the moderates of Hashomer Hatza'ir and former Hapoel Hatza'ir members of their own party, on the one hand, and Le'achdut Ha'avodah on the other. While M. Nemirovsky (Namir; later minister in Moscow and minister of labor), vehemently supported unity with the IZL and Lehi, citing the French Resistance, which embraced the entire spectrum from the extreme right to the extreme left, Lubianiker warned against a repetition of Massada.[28]

Ben-Gurion, now back in Palestine, relied not only on the United Resistance Movement but on the Haganah apparatus in Europe to organize the movement of 250,000 Jews from Eastern Europe to the American Zone in Germany, thus creating pressure on Truman to send them to Palestine. For him, unity was necessary for an effective resistance to Britain.[29]

By the time Ben-Gurion came to justify his policy before the Elected Assembly, relations between the Yishuv and the British government had further deteriorated. In the name of the United Resistance Movement, the Palmach (shock troops of the Haganah), following the "linked struggle" school (after the British captured the illegal immigrant ship Berl Katzenelson) attacked the police stations at Givat Olga and Sidna

Ali (25 November). The next day British forces surrounded and searched the nearby kibbutzim of Shefayim and Givat Haim (to which the tracks of the saboteurs led), and Moshav Hogla. Thousands of people from the surrounding settlements converged on the search sites and tried to break through the British lines. The troops opened fire, killing eight Jews. The Palmach, led by Yitzhak Sadeh, acting chief of staff of the Haganah, and Yigal Allon, its commander, prepared a plan to fight the (British) "enemy" by attacking its units on the main roads. This plan, however, was rejected by the leadership as constituting a diversion from the limited ("linked") struggle that had been decided upon and as irreconcilable with Sneh's frequent protestations of the Yishuv's basic loyalty to Britain.[30] With fourteen Jews having been killed in anti-British riots in Tel Aviv (14 November) and in Emek Hefer (26 November) in less than two weeks, Ben-Gurion, and the Yishuv in general, became far more aggressive. In a despairing mood, he conceded that the pro-Zionist Labour Party in Britain had irrevocably lost its fight against the anti-Zionist Foreign Office.[31]

But a definitive decision on the form of struggle to be pursued had not yet been made. Ben-Gurion faced systematic and powerful opposition on the part of such figures as Kaplan, D. Remez, Sprinzak, and Lubianiker, who all decried the constant wavering between the linked and "continuous" forms of struggle.[32]

In a closed meeting of the Va'ad Leumi in early December 1945, during a heated discussion on the use of force, Ben-Gurion sought to dampen the conflict between Britain and the Yishuv. There was conflict between those like Sprinzak and M. Neustadt, who felt that a confrontation with Britain would lead to disaster—"we have had enough Massadas, such as the Warsaw Ghetto"—and those like E. Lulu and David Hacohen, who felt that Britain left the Yishuv no alternative.[33]

But the most impressive, and extreme, ideologue of activism remained Liebenstein. Liebenstein's uniqueness on the Yishuv political map and his dedication to activism were exemplified by his ardent support for the United Resistance Movement, although in fact he leaned toward the more extreme (continuous) line of struggle and thought that coordination with the breakaways IZL and Lehi should be strategic and more permanent. This approach, however, was unacceptable to both Ben-Gurion and Shertok and more so to Sneh. Liebenstein's radicalism culminated, in the spring of 1947, in his removal as editor of the Haganah monthly *Eshnav*, for publishing photographs of IZL martyrs together with those of illegal immigrants killed by the British. Besides being a member of Mapai Center, as an editor of another activist journal *(Milchamtenu,* later *Beterem),* and a frequent contributor to *Davar,* he had considerable influence on public opinion. Liebenstein evaluated the struggle as a turning point in the history of Zionism and suggested a new interpretation of Zionism, which was vital, in his view, at the peak of the Zionist campaign for survival: "We now confront the end of Emancipation. The Gentiles are unwilling to tolerate the Jews in their midst as a separate entity with equal rights." Resistance twinned with moral force was the key.[34] I. Gurfinkel (later Guri, a Knesset member) pointed out perceptively that many in Mapai were experiencing "serious psychological confusion" because the very foundations of their Zionist worldview were being shaken. They had been taught, in the Labor-Zionist conception, that offensive rather than defensive force was basically immoral.[35]

As the debate raged on, virtually the entire Yishuv was able to reach unity on three issues, as Ben-Gurion wished: immigration, settlement, and the right to defense. Nonetheless, in the Va'ad Leumi, where every party was represented, Felix Rosenblueth, leader of Aliyah Hadashah, questioned the Yishuv's ability to pursue even the so-called moderate, linked struggle (see chapter 7). S. Z. Shragai gave vent to the general feeling in the Orthodox Hapoel Hamizrachi when he denounced the slogan "A war of desperation even if there is no chance," saying that as a religious Jew he could not accept it. There was no shred of Fishman's former sympathy for the IZL in his words. On the contrary, he praised the fact that no shooting had taken place on the Jewish side. Indeed, both national-religious parties, the Mizrachi, and its more "leftist" ally Hapoel Hamizrachi were Ben-Gurion's surest allies in the Jewish Agency Executive, even more than the divided General Zionists, whose messianism was always tempered by realpolitik. The pragmatic leadership that had made them trusted coalition partners since 1935 would later make possible the "historic alliance" between Mapai and the national-religious parties (lasting until 1977).[36] The leadership felt they had to make more of an impact on the British by mounting offensive attacks on airfields, thus moving some way toward continuous struggle. In the Haganah's Plan for Japheth (= British) Affairs the British were called "the enemy" because they might try to hinder the "constructive Yishuv work (immigration and settlement)" or launch a sweeping action against the Haganah, including systematic arrests and major arms searches. In addition, the authorities might declare curfew and martial law in the country. Hence the need to react on an unprecedented scale utilizing sabotage and harassment and not excluding retaliatory acts against individuals. Clearly, however, the plan was subordinated to the political line of the Yishuv. The Plan for Japheth Affairs foresaw three phases of escalating action: (1) if limitations were placed on the Yishuv's "constructive work" within the civil law, the reaction would be primarily passive, although in some cases active methods could be adopted against selected targets such as the navy and radar stations; (2) in response to systematic "enemy" acts against the Yishuv, the Haganah should itself operate systematically against government facilities, including communications, CID offices, garages, and Police Mobile Force (PMF) stations, as well as by sabotaging the railway and road systems and civilian air and sea ports, and by freeing prisoners; and (3) actions against "imperial" targets such as the oil pipeline, refineries, and telegraphic cable system, military targets such as storage depots (including fuel resources), airports, and army camps, and imperial targets outside the country. Phases 2 and 3 could be accompanied by mounting civil resistance. Phase 3 was added even before the Black Sabbath (29 June 1946) with its mass arrests and arms search in Yagur and the threat to raze settlements and implement mass deportations of Yishuv leaders.[37] Fortunately for the Yishuv, the second phase was implemented only in part, because the Jewish Agency was able to stop the United Resistance Movement from deteriorating to the level of the terrorist actions perpetrated by the IZL and Lehi. The agency accomplished this by shifting the weight of the struggle: by the summer of 1946 it had purchased large ships and assembled enough Jewish refugees to launch a campaign of illegal immigration.

The Anglo-American Committee of Inquiry as a Soothing Diversion

It is clear that the Anglo-American Committee played a key role as a soothing diversion for frustrated expectations and helped to prevent violent escalation of the type espoused by the IZL and Lehi breakaways from dominating the Yishuv frame of mind. The establishment of the committee forced the bitterly disappointed Zionists to countenance political as well as violent means to salvage their enterprise in Palestine. The prime mover here was Shertok, who realized the potential advantage latent in the committee for the Yishuv because it got America involved in the Palestine problem. It would be highly counterproductive to boycott the committee, as some were suggesting.

Ben-Gurion suggested that only members of non–Jewish Agency bodies testify, but he remained in the minority. The committee, he told the Mapai Secretariat, "is an instrument [for Britain] to evade its undertakings." He feared that the committee might define the Jews as foreigners in Palestine or find that Jews did not wish to go to Palestine, or that Palestine was incapable of absorbing them. To appear before the committee was tantamount in his eyes to abolishing the legal foundation of the Jewish presence in Palestine.

Later in the debate Ben-Gurion raised a new point. He was concerned that the committee might be swayed by non-Zionist Jewish representatives, who would argue that there was no connection between Palestine and the Jewish problem. Ben-Gurion said he would agree to the Jewish Agency's appearance if it were the sole Jewish representative but not otherwise.

Dobkin and Berl Locker criticized Ben-Gurion's approach. Lubianiker declared: "Our position is too tragic to afford the luxury of replacing political struggle with an empty demonstration" and reiterated Shertok's point that there was nothing to lose by appearing before the committee. Liebenstein, however, thought that the committee was less significant than the resistance actions. The committee's makeup, he claimed, made it an instrument in Bevin's hands, and therefore the Yishuv should not cooperate with it. As expected, the Mapai moderates favored cooperation. To boycott the committee at a time when Zionism was itself ostracized was tantamount to eliminating the Jewish Agency as a public political body, Sprinzak argued.

Shertok, in a moving speech, called for cooperation with the committee in order "to salvage what we can from the debris of the Mandate and the Balfour Declaration." Finally, and most significant, even if the committee held center stage, the Yishuv "must recruit forces to ensure that the struggle and illegal immigration will continue and that courageous acts will be performed precisely when the committee is in session." Not to appear, Shertok said, would be to "disappear from the political stage." Nemirovsky supported Ben-Gurion, and by a margin of 16 to 2 Mapai's Political Committee decided to cooperate with the Anglo-American Committee.[38]

Dominated by Mapai, the General Zionists and the Mizrachi, the Small Zionist Actions Committee voted 15 to 3 (7 abstentions) in favor of the executive's motion, which spoke of "stepping up of the struggle of the entire Jewish people in the country and the Diaspora against the White Paper regime." The vote in favor of cooperating with the Anglo-American Committee, though less overwhelming (16-11), was no less clear-cut and was binding on the Jewish Agency and the Yishuv.[39]

It would be a mistake to think that Ben-Gurion's conceptual thinking at this period was limited to the Resistance Movement. He never swayed from his basic assumption that every Zionist consideration should be guided by politics, not by force. The preparations for the Anglo-American Committee, however, shifted the focus in Yishuv politics. One consequence was that the IZL and Lehi decided to act on their own as well as within the Resistance Movement framework. On 27 December they attacked police stations in Jerusalem (and in Jaffa and Tel Aviv), resulting in seven British fatalities. High Commissioner Sir Alan Cunningham asked Ben-Gurion and Shertok point-blank whether the Jewish Agency "associated itself" with this attack. The reply, that the Jewish Agency had exactly the same connection with the operation by the breakaways as the high commissioner had, surprised the latter. Ben-Gurion also rejected Cunningham's request for the Jewish Agency to renew its collaboration with the authorities. This, he said, was not feasible in view of the government's "unlawful" activity. The public, Ben-Gurion said, was becoming increasingly angry, and the Jewish Agency could not easily impose law and order. If the Jewish Agency were to cooperate with the British, it would alienate itself from the public altogether. Unwittingly, Ben-Gurion thus admitted that the Jewish Agency had effectively lost control. Exaggerated as this assessment was, Ben-Gurion nevertheless soon had to escalate the Resistance Movement's operations, and not only to satisfy the Yishuv's frustrated activists and to restrain the breakaways; he also had to demonstrate to the committee the Yishuv's military prowess (discussed later).

Notwithstanding his former objections to cooperating with the inquiry committee, Ben-Gurion now prepared himself intensively for that purpose. Although he maintained that the main thrust of the issue would be political, he encouraged the Jewish Agency's Planning Committee to concentrate on Palestine's economic capacity. Two key points, besides the country's enormous potential, were that the Arabs, far from suffering because of the Zionist enterprise, actually benefited from it, and that 100,000 Jewish immigrants could be absorbed immediately.[40]

Meanwhile, however, the British were doing all they could to prevent the unauthorized arrival of such immigrants. On 17 February 1946, they intercepted the illegal ship *Enzo Sereni* with 915 refugees on board. Three days later the Palmach retaliated by destroying the Coast Guard station at Givat Olga for the second time, though another operation, against the radar station at Haifa, was foiled.[41]

Liebenstein, though, took issue with the leadership's approach. He told a meeting of the Mapai Council in early 1946 that it was a mistake to place the emphasis on "refugee Zionism," since the problem of 100,000 or 150,000 refugees could in fact be solved outside Palestine.

He wanted to avoid the kind of anti-British revolt at which Sneh had hinted. The atmosphere in Mapai was against a broad struggle, military or otherwise. Consequently, the Yishuv should accept Britain's willingness to continue the quota of 1,500 immigrants per month. In any event, as Meyerson said, there were no large ships available which could break the "shameful" limit. L. Shkolnik (later, Eshkol) agreed that the Yishuv should take whatever it was offered. Zionist policy makers also feared that, if rejected, potential immigrants might prefer America.[42] In the light of this atmosphere, it was not surprising that the Mapai Council also decided overwhelmingly, binding the party, in favor of appearing before the Anglo-American Committee (46 to 2, with 5 abstentions).

At a meeting of the Elected Assembly, Shertok was concerned to contain extremists from Hapoel Hamizrachi and Le'achdut Ha'avodah who refused to cooperate with the committee. For the first time, speaking for Ben-Gurion too, he hinted at the Jewish Agency's readiness to accept partition ("Zionist policy is not 'all or nothing'"). The defection of Hamizrachi did not substantially reduce the majority in the Elected Assembly (the vote was 63 to 32) in favor of appearing before the committee, of protesting against the White Paper and granting independence to Transjordan, and of accepting the limited quota for the refugees in Europe.[43]

The British hope that the Committee of Inquiry would stave off at least temporarily the violence of the Yishuv was disappointed. Pressure from below, and in particular the slow trickle of illegal immigration (only 2,200 arrivals in three months), again made the option of force more attractive. On 22 February 1946 the Palmach attacked four PMF camps, suffering four fatalities. Three days later the IZL and Lehi, with official approval, successfully attacked British aircraft, destroying twelve planes and damaging eight. The cost to the RAF was £750,000. Nerves in government were stretched to the limit.

As the leadership was looking for ways to consolidate the Yishuv, Mapai was debating whether to run together with Hashomer Hatza'ir and Le'achdut Ha'avodah in the Histadrut elections. The activists, led by Ben-Gurion, were uncompromising. Their argument was that, unlike in 1939, this time Mapai must hoist the banner of the Jewish state, otherwise that slogan would be usurped by the right-wing Abba Hillel Silver in America, and by the Revisionists. Hashomer Hatza'ir would not, however, forsake its binationalist formula, so that a joint election list seemed to be ruled out. Instead, Ben-Gurion suggested a general labor list "on the basis of a committed program. . . . We will not impose anything on them . . . if they reject it." The list would be based on a compromise, though not on the concept of a Jewish state.

Although Ben-Gurion was still bitter at Le'achdut Ha'avodah for its split in 1944 from Mapai, he preferred them now to Hashomer Hatza'ir, as the latter opposed both a Jewish state and an activist approach. Whatever the shortcomings of Le'achdut Ha'avodah, Ben-Gurion said tellingly, "it is unwilling to take orders and instructions from Russia." As for Hashomer Hatza'ir, it held "the fate of the Russian empire and a binational state to be more important than anything else," even to the point of not acting against the British. Ben-Gurion persuaded Mapai to opt for talks with Le'achdut Ha'avodah.[44]

On the eve of the Anglo-American Committee's arrival, Ben-Gurion was preoccupied with the urgency of Jewish immigration to achieve the first million. Shertok was more skeptical for, in practical terms, the DPs were ready to go, but only 60 or 70 percent, about 200,000 people, would probably make the move. He was even more unsure about Oriental Jewry, despite their "great love for Zion." Ben-Gurion insisted that the Jewish Agency, controlling *aliyah* and expropriating land, could bring in a million Jews in order to establish a state, though even 100,000 new immigrants "could shake Palestine from top to bottom."[45]

Consensus was the order of the day in the Jewish Agency Executive on the eve of the committee's arrival, and Rabbi Fishman, who demanded a Jewish state on both sides of the Jordan River, remained isolated. Similarly, Ben-Gurion won on the proposal for the first million without any commitment to a specific time frame. There was also a majority for a unified appearance by the Yishuv and a ban on separate testimony. Shertok voted with Ben-Gurion, allowing him a convenient majority in the Jewish Agency Executive (5 to 2, with 2 abstentions). But his greatest victory was in the parliamentary body—23 to 3 with 7 abstentions.[46] In his appearance before the committee, Ben-Gurion emphasized the plight of the destitute Jewish refugees in Europe and stressed the Jews' historical claim to the Land of Israel. He underlined two basic principles: that Jews deserved the same rights as any other nation or any other human beings; and that Palestine has always been the Jewish homeland. "We are here as of right," he declared, and "not on the strength of the Balfour Declaration or the Mandate." Ben-Gurion sought to explain that Zionism had not sprung from anti-Semitism but from the Jews' refusal to be dependent on others, and from discrimination, which was not always legal, political, or economic in character but in some cases was moral discrimination. Quoting Churchill's criticism (1939) of the White Paper as a "mortal blow," he added that tens of thousands of Jews could have been saved during the Holocaust, if the gates of Palestine had been open. He lashed out at the "conspiracy of silence" during the Nazi genocide and recalled that attempts by the Yishuv to tell the world about the atrocities were dismissed as Jewish propaganda. Even now, in Poland, where out of three million only 30,000 remained, pogroms were a daily occurrence. After explaining the role that the concept of Zion had played throughout Jewish history (whereas Palestine had fulfilled no role in Arab history), Ben-Gurion said that the contemporary Jewish generation was determined to build a "Jewish commonwealth" in Palestine and to reinvigorate the land. He listed the Yishuv's accomplishments in seeking this goal—in agriculture, industry, culture, the arts, and in science—and noted pointedly that Jewish security was based solely on the concept of defense. With a view to the committee's American members, Ben-Gurion likened the Yishuv's struggle to that of the colonies in America against the British. Like them, the Jewish settlers believed that the colonial administration was acting against their interests. In Palestine, he said, it had failed in its task as stipulated by the terms of the Mandate. The solution, he said, was a Jewish state in which the Jewish national home could be built and the Jewish question resolved.[47]

Ben-Gurion's presentation was not to the taste of all the committee's members, as one of them, Richard Crossman, the British Labour MP, disclosed in his diary: "[Ben-Gurion] made a bad impression on the Committee. His speech was obviously propaganda to his own people." But his main complaint was Ben-Gurion's refusal to condemn Jewish terrorism, as Weizmann had done in his testimony. Crossman felt that Ben-Gurion wanted to have his cake and eat it: to abide by the law as head of the Jewish Agency, but also "to tolerate terror" in order to put pressure on the British authorities. In this Crossman was absolutely correct. Not only did Ben-Gurion tolerate terrorism; he directed it. This was a "doubtful policy," Crossman thought, and he recommended that Ben-Gurion either go underground, like the Irish leaders, and declare war on Britain or emulate "Weizmann and the moderates," who considered it wrong to use force.[48] Crossman, though, missed the point: this was exactly Ben-Gurion's political sagacity. The logic behind his policy of cautious resistance was to combine force and diplomacy, since diplomacy alone did not work. The full extent of this policy was revealed to the British on the Black Sabbath, when Ben-Gurion's direct involvement with terrorism, and his collaboration with the IZL and Lehi, were exposed in documents seized in a search of the Jewish Agency's headquarters.[49]

A more positive note was struck between Ben-Gurion and Crossman on the issue of partition when the two met privately on 21 March 1946. The decision to accept partition had been taken, at both the ideological and political levels, in 1937. But its operative reaffirmation in the spring of 1946 was an act of courageous statesmanship, supported by Weizmann and Shertok, and made despite the absence of backing from Sneh and Fishman. Another four months had to pass, with the collapse of the Resistance Movement, to convince the rest of the Jewish Agency Executive that there was no viable option but partition. What moderates like Weizmann and Goldmann did not grasp, however, was that even partition would entail fighting the Arabs. Thus, in his appearance before the committee, Ben-Gurion was not trying to manipulate Zionist policy but to strike a balance between moderates and activists by exploiting to the maximum Zionist politics and resorting to limited force. Now, finally, Ben-Gurion and Shertok revealed their support for partition,[50] though both Kaplan and Sneh showed their lack of faith in its feasibility.

The frequent meetings of Mapai institutions and the leadership's appearances at them testify to the need to maintain contact, to update the party about current decision-making policy, and to sharpen its differences with other parties, particularly those of the labor movement, in view of the forthcoming elections to the Zionist Congress. The problem was that political achievements were slow to come both from the United Resistance Movement and from the Anglo-American Committee. This was against the background of the deteriorating relationship between the Yishuv and the British authorities, characterized by two episodes in March, one connected with the settlement enterprise, the other with the illegal immigration effort. The first was the British forces' discovery of arms near Biryah, in Upper Galilee, where a Palmach unit was stationed. The unit's members were arrested and tortured (the Haganah responded by killing the officer in charge). The Jewish Agency called on the Haganah to make this a test case by assembling thousands of people at the site as an act of protest. Finally the authorities agreed that twenty people could remain. The Palmach members were sentenced to prison terms ranging from one year to four years. Nonetheless, the Yishuv saw the episode as a victory for its basic principles of settlement and armed defense.

The second episode involved an old dream of Ben-Gurion's to provoke a clash with the authorities on the immigration issue, not in broad daylight but well into the night. It had been planned to land the *Wingate* with 248 illegal immigrants on board, in Tel Aviv, under the protection of three rows of Haganah guards in order to prevent their arrest. The ship was intercepted at sea, and in the ensuing clash a young woman was killed. These two episodes were doubtless intended to impress the Anglo-American Committee as well.

There was also a danger from the left, with Hashomer Hatza'ir calling for a binational state rather than supporting the struggle for a Jewish state, and Le'achdut Ha'avodah calling for a new mandate to be controlled by Britain, the United States, and Russia.[51] The moderates, led by Sprinzak (and Kaplan), favored a unified Histadrut list to the Zionist Congress, playing down the differences with the leftist parties over the methods of the anti-British struggle and over the state question. Sprinzak, though, got no comfort from Hashomer Hatza'ir, which refused to accept Ben-Gurion's conditions for a unified list and demanded that its binational state plank be added to Mapai's Jewish state program.[52] In any case, the divisions within Le'achdut Ha'avodah prevented unity with Mapai.[53]

The Report of the Anglo-American Committee of Inquiry (signed on 20 April but released on 30 April 1946) was a pro-Zionist document, as Arab negative reactions testified. The Jewish Agency Executive cautiously refrained from hailing it publicly, however, lest the Arabs bring "tremendous pressure" to bear on the British government.[54] Although the report fell short of Zionist expectation for a state, it was a turning point in terms of its recommendation to repeal the White Paper.

Ben-Gurion's first reaction (to a summary of the report) demonstrated his ability to bridge the gap between the utopian dimension of his leadership and his realpolitik approach. Underrating the tactical importance of the report's two achievements for Zionism (repeal of the Land Laws and permitting the entry of the 100,000 DPs), he thought the document was remiss with respect to two pillars of Zionism: the concept of the homeland and the Jews' historical bond with Palestine.[55] He took a more realistic approach, however, in a secret meeting with British Zionists.[56]

Within a day of the publication of the committee's report, however, Attlee effectively dashed remaining Zionist hopes by making the report's implementation conditional on the disarming of the Jewish "private armies." Ben-Gurion's guarded optimism (if not guarded pessimism) turned out to be justified, and the gap between activists and moderates was narrowed. Remez, an anti-activist, cautioned against resuming Resistance Movement operations, while E. Liebenstein (later Livneh) regarded the report as the first Zionist success since 1931 and as proof of the positive impact of resistance actions, as well as of American pressure. Mapai, however, refused to lose hope after Attlee's announcement, deciding to prepare both for the worst (the violent consequences of an Arab general strike) and for the best (the arrival of the 100,000).[57]

Yet, with the British adamantly rejecting the Jewish state demand and adhering to the White Paper, they played into Ben-Gurion's hands: instead of dividing the Yishuv, they brought about its cohesion.[58] Though rejecting the solutions suggested by Attlee and the committee as impractical, Ben-Gurion gave strict orders against taking "rebellious" action, calling on all forces to maintain national discipline and to conduct only political activity.[59]

What impact did the committee's report have on Ben-Gurion's grand strategy? On the face of it, very little, since it recommended that neither a Jewish state nor an Arab state should be established. In practice, though, it made him more tenacious about the need to achieve the definitive solution—a Jewish state—since the continuation of the Mandate was plainly impossible in view of the government's hostile attitude toward Zionist plans for the Yishuv's growth.[60] Bevin's speech to the Labour Party Conference on 12 June was ominous: "If we put 100,000 Jews into Palestine tomorrow," he declared, "I will have to put another division of British troops there. I am not prepared to do it."[61]

The result was a major, albeit final, Resistance Movement operation (Night of the Bridges, 17 June 1946), in which ten bridges connecting Palestine with the neighboring states were destroyed with no casualties. The eleventh bridge, however, cost the lives of fourteen Palmach men. In addition, the IZL kidnapped five British officers, and Lehi blew up the railway workshops in Haifa, losing eleven of its members in the process. Ben-Gurion, meeting in London with the colonial secretary, denied Haganah involvement, claiming that the Jewish Agency dealt only with immigration and that he, too, was distressed by the actions of the breakaways. But from G. H. Hall he got no more than a hint at a binational state, which Ben-Gurion took to mean some sort of cantonization.[62]

Although Black Sabbath on 29 June jolted the Yishuv, Ben-Gurion's long-term strategy remained unshaken: accumulation of strength through illegal immigration and the building of a strong military force; persistent advocacy of a Jewish state; reliance on the Anglo-Saxon world and its Jewish population; and recruitment of East European and Oriental Jewish communities for the state-building process. A few days before Black Sabbath, the news from the Arab League's conference at Bludan (see "The Missed Opportunities of Eliahu Sasson," chapter 3) made it clear to the Yishuv leadership that the countdown for an Arab-Jewish military confrontation had begun. June 1946, then, was a turning point not only in the saga of Anglo-Zionist relations but in the Arab-Jewish conflict. Ben-Gurion was the first to become aware of this, after the Jewish Agency's Arab Section disclosed Bludan's militant plans for the Arab states' occupation of Palestine.

Anti-British Activism, or Preparing for an Arab-Jewish War: June 1946–November 1947

Unlike the breakaways, who were obsessed with the British "enemy" to the point where they completely ignored the Arab factor, the Haganah under Ben-Gurion's political guidance considered both the British and the Arabs serious opponents, albeit of different orders. By May 1946, even before Bludan, it became obvious that Plan B, drawn up by the Haganah command against a possible Arab attack, had to be revised. From now on, the assumption would be that the local Arabs would not repeat their 1936–39 tactics but would operate according to a plan. The Haganah's Plan D of March 1948 originated with the revised Plan B of May 1946. For the second time since September 1945, the Jewish Agency's military arm drew up an offensive-defensive plan. This time, however, it spoke bluntly about "taking the initiative from the Arabs and containing them in the shortest possible time." The detailed plan for a counterattack called for "striking at any element, at the very outset of Arab operations, which might deter the perpetrators, and prevent the Arab masses from offering assistance. Strong hard strikes can pinpoint and isolate the activist elements." At the time the plan was formulated, the perceived balance of forces was such that the Haganah did not think it could meet the Arabs head-on, and therefore "our counterattack will be expressed, in most cases, as retaliatory action," which might also be directed at secondary or supportive targets. The Arab hinterland was targeted as well, in order "to shake Arab self-confidence." However, Plan B, unlike its successor, Plan D, did not call for deliberate assaults on the innocent civilian population, such as the burning of whole villages or expulsion. (That escalation can be explained only within the context of the hostilities that began in late November 1947.) Still, the seeds of Plan D were planted: the May 1946 plan took into account attacks on Arab villages that were a haven for gangs: "If the goal is general punishment, then everything possible should be burned and the houses of the agitators or the activists should be blown up."[63]

Yet, in mid-1946 a full-scale British-Jewish war seemed, for a time, as much of a possibility as an Arab-Jewish war. The British authorities' sweep against the Yishuv on 29 June 1946, called Operation Agatha but known to the Yishuv as Black Sabbath, in fact failed to accomplish two of its three objectives. The idea had been to cripple the Palmach, which was believed to be responsible for the most destructive operations, to leave the Haganah leaderless by arresting the Jewish Agency Executive officials known to be involved with the force, and to unearth documents providing clear-cut evidence of the agency's illegal action and shedding new light on the nature of the Haganah. Only the third objective was achieved. About 200 Palmach members were arrested, but Ben-Gurion (who was abroad), Sneh, Sadeh, and the majority of the Haganah leadership escaped. Some activists, such as Shertok, Fishman, and Bernard Joseph, were arrested, but so were moderates like Gruenbaum and Remez. The historic significance of the operation was that it imposed a tactical shift of direction on the Jewish Agency Executive. Black Sabbath was the primary motive for the disbanding of the United Resistance Movement; and from this time the practical aspect of the struggle was concentrated almost exclusively on illegal immigration and only slightly on settlement, though the military buildup continued.

Ben-Gurion, in Paris, condemned Operation Agatha as a "pogrom" worthy of Tsarist Russia and Hitler (he mentioned Lidice) but did not declare a break with Britain.[64] Instead, he rushed from unhelpful France to America, where pressure could be applied on Britain. There, privately, he told Felix Frankfurter, the Supreme Court justice and a veteran Zionist leader, that the Anglo-Zionist chapter had come to a close and that Palestine must be "freed" from the British.[65]

Internally, the official leadership, still reeling under the impact of Black Sabbath, suffered another serious blow three weeks later, when the IZL blew up the King David Hotel (22 July). Cunningham suggested that in response, legal immigration be stopped and illegal immigrants transferred from Palestine territorial waters to other countries. London, however, opted for a more moderate line, in keeping with its new policy for a political solution in Palestine. This was the Morrison-Grady proposal of 31 July, which inflicted a third blow on the Zionist-Yishuv leadership (see chapter 1). This proposal was for Palestine's division into Jewish and Arab cantons, apart from the Negev and Jerusalem, which would be ruled by the British high commissioner. The Jewish and Arab provincial autonomies could evolve into unitary entities or a binational state or could undergo partition. Truman, however, influenced by the Zionist lobby in America, refused to support the plan.

Against the background of these contradictory developments, an atmosphere of confusion and distress prevailed at the historic convention of the enlarged JAE, held in Paris in early August 1946, where it was officially decided to adopt partition (a "viable state").[66] Unlike Shertok, who was still imprisoned, Ben-Gurion had no intention of retreating from his Jewish state program, Morrison-Grady notwithstanding. His pragmatic activism tactics won the day, by maneuvering between the activists and the moderates, and it was decided to initiate moves toward partition by sending a mission to Washington headed by Nahum Goldmann.

The plan worked out by Goldmann, who was a member of the Jewish Agency Executive, was to present Truman with a concrete program for partition and the immediate immigration of the 100,000 in the transition period, granting the Jewish Agency control of immigration.[67] The fact that Goldmann's mission was approved by a majority of the Jewish Agency Executive also helped bring closer the basically opposing schools of Weizmann and Ben-Gurion and was instrumental in deferring the final break with Britain until February 1947, when Bevin announced the transfer of the Mandate to the UN. Had the break with Britain occurred earlier, war with the Arabs would also have begun before late November. This could have been crucial because not until the Paris meeting did the enlarged executive allocate an extra three million dollars for defense needs. In the meantime, relations with Britain deteriorated further with the government's decision to expel the illegal immigrants to Cyprus (12 August). This symbolized the practical end of the Zionist orientation toward Britain without endorsing the Resistance Movement in Palestine.[68]

Until Truman came forward in clear support of Zionism, on 6 October 1946, there was little Ben-Gurion could do about the political situation. Absent from the country at the time of the great crises of June–August 1946, and still in Paris on 23 August, he attempted to consolidate his tottering leadership (regarding the group of intellectuals who demanded his resignation, see chapter 6) by boosting the morale of Mapai members following the recent setbacks. His command of the day to the party, the Zionist movement, and the Yishuv was: "Neither Massada nor Vichy." In other words, Zionism must neither let it itself be placed in an impossible situation nor fatally compromise its principles. "Either way is downfall," he wrote to the Sixth Mapai Convention from Paris in September. Kaplan, the leading moderate, however, thought this presentation of the situation—"surrender or activism"—was actually "deluding the public, [for] what is called activism could bring shameful surrender."[69]

"Neither Massada nor Vichy" should be seen as a tactical line in the service of Ben-Gurion's strategic goal of unifying activists and nonactivists in favor of partition—another indication of the primacy of his *Innenpolitik.* This line was approved by the two key Mapai institutions by a large majority, according to the Paris formulation of a "viable Jewish state" (14 to 1, with 3 abstentions).[70] Mapai was also looking for a common denominator on the issue of struggle. One "plan of actions" was suggested by Shkolnik, who found that he and Kaplan could agree on it through the establishment of settlements.[71] (The results would be seen on the night of 6 October, when eleven new settlements went up simultaneously in the Negev.)

The debate in Mapai's Sixth Convention over the methods of struggle—taking into account that at Paris the military struggle was subordinated to political considerations, not the reverse—was dominated by the party's representatives in the Jewish Agency Executive, who had already decided to continue the Resistance Movement. As noted, however, "Neither Massada nor Vichy" was a flexible enough formulation to enable Ben-Gurion to pursue the activist policy by a different method: illegal immigration.

No leadership could ignore as distinguished a group as the Mapai moderates, whose arguments were rational, not emotional, though organizationally the group was weak. Apart from a major speech by Lubianiker against Liebenstein (warning against a new Massada), their ablest spokesman was perhaps Israel Gurfinkel (Guri), who pointed to the strategic assumptions behind Britain's anti-Zionist policy and consequently to the small weight that moral arguments could carry. He warned that the use of force might prove counterproductive in three ways: by increasing Arab fear and hatred; by disastrously affecting the internal front; and by destroying the constructive plans of the Yishuv for demographic and economic buildup. Still, not all the counterarguments of the activists could be dismissed as emotional. Meirov, who was in charge of Aliyah B (illegal immigration), warned of the danger that the more than 100,000 Jews in the camps in Germany might be lost to Zionism if the Yishuv refrained from struggle.

Another future Israeli statesman, Shimon Persky (Peres), saw danger in both "Massada" and "Vichy" but preferred the risk of battle:

"The road of struggle endangers the present, but the way of self-restraint jeopardizes the future." In the final vote on the line of struggle in the Sixth Mapai Convention, the pragmatic activist line that had been formulated by Ben-Gurion in "Neither Massada nor Vichy" won by 340 against 101 (22 abstained and 144 did not vote).[72] The convention was a turning point in Mapai party politics in the sense that its policy, following also the outcome of the Jewish Agency Executive's conference in Paris, was now focused on partition and a limited activist struggle, to Ben-Gurion's satisfaction.

But the consensus in Mapai did not reflect a consensus in the Yishuv leadership, notwithstanding Mapai's dominance in the executive, a fact signified by Sneh's resignation from the Haganah National Command (21 September) after Weizmann's demand, in his capacity as president of the Jewish Agency and the Zionist Organization, to stop the Resistance Movement actions in July. Sneh agreed to stay on temporarily, but the Yishuv's inaction in the face of British harassment (searches, expulsion of illegal immigrants) and Weizmann's readiness to negotiate with the British government unconditionally (at the London Conference on Palestine) left him no choice but to resign. In his view the Jewish Agency Executive in its current composition was not capable of "lengthy and persistent resistance" and therefore "not worthy of the task." Ben-Gurion told Sneh that he too would like to resign but could not bring himself to do it because of the gravity of the situation. No doubt, Ben-Gurion was closer in his overall policy to Sneh than to Weizmann, but he urged the members of the leadership not to follow Sneh's example, as this would show the British that the Yishuv was split between moderates and activists.

It was, however, the success or failure of the *ha'apalah*—the campaign to bring Jews to Palestine despite the British prohibition—that Ben-Gurion regarded as the acid test of his policy.[73] The *ha'apalah* movement was a great success both in terms of increasing the number of immigrants and in pressuring Britain through world opinion to surrender the Mandate even though the majority of immigrants were exiled to Cyprus. The thirteen ships the Haganah successfully brought from Europe to Palestine between August 1946 and January 1947, carrying a total of 12,656 immigrants, constituted a breakthrough in the history of the Yishuv, long before the *Exodus*.

Ben-Gurion had to steer a middle course between Weizmann's pro-British line and Sneh's anti-British one. Hence his willingness to negotiate with the government provided a "viable [i.e., partitioned] Jewish state" were the premise underlying the talks. At the same time, to maintain his credibility as Zionism's supreme leader, he felt constrained to add some militant rhetoric: "We always revolted as the weak against the strong, the few against the many."

The greatest surprise of the twenty-second Zionist congress had been Rabbi Fishman, who now repeated to the JAE what he had said in Paris: "I love the Land of Israel, and I love the people of Israel too. But the people takes precedence over the land. If the people is annihilated, there is no hope that we could live under any regime, including Britain's . . . even with the Messiah's appearance Nablus would not belong to the Jews. We can only hope that we shall get a state in part of the Land of Israel."[74]

Ben-Gurion on the threshold of 1947 did agree to hold "personal talks" with the British after an interval of six months.[75] He managed to get Weizmann rejected as a member of the Jewish Agency delegation, but instead of Weizmann he had to accept Silver on his side. Weizmann was an easy scapegoat on the altar of the new-old coalition, in which Sneh was an ally of both Ben-Gurion and Silver, notwithstanding the rightist character of the latter. In a coalition of nineteen members of the Jewish Agency Executive, nine would be based in Jerusalem, the rest in London and the United States. Ben-Gurion made sure that the final decision on all questions would always be made in Jerusalem. The Zionist Congress had shown that on political matters, Mapai was closer to the right-center parties of the General Zionists and the Mizrachi than to the two leftist parties, particularly Le'achdut Ha'avodah, now condemned as a Bolshevik party.[76] In fact, Ben-Gurion, through his dominance in the Histadrut and the Haganah, also controlled the leftist parties, though they rejected partition. Silver was upgraded, at Weizmann's expense, but Ben-Gurion remained the arbiter of the Zionist decision-making bodies.[77]

The talks, however, proved conclusively that the policies of the government and of the Jewish Agency were irreconcilable. On 13 February 1947 Bevin told Ben-Gurion point-blank that in his opinion, the establishment of a Jewish state would mean war with the Arabs, which Ben Gurion disputed in vain.[78] The British presented a new plan, which to Ben-Gurion was even worse than Morrison-Grady, merely another version of the 1939 White Paper. With the British chapter effectively ended, the Jewish Agency prepared itself for the next campaign—in the UN.

Significantly, as the critical stage of the struggle approached, Ben-Gurion—unlike his colleagues—refused to regard the breakaways as lost to the Yishuv, though he continued to see the Revisionists as basically mistaken in their methods. He was especially upset that the young Oriental Jews had been neglected by the Yishuv establishment and had turned to the IZL.[79]

In his approach to the problem of the IZL and Lehi, Ben-Gurion was guided by his belief that internal unity was a sine qua non for success on the external front. Thus, although the Haganah was enlisted on a small scale to contain the IZL, Ben-Gurion adamantly refused to mobilize the Histadrut for this purpose, as such a move might generate a true civil war.[80] Indeed, *Innenpolitik* was triumphant across the entire period under discussion.

With *ha'apalah* the agreed focus of the Yishuv struggle according to Ben-Gurion, Shertok, and the rest of the leadership, an internal consensus became easier to achieve. Only the IZL and Lehi remained outside the consensus.[81] The hanging of four IZL members by the British and the suicide by two other members of the breakaways in April 1947 intensified the internal debate in Mapai over the use of terrorism. In this debate Liebenstein, though dissociating himself from the methods and worldview of the IZL and Lehi, urged the revival of the United Resistance Movement. But he represented a minority view in Mapai. The majority supported Ben-Gurion's line that these "gangs" constituted a danger to the Yishuv's unity of policy and action.[82]

Indeed, Ben-Gurion was aware that one of the issues that could cause the collapse of the coalition in the Jewish Agency Executive was the support of some right-wing elements for terror tactics. A similar outcome would result if opponents of the Jewish state were to get the upper hand in the executive. This, however, remained a hypothetical danger. Although the right wing had become stronger in the Jewish Agency Executive, expressing sympathy for Menachem Begin, the Mapai Center continued to support the executive as it was then constituted by a substantial majority (32 to 4, with 4 abstentions, in a vote on policy toward the use of terrorism).[83]

Since late March 1947, Ben-Gurion, in his capacity as Jewish Agency Executive chief of defense, had conducted a thorough examination of the Yishuv's military situation. With 2,200 combatants in the semi-trained Palmach and fewer than 6,000 in the even less trained Hish (initials for the Field Force), and none of the commanders having experience in commanding even a battalion, he was naturally worried about the Yishuv's ability to face the Arab states. Ben-Gurion's military advisers told him that some 40,000 troops would be needed for an efficient defense. Thus, six months before the start of hostilities, Ben-

Gurion was genuinely worried about the capability of the Haganah and the Palmach.[84]

Ben-Gurion felt it was essential that there be no opposition before the forthcoming UNSCOP committee (see chaper 1). He made it a point to meet with opposition representatives on 18 June to obtain the clear-cut support of the convention held in Paris in August 1946 regarding a viable Jewish state. For this resolution he won a majority of 7 to 5 ow-ing to the split in the General Zionists between the radicals, Bernstein and Sneh, and the moderates, Goldmann and Gruenbaum.[85] In this spirit Ben-Gurion demanded, in his statement to UNSCOP, the estab-lishment of an independent Jewish state in Palestine. Only in the cross-examination did he concede that the Jewish Agency was ready for a compromise—that is, for partition.[86]

Although to UNSCOP he played down the danger of an Arab-Jew-ish war, seeking the committee's political support, Ben-Gurion knew very well that such a war was likely in the near future. He said so bluntly to the newly established Security Committee, consisting of representa-tives of the Yishuv's Zionist parties and accountable to Ben-Gurion him-self. The Haganah's structural weaknesses were glaring, and its dedi-cation and optimism alone would be insufficient in the coming war. It was necessary to establish an army founded primarily on the Palmach, the former Jewish Brigade, and the Field Force (Hish). In the mean-time, on 18 June, the day he also brought the partition formula to the executive, he instructed the Haganah National Command to prepare for an Arab-Jewish war. As for the British front, he explained, it was basically a political one, and the IZL was misguided to think other-wise.

In fact, the division of opinion in the Jewish Agency Executive pre-vented Ben-Gurion from taking a strong hand against IZL extremism. That organization indeed intensified its anti-British campaign dramati-cally at the end of July 1947, hanging two British sergeants in retalia-tion for the same punishment meted out to four of its activists. This act, together with the episode of the *Exodus*, the largest *ha'apalah* ship ever to reach Palestine (it carried 4,530 would-be immigrants), prompted Ben-Gurion to launch what was perhaps his most vitriolic attack against the IZL. He branded them "Jewish hooligans" who by their terrorist acts had diverted world opinion away from the immi-gration drive. The IZL's hanging action, he said, was tantamount to a "Nazi operation." Ben-Gurion launched a second denunciation after the IZL accidentally killed a Jewish bank clerk, calling the organiza-tion "a plague," and "a gang of Jewish Nazis" (though he would not say so in public because of "Jewish solidarity"). If Begin himself were hanged he, Ben-Gurion, would not commiserate in his martyrdom. Meyerson's apology to Cunningham ("we never felt more ashamed than at this time"), notwithstanding her rejection of the "open cooperation" he demanded, was sincere.[87] Despite his rhetoric, Ben-Gurion treated the IZL largely as little more than a nuisance, though its continued provocations led him to promise that the time to deal "militarily" with the breakaways would come, but not under foreign rule. In any event, none of this affected Ben-Gurion's "integralist" concept of struggle: "*Aliyah,* construction, political action, negotiation." The struggle was to be decided politically, and only if these means should prove insufficient would sabotage be resorted to (as in the case of the *Exodus,* when a British "expulsion ship" was damaged by the Haganah).[88]

The UNSCOP Report published in August 1947 recommending partition was, despite all its faults, a great Zionist victory, according to Ben-Gurion, who called it "the beginning of redemption, if not more." Obviously, he was unhappy about the exclusion of Jerusalem and Western Galilee, but he saw the partition recommendation as a "moral victory," and he had always believed that moral superiority was a vital element in any national struggle. The report was also the coup de grâce to the minority opposition on both the left and the right: the Greater Zionist Actions Committee accepted the report by an overwhelming majority of 51 to 16.[89] Ben-Gurion's granting of priority to *Innenpolitik* was now legitimized by UNSCOP; here, finally, was the proof that there was no alternative to partition on the agenda of either Zionism or the great powers.

Preparations for war with the Arabs were now in high gear. Ben-Gurion involved himself in the minutest details of military preparations: budgets, the cost of manufacturing ammunition, manpower for the various units, and acquisition of aircraft and recruitment of pilots to fly them. A sense of drift had been replaced by immersion in the concrete realities of planning at both the military and diplomatic levels.

As for the borders of the Jewish state, Ben-Gurion would say only that if the UN decision turned out to be "convenient," the Jewish forces would "occupy only those areas allotted to us . . . we will not fix territorial parameters." He pledged that a positive decision by the UN would place limits on Jewish expansion: "The Jewish state will not conquer that part of Palestine not designated for it. Jews will remain in that [Arab] area. Nor will the Jewish state wish to occupy Jerusalem and Kfar Etzion."[90]

For the first time, Ben-Gurion admitted that the Haganah was prepared only to do battle with the Palestine Arabs but not with the Arab states. The full picture of the Yishuv's military weakness, though, was made known only to the Security Committee.[91] There Galili admitted that Plan B was outdated and dealt only with an Arab uprising inside Palestine, but he did not have the authority to change it; only Haganah General Headquarters could do this.[92] Chief of Staff Y. Dostrovsky (Dori) presented the old plan to the Security Committee as late as 13 November 1947, although it failed to take into account the intervention of neighboring Arab countries. In view of Plan D of March 1948 (see chapter 5), it is astonishing to read the following remarks uttered by Galili only four months earlier: "The Haganah is not built for aggression; it does not wish to subdue; it respects human life; it wishes to strike at only the culprits; it does not wish to set fire but to extinguish it."[93]

What is the reason that no one on the Security Committee reprimanded the Haganah Command for not preparing a revised plan, and least of all Ben-Gurion? The answer lies in the latter's approach. He was aware of the limited strength of the Arab armies, but he knew also that they could not be treated with contempt. Given the proper preparations (and some encouragement for his despondent colleagues), he believed, there was no reason for fear, "because we have two moral advantages, which are also of crucial military value: [our] moral and intellectual superiority, [and] the world's recognition of the justice of our cause and our goal."[94] Three days before the eruption of hostilities, the Haganah still had no new strategic plan to replace Plan B and relied heavily on the Home Guard. Unlike others, such as Galili and Shkolnik, Ben-Gurion did not deny that "serious fears" and "hesitations" existed about establishing a state. Nevertheless, he declared unhesitatingly that the solution was "to establish a Jewish force, and not to ask the British to stay on." The leftist parties finally accepted the Jewish Agency's authority in full, as discussed later, but would not countenance the continued separate existence of the breakaways and suggested that they disband.[95]

Leadership at War: Trial and Error

Although Ben-Gurion regretted the relatively small area allotted to the Jewish state, in contrast to his initial enthusiasm, he was convinced that the new state would be economically viable. The desolate Negev could be built up, and there were also the long coast and the Gulf of Eilat, which would make Israel's use of the Suez Canal unnecessary.

The most serious shortcoming was the dearth of Jews. The population distribution—520,000 Jews (excluding 100,000 in Jerusalem) and 350,000 Arabs—gave him great anxiety, but he did not mention transfer as a solution. Rather, the immigration of a million and a half Jews was the first commandment.[96] The Negev, with its vast agricultural potential, was the key to the state's existence. "The desert," he said, "is more real than Tel Aviv."[97] Although he wished ardently that Jerusalem should be part of the Jewish state (by means of a corridor from the Dead Sea), he reconciled himself to the idea that the city might remain internationalized and could not, therefore, serve as the country's capital. Nevertheless, it should be the capital of the Jewish people, organizationally, scientifically, culturally, and educationally. Ben-Gurion rejected the seizure by force of Jerusalem and seems to have been sincere in objecting to Jewish expansion beyond the UN borders (provided the Arabs behaved likewise); he was satisfied with the 55 percent of western Palestine allotted to the Jewish state.

Ben-Gurion put the defense of the Yishuv at the top of the agenda as Arab attacks intensified. Three weeks after the beginning of hostilities on 30 November—hostilities triggered by the Palestine Arab leadership and involving local irregulars and volunteers from the neighboring countries—Ben-Gurion appointed four senior officers to prepare a new military plan and a budget for the Jewish army. The revised Plan B of May 1946 was no longer relevant, given the heavy Jewish casualties during the first two weeks of fighting (94 dead and 100 wounded).[98]

Ben-Gurion saw the Arabs' military effort as an attempt to destroy the Yishuv and certainly to prevent the establishment of a Jewish state.[99] The Yishuv must be prepared both for a war of protracted attrition and for a major invasion. Ben-Gurion preferred what he called an "offensive defense" to a "static defense," in order to undermine the Arabs' capability as quickly as possible.[100]

Within six weeks of the beginning of hostilities, Ben-Gurion realized that the next seven or eight months would be crucial for the coming "hundreds or thousands" of years of Jewish history, for in that brief period the war would be decided. The Jewish people's lengthy confrontations—with the likes of the Romans, the Byzantines, the Crusaders, and with Chmelnitzky and Hitler—were only "episodes" in a continuing struggle. Now the final battle was at hand.[101] The current generation of defenders, he said, was one with "the heroes of Israel through the ages, going back to Rabbi Akiva and Bar Kochba, to the defenders of Yodfat and Massada."[102] Yet the quality of the Haganah, just emerging from a lengthy period as an underground force, was now sharply questioned by former British officers who were close to Ben-Gurion, such as F. Eshet (Eizenstadt).[103]

Ben-Gurion knew that victory would depend on the arrival in time of heavy equipment. Shertok, on the other hand, believed that an international force was vital, since he doubted whether the Haganah could establish Jewish domination within the borders determined by the UN. To this Ben-Gurion replied that he was certain the Yishuv could cope with the Arabs given "enough equipment, of the right quality and by the right time (before 15 May)." This was "no mystical faith, but cool judgment based on practical examination."[104]

While he was preoccupied with turning an underground force into a regular army, Ben-Gurion was also working to form a provisional government to resolve the division of authority between the Jewish Agency and the Va'ad Leumi. On 25 March 1948 the Jewish Agency Executive decided to create the People's Administration (Minhelet Ha'am or "The Thirteen"), comprising the thirteen members of the executives of the Jewish Agency and the Va'ad Leumi, thus forming what would become on 14 May Israel's provisional government. Indeed, it functioned as a government with full powers except in the formal sense, including foreign affairs. Commensurate with the Yishuv's democratic character, a People's Council of thirty-seven members was created as a parliamentary body according to the parties' proportional strength in the recent elections to the Zionist Congress (1946) and the Elected Assembly (1944). Aliyah Hadashah, Agudat Israel, and the Sephardim joined the People's Administration, as Ben-Gurion wanted to show that even the non-Zionists accepted the Zionist consensus. The Revisionists were members of the People's Council, but not of the People's Administration, because of their sympathy for the IZL, which was still negotiating the conditions for dissolution (discussed later).

Ben-Gurion sought to reorganize the military. He regarded the Haganah Command as superfluous, a throwback to the "primitive" period. On 26 April 1948 he accused the Palmach of being a "sectorial army" of Mapam, the left-wing Zionist party created in January (see chapter 10). Defense affairs, he declared, must, as in wartime Britain, be concentrated in a war cabinet and "the last word must belong to the civilians, not the soldiers." War, Ben-Gurion said, is finally a "political issue."[105]

The establishment of the People's Administration was a watershed: seven weeks before the British withdrawal, the first Jewish government in Palestine after nearly 2,000 years of exile. More immediately, it put an end, at least temporarily, to the internal bickering between Mapai and the radical left and Aliyah Hadashah, though not with the Revisionists and IZL, the radical right. However, both left and right complained that the new body legitimized Ben-Gurion's "dictatorship" in the Yishuv, although he pointed out that Mapai was represented only by four members among The Thirteen (Mapam, the General Zionists, and the Mizrachi had two each, and Aliyah Hadashah, Sephardim, and Agudat Israel one each).[106]

Operation Nachshon, launched by the Haganah on 1 April 1948 (lifting the siege of Jerusalem, if only temporarily), became the turning point of the entire intercommunal war with the Palestinian Arabs. It obviated the need for the convoy system by which isolated areas were supplied, since the Arab villages that dominated the crucial roads in the Judean Hills were now permanently occupied, having been destroyed and having had their inhabitants expelled (the expulsions exceeded the instructions of Plan D). Ben-Gurion, though, did not regard this as the prelude to a strategic victory because of the plan's limited objectives. He drew a bleak picture of the dangers that still lay ahead: 900 Jews had been killed so far, thousands of Arab League volunteers were streaming into the country; the British authorities were inimical, their rule was breaking down, and they provided arms only to the Arabs. It was therefore urgent, Ben-Gurion insisted, to reorganize the civil-military administration and adapt it to the war's needs. The Yishuv was coping and many Arab villages had been captured or their inhabitants had fled "in fear," but no Jewish settlement or quarter had been evacuated.[107]

By now, Plan D, which was blatantly offensive in character, was ready for implementation. Operation Nachshon had been a sideshow in comparison to what lay ahead. The plan assumed that both regular and irregular forces, including Jordan's British-trained Arab Legion, would invade Palestine. Their objectives would be to cut off, or occupy, Galilee and the Negev, and to effect a "deep penetration" in the Sharon region and around Emek Hefer toward Kalkilyah-Herzliyah and Tul-Karem–Netanyah. Air attacks on settlements and urban centers were also anticipated. Foreseeing a situation of total war, the plan recommended "annihilating (burning, blowing up, and leveling)" Arab villages lying inside the Jewish defense grid. Such villages were to be surrounded and searched, and if there was resistance, the course to follow was "the extermination [*hashmadah*] of the armed force and the expulsion of the population across the borders." In the big cities the plan called for the "seizure" of isolated quarters, and again, in the event of resistance, the population would be "expelled to the Arabs' major urban area." Though survival was the Jewish superior goal, Plan D could be construed to mean what a later era would call "ethnic cleansing." However, it did not, "generally speaking," call for conquests beyond the Jewish state's designated borders. "Nevertheless, several enemy bases which are directly near the border, and which might become a springboard for penetration into key spaces of the Jewish state, will be captured temporarily and mopped up . . . and become, until the end of the operations, part of our defense system." Ultimately, Plan D did not become operational until 14 May, in accordance with the strategic deployment of the Haganah brigades.[108]

Yet Ben-Gurion was not motivated by the Haganah's local successes between 1 April and 14 May; he was driven by the fear that the Yishuv lacked sufficient arms to prevail against invading Arab armies. The victories against the poorly equipped local Arabs would thus evaporate into thin air. The first breakthrough in the arms acquisition campaign occurred when Ehud Avriel, hitherto the senior activist of Aliyah B in Europe, negotiated an arms shipment with Prague in early January 1948. The first and second arms deals were crucial to the Haganah's successes in April.[109] By mid-April, however, Haganah GHQ reported to Ben-Gurion that 40 percent of its forces lacked weapons, 75 percent had no access to vehicles, and 50 percent of the required equipment was not yet available.[110]

As the date of the of the British withdrawal approached—15 May, according to the colonial secretary's announcement on 11 December 1947—Ben-Gurion turned cautiously optimistic. Although rejecting as mere "speculation" the experts' opinion that Iraq and Syria would not intervene militarily because of their minorities problems, he nevertheless foresaw an improvement in the Yishuv's manpower situation. Certainly there was no place for despair, he thought, especially in view of the Jewish occupation of Tiberias, Haifa, Jaffa, and Safed in the run-up to 14 May. He warned, however, that nothing could be considered final before the actual confrontation with the Arab states.[111]

Ben-Gurion's proclamation of the State of Israel in Tel Aviv on 14 May 1948 meant little in military terms: the invading Arab states were determined to nip Jewish independence in the bud. With no international force to defend it, nascent Israel was thrown back on its own meager military and financial resources, though it did have essential diplomatic support and arms supplies from the Soviet Union.

There was much concern over the fate of besieged Jerusalem, particularly after the surrender of the Jewish Quarter of the Old City. Operation Nachshon had proven only a temporary respite, the Arab Legion again placing Jerusalem under tight siege. Militarily the loss of the Jewish Quarter was of little consequence, but it was a severe jolt to morale. Ben-Gurion's first target, however, was Lebanon ("the weakest link"), in which he wanted to establish a Christian state ("Muslim rule there was artificial"). Syria would then fall, and if Egypt dared to continue fighting, Port Said, Alexandria, and Cairo would be bombed. Domestically, Ben-Gurion, with the backing of the small parties, rejected an idea put forward by Mapam and Mizrachi to establish a small war cabinet, pointing out that the candidates (Gruenbaum, Kaplan, Shapira, and Ziesling) were unversed in military affairs.[112]

On 31 May, following a decision five days earlier by the provisional government, the Israel Defense Forces (IDF) officially came into being; all other independent forces were barred. On 1 June, the IZL and Lehi joined the IDF. It was a traumatic event for the breakaways, who tried to maintain an independent presence in Jerusalem, which was not officially annexed to Israel (see later discussion of the *Altalena* affair and Bernadotte's assassination). The first cease-fire, initiated by the UN and lasting from 11 June to 9 July 1948, gave the IDF a much-needed respite during which it could regroup for the renewal of hostilities.

Ben-Gurion now recast his grand strategy. His basic assumptions were that the partition resolution of 29 November was dead and that the Palestine question would be decided by force. The war was a zero-sum game: for Israel to lose would mean destruction, though Israel sought only the eradication of the Arab armies, not the Arab nations.

As the new state struck roots, Ben-Gurion was increasingly concerned by the relations between the military and civilian sectors. The army, he told the Mapai Council, must be subordinate to the civilian government. From this point of view, he was less worried about the IZL than about the Palmach, which he considered the "private army" of Le'achdut Ha'avodah, now part of Mapam. Ben-Gurion had therefore laid down certain conditions before accepting the defense portfolio, especially that there must be only one army, exerting one authority.[113]

Although he considered the Palmach the immediate danger, he chose the IZL, an easier target, as the first victim of his decision to eliminate private armies. The result was the *Altalena* affair, revolving around an IZL arms ship, which arrived off the coast of Tel Aviv on 22 June, too late to contribute significantly to the military situation. Already on 20 June the cabinet had decided unanimously to use force if necessary to prevent the ship from landing. IZL members had deserted their army units to assist in the delivery of *Altalena* arms to IZL bases, and the army was ordered to use force against them and in the last resort to sink the ship. Ben-Gurion saw the *Altalena* episode as an attempt to "assassinate" the state, which would effectively cease to exist if there were no civilian control over the armed forces. He was outraged at what he saw as an attempted IZL coup d'état. Lashing out at the IZL's supporters in the cabinet and elsewhere (Gruenbaum, Fishman, and Shapira and a group of rightist mayors), he pointed out that the war was still raging and Arab forces were still occupying parts of Israel. Despite the resignation of Fishman (for two weeks) and Shapira (for four days), the State Provisional Council, the parliamentary body that was the forerunner of the Knesset and that replaced the People's Council after 14 May, stood by the government action against IZL by a majority of 24 to 4, with 5 abstentions.[114]

Ben-Gurion was also able to resolve the other internal crisis during the truce and thus strengthen his war leadership, which despite the IDF's victories came under occasional question by various ministers. This crisis, he suspected, in view of an earlier intention to fire Galili, had been deliberately fomented by Mapam to obtain a share of the war's fruits. On 1 July 1948, far from the public eye, the heads of the departments in GHQ (Yadin, Z. Ayalon, E. Ben-Hur, and Galili) submitted their resignations to Ben-Gurion.

The best witness to Ben-Gurion's state of mind is his diary: "I do not know whether Israel [Galili] is the victim or the initiator of a persistent intrigue by his party [Mapam] to dominate the army, and thus get rid of me. . . . The Mapam machine is working."[115] Mapam ministers now launched a full-scale attack on Ben-Gurion's military capability. M. Bentov, for example, was enraged at Ben-Gurion's interference in the small details of the military. Mapam was prepared to accept Ben-Gurion's strategic leadership but not to countenance his involvement in day-to-day affairs. Nevertheless, Ben-Gurion was invited by the cabinet to return to the Ministry of Defense by a majority of 6 to 0 with 2 abstentions, and as a result the senior officers retracted their resignations. His fight for total control of the war was complete ("I see things better than the GHQ personnel. I say so as a result of a year and a half's experience").[116] Ben-Gurion could abandon his mea culpa attitude after his triumph in the controversy with GHQ.

When hostilities resumed, the victories of the so-called "Ten-Day War" consolidated Ben-Gurion's rule even more solidly. Drawing biblical analogies was, as usual, a sure way to enhance his charismatic leadership at home and abroad but also to obtain historical legitimacy.

Speaking to the Provisional State Council on 12 July, he quoted from the Book of Joshua (12:7–24): "And these are the kings of the country which Joshua and the Children of Israel smote."[117]

On every front there was unfinished business. Although some ministers doubted that a decisive victory was possible, the cabinet unanimously supported Ben-Gurion's policy to end the truce and renew the war with Egypt (to decide the fate of the Negev) and with Transjordan (to widen the corridor to Jerusalem). The moderates' views, particularly their skepticism about Israel's ability to achieve a strategic victory, did not destroy the consensus generated by the continuing successes.[118] It was a consensus more easily achieved in foreign affairs than on the internal front. The IZL refused to accept the government's authority in Jerusalem, as the city had not been officially annexed (although Israeli law had been applied to the city). The IZL, Gruenbaum reported to the cabinet, wanted to play General Zeligowski's role in Vilna in 1920 (i.e., annex Jerusalem without prior official approval). The ministers of the majority objected to Gruenbaum's tolerance of the IZL in Jerusalem after it had disbanded in the rest of the country—its presence, they argued, might spark civil conflict at the worst possible time. Mapam and Mapai, seeking to avert bloodshed, yielded to Gruenbaum's pressure and extended the deadline for the dissolution of the breakaway groups, but to no avail. On 17 September 1948, the Stern Gang (Lehi) took advantage of the situation and assassinated Count Bernadotte, the UN mediator, who had proposed a reduction of Israel's territory. Even then, Gruenbaum tried to save the IZL's prestige, but the cabinet reacted with an ultimatum to the IZL to join the IDF within twenty-four hours or face the consequences.[119]

Nor was the Palmach issue yet resolved, for the danger that the Palmach would act as a private army continued to haunt Ben-Gurion. He was not persuaded by the left's claim that the Palmach's existence might prevent a civil war with the IZL—clearly the IDF could also quell domestic violence. A last attempt by Mapam to preserve the Palmach's independence through the Histadrut was also foiled.[120] Ben-Gurion, then, feared both right-wing and left-wing coups d'état and treated both sides high-handedly.

Ben-Gurion saw no option but a continuation of the war. Following the cabinet's refusal to sanction an attack on the central front, Ben-Gurion shifted his strategy to the south. Here the support of Shertok convinced the ministers that an operation in the Negev would not entail a confrontation with the UN.[121] The outcome (only three voted against) was yet another demonstration that Ben-Gurion could afford to include in his cabinet moderates such as Kaplan, Remez, or even Bentov and Rosenblueth: all cooperated in the war effort, though occasionally questioning some of Ben-Gurion's more audacious tactical moves. Mapam, which had already gained legitimacy by its very co-option to the coalition, could no longer be accused of taking orders from Moscow against Jewish interests (as Ben-Gurion had charged before Gromyko's pro-Zionist declaration on 14 May 1947; see chapter 2).[122]

The great victory in the south from 15 to 22 October, and in Galilee a week later, showed the fluid nature of Israeli tactics. Kaplan underlined the deteriorating economic situation, compounded by a debt to Czechoslovakia of $6.5 million for arms, leaving no funds to purchase food or additional weaponry: "We are on the edge of the precipice," he warned.[123] Ben Gurion was determined to press Israel's advantage.[124] "Conquest by settlement," he believed, was no less important than "conquest by arms."[125] This applied to Upper Gallilee as well as the Negev, even at the risk of provoking the UN.[126] In any case, military victories alone could not ensure the state's survival. "The task of the economy after the war," he wrote, "is not to build on military conquests but on economic and spiritual conquests."[127]

By the end of 1948, Ben-Gurion could hail Israel's achievements as a watershed in Jewish history. "The Jewish people is conscious of its moral superiority and humanitarian uniqueness, and therefore has been able to maintain its independence. In its heart it did not succumb even when physically defeated."[128] Now he could also mock radicals of both the right and the left who, in the name of "international fraternity" or of "historical borders" or of "tomorrow's forces" preached trusteeship, an international mandate, a binational state, and "other futile programs." By January 1949 the conquest of the south was complete (apart from the southern Negev, which would be taken in March). Ben-Gurion envisaged five conditions for the Jewish state's future security: rapid, large-scale immigration, which would help build a strong, durable army; speedy settlement of the empty areas; a pacific foreign policy; the development of industry and industrial agriculture; and military security—a quality army to counter Arab quantity.[129]

Mapai's victory in the general elections for the First Knesset, held in early 1949, with 35.7 percent of the votes, enabled it to form a coalition with the least ideological parties (in right/left terms): the religious parties, the Progressive Party (formerly Aliyah Hadashah), and the Sephardim. Ben-Gurion declared that his government espoused friendship and cooperation with both Russia and America, a Jewish-Arab alliance, support for the UN, and the consolidation of peace; it was a coalition where the workers held the majority and with civil equality for women. It was by no means a government that was committed to a socialist ideology, since it would welcome the injection of capital from abroad and wanted to encourage private enterprise to develop the country and facilitate immigrant absorption on a mass scale: "As we are obliged to rescue the survivors [of the Holocaust]," Ben-Gurion asserted, "so must we save the remnant of Jewish [human] capital in the Diaspora." His Zionist-socialist vision, he declared, derived from the millenarian vision of Israel's prophets. Speaking to the nation in a major radio broadcast, he omitted any mention of the Zionist-socialist pantheon, citing only Herzl as the prophet of a Jewish state based on a cooperative society.[130] These pronouncements did not entail a policy shift, as Ben-Gurion had always made it clear that his goal was a national revolution that would enable the Jewish state to become an integral part of the free world.

Mapai's victory in 1949 was largely the result of Ben-Gurion's leadership, and it gave him leeway to form any coalition he wished. With the mandate he won he could articulate a two-pronged grand strategy for Israel's future based on a dual partnership: between Israel and the Diaspora, and between "the Jewish worker and the other constructive forces in the nation." This was in line with the strategy he had formulated as early as the 1930s, encapsulated in the slogan, "from class to nation." Then as now, he was guided by the concept that periods of crisis called for emergency coalitions; hence his readiness in 1949 to form a coalition with any Zionist party (apart from Begin's Herut). His task was facilitated by his goals being primarily nationalist rather than socialist. As in the past, he rejected "maximalist declarations," whether from the right or the left, and espoused "independence and activism." By this he meant not so much political as moral and ethical independence, "without blind imitation" of others. Zionism, he said, was neither "reformist" or "revolutionary," it did not emulate German social democracy, the British Labour party, or Russian communism. In fact, Ben-Gurion distilled what he needed from each of those movements and wove the result into the distinctive fabric of Zionism, in this following the classical labor-Zionist ideologues: B. Borochov, N. Syrkin, and B. Katzenelson. But Ben-Gurion was no ideologue; his priority was pragmatism in the quest to achieve his only goal: the establishment of a durable Jewish state.[131]

His decision to omit Mapam and the majority General Zionists from the coalition was due to their excessive demands in terms of ideology and portfolios. The latter, for example, refused to tolerate even Ben-Gurion's mild form of socialism, though the real obstacle was its ministerial demands.[132] Nor did Ben-Gurion make apologies for what Mapam called his "reformist-clerical" coalition, countering that this was the same coalition he had led for the past fifteen years, with optimal results in immigration, settlement, education, and defense. Ben-Gurion's large Knesset majority left the door open to both Mapam and the General Zionists to join the government at a later stage, which they did (though doubts about Mapam's ideology grew as the Cold War intensified).[133]

Ben-Gurion's decision to compromise on strategically inconvenient borders was based on his conviction that "no border is absolute" and his view that "Israel's central mission now is to absorb immigration." Moreover, many Jews in the Diaspora were threatened by annihilation and "Israel must spare no effort in rescuing them."[134] Israel, in fact, was not yet truly consolidated as a state, having a population of only 800,000 in a truncated area. Martin Buber had been right to ask: "A state—what for?" Without supremacy of the spirit, Ben-Gurion replied, Israel would not survive. But spirit could not exist without matter. The messianic belief that had spurred Jewish faith for thousands of years was still the raison d'être of the Jewish people.[135] So it was to Moses that Ben-Gurion looked as the prototypical prophet and nation builder.[136]

Pragmatism, democracy, and a studied orientation toward Western civilization were Ben-Gurion's policy guidelines. In retrospect, it is clear that neither of the two main opposition parties, on the right and the left, fitted this pattern. Linkage between internal political integration and a non-ideological foreign policy was essential but required a mainstream domestic consensus, which precluded the co-option of Herut's chauvinism and Mapam's communism. As far as Ben-Gurion was concerned, this was the key to his politics of state building: *Innenpolitik* conditioned *Aussenpolitik*.

5

Chaim Weizmann and the Collapse of the British Orientation

An Alternative to Activist Politics?

Although Ben-Gurion and his limited activism won the day in 1948–49 in the realms of politics, the military, and economics, that victory would not have been possible without the infrastructure laid by Chaim Weizmann between 1914 and 1931. Nor should Weizmann's subsequent contribution to the national effort be underestimated either, even though he was forced out of the presidency of both the World Zionist Organization and the Jewish Agency in 1946. His main disadvantage, beyond his lack of a political constituency, was his physical remoteness from the Yishuv. Weizmann visited Palestine only occasionally, usually in periods of crisis: he believed that the center of power lay in London. Still, he was not entirely isolated in the Yishuv. He had support from elements in the General Zionists, although their influence was greater in Britain than in Palestine or America. But when the German immigrants organized their own party, Aliyah Hadashah, in 1942, they found in Weizmann their spiritual mentor. This was, however, a one-sided affair. The party itself was a minor actor on the Yishuv political stage, but its moral influence, together with that of J. L. Magnes's Ichud intellectuals, contributed significantly to easing the Anglo-Zionist dispute, though it conspicuously failed to resolve the Arab-Zionist conflict.

Ben-Gurion bore no responsibility for creating the connection with Britain, since he was not yet a decision maker in the formative period of the Anglo-Zionist relationship. Not so Weizmann, who was the matchmaker of this marriage of convenience, which was bound to end

in divorce. The unresolved historians' debate as to who initiated the
Balfour Declaration seems to have been reduced to the proposition that
"had there been no Zionists at that time the British would have had to
invent them."[1] Weizmann built his policy, which lay in ruins after the
1939 White Paper, on his belief in the support of the British establishment, headed by Churchill; he placed great hopes in the latter's advocacy of Zionism, failing to realize that this position was motivated
largely by imperialist considerations. Weizmann's most triumphant
moment in this period came when Churchill, acceding to the Jewish
statesman's impassioned plea, appointed a cabinet committee at the
height of World War II to consider the political future of the Middle
East. Churchill cautiously encouraged Weizmann to believe that serious deliberations could be held on the creation of a Jewish state.[2] But
Weizmann's diplomatic edifice was brought down by the assassination, by Lehi extremists, of Lord Moyne, the British minister of state
resident in the Middle East (who supported partition and a Jewish state
within a regional federation) on 6 November 1944. Weizmann rushed
to Palestine to stop the rising tide of terrorism by the breakaway groups
Lehi and IZL. But Haganah literature (supplied to him by Aliyah
Hadashah), which stunned him with its flagrant chauvinistic-activist
tone, showed him that the organized Yishuv, led by Ben-Gurion, was
also engaged in anti-British propaganda. Fearful of Churchill's warning to the Zionist movement (on 17 November 1944) that he might "reconsider" his attitude to Zionism's "dreams," Weizmann willingly vol-
unteered to assist Ben-Gurion in the *saison*, the name given to the campaign in which the organized Yishuv collaborated with the British in
an attempt to eradicate Jewish terrorism.[3]

In fact, Weizmann's personal diplomacy, which relied on Churchill,
failed totally even before the latter's fall from power, because Ben-
Gurion had usurped power from him at the Biltmore conference in the
United States. Nor did Weizmann demonstrate innovative leadership
on the Arab question.[4]

Churchill's loss of power finally put an end to Weizmann's illusions
about Anglo-Zionist relations. But neither did he pin many hopes on
the United States—where the new president had not yet clarified his
Palestine policy—though he warned of enmity from the State Department and the OSS (Office of Strategic Services, predecessor of the CIA)
as well as about the influence of Arab oil.[5] Yet, as we have seen, it was
America, under Truman's leadership, that gave Zionism its first boost
after the war by urging Britain to permit 100,000 Jews to enter Palestine. Weizmann believed that only Britain could deliver the goods, hence

his rejection of Ben-Gurion's ban on meetings with Bevin until the White Paper was abolished. By this time Ben-Gurion had instructed Sneh to launch the operations of the United Resistance Movement against British targets.[6]

Nothing shows more strikingly the decline of Weizmann's influence than the fact that he learned about the Resistance Movement's first major operation from the press—but was summoned by Bevin to take a dressing-down about his responsibility for the Jewish violence in Palestine. No wonder he was "overwhelmed and towering despair fell on him."[7] Still, even though Bevin used "brutal, vulgar and anti-Semitic" language, which hinted at his "nature," Weizmann saw a new glimmer of hope in the establishment of the Anglo-American Committee of Inquiry.[8] And he still struck a forceful attitude, in public and in private: "You are wrong," he warned Lord Halifax, the British ambassador in Washington, "if you think you can overcome us by committees or that you can suppress the Yishuv by force." Ideologically, though not operatively, he was closer to Ben-Gurion than to Magnes. The arguments he adduced were typical of the Jewish Agency's Zionist propaganda, such as Palestine could absorb 4 million inhabitants, and Bevin reminded Weizmann of the Nazi ideologue Alfred Rosenberg.[9] At bottom, Ben-Gurion and Weizmann made the Zionist case in similar terms, their tactical differences on policy toward Britain notwithstanding. The fact that Zionism's only external bulwark, Britain, was temporarily out of the picture, as Weizmann believed, and that no other had yet replaced it, narrowed the gap between the two Zionist leaders, who after all shared Zionism's basic goals. The main difference was that Weizmann did not believe in accelerating the creation of the Jewish state. Thus, their common outlook on Arab policy was their strongest bond: the danger posed by the Arabs' total rejection of Zionism required the creation of a common front between moderates and activists. Weizmann, though, shared no responsibility for building the military force.

For Weizmann, the Jewish people's fate in the aftermath of the Holocaust was a matter of moral and historical justice, not of power politics. His testimony to the Anglo-American Committee, although far briefer than his five appearances before the Royal Commission nearly a decade earlier, constituted his most comprehensive, cogent, and balanced evidence to a foreign commission.[10] The ceaseless persecution of the Jews and, in particular, their most recent suffering, demonstrated the need for a Jewish national home. Although resorting to the classic Zionist propaganda that a Jewish community had "always" existed in

Palestine (except for brief periods), Weizmann generally painted a realistic picture of world Jewry and the Yishuv. The difference was that the latter had lost "all the marks of the ghetto," whereas even the Jews of America suffered from "occasional" discrimination and were not identified with "the basic performance of American life . . . agriculture . . . [and the] great industries [of] iron, coal, railways, shipping." As did Ben-Gurion, Weizmann likened the Jews who were arriving on the leaky ships of the *ha'apalah*—the illegal immigration movement—to the Pilgrims' arrival in America on the *Mayflower*. The new model for the future Jewish state was no longer Belgium, as it had been during World War I, but Switzerland, which also lacked raw materials yet could boast of magnificent industry.

On the Arab issue, Weizmann in 1946 was more muted than he had been in 1936. In 1946 he stated boldly that he wished the committee to "move on the line of least injustice." Only "some slight injustice politically" would be done, though not to Arab individuals, who would actually gain, economically, culturally, and spiritually. "Their [the Palestine Arabs'] national sentiments can find full expression in Damascus, and in Cairo, and in Baghdad."[11]

Nonetheless, on the political solution he remained an ardent advocate of partition. Like Ben-Gurion, he would be satisfied with two-thirds of western Palestine, which would be "adequate," as he admitted to Crossman four days after his testimony.[12]

Some on the Jewish Agency Executive, however, were critical of Weizmann's testimony regarding the pace of immigration. Dr. Emil Schmorak claimed that Weizmann had effectively nullified the concrete results of the committee's investigation by not insisting that the promised 100,000 immigrants must arrive within a year. Refugees at risk should not, moreover, be judged by economic considerations. Weizmann was said to be unaware of official Zionist policy. Shertok agreed that there had been a "serious mistake"; Weizmann should have known that the rescue of Jewish DPs was not conditional on the Yishuv's supposed absorption capacity. Fishman asked who had authorized Weizmann to declare that "in the era of his sons and grandsons we will not need more than western Palestine."[13]

Weizmann retorted that he did not understand the "fuss" being made over a tactical matter. He was annoyed that the Yishuv leadership had forbidden Hashomer Hatza'ir and Aliyah Hadashah to appear. Such "totalitarian methods," he warned, would have "very grave consequences" for the Zionist movement. Since these were the parties that displayed the greatest admiration for Weizmann (less so the other way around), his strongly worded protest may have been only natural.[14] Overall, though, his attitude was vitiated by a certain vagueness, as he tilted between wishful thinking that a Jewish state should emerge, miraculously, by peaceful means, and his despairing acceptance of Ben-Gurion's faits accomplis.

Indeed, Weizmann was aware of his waning authority in the Zionist movement, yet he refused to believe that Mapai and others would allow Silver to replace him, given Silver's strong right-wing identification. Still, rejecting the role of "figurehead," he considered the renewal of his authority justified, because of his personal alliance with senior British statesmen against a possible attempt to abolish the Jewish Agency and because of his efforts to convince the British government to act as an honest broker between the Jewish Agency and those Arab states that had allegedly accepted partition (Transjordan and Egypt as well as Iraq) in a common front against the Russian menace.[15] Weizmann naturally saw the Report of the Anglo-American Committee as a victory for his concept of Zionism, as it offered what he had always striven for—Jewish immigration and settlement—though not statehood, which he considered less pressing. British imperialism, he held, would also benefit from the existence of a Jewish state in part of Palestine. However, Attlee's statement that implementation of the report would be conditional on the Yishuv's disarmament came as a "terrible blow" to Weizmann, leaving him "absolutely bewildered."[16] Theoretically, the way was now open for a reconsideration of Ben-Gurion's ad hoc coalition with the breakaways. This might have been feasible if Attlee had made the report's acceptance conditional on a complete end to terrorism of the sort perpetrated solely by the breakaways, thus also driving a wedge between the Haganah and the IZL-Lehi. Weizmann, though, was out of touch not only with Zionist decision making (he completely misread the position of the Jewish Agency Executive on the question of anti-British violence), due to Ben-Gurion's machinations, but also with the realities of British policy. "I am quite sure the Haganah will, if the Report is accepted, abandon all aggressive intentions," he noted.[17]

The violent events in Palestine on 17 and 18 June 1946 (Haganah raids and IZL kidnappings, and retaliatory measures by the British) caused Weizmann to ponder again the relevance of his leadership. He had been deeply perturbed for some months at the Haganah's use of violence. Now he spoke of the possibility that Zionism was "sinking to the level of gangsterdom." Nonetheless, he conceded that British provocations were to blame for this state of affairs (the Mufti's reappearance in the region, a speech by Bevin at Bournemouth again repudiating the committee's report, and, crucially, the British military's attempt to destabilize the Yishuv on Black Sabbath). Why, then, was Weizmann so critical of Haganah operations, which usually caused no loss of life? Certainly he was deeply distressed at the Haganah's collaboration with the breakaways. Perhaps this was because no one in the Jewish Agency Executive bothered to explain to him that the Haganah's use of violence was not an end in itself but was meant to bolster the organization's increasingly weak political position. Weizmann continued to argue (very much like the intellectuals around Magnes) that "*our* only force is moral force" and to assert his belief that the leadership should wield power in the Yishuv solely by means of "constructive achievement." Weizmann was not alone in holding this view; it was shared by a significant, if powerless, minority in Mapai (see chapter 4), Aliyah Hadashah, Ichud, and Hashomer Hatza'ir. But only the latter tried actively to exercise influence on the Haganah in an attempt to prevent violence. It took Black Sabbath, which dealt the Yishuv a shattering blow, for Weizmann to reemerge, however briefly, as a central figure in Zionist diplomacy.

Weizmann's basic assumption, typical of moderates of all shades, was that Zionism, unlike other national movements—of the Arabs, the Irish, or the Boers, for example—must refrain from using violence. He abhorred violence in principle: "It is a method; and it is both inconsistent and useless to condemn one single act unless the whole method is discarded." Weizmann was able to engineer a suspension of the activities of the United Resistance Movement until the Zionist Congress in late 1946 (with the exception of the King David Hotel bombing).[18]

In the wake of Black Sabbath and other such British sweeps, Weizmann warned Cunningham in the strongest possible language that notwithstanding the suspension of violence he had achieved, "the Haganah will split, and the younger elements will join the more extreme terrorist groups. And then may God help us! . . . I had already heard people say: 'Rather die fighting than turn Vichy!'" This of course was a total misconception. Ben-Gurion had the situation under control, and there was no danger of a split in the Haganah (see chapters 7 and 8).

Yet Weizmann did understand that the British grip on Palestine was very loose indeed and that in the long term, a return to the Peel proposal was inevitable. Nor was he blind to short-term needs: the release of the incarcerated Yishuv leaders; the issuing of 100,000 immigration certificates; and the reestablishment of civil authority. British experts said that allowing 100,000 Jews into Palestine would spark an Arab revolt. But Weizmann, unlike Ben-Gurion or his supporters in the Yishuv, remained dogmatic, even old-fashioned, on Arab affairs, and he was totally in the dark about the new approach taken by Ben-Gurion and the Haganah to the Arab question. Astonishingly, he was not aware that Ben-Gurion had ordered the Haganah and the Palmach to prepare for battle not against the British but against the Arabs. He was certain that "once the Jewish state has been established the Arabs and the Jews will have to get together on the basis of their common interests."[19]

If heeded, could Weizmann's school of nonviolence have triumphed? The problem was that the major decisions were made by the Jewish Agency Executive in Jerusalem, a body in which Weizmann had lacked influence since the previous November. Weizmann's only stronghold lay in the British Zionist movement. Aliyah Hadashah, the closest to him of all the Yishuv parties, was unrepresented in both the Jewish Agency Executive and the Haganah. Nor was he a source of encouragement to Hashomer Hatza'ir, which espoused Marxism and binationalism. Weizmann's efforts to reorganize moderate, sometimes marginal forces in world Jewry, such as the American Jewish Committee, or to revive the moribund 50:50 arrangement in the Jewish Agency, between Zionists and non-Zionists who would accept his nonviolent approach, were fiascos.[20] In any event, the moderates were put on the defensive by Britain's adherence to the White Paper policy against the background of the Holocaust trauma, and Weizmann was overoptimistic about London's willingness to compromise.[21]

Weizmann's views actually prevailed at the historic Jewish Agency Executive meeting in Paris. Although he himself refused to attend, owing to his angry mistrust of Ben-Gurion and Sneh, he wielded influence through proxies: Dr. N. Goldmann, Professor Z. Brodetsky, and Sir Simon Marks. Goldmann put forward a partition plan on the Weizmann model, adding that only if the Zionist struggle rested on a moral foundation would it persevere. Moreover, if the effort to build a Jewish state were not expedited, half the DPs in Europe would remain there or settle in America and Brazil. (Goldmann's mission to the United States in August 1946 would prove a breakthrough in the history of Zionism; see chapter 1). E. Z. Hoofien, director of APC Bank (today's Bank Leumi) argued, along Weizmann's lines, that even a nonviolent civil struggle was feasible only in the conditions of a primitive economy—in India, for example. Sir Simon Marks said Sneh's notion of presenting an ultimatum to Britain recalled Bar Kochba and might bring about Zionism's eradication. Suicidal heroism must be rejected, Sir

Simon said. In a similar vein, Brodetsky argued that continued resistance might cause Zionism to end up as one more movement driven by false messianism. Kaplan, a Mapai Weizmannite, said that 25 percent of western Palestine would suffice for a Jewish state and could absorb a million and a half Jews.[22]

But Weizmann's proxy success in Paris was short-lived. Britain rejected partition, as shown by the failure of the London Conference on Palestine and the subsequent cabinet decision (18 February 1947) to refer the issue to the UN. Still, his momentary success enabled Weizmann to eschew the appeal by the intellectuals around M. Smilansky and S. Zemach to form a new group of moderates. Weizmann knew all too well that if he joined them, not only the breakaways but the entire Yishuv would brand him a quisling. His attempt to take the diplomatic initiative also rested on shaky ground: the illusion of Arab agreement to partition; Truman's future support; the aid of Churchill and of other prominent Conservatives; and the sympathy of the London *Times* and the *Manchester Guardian*.[23] In reality, none of these factors affected British realpolitik considerations. But if Weizmann's ability to sway British policy proved nonexistent, he exercised enormous influence on Zionist policy at this time, by helping to dissuade the Yishuv leadership from declaring all-out war on Britain. His last success was to convince Ben-Gurion to attend the London Conference, "even if our point of view is not accepted beforehand," on the basis of the Paris decision for a "viable" (partitioned) state.[24]

Even though Weizmann's policy on partition and ending resistance prevailed, he was not reelected president of the Zionist movement at the 22nd Zionist Congress, due to Ben-Gurion's and Silver's manipulations. The vote, 171–154, with Hashomer Hatza'ir deciding against Weizmann (because of his pro-partition line; see later discussion), was a clear signal that his era was over. Ben-Gurion engineered the defeat after Weizmann rejected on principle the policy of simultaneous building and struggling. Weizmann's basic approach—"No warm frost!"—was unacceptable to Ben-Gurion. Moreover, unlike Ben-Gurion, he still believed that Britain was not yet lost to Zionism. In spite of the Morrison-Grady cantonization plan, Weizmann maintained that the future Jewish state would "freely concede to Great Britain all the facilities and opportunities commensurate with its special strategic position."[25] This also dovetailed with the Jewish Agency Executive's pro-Hashemite orientation, with which he was well acquainted.

Rejecting Ben-Gurion's offer to become honorary president of the World Zionist Organization, Weizmann tried after the congress to form a "progressive group" of General Zionists with the assistance of long-time associates such as H. Sacher, S. Marks, L. Stein, A. Eban, and I. Berlin in Britain, and R. Szold, S. Wise, D. Ginsburg, L. Lipsky, and M. Weisgal in America. But it was impossible to revitalize the old Zionist political framework.[26] Unaware of Ben-Gurion's preparations for war with the Arabs, Weizmann feared, much like his moderate supporters in the Yishuv, that the outcome of the London Conference would plunge Palestine into chaos.[27] His failure to regain the presidency of the Zionist movement did not alter his political views, which remained midway between the Jewish Agency Executive and the moderate opposition. In other words, although rejecting the use of violence, he supported partition.[28]

Despondent over the waning of his political influence, Weizmann immersed himself in work at the Hebrew University and at the Sieff Institute, in Rehovot, which would later bear his name. The direction of Zionist politics left him with little enthusiasm. He foresaw a "fascist development" in the Zionist movement. Mapai would soon find itself in the position of the socialists in Germany at the outset of the Hitler era. The Revisionists were talking about ousting the moderates, Kaplan and Goldmann, from the Jewish Agency Executive.[29] Yet this was far from an objective view. It was what Weizmann saw through the prism of his tragic situation, cut off from the center of decision making. It was not the Jewish Agency Executive that was losing touch with the Yishuv ("because of its impotence, and being divided against itself") but Weizmann himself, who was weary and sick. He saw himself reflected in the Yishuv: close to collapse, economic and otherwise.[30] As late as 27 March 1947 he still thought that "we can do nothing and we shall not succeed unless we re-establish confidence between the [Zionist] Movement and the British Government and the British people. . . . It is a grave mistake to believe that what we have lost in England we will recover in America." Lamenting that he was a victim of "political assassination," he feared that Silver—other than Ben-Gurion, his worst enemy—if elected president of the movement, would introduce a "totalitarian regime," certainly in America, where "the sickness in the Movement has gone so deep that only a major operation can cure it."[31]

Still a prisoner of concepts that were little more than Zionist propaganda, such as his contempt for the Arabs ("who may shout at present, threaten and blackmail as they always do," but "would accept a reasonable project of partition, with safeguards for themselves, if they knew that England and America are determined to put it through"), he also refused to take seriously the Zionist "extremists," having harbored little respect for Jabotinsky and less for Begin ("Whether he is just a fanatic or a charlatan or both is difficult to say"). In his despair he believed that only his old associates in America, such as Frankfurter, Morgenthau, and Wise, could stop Zionism from hurtling into the abyss.[32] Yet despite his pervasive melancholy (for example, he ignored Gromyko's crucial statement of 14 May), his appearance before UNSCOP was magisterial.[33] He called for "a form of partition which would give both the Jewish and the Arab areas a large and gradually increasing measure of autonomy (including, from the start, control of immigration), and which would close the door neither to complete separation after a transitional period nor the maintenance of some link (especially in the economic sphere) between the two areas, if both desired it." Weizmann accepted a proposal by Leonard Stein (for a "halfway house between the Morrison-Grady Plan" and a "more radical" partition), "provided we can really get proper frontiers for the provinces and also have the Negev, wholly or partly [he would accept less than a fifth of the total area]. . . . If an agreement could be reached with [the] Government on the provinces which should correspond to something like the Peel line and [part] of the Negev . . . we could leave it for the next generation to look further ahead."[34] But Weizmann's political views took second place to his value as a symbol for the Zionist movement.

Since the Yishuv, under Ben-Gurion's guidance, had begun to develop a serious security force, the Haganah, after the eruption of the Arab Revolt in 1936, Weizmann's emphasis on personal diplomacy had become of diminishing significance. The final failure of his approach was brought about by the 1939 White Paper. Nor was he successful in his attempt to build a new force in Zionism, a "progressive" camp, based not on the existing left-center parties but on a few politicians who all derived their power from their association with Weizmann himself, or from outside Zionism. By the time he was ousted from the leadership, in late 1946, the name of the Zionist game was party politics, based on ad hoc alliances, like the one between Ben-Gurion and Silver. Weizmann was not cut out for power politics. He believed that his personality transcended most Zionist parties. But at a time when the struggle for the Jewish state necessitated the use of force even if only for tactical purposes, Weizmann's approach, founded largely on (declining) British imperial considerations, was a death blow for his theory and practice of Zionism.

He was, moreover, oblivious to the escalating Arab military threat, still captive to the obsolete 1919 agreement with Faisal. Weizmann did not realize that even if any Arab leader had held a positive view of Zionism, his aim would be to consolidate his country's independence, not to promote Zionist ambitions. In any event, an isolated case could not serve as an opening for Arab-Jewish political cooperation.[35] Weizmann failed to foresee the Arab violence that was triggered by the 29 November resolution. As late as February 1948 he told the British colonial secretary that it was not the British government, or people, who were to blame, but Bevin himself, who "suffer[ed] from a Hitler complex. He hated the Jews and wanted to destroy them. . . . Bevin would suffer Hitler's end."[36] By contrast, Weizmann reconciled himself to Ben-Gurion's "great success" in war—he is "thoughtful, calm, resolute and a man of enormous courage," he wrote of Ben-Gurion— but was skeptical about his leadership in peace, citing Churchill's election defeat in 1945.[37]

Weizmann's career ended in a blaze of false glory. On 16 May 1948, two days after the establishment of the state, he was elected president of the Provisional State Council. On 13 February 1949, the newly elected First Knesset made him Israel's first president by a large majority over Y. Klausner, the candidate of Herut and the political successors of IZL and Lehi. Ben-Gurion had capped his victory over Weizmann by installing him as a ceremonial president with no power. The formal usurpation of power had taken more than a decade. But from a historical perspective Ben-Gurion had continued from the point at which Weizmann lost much of his power in 1931, when for the first time he was removed from decision making after making an unfortunate statement about his lack of enthusiasm for the idea of a Jewish state. Weizmann's work with the Zionist labor movement was instrumental in laying the political, social, and economic infrastructure for a future state. Both he and Ben-Gurion were towering figures, but there were immense differences between them, and not only in tactics. For example, Weizmann's political lobbying for the establishment of a Jewish military force during World War II was intended to enhance the Zionist movement's moral and political standing, and not, as Ben-Gurion wanted, as an investment to prepare the Yishuv for Armageddon. Yet, despite their antagonistic personalities, Weizmann and Ben-Gurion complemented each other during the Mandate period. Ben-Gurion's brilliant, albeit brutal, manipulations of Zionist power in the late 1930s and through the 1940s would not have been possible without Weizmann's achievement in the 1920s, especially in helping to draft the Mandate and ensure its acceptance by successive British governments.

In the period under discussion, Weizmann was influenced strongly by the Ichud intellectuals' binationalist ideas, and by the German Zionists who gathered around Aliyah Hadashah. Their dialogue, however, proved unsuccessful in terms of power politics. In the end Weizmann, like Aliyah Hadashah but not the intellectuals, clung to Ben-Gurion's point of view as the least of all evils.

6

The Intellectuals

Ichud and the Politics of Binationalism

The copyright on the politics of moderation in Zionism belongs to a small group of intellectuals who were associated with the Hebrew University. In the mid-1920s this group established Brit Shalom (Covenant of Peace), which openly announced its support for a binational state in Palestine. The group collapsed in the early 1930s because of weak leadership and a lack of public sympathy, only to be revived in 1942 by Ichud, which by then had a stronger leadership. (In 1939, the League for Jewish-Arab Rapprochement and Cooperation was established, but failed to make headway, because it was largely controlled by the leftist Zionist parties.) The leader of Ichud was Dr. J. L. Magnes, the president of the Hebrew University, a former American Reform rabbi, and an active pacifist during World War I. Magnes was the dominant figure in the propagation of the binational idea after 1929. He believed that there were only two policy options in Palestine: Jabotinsky's approach, which was based on "militarism and imperialism"; or a "pacific policy that treats as entirely secondary such things as a 'Jewish State,' or a 'Jewish majority,' or even 'the Jewish National Home,' and sees as primary the development of a Jewish spiritual, educational, moral and religious center in Palestine. . . . The question is, do we want to conquer Palestine now as Joshua did in his day—with fire and sword? Or do we want to take cognizance of Jewish religious development since Joshua—our Prophets, Psalmists and Rabbis, and repeat the words: 'Not by might, and not by violence, but by my spirit, saith the Lord'."[1] In 1929 Magnes supported a plan put forward by St. John Philby that would recognize the Arab majority and leave the Jews in the minority. However, when this was rejected even by Chaim Weizmann, Magnes, fearing he would become a virtual outcast in the Yishuv, returned to the Zionist fold by reembracing the Balfour Declaration and the Mandate.[2]

Magnes was not the only dissenter in Zion. Other leading intellectuals joined the struggle for binationalism and moderation, such as Shmuel Hugo Bergman, the philosopher; Hans Kohn, the historian; Gershom Scholem, the authority on Jewish mysticism; Ernst Simon, a future professor of education; and others. Significantly, these intellectuals considered Weizmann a kindred spirit, ideologically. To Brit Shalom in 1931, Weizmann's reservations about the concept of Jewish majority and his alleged support for binationalism (which, as noted, later led to his ousting from the presidency of the World Zionist Organization and of the Jewish Agency) elevated him to the status of true leadership "above the instincts of the masses . . . those who are impatient."[3] In fact, Brit Shalom was wrong to think that Weizmann was its ally. As for Ben-Gurion, he considered Magnes too naïve to be involved in politics, as he could be easily duped. He pledged to remove the political influence of Magnes and his associates.[4] Invited by the JAE to report on his contacts, Magnes claimed that he had never agreed to a permanent minority status for the Yishuv.[5] His views on the Jewish Agency's Jewish-state politics, however, were well-known to the executive. Indeed, following the publication of the Peel Commission Report, he warned the Jewish Agency's council, in the presence of Ben-Gurion and the executive, that the establishment of a Jewish state would cause perennial bloodshed.[6]

The establishment of Ichud (Union) by Magnes, Ernst Simon, Martin Buber, Moshe Smilansky, and Henrietta Szold was a last-ditch attempt to persuade both the Zionist leadership and the British—less so the Arabs—to accept a compromise politics: binationalism combined with moderate Jewish immigration until population parity was reached. Like Brit Shalom, Ichud, its successor, wished to remain aloof from party politics and to function as an intellectual association disseminating ideas—binationalism, immigration, and settlement—in the Yishuv. Simon, active in both Ichud and Aliyah Hadashah, accused the Mapai leadership of abandoning its "former slogans against domination [of the Arabs] and in favor of political equality." Ichud, he said, was a Zionist body since it "strives to create a political and economic situation which will enable the maximum of Jewish *olim* [immigrants] to the Land of Israel." By contrast, the Biltmore program (the 1942 Zionist declaration of intent to establish a Jewish state, approved by the JAE, which did not mention the Arabs, "contains grave dangers for the establishment of the National Home and its expansion."[7]

In fact, it was Biltmore that brought about the creation of Ichud. From the outset, then, Ichud found itself in a shaky alliance with both Hashomer Hatza'ir (not yet a party) and Aliyah Hadashah (founded in 1942 by German Jewish immigrants; see chapter 7). The Holocaust caused Magnes to change his operative ideology and to remain within the Zionist consensus. In early 1943, he put forward a new program that had the primary goal of preventing an Arab-Jewish war. A compromise solution, Magnes said, required, as an "indispensable prerequisite," that "America's moral and political authority be thrown into the balance." The core of his proposal was "the great idea of union," which must guide the UN in its attempt to build a new world in place of the old "narrow chauvinism." This union should be threefold: "(1) Union between the Jews and the Arabs within a bi-national Palestine. (2) Union of Palestine, Transjordan, Syria and the Lebanon in an economic and political federation. . . . (3) Union of this federation with an Anglo-American union which is assumed to be part of that greater union of free nations." Within this framework binationalism must be constituted on equality of political rights. Though rejecting Biltmore's Jewish state thrust, Magnes proclaimed a Zionist stand on immigration by rejecting the 1939 White Paper and accepting the demand for flexible economic absorption. Retreating from his stance of 40 percent minority status, he now demanded no less than 50 percent, which would enable "several hundred thousand Jewish refugees" to be admitted to Palestine. The Palestine Arabs would no longer fear that they would be swamped by Jews, thanks to the creation of an Arab federation. Nonetheless, the Mandate should be replaced by a trusteeship.[8] With the benefit of hindsight, it is clear that although Magnes suggested gradual development toward a binational state, this had no chance of implementation after the Arab Revolt of 1936–39.

Smilansky, the leader of the Farmers Association, expressed Ichud's complete rejection not only of the use of violence by the breakaways, whose terrorism reflected a "Gentile Balkan heroism," but also by the other "group of murderers," the Haganah, who bore the blame, he said, for the drowning of 267 [sic] Jews (the *Patria* tragedy).[9]

Ichud's prime mover and ideologue was the renowned Galician-born philosopher Martin Buber, who had been in Palestine since 1938. Buber rejected Ben-Gurion's claim that the UN would grant the Yishuv the right to become a majority. He accused Ben-Gurion of relying on "imaginary prospects which have no reality except that of a stratagem, sometimes only for an election campaign." Moreover, the "basic defects of our foreign policy are that it is not based upon a recognition of the real interests of the peoples involved in the decisions."[10]

Buber regarded the Biltmore policy as a "fata morgana" which was incompatible with a moral outlook, "because it is impossible for any length of time to build with one hand while holding a weapon with the other."[11] Simon, who had a more practical approach, envisaged a better future for Palestine through various development projects.[12] At the same time, Simon warned about the consequences of the "moral cynicism" of Zionism and the Yishuv, and the "myth of sacrificing youth" in particular. As Nazism had shown with respect to the great German tradition, no one, including the Jewish people, was immune to moral degeneration. Quoting Friedrich-Georg and Ernst Juenger's book (*Aufmarsch des Nationalismus*, Leipzig, 1926), he explained how they had prepared the spiritual ground of the Nazi revolution by preaching against reconciliation and admiring the cult of force and war.[13]

Of all the senior Zionist leaders, Weizmann was closest to Ichud's views, though he himself might have disagreed with this conclusion, if asked in public. But the Ichud perception of Weizmann was based on intimate meetings with him. He saw eye to eye with Ichud about the anti-British atmosphere that had engulfed the Yishuv, but Ichud members themselves admitted that they had failed to sell Weizmann their binational plan as an alternative to Biltmore—he was too "bound" to that plan by his speeches and articles. Still, Magnes said that Weizmann had acknowledged being "favorably impressed" by Ichud's plan. In any event, it was understood within Ichud that with the rising tension between the two groups, it was important to keep in touch with Weizmann.[14]

Weizmann was never condemned by Ichud, perhaps because he was viewed as an unwilling prisoner of Jewish Agency politics. Smilansky painted Weizmann as a man who always put facts before declarations. Had Weizmann been heeded in 1939, he said, the Yishuv could have numbered one million, not half a million. Smilansky focused his ideology on Ahad Ha-Am's interpretation (quoted by Weizmann at the 17th Zionist Congress) of the "double promise" granted by Britain to both Arab and Jew to build their national homes. Smilansky's Zionism consisted of two demands: to open the country's gates to 100,000 Jews and exhaust the country's absorption capacity, and to extend the right to buy land without damaging either the *fellah* or the tenant.[15] At the same time, Smilansky vehemently opposed the establishment of a Jewish state. More exactly, he objected to small, independent states in general, believing only in confederations or federations such as the British Commonwealth, the Soviet federation, and the United States.[16] Smilansky disclosed in an Ichud internal meeting that Weizmann had confirmed to him his opposition to *ha'apalah*. Weizmann had objected, Smilansky said, in an "emergency Zionist committee" to Ben-Gurion's policy of rebellion.[17]

Weizmann was regarded as a moderate politician who did not demand a state; however, since Biltmore, Ben-Gurion had been perceived in Ichud circles as a "false prophet" because he wanted Jewish statehood "while the Yishuv is disintegrating. . . . Instead of democratic equality [there is] fascist terrorism and oppression of [political] minorities." Ichud's program was thus based very much on an imaginary Weizmann, who, unlike Ben-Gurion, did not publicly advocate a Jewish state but did his best to enlist the British government for its establishment. In truth, very much like Ichud, Weizmann deluded himself that the state could be established without the use of force. Moreover, as we have seen, Weizmann, like Ichud, was a great believer in an exclusive British orientation; neither he nor Ichud trusted America. Dr. Robert Weltsch, an old Weizmann hand, formerly the editor of *Jüdische Rundschau*, echoed Weizmann's fear that the Silver-Neumann brand of right-wing General Zionism in America might undermine the Yishuv's British orientation.[18] Unfocused, fearful of the Zionist leaders' ambition, and last but not least, having no constituency of its own in the Yishuv, Ichud had little prospect of influencing future events.

Ichud's program at the end of World War II rejected partition, which, in Magnes's words, would create two irredentist states. As in the Balkans, this would invite perennial war. The Palestine problem, in view of its international and interreligious significance, must be resolved with cooperation of the UN, the Arab League, and the Jewish people. The UN should establish a Middle Eastern Council, to be responsible for the security of Palestine and to guarantee any compromise that might be achieved. Optimally, there should be a binational constitution, the details of which Magnes failed to specify except for citing Switzerland as a general model. However, the permanent principle was that neither Jews nor Arabs should predominate; both should rule in cooperation, thus creating a bridge to close the gap between the two peoples and between them and the British. (The latter, in view of their interests and experience, should be well represented on the regional council, with an unspecified UN member state to bear the main responsibility for governing the country.) The government itself should be equally divided between Arabs and Jews. Magnes said there should be numerical parity between Arabs and Jews, and quoted Weizmann to bolster his claim for the "immediate *aliyah* of 100,000 children," which he naïvely believed would be supported by a "great majority" in the Muslim world.

In the post-Holocaust period, Magnes took a basically Zionist position, justifying the principle of numerical parity on the grounds that this would effectively "liberate the Jews from their minority status [as a people]." Such a situation, he argued, would not disturb the political balance in Palestine. Magnes also maintained that once equality of population was achieved, the Jews should be entitled to more *aliyah*, to offset the Arabs' fertility rate, which was twice as high as that of the Jews. His great hope was for an early meeting of leaders from both sides. Magnes had the vision and the courage, as well as great naïveté, given the realities, to believe that since the cradle of human civilization lay in the Middle East, the new civilization that humanity so urgently needed would also find its origins in the region. Quoting an unnamed Egyptian diplomat (Mahmud Fawzi Bey), he said that both sides needed each other. The Arabs did not need Jewish money, though, only their experience and education.[19]

Magnes saw no reason to revise his operative program after the end of the war. He did not retreat one iota from the idea of binationalism as the principle for a political solution; now, though, he said that a UN trusteeship should be established without delay, with Britain to serve as the administrative authority. The UN Trusteeship Council should direct both Jews and Arabs to cooperate in a binational state. Magnes continued to reject partition as an "imaginary and superficial" solution which would "Balkanize" Palestine. It was not *aliyah* as such to which the Arabs objected, he thought, but to the fact that this would create the foundation for a Jewish state. However, a binational state would remove one of the "main psychological barriers to Jewish *aliyah*." Not even the most extremist Arab leader would be able to arouse the Arab peoples, inside or outside Palestine, to resist such a plan. Magnes's lack of realism reached new heights when he stated that once the Arabs agreed to the immigration of suffering Jewish refugees, they would understand that they were performing a humane act in their best tradition and adding to the luster of their good name. To achieve numerical equality, he estimated, another half a million Jews would be needed, and "perhaps even more."[20] To the attack on Magnes by prominent Palestine Arab leader Dr. Husayn al-Khalidi for changing his mind since 1936, when Magnes had agreed to a solution in which the Jews would constitute only 40 percent of Palestine's population for a ten-year period, Gabriel Stern, Magnes's Arab affairs adviser, responded (privately, to Magnes) that times had changed. Furthermore, "our circle never concealed its final aim: to arrive gradually at an agreement with the Arabs on maximum *aliyah* according to economic absorption capacity; [Ichud is] against a Jewish state and against a population transfer." Khalidi might argue that Ichud was only a small minority without real influence, but he could not doubt its "moral persistence."[21]

But this was not the final shape of the Ichud plan. One defect, Magnes knew, was the absence of a workable formula for elections to the legislative council in the binational state. This led him to suggest a cantonal system: enabling Jews and Arabs in mixed districts to vote for members of both communities.[22]

If not a party, was Ichud then a homogeneous body in the ideological-political sense? An open debate between W. D. Senator (Magnes's right-hand man in the Hebrew University) and Buber on basic attitudes toward the Arabs sheds some light on this. Being a member of the JAE, where he represented the non-Zionists, Senator was worried that Ichud's attitude on this score would result in "the exclusion of our circle from the political society of the Jewish people in the Land of Israel. A great danger to our circle, to its political activity, and to Zionism in general." Senator called upon Ichud to revise radically its approach to the Arab question by taking into account only realpolitik considerations, not moral ones. Senator did not think the Jewish state as such was a "nightmare." Nor did he agree with Magnes's numerical equality. The Arabs themselves admitted, said Senator, that the Jews' "qualitative traits" so far exceeded those of the Arabs that they were in fact the country's rulers. Numerical or any other form of equality was insignificant in the face of this consideration. Of far greater importance was mutual understanding with regard to basic political facts. If this were achieved, either Arabs or Jews might agree to numerical inequality. The main agreement must be on a binational state, "which means equal rights in practice and guarantees for them to be upheld." But Senator hinted at the transfer solution: "Today more than at any time before it is impossible to isolate the Jewish-Arab question from similar national issues in eastern and southeastern Europe and the Near East."[23]

Buber, Ichud's chief ideologue, dismissed Senator's views outright. Far from wishing to be excluded from the Zionist consensus, Buber set the limits of Ichud's ideology: "With regard to the issue of 'necessity,' there is a crucial difference between expansive settlement, seeking to enlarge the borders and property and rule of the colonizing nation, and concentrative settlement, in which a nation which has lost its organic center seeks to return to its origins. . . . If one has the intention of driving people who are bound to the soil out of their homeland, then one has exceeded those limits."[24]

Thus, when the United Resistance Movement launched its violent operations, particularly the attack on the railway system (see chapter 4) on the night of 31 October–1 November 1945, Magnes took advantage of a degree-granting ceremony at the Hebrew University to declare his objection to what he considered an "insurrection" by the Yishuv. Magnes denied that he opposed rebellion in principle (citing the Maccabees and the Warsaw Ghetto uprising as justified) and pointed out that he himself had been brought up in the American tradition that "every people has the natural right to rebel against its oppressors." The Yishuv had not yet, however, "reached such a desperate pass."[25]

Ichud lost its sole member of the JAE when Senator resigned on 24 December 1945 in protest at the decision to cooperate with the breakaways in the United Resistance Movement. But he did not change his mind on transfer, arguing that "a workable partition seems to be possible only if at least a partial transfer is effected. I don't say that it is impossible, or immoral, but I doubt whether any partition could be arrived at which would be feasible from the economic, political and military points of view."

Ichud's claim to be within the framework of the Zionist consensus should not be questioned, even if it objected to a Jewish state. Not only its full support for *aliyah*, including illegal immigration in many cases, but also its backing of extensive settlement projects should be taken into account. Veteran Zionist agriculturists and authors like Moshe Smilansky and Shlomo Zemach must be regarded as being loyal to the Zionist tradition (both came to Palestine before World War I). Zemach, though officially not an Ichud member, was very close to its views; working the land was his touchstone for Zionism's claim to be an authentic national movement. In contradistinction, the Palestine Arabs did not meet this criterion as a national collective but only as individuals. "There is no Palestinian Arab nationalism," he wrote. "There is no Palestinian Arab nation. There are only Arabs who dwell in Palestine, and therefore their connection to the land is more tenuous."[26] Despite such views, Zemach's sympathy for Ichud was never questioned, yet he reacted with irony to Magnes's self-righteousness.

Ichud was also close to the mainstream Yishuv consensus on the issue of finding common ground between Arab and Jewish workers.

Gabriel Baer, a future professor of social history of the Middle East at the Hebrew University, argued that even though Arab-Jewish workers' solidarity would not come about without a political solution, various manifestations of such solidarity showed that the workers were the foundation stone for such a solution.[27]

The Mapai leadership was Ichud's main target of criticism. Ben-Gurion was accused of ultra-activism (Biltmore), while Berl Katzenelson was chastised for setting the labor movement on a narrow nationalist course and diminishing its internationalism. While containing Marxism, he introduced fascist elements. Instead of seeking accommodation with Liebenstein and his cronies, he should look toward Georg Landauer, Aliyah Hadashah's moderate leader (see chapter 7), and Hashomer Hatza'ir.[28] Bevin's notorious speech (13 November 1945), however, had the effect of solidifying Ichud's loose ties with the Yishuv. Ichud was disappointed by the speech for not offering political solutions, although the way was opened for a revision of the White Paper. The Anglo-American Committee of Inquiry was welcomed by Ichud, which warned the Jewish Agency that it must choose between an explanatory and a militant policy. It was impossible to combine both.[29] The Anglo-American Committee presented Ichud with a wholly new challenge: to present its case before an official body of the Western powers. It did so against the wish of the JAE, maintaining that the prohibition against appearances by the opposition distorted reality by showing the committee only one (official) Zionist voice, while in fact there was a multiplicity of views. Albert Einstein (in Washington) and Lord Samuel (in London) had already presented non-Biltmorist views to the committee. Moreover, the right-wing opposition had been permitted to appear. Greatly excited by its opportunity, Ichud was the only body that rehearsed by means of a simulation game.[30]

Ichud's starting point was that because Palestine was sacred to the three monotheistic religions, it could not be exclusively Jewish. Nor could it be an exclusively Arab land, given "the indissoluble historical association of the Jewish people and of Judaism with this land." On the other hand, the Arabs had "natural rights" in Palestine. Ichud envisaged three stages toward a political plan: the present Mandate; trusteeship under the UN; and a binational Palestine as a self-governing unit in a regional union. The plan to allow in 100,000 Jewish immigrants should be implemented in the first stage, and Ichud believed that Arab opposition would not take "an extreme form." An annual immigration rate of below 30,000 would never let the Jews "catch up with the Arabs." According to Lord Samuel, Palestine had the economic potential to absorb 4.5 million Jews. In the third period, Jewish immigration would be reconsidered, following the establishment of a regional union.

Heading off the anticipated Arab opposition to its plan, Ichud claimed that "the whole history of Palestine shows that it just has not been made for uni-national sovereign independence. . . . [The Arabs] can enjoy independence in a bi-national Palestine." To counterbalance this major Arab concession, the Jews too would give up their claim to a sovereign state. The breakdown of the legal minority guarantees provided for by the Versailles (Paris) peace treaties was proof that the only safeguard for a minority was equality with the majority in a binational state. The multinational state was an effective method, as Switzerland proved, to ensure full protection of national language and culture, and the multinational models of Soviet Russia and Yugoslavia were also cited approvingly. The advocates of self-determination had failed to demonstrate the workability of their idea, the Ichud spokesman argued; citing Professor A. Cobban, Ichud claimed that the federative union was a more modern and more hopeful concept than the unilateral national state.

With respect to self-government, Ichud suggested that, as already in the Mandatory period, Jews and Arabs should be appointed to executive positions in equal numbers at all levels—from the Executive Council to district commissioners—in addition to a consultative body to be chaired by the high commissioner. A bill of rights would guarantee religious, educational, economic, and national freedom to all. The head of state would be appointed by the UN, possibly upon nomination by the legislature, for four years. Ideally, the federal legislature should be elected on a geographical rather than a communal basis, this in order to avoid enhancing separate national interests and instead placing the focus on fields of endeavor that might draw the two sides closer together. Quoting Professor O. Janowsky on the Swiss cantonal system, Ichud sought to demonstrate how broad autonomy could be further developed. Palestine thus was envisioned by Ichud as a Switzerland in the Middle East.[31] Committee member Richard Crossman, not to mention Shertok, questioned the practicality of Ichud's proposals. Magnes admitted that Ichud had only a small membership ("a few hundred"), it was not a political party, and about 500 people subscribed to its monthly, but "a large part of the inarticulate section of the population believes more or less as we do." Crossman, in his book on the Anglo-American Committee, noted that Magnes had spoken "extremely well in favour of binationalism" but that his ideas were irrelevant to the local political situation. They might have been germane twenty-five years earlier, but "it's too late for it now." The Arabs, in any event, could not accept his plan as "genuinely conciliatory." To prove his point, Crossman said that when Magnes was asked about the Hebrew University, he had replied that it was meant to be "the university of all the Jewish people," hence the name—rather than, as the questioner had suggested, the University of Palestine. This, together with the notion that the "just society" must first be established "by the Jews among the Jews," constituted, in Crossman's opinion, a "complete contradiction . . . of the binational politics he had been talking throughout his speech."[32]

With this testimony, Ichud reclaimed its place within the Zionist consensus. "At this moment," Sally Hirsch wrote, "there is only *one political target*—and it is shared by both the JAE and the opposition— to abolish the White Paper and thus open the country's gates to massive *aliyah*. All the political plans are *only means* toward this goal."[33] Although the Anglo-American Committee's report was encouraging to Ichud, since it recommended the repeal of the White Paper and the immigration of 100,000 Jews, Attlee's announcement making the report's implementation conditional on the disbanding of the Yishuv's "private armies," was seen as a serious blow.[34] Ichud's only hope remained its problematic alignment with Hashomer Hatza'ir and Aliyah Hadashah, the only "healthy" parties, according to Simon, in the "seriously ill" Yishuv. Weizmann proved a disappointment after he cut himself off from such colleagues as Gruenbaum and Sneh in the "A" faction of the General Zionists. Under Sneh, General Zionism had "deteriorated" into "chauvinist nationalism."[35] Ichud received considerable support from the daily *Ha'aretz* and its editor, the German-born Gershom (Gustav) Schocken. *Ha'aretz* was an independent liberal paper read by the Yishuv intelligentsia, and Schocken was affiliated to Aliyah Hadashah. The paper gave generous space to Ichud members, particularly Smilansky and Zemach, and gave Ichud's stands strong editorial backing, though not clearly favoring a binational regime. After the Night of the Railways, for example, *Ha'aretz* wrote that despair was "our adviser," and that the Holocaust was not a reason to show contempt for the sanctity of human life. Certainly the paper rejected the collaboration with the breakaways, lamenting the blur between goals and means. However it supported *aliyah*, settlement, and nondomination by "others over us."[36] *Ha'aretz* did not lose heart after Black Sabbath, but its patience ran out after the King David Hotel bombing. "A huge mine has been detonated under the very foundations of the search for a political solution," the paper wrote. "What value will the state have if, in order to gain it, we must alienate ourselves from all our traditional values and defy all the commands between man and man?"[37] The next day its editorial called upon the national institutions to resign. A few days later Buber published an article. "All of us are part of the same crime," he wrote, adding that it was vain to believe that a people's rebirth could be achieved "by means of violent acts. This is not the way to liberation or healing, but to new decadence and new oppression. We must repent."[38]

But Ichud's own tragedy was that it lacked support in the Yishuv, apart from Aliyah Hadashah and Hashomer Hatza'ir (both with reservations).[39] The most radical critics of official Zionism were Smilansky and Zemach, as shown by their appeal to Weizmann to take over the leadership from Ben-Gurion.[40] This was not, however, the official line espoused by Buber, Magnes, and Simon, who masterminded Ichud's political propaganda. Overall, Ichud was more realistic, while still regarding Ben-Gurion's policy as dangerous. Ichud continued to support the Morrison-Grady plan, for despite its many faults it contained a binational element and offered a "general framework." Yet, the proposed area of the Jewish province was too small, even from Ichud's viewpoint, and the plan stipulated nothing about the development of the Negev. The best thing about this plan was that it promised the immigration of 100,000 Jews and a joint development and planning committee, a starting point for cooperation between the two peoples.[41]

Simon went even further in an attempt to prevent Ichud's isolation. He explained that the British government, by arresting the Yishuv leaders, was elevating them to the rank of martyrs in the public eye and creating anarchy.[42] "If England wished to boost the status of the moderates and take the wind out of the extremists' sails, it need only increase significantly the number of legal *olim* (new immigrants) above the ridiculous and arbitrary number of 1,500 per month."[43] At the same time, the violence initiated by the IZL and Lehi after the Resistance Movement collapsed alarmed Ichud.[44]

Despite the steady deterioration in the Palestine situation, Ichud did not lose hope, still clinging to the recommendations of the Anglo-American Committee. Ichud's main task, as seen by its ideologues, was to inculcate its binational and nonviolent approach in the Zionist camp, not to take the role of a formal opposition party. At the same time, Ichud relied on three opposition groups to put forward its general principles. These were Hashomer Hatza'ir and Aliyah Hadashah, both political parties, and the anti-activist minority in Mapai. The latter was

Ichud's greatest disappointment, because it had lost its "spiritual, Zionist, and organizational independence." It now served the "totalitarian" majority in Mapai, which aimed to create a one-party regime. But the two parties proved little better. Aliyah Hadashah, though anti-Biltmore, anti-terror, pro-*aliyah* and pro-settlement, deserted the binationalist camp. Hashomer Hatza'ir, although seeing eye to eye with Ichud on all these issues, had one glaring fault: it favored a Jewish majority. Ichud also sought to become a magnet for dissident groups in the large parties (Mapai, the Mizrachi, General Zionists).[45] To a degree, this was accomplished through the League for Jewish-Arab Rapprochement and Cooperation, which had been created in 1939 by former members of Brit Shalom together with Hashomer Hatza'ir and the Left Poale Zion. However none of these bodies was able to increase popular sympathy for binationalism. The elections to the 22nd Zionist Congress showed that both Hashomer Hatza'ir and Aliyah Hadashah were still *quantités négligables* in Zionism. The masses wanted activism.

Bevin's announcement that Britain was referring the Palestine problem to the UN did not change Ichud's basic approach. Magnes, who congratulated Bevin for his fortitude and political wisdom, was not discouraged by the failure of the tripartite London Conference. (Magnes and Senator had turned down an invitation to attend the conference, not daring to act in defiance of the Jewish Agency, which boycotted the meeting.) Working to create an American Association for Union in Palestine with the assistance of the American Jewish Committee, Magnes took heart from "responsible persons" who regarded Ichud's ideas as "the best politically and morally." Still, he was aware that such ideas continued to be regarded as "impractical," leaving the arena to the "extremist" Zionist leadership.[46]

Buber, on the other hand, did not meddle in politics so much, apart from appearing before the different inquiry committees, mainly to support Magnes. Well aware that he played at best the role of Cassandra and at worst that of a quisling, he lamented that the Zionist political leadership had committed a "basic error" by pursuing a "traditional colonial policy" instead of being guided by "intra-national rather than international considerations." Binationalism, he believed, was not just a compromise for its own sake, but "the indispensable postulate" for the solution of the Jewish people.[47]

The reality was different. Weizmann's removal from the presidency of the Zionist Organization deprived Ichud of any serious chance to advance binational ideas. It remained only to eulogize Weizmann's achievements.[48] Ahad Ha-Am's slogan of a "double-promise for two national homes in Palestine" was the Ichud's guiding principle. So deeply ingrained was binationalism, both as an ideal and as a policy, that no one in the group foresaw the possibility that Britain's referral of the Palestine problem to the UN was an irreversible policy, leading inevitably to the end of British rule.[49] Senator warned the new JAE: "The foundations of a dwarf-state, its frontiers strategically indefensible, its economic situation complex, and without Jerusalem," might be a temporary salve for "the ambitions of political leaders," but in the long run "the perpetual enmity of our neighbors will show that the advantages were imaginary."[50]

Ichud was not deterred by the fact that less than a dozen Arabs secretly signed a declaration of support for its binational program. The assassination of Fawzi Darwish al-Husseini, who headed the tiny Filastin el-Jadida (New Palestine) party, on 23 November 1946—when twelve days earlier he had signed the document calling for a vague binational state, which spoke of political equality and *aliyah* according to the country's economic absorption capacity (no mention was made of numerical equality)—seemed to deepen Ichud's inner conviction. The document was the initiative of the League for Jewish-Arab Rapprochement and Cooperation and was signed by three Ichud members, the veteran binationalist H. M. Kalvarisky, as well as E. Simon and G. Stern and by A. Cohen for Hashomer Hatza'ir. To Ichud, al-Husseini's assassination did not signify—as it should have—the Mufti's complete domination of the Palestine Arabs. The Mufti's anxiety, as Ichud saw it, stemmed from his "fear" that the young Arab generation was falling under the thrall of binationalism. Ichud generously assisted Fawzi's family.[51]

Ichud's failure to crystallize an antipartitionist front either with Hashomer Hatza'ir or with Aliyah Hadashah did not bode well for its future. The former's vote against Weizmann at the 22nd Congress further split the antipartitionist front. Hirsch, a prominent member of both Ichud and Aliyah Hadashah, refused to continue the cooperation with Hashomer Hatza'ir.[52] Magnes admitted that Ichud had not been effective, and perhaps disintegration was called for since Arab-Jewish understanding had "thus far been advanced in a most amateurish way."[53] Many Ichud members were in despair over Britain's coming withdrawal and a possible Arab-Jewish war. Simon warned against messianic tendencies within the Zionist movement, in the light of the fate of other liberation movements.[54] In their despondency, Ichud leaders continued to believe that the JAE would not be able to unite in favor of partition and that this would lead to a general crisis in the Yishuv.[55]

The unrealism of these scenarios became clear on the eve of UNSCOP's visit to Palestine: Ichud suffered a severe blow when it became known that Aliyah Hadashah had deserted the antipartitionist front.[56] (Hashomer Hatza'ir would follow suit after the commission published its report, as described later.)

Yet despite everything, there was a feeling in Ichud that its position was strengthened by Gromyko's historic speech of 14 May 1947, in which the Soviet Union made binationalism the first priority for the solution of the Palestine problem. Internally, though, Senator was concerned that the Soviet line was based on "political reasons of their own which have very little to do with our aims." Senator called for the establishment of an Anglo-American trusteeship, alongside self-governing institutions that would "force" Arabs and Jews to work together in the central government. The demands of Jewish immigration must also be satisfied. Gabriel Stern, Ichud's Arab affairs expert, warned that a "good solution" (Peel plus the Negev) would include such a large Arab minority that to all intents and purposes a binational state would be created. India's failure to preserve unity reinforced Ichud's conclusion that partition would be the death knell for the development plans that depended upon the Jordan waters. Stern ruled out a separate Arab state because it would be "a fortress of fanatical and narrow-minded chauvinism." His binationalism was obsessive and little more than wishful thinking. It was based on the "tremendous" convergence of the two peoples' economic interests and on the fact that there was "no enmity whatsoever in daily life."[57]

Ichud's final public activity of any significance was its testimony to UNSCOP. There were few changes from the case it had put to the Anglo-American Committee about sixteen months earlier. Magnes urged UNSCOP to correct the "main weakness" of the Anglo-American Committee, namely that it did not propose a constitution for a binational state. There should be a federated state, which would help revive the two surviving peoples of the Semitic world. Naturally, Ichud did not fail to mention the encouragement given the binational idea by Gromyko. Magnes, oblivious of Professor Richard Koebner's public warning that Palestine did not constitute a vital part of British interests, recommended that Britain should be the trustee power because of his admiration for the British liberal tradition, particularly now when there was an effort to shift from imperialism to a commonwealth, in India, Burma, and Egypt. He drew a comparison with the Yugoslav federation, where the Croat language, albeit different from the alphabet of the "other languages," had the same "basic roots" and basic forms. In Palestine, though Hebrew and Arabic were closely related, future prospects for cooperation must rely on the "common ancestry" of Jews and Arabs as Semitic peoples. There was no racial animosity and "many points" of affinity existed between Judaism and Islam. Magnes's idea of federalism was that of a "joint Arab-Jewish Commonwealth" with no boundaries such as would inevitably give rise to irredentism on either side of the border.[58] At the same time, Ichud's antipartition case contained typical Zionist arguments, such as the need to preserve the integrity of the country for new Jewish immigration. A more cogent argument was that a Jewish state in a partitioned Palestine would "in effect be a binational state" whatever its boundaries.

UNSCOP, however, treated Ichud's proposals as impractical from both the Arab and Jewish points of view.[59] The commission's majority decision on partition was a "defeat" for Ichud, leaving the association's future unclear, according to Magnes.[60] Magnes, however, did not give up. Citing pro- and anti-Zionist arguments indiscriminately (such as the imminence of an Arab-Jewish war and the reduction of the Jewish area), Magnes said that partition would deprive Jews of the ability to purchase land and settle in the Arab area, undermining Ichud's case for a binational state. Oddest of all, Magnes seized on the UNSCOP Minority Report (because of its federal idea) as a "basis of discussion," although demanding certain corrections. Simon was sharply critical of Magnes, saying he had made "a serious tactical mistake" by relying on the minority report. Simon was more alarmed by the majority report than was Magnes, seeing the situation as "extremely serious." Britain's threat to withdraw was very real, and the "danger of anarchy" loomed. Simon was the first to admit failure when UNSCOP decided on partition.[61]

Nonetheless, Ichud's members refused to own up to their failure in public. On the contrary, they interpreted the eruption of the Jewish-Arab war the day after the 29 November 1947 partition resolution as a missed opportunity, since their proposal for a solution had not been considered by the UN.[62] Ichud in fact faced total isolation, with Hashomer Hatza'ir and Aliyah Hadashah both opting for partition.[63]

Nevertheless, Ichud did not stop disseminating ideas. Even though Palestine was engulfed by war, Ichud still called on the two emerging "sister states" to fight for "the lofty ideal" of close unity. At the same time, the forthcoming Jewish state was considered by Y. Luzitanus (Y. R. Molcho) to be a "historical turning point." There was a "sacred obligation" to ensure the Jewish state's success, he wrote, and ultimately, "together with the ingathering of the exiles and the Yishuv's prosperity," partition would fall away in a "fraternal alliance between the two Semitic peoples."[64] Stern concluded that the Arab-Jewish war was the direct result of the catastrophic partition decision and as such a self-fulfilling prophecy.[65]

The bitter reality of events led Magnes to lay the blame at Buber's feet. Magnes (whose nerves were "not in good shape," according to Buber) wrote ruefully: "You thought and believed that Zion could be built not with blood and fire but through tireless creative work and mutual understanding with our neighbors. You know very well that in the history of mankind states have almost invariably been built only with blood and injustice. But you counted too much on the great miracle . . . we have fallen prey to the Fata Morgana of the state."[66] When Buber, Magnes, and Senator made a public appeal to the people of Jerusalem, in the midst of the war, to desist from mob reprisals, it was condemned by the editor of the *Palestine Post* as "quislingism and a stab in the back of the Jewish cause."[67]

Yet during the débâcle the disillusioned Ichud drew some hope from America's trusteeship proposals to replace partition.[68] An interim trusteeship could serve as a new opening for binationalism.[69] Buber now claimed that a state was not needed. Development of the country, *aliyah*, and settlement could be well served without it. A treaty with the Arabs should be concluded "based on faith."[70]

The Deir Yasin massacre (which Rabbi Benyamin—Y. Radler-Feldman—likened to S.S. atrocities) and the Arabs' revenge in the form of the attack on the Hadassah Hospital convoy to Mount Scopus, in which 77 Jews were massacred, constituted a turning point for Magnes, who left for America soon afterward.[71] Evidently, Magnes believed that his solution could have meant another twenty or thirty years of "fruitful progress." The alternative was permanent war. True, the Jews could "'take' Haifa, Tiberias, Jaffa, and many other points, but we will be like the Germans—we will lose the war." The Yishuv could not stand up to the "millions upon millions of Muslims in the world." Moreover, the Arabs "have time" while the Jews "are in a hurry because of our tragedy," the Holocaust.[72]

To preclude a situation in which the new State of Israel would have to live by the sword, Senator recommended that Israel be a member of "large alliance of states," like free Ireland vis-à-vis the British Empire. His dream was a United States of the Semitic Middle East.[73] Buber was more pessimistic. Though yearning for a federated "covenant" with the Palestinian Arab state, he did not believe that the nascent Jewish state would forsake sovereignty, which he despised (and feared).[74] The remaining leadership, fearful of a second Spain, relied on Ben-Gurion's assurances of national equality for Israel's Arab citizens.[75] Few if any in Ichud foresaw the cardinal problem of the Arab refugees. Rabbi Benyamin and Gerda Luft also used the conventional terminology, referring to the Arabs' "flight." The exodus was considered unfortunate, because the Palestine Arabs were, in the Ichud conception, supposed to serve as a "bridgehead" for far-reaching social change.[76]

Against this background, it is clear that Ichud took a positive view of the mission by the UN mediator Bernadotte. Notwithstanding the "serious shortcomings" of Bernadotte's first plan, Stern said, compromise with Abdullah was preferable to "total" Jewish-Arab war. After Bernadotte's assassination, Stern praised him for his "humane and realistic" line toward the Arab refugee problem.[77] In fact, the best proof that Ichud was in harmony with the Israeli consensus on at least one issue was its attitude toward the Arab refugees: they were said to have brought on their own plight. Ben-Gurion's frequent declarations on the need for peace with the Arabs were very much to Ichud's taste. Ben-Gurion the prime minister was more credible in Ichud eyes than was Ben-Gurion the chairman of the JAE, who was often represented as an extremist, if not an adventurer. Now his warning that the Arabs would not accept the Jewish victory as a fait accompli was hailed by Ichud as proof that its own approach was justified. The Palestine problem bore a political and not a military character.[78] Shertok, too, was hailed as a sober statesman who was not "intoxicated" by the military victories. He was said to be "sincere" in his approach to peace, albeit lacking "vision and initiative." Naturally, refugees could not be permitted to return in wartime. But why, Stern asked, was "no declaration made concerning the refugees' right, as a matter of principle, to return, just as the Jewish people had a right of return"?[79] Rabbi Benyamin also endorsed this right of return, and compared the militaristic origins of the new state with that of the united Germany in 1870–71.[80]

At the same time, the Ichud journal cited a newly published book by W. Kolarz, *Myths and Realities in Eastern Europe*, in which it was argued that the Turko-Greek "transfer," which was mentioned by Begin as a "precedent," had been far from successful.[81] Within a month, however, Stern had changed course, wishing to remain in the Israeli consensus. He no longer recommended a mass return either, as no one could assume the "military, political, and moral responsibility" for such a step. But small numbers of refugees, from Jerusalem and Haifa, where friendly relations had existed, should be permitted to return as a gesture of goodwill. Since the Arab governments were responsible for the refugees' lot, according to Stern, they should share the financial burden with Israel, besides refugees receiving aid from the international community. Arab and Jewish associations would also slowly extend their cooperation to other political and economic fields.[82]

Ichud called upon the Arabs, both in Palestine and the region, to turn the temporary truce into a peace alliance and to recognize Israel as a fait accompli. As for the country's borders, those set by the UN were perhaps acceptable, but "free" negotiations could produce better ones. Jerusalem, if not partitioned by the UN, should be a single organic unit, a kind of condominium. Ichud hoped for the establishment of an independent state alongside Israel and economically united with it, according to the UN decision. The question of *aliyah* would be decided on the basis of the country's potential to absorb new immigrants. As for the Arab refugees, this position paper also said that a full solution would have to await a full peace. Israel could not, at present, cope with such a great burden, though there was a recognition of their right to return.[83]

The last word for Ichud in the emerging new Middle Eastern order should go to Magnes. Despite everything, he insisted that the 1948 war had not killed the idea of confederation. He called for a federation, based either on the American model or on that of the former Austro-Hungarian Empire. Magnes was proud of the fact that his proposals were akin to Bernadotte's first proposals (except on Jerusalem). In particular, he accepted the mediator's concept of free immigration for two years, following which the decision would be made by the confederation or, if disagreements arose, by the UN. Magnes's confederative ideas were utopian in the context of 1948. Naïvely, he thought that his "United States of Palestine" idea could compensate for growing Cold War rivalries.[84]

Ben-Gurion's victory over Ichud after a long struggle (dating back to Brit Shalom in the 1920s) not only demonstrated his systematic and abiding belief in the concept of *Innenpolitik;* it also symbolized the triumph of his version of Zionism—living by the sword—the negation of Ichud's ideology. At least one member of Ichud conceded to Ben-Gurion that the movement had been defeated and congratulated him on his victory.[85] Yet, Magnes and Ichud should not be seen as intellectual Don Quixotes; the group constituted an intellectual leadership, though without party affiliation. The Zionist movement's ambition for statehood, Ichud argued, portended incessant war. Magnes, then, was a minimalist Zionist. He had to create his own nonparty group because he found himself unable to participate in bodies such as the League for Jewish-Arab Rapprochement, in which Hashomer Hatza'ir and Left Poale Zion gave vent to their idea of mass immigration, a concept unacceptable to Magnes.

7

Aliyah Hadashah

Ideology and Practice of Nonviolent Zionism

Aliyah Hadashah (New Immigration—referring to the Zionist immigrants from Germany and Austria) was the only "political faction" or "movement"—it refused to call itself a party—that supported Weizmann wholeheartedly, apart from the General Zionists A. Like Ichud, it was established in 1942 on the ruins of an older party, Achdut Ha'am (Unity of the People), itself a breakaway from General Zionism. Achdut Ha'am espoused political parity: six Jewish provinces and six Arab provinces.[1] It was founded in the wake of the German Zionists' disappointment at being underrepresented in Yishuv institutions. The movement's foremost leaders were Felix Rosenblueth (later Pinchas Rosen) and Georg Landauer. Rosenblueth was chairman of the Zionist Organization in Germany and a member of the Zionist Executive in London, while Landauer headed the WZO's departments of German Jewish Immigration and Youth Aliyah. Landauer represented Aliyah Hadashah in the Va'ad Leumi Executive, which gave him just a little influence on decision making in the Yishuv. Paradoxically, his rival Rosenblueth carried more weight as the president of Aliyah Hadashah. Unlike Ichud, Aliyah Hadashah sought to influence Zionist politics directly, through a party drawing its strength from Central European immigrants. Like Ichud and Hashomer Hatza'ir, it found itself caught up in a serious conflict between its Zionist aspirations and its universal faith. To remain within the Zionist consensus, Aliyah Hadashah had to give its full support to *aliyah* and settlement and reject the 1939 White Paper. Aliyah Hadashah claimed to stand for four principles: (1) *aliyah* and settlement as a priori conditions for the fulfillment of Zionism; (2) the Zionist Executive should present the government with a well-argued plan for building the country, demanding the empty areas for Jewish settlement, this to be confirmed by the victorious Allies; (3) in order to get the Allies' consent to such a plan, "every possible attempt" should be made to "coordinate the essential needs of the Jewish people and the Arab people on the basis of mutual recognition of their rights . . . with no surrender of the Zionist goal and the fundamental conditions for its fulfillment, without harming the Arab nation's national interests"; and (4) the UN should come to the rescue of persecuted Jews, and all possibilities granted as part of the Jewish national home (i.e., the Mandate charter) should be exploited.[2]

In fact, though, Aliyah Hadashah had no clear program and indeed took pride in not being committed to any particular plan for Palestine. Its chief raison d'être was its opposition to the Biltmore plan, leading Ben-Gurion to criticize it for being alienated from the thrust of Jewish independence. Aliyah Hadashah was never able to get rid of its image as a *Landsmanschaft*, as Rosenblueth admitted.[3] Its main contribution to Yishuv politics was its insistence on moderation. It demanded an exclusive British orientation and condemned the terrorist methods of IZL and Lehi, not hesitating to liken the "falsified heroic legend" of the latter to that of the Nazis and Chmelnitzky, as did G. Krojanker, editor of Aliayh Hadashah's German-language journal *Mitteilungsblatt*.[4] Aliyah Hadashah, although showing social consciousness, was basically a nonclass party. It called for labor legislation and advocated free enterprise; it promised to be neither proletarian nor bourgeois in character. Internal debate did not resolve the problem of the party's social identity.[5] Mapai was its main target of criticism, largely because the Biltmore program had, in its view, "usurped" Revisionist policy.

Weizmann's commitment to Biltmore did not diminish Aliyah Hadashah's blind faith in the aging leader. In his policy, so the movement believed, vision and reality complemented each other. Rosenblueth misread the situation, being confident that the overwhelmingly positive attitude toward Weizmann in the Yishuv reflected "healthy instincts." The party's moderate policy drew also on Professor Roberto Bachi's prognosis, which warned that foreign policy must be built on a clear recognition of the demographic facts. A Jewish majority could not be achieved only by *aliyah* but required also the Yishuv's natural growth.[6] But Aliyah Hadashah, like most parties in the Yishuv, was not haunted by the demographic danger as much as members were fascinated by new ideas for development such as the Lowdermilk plan. Yet they understood that there was an element of optimism, verging on naïveté, in this plan. Because of their implications for the Arab population, such plans could only be implemented by the British; the main goal of Zionist policy, according to Aliyah Hadashah's representative in the Va'ad Leumi Executive, should be to obtain the great powers' consent for the execution of these development projects.[7]

Aliyah Hadashah wielded little concrete influence because it was not represented on the Jewish Agency Executive, although, as mentioned, it was temporarily represented on the Va'ad Leumi Executive and on the Zionist Organization's Small Actions Committee.[8] However, its leaders kept in touch with Mapai, trying, to mitigate its policy of "activism," labeling this "adventurism." Mapai in turn retorted, accusing Aliyah Hadashah of trying to "ingratiate" itself with the British. Sprinzak agreed that the anti-British struggle was misguided and that Biltmore was a "fatal" mistake, but he criticized the "moral conceit" of *Mitteilungsblatt*.[9]

Aliyah Hadashah, which claimed to be neither right nor left, belonged to the World Confederation of the General Zionists. As such, it tried occasionally to find common ground with other "progressive" elements of this rightist confederation. Evidence of one such futile attempt is a meeting the party held, in July 1945, with representatives of the General Zionists B and of Ha'oved Hatsioni, which was established in 1936 as a faction of the General Zionists in the Histadrut, and as such was closer to the General Zionists A. Among those taking part for the General Zionists was Moshe Sneh, who denied that he was against compromise but refused to make this position an end in itself. Rosenblueth did not rush into unity, as Sneh and Moshe Kolodni (later Moshe Kol) wanted, since a common language existed only in internal matters. When it came to external affairs, Aliyah Hadashah insisted that a Jewish state could survive only with British assistance in the face of Arab strength. Rosenblueth secretly—in view of Landauer's opposition—accepted partition as the only means by which to create a new society. But the party as such could not publicly come forward in favor of partition because Rosenblueth did not have a majority before the summer of 1947. He would obey the national authority but he was against "maneuvers" that made Britain hated by the Yishuv. "We believe that the world has a conscience," Rosenblueth told the meeting. "Zionism is based on the assumption that there are forces in the world which consider it a moral precept to create a national home for the Jews. . . . It would be a burden on the British conscience to forsake us." Sneh, in July 1945, was ready to accept dependence on Britain but only within the framework of a state. History, he claimed, would justify a collision with the British over illegal immigration and the Biltmore plan.[10]

But what was Aliyah Hadashah's alternative to Biltmore? The party refused to commit itself publicly to any specific plan until Bevin's speech of 18 February 1947, when it resigned itself to partition. As for anything more concrete, Rosenblueth, though against binationalism, refused to go beyond the words of the Zionist anthem: "To be a free people in our land."[11] Landauer believed that the Yishuv's fate would be "to remain for generations a minority." Immigration combined with natural growth would still not enable the Yishuv to constitute more than a third of Palestine's population. Landauer's ideal was an improved Mandate; partition would be dangerous. Zionism could be destroyed even if Britain permitted immigration on a far larger scale, as this would trigger an Arab revolt and bring about a far worse White Paper. Rosenblueth, far more optimistic, would have agreed with Landauer's position if the British were to grant 50,000 immigration certificates per year. As it was, he urged an "acceptable partition."[12] In the short term it was Rosenblueth who capitulated, not Landauer. Aliyah Hadashah's support for partition was never mentioned in public, and this omission was a major cause of the party's débâcle in the elections to the 22nd Zionist Congress in October 1946. Instead, the emphasis was placed on Landauer's idea that a small Jewish state would have limited staying power and would not be able to cope with mass immigration or, more crucially, to hold its own in an inimical Arab region. Nor was Landauer isolated within the party. Nothing more than cantonization, within the framework of the "responsible power" and in cooperation with the regional peoples, was palatable to the editor of its journals in both German and Hebrew, Robert Weltsch. He feared that in a Jewish state the rulers would adopt totalitarian methods, instead of becoming "spiritual leaders who will guide [the people's] moral and intellectual conscience."[13] It was in this spirit that Aliyah Hadashah construed Britain's decision to continue the White Paper—a policy which the official Zionist leadership considered a terrible blow—as the death knell for Biltmore. Aliyah Hadashah also rejected the White Paper but urged only passive resistance. Indeed, on the eve of the United Resistance Movement's anti-British operations, Weltsch warned—without knowing what was afoot—that an armed uprising by the Yishuv would result in its destruction, ending "any chance of a renaissance of the Jewish people . . . for decades if not centuries."[14]

Following the Atlit incident (when the Palmach forcibly released some 200 illegal immigrants from the British prison there), Aliyah

Hadashah demanded that a "national emergency committee" be established by the Jewish Agency and the Va'ad Leumi with Weizmann as its head. Sensing that some sort of resistance movement was in existence, Aliyah Hadashah said that the new body should have the character of *"active resistance without the use of arms, as long as the British do not touch it* [emphasis in the original], *aliyah* under all circumstances, settlement everywhere, etc." The plan, though, would have value only if it were implemented "incrementally" and not "in a catastrophic one-time act." Rosenblueth called for the Yishuv leadership to emulate Gandhi's example of fasting as a type of passive resistance that would win public sympathy. The top leadership should fast until the British permitted 100,000 Jews to immigrate—and, if necessary, they should fast until death.[15] The editor of *Ha'aretz*, G. Schocken, objected, arguing that fasting suited the Indians but not the Yishuv. The maximum plan, suggested by H. Foerder (later a Knesset member), was three-fold: breaking the ties with the government; support for illegal immigration; and no use of arms unless an attempt were made to confiscate them.[16] Publicly Rosenblueth committed his party to a policy of rejecting the use of terror and supporting *aliyah* and settlement "under any conditions." This, he was confident, would keep Aliyah Hadashah within the Zionist consensus. But internal party constraints did not permit him to go beyond generalities such as "national freedom and territorial crystallization."[17]

The party was united in its objection to violence and in its faith in political negotiations. The United Resistance Movement's sabotage against the railways was condemned as an "act of despair" and virtual "madness," since the British had not yet made a final decision. In an article that was partly censored by the British, Rosenblueth went as far as to call on Ben-Gurion and the leadership to instruct certain groups of citizens to stop paying taxes, to boycott British goods, and, again, to stage a protest fast against the ban on immigration. Nonviolent civil resistance must become the order of the day. Conditions might arise in which there would be "no more suitable place for Weizmann than in prison."[18] Bevin's "anti-Jewish" speech of 13 November 1945 gave impetus to the Rosenblueth school of partition, since the British foreign secretary took a *non possumus* stance with regard to an Arab-Jewish compromise. The appearance of a new factor, American participation on the Anglo-American Committee, was a further boost for Rosenblueth's optimism. Moreover, Hashomer Hatza'ir's condemnation of the Night of the Railways ensured that Aliyah Hadashah would not remain isolated.[19]

Aliyah Hadashah's negligible influence on the Va'ad Leumi brought home to its leadership that it had "very little chance" to alter Ben-Gurion's line, since the majority formally opposed Weizmann. At long last Aliyah Hadashah leaders realized as well that Hashomer Hatza'ir was closer to Ben-Gurion.[20] Thus their role now became one of moral opposition rather than a practical impact on the decision-making process. Indirectly, Aliyah Hadashah exercised a moderating influence on the policy of the Resistance Movement. However, any attempt to replace Ben-Gurion with Weizmann was bound to fail. In fact, Ben-Gurion and Rosenblueth understood each other (Ben-Gurion would appoint him Israel's first minister of justice). By maintaining the line of large-scale *aliyah* and large-scale settlement, notwithstanding his vague formula of "political conditions promising freedom of life," Rosenblueth was ideologically within the Zionist consensus. His disagreements with Ben-Gurion were confined to the operative level, revolving around the character of the struggle. But his basic belief that Zionism had a future only if it relied on Britain was more than tactical. Although it was up to Britain whether it would support Zionism, this absolute reliance was a matter of strategy. Later on, Rosenblueth would admit that this had been his party's major mistake: its failure to appreciate that Britain no longer had any common interests with Zionism. But in late 1945 he believed that sheer hatred of Britain in the Yishuv would end the Anglo-Zionist relationship. Moreover, the use of sabotage would deteriorate to individual terrorism on the model of the Stern Gang. He objected to the United Resistance Movement's "flexible" line of "linked struggle" (i.e., directly linked to the efforts of *aliyah* and settlement) instead of "continuous struggle" (as urged by the IZL and Lehi), since in his perception the former also produced bloodshed, as seen in Palmach attacks on British radar stations. This so-called flexible line was extremely dangerous because in practice it was a blank check for "unhindered operations."

What alarmed Rosenblueth even more than the terror perpetrated by Jabotinsky's disciples was the "perilous" concept inherent in the idea that "we must strike at our friends in order to prove that we are strong." This idea was propagated by the radical-left Le'achdut Ha'avodah movement member, Israel Baer, quoting Marx: "There are moments in which a war of despair is needed without any chance of success in order to educate the masses and to prepare them for the next campaign." Rosenblueth believed that partition could be achieved without such a gloomy prelude. However, it could not be implemented by the "broken" Holocaust survivors, only by Western Jewry. Weizmann

alone could bring about such a solution.[21] The problem was that Aliyah
Hadashah had been cut off from the Zionist decision-making process
since Senator's resignation from the Jewish Agency Executive—a step
Rosenblueth regretted Senator had taken without first consulting him.[22]

Aliyah Hadashah's goal was to convince the Yishuv that Biltmore
was an unrealistic plan.[23] But the party was split on the political plan
that should be presented to the Anglo-American Committee.

Dr. Elias Auerbach, the party's deputy president, recommended cantonization. By contrast, S. Hirsch believed in continued building of the
Yishuv for another ten years under a trusteeship not worse than the
Mandate. In the party's executive, Rosenblueth's partition proposal
received only five votes, Auerbach's cantonization eight, and
binationalism under trusteeship seven.[24] In the Aliyah Hadashah Center, partition received twelve votes but cantonization garnered thirteen,
and a combination of binationalism and trusteeship got fifteen.[25] Only
on the issue of nonviolence was the party united. On this basis it demanded, at Landauer's initiative, that Ben-Gurion resign because of
the growing use of violence.[26] As for the party's appearance before the
Committee of Inquiry, Rosenblueth said it could not support the status
quo; it must decide between partition and a combination of the trusteeship and cantonization plans.[27] In the meantime, no consensus was
reached, and the party decided to appear before the Committee of Inquiry only if Hashomer Hatza'ir also testified.[28] Ichud influence on
the party was considerable, Simon explaining that he favored
binationalism because the alternative was war with both Britain and
the Arabs.[29] Landauer warned that if Britain withdrew the result might
be an Arab state controlled by Russia.[30]

Nothing of the party's internal confusion was revealed in its manifesto, which espoused "systematic extension of territorial and personal
autonomy. The Yishuv must obtain political recognition as a national
body." Compromise between the Auerbach, Hirsch, and Rosenblueth
schools was an urgent necessity. Dr. Auerbach's plan calling for
binationalism and cantonization—two autonomous areas, one for Jews
and another for Arabs, and a mixed area—was published by the party
in its Hebrew journal *Amudim*, next to the aforementioned manifesto.[31]
Aliyah Hadashah's fasting proposal was applied by the Jewish Agency
in the episode of the illegal-immigrant ship *La Spezia*, but it proved
ineffective. Landauer applauded the fact that the party did not participate in the fast (and he regretted Senator's participation), thus avoiding the "general psychosis."[32] The Report of the Anglo-American Committee saved the party, momentarily at least, from disintegration. Since

it complimented Aliyah Hadashah for its constructive line, Landauer considered his policy of opposition to a state vindicated. But he understood that the Yishuv faced a dilemma: a choice between receiving immigration certificates and disarming. The situation was full of contradictions, said Landauer, and needed Weizmann's intervention, according to Hirsch.[33] The price for the blunder of dissociation from the Yishuv during the *La Spezia* episode would be paid in the next elections to the Zionist Congress. In the meantime, Rosenblueth, who called official Zionist policy makers "fascists" and continued to advocate "civil resistance," objected to accepting the committee's report without reservations, as other party leaders favored doing. Expressing great pessimism as to its implementation, he explained that he could not rely on the British. Hans Kaufman reminded his colleagues that the majority in the Yishuv wanted a state, to which Auerbach replied that this should be the line "one day" but not now.[34]

Bevin's defiant speech at Bournemouth in June 1946 increased the confusion in Aliyah Hadashah. Landauer said he was optimistic about the abolition of the White Paper but not about Zionism's long-range prospects.[35] Rosenblueth yielded to Landauer's line, accepting his thesis that the time was not ripe for a definitive solution. The two were in closer agreement about reliance on Britain. Landauer adduced a moderate line, hoping that common sense would prevail and the Yishuv would be saved.[36] However, Britain's inability to deal with the Palestine morass, combined with what Aliyah Hadashah perceived as Ben-Gurion's tottering leadership, again upset the party's fragile political balance. After the Black Sabbath, even Landauer grasped that the Jewish Agency's very survival was at stake. Weizmann naturally seemed to be the only possible savior. Members of the party's executive called on him to seize the reins of power again, assisted by moderates from Aliyah Hadashah, Hashomer Hatza'ir, and the opposition in Mapai. Inwardly, Rosenblueth—who appealed to Weizmann in his capacity as president of the Jewish Agency and the World Zionist Organization to take power from Ben-Gurion—was doubtful whether Weizmann would take the responsibility and establish a caretaker Jewish Agency Executive. Landauer was certain that the rule of Mapai was over. Surely the Jewish Agency Executive had lost its grip.[37] The party's center formally called on the Jewish Agency Executive to resign.[38]

Despairing of the possibility that the opposition in Mapai would take the initiative against Ben-Gurion's line, Rosenblueth was convinced that he could effect a change of policy, including the formation of an anti-activist Jewish Agency Executive, only from within the Yishuv institutions. He accepted the Morrison-Grady provincial autonomy plan as a basis for negotiations, although noting that it should be improved in the direction of partition. But the Jewish Agency's rejection of Morrison-Grady and the expulsion of illegal immigrants to Cyprus again threw Aliyah Hadashah into pandemonium.[39] Its German journal published an article on the latter issue, which Auerbach said "put us beyond the pale of public opinion [in the Yishuv]." G. Luft, however, pointed out that though the illegal immigration was politically motivated, the recent expulsions must be fought.[40]

The party placed great hopes for a victory of moderate policy in Rosenblueth's appearance before the historic Paris meeting of the enlarged Jewish Agency Executive in August 1946. In fact he spoke to the converted, since that body had decided on 5 August 1946, thirteen days before his speech, to support partition and to put an end to the violence. Nonetheless, he courageously condemned Ben-Gurion's boast to the Committee of Inquiry that the Yishuv could hold out alone against the Palestine Arabs, or even the Arab states, without Britain, as "sheer bluff and propaganda." Expressing his support for partition, which he said was also his party's line, he stated that "security demands continued cooperation with Britain until an understanding with the Arabs has been reached, which at the moment is a far-off goal."[41] Cooperation would, however, definitely not be against other Zionist groups, and he turned down the British invitation to attend the London Conference. Aliyah Hadashah's democratic character and Zionist goals ruled out the danger of collaboration behind Ben-Gurion's back.[42]

As soon as it became public knowledge that partition was the official Zionist program, replacing Biltmore, Rosenblueth urged his colleagues to support it rather than the Morrison-Grady plan. He consoled himself that the opposition in Mapai, led by Kaplan and Sprinzak, needed the backing of Aliyah Hadashah. However, diplomacy alone was not enough; illegal immigration, passive resistance, and a British orientation were also necessary, Rosenblueth said.[43] By contrast, Simon argued that binationalism might prove attractive to the peoples of the Soviet Union, the Jews included.[44]

However, the continuing internal split (Landauer still espoused binationalism, and Ernst Simon objected to the "one-sided alliance" between Zionism and Britain) did not enable the party to contest the elections with a distinct line that would have brought it nearer to the Yishuv majority. The Morrison-Grady plan, like the Report of the Anglo-American Committee, temporarily saved it from disintegration. The party demanded that this plan be accepted as a basis for negotiations leading to two federally connected independent states or one binational state. In the highly nationalistic mood of the Yishuv, this moderate plan had little appeal: "British policy and Jewish hysteria" joined hands, Rosenblueth said. He indicated to Weizmann that Ben-Gurion's name commanded the support of "large masses of the electorate."[45] The result was a devastating defeat; the party's strength was reduced from 10.6 percent in the Elected Assembly of 1944 to 5.9 percent in the 1946 elections (unlike the left-wing parties, which retained their overall representation). Rosenblueth tried to grasp the reasons for the débâcle. The easiest explanation was that the majority in the Yishuv, Mapai included, had voted for activism and against partition. He was confident that the very name Aliyah Hadashah was another reason for the defeat, as it sounded sectarian to the public, and he noted also the party's poor campaign and faulty organization. Aliyah Hadashah was the only party that was seen to favor cooperation with Britain, hence its unpopularity. Another major mistake was the party's line over the expulsion of illegal immigrants, which was seen as not sufficiently anti-British.[46]

At the Zionist Congress itself, Rosenblueth made a last plea against activism. Now he spoke in favor of "political self-rule," concealing the party's split over cantonization vs. binationalism. Unable to speak cogently for partition, he fulminated against activism, an issue on which the congress was split. Comparison to Ireland was false, because Zionism needed the British for *aliyah*. The Irish nationalists, whose struggle had lasted hundreds of years, used Lehi's methods, which were rejected by the Yishuv. Although the United Resistance Movement with IZL and Lehi had been dissolved in July, Rosenblueth's nightmare was that this combination could be revived: "'He who sups with the Devil should have a long spoon,'" he argued, and added: "Ours has not been long enough." Sneh, once a potential ally, was Rosenblueth's main target, as both a protagonist of activism and the espouser of an anti-British orientation.[47]

It was a pugnacious speech, but the battle had been lost—and not only by Aliyah Hadashah. The party's chief hope and ally, Weizmann, to whom Rosenblueth made a last appeal to take upon himself a Hindenburg-like role as president, was ousted from power with no hope of recovery.[48] Rosenblueth would, however, soon impose support for partition on his colleagues in order to save the party from oblivion. Bevin's historic speech of 18 February 1947 overwhelmed the party as no other event did. At one stroke the main anchor of its Weltanschauung disappeared.[49] Apart from Bevin's speech, it was Gromyko's statement of 14 May 1947, three months later, that cemented Rosenblueth's final victory over Landauer. Rosenblueth, however, did not accept Ben-Gurion's plan (independence in part of the country and the Mandate in the rest), instead regarding partition as a final solution. Partition, according to Rosenblueth, had the best chance of gaining the agreement of the Arabs. Landauer's last-ditch argument was that as long as the Jews were a minority in Palestine, they must have a transition period under international control. Partition in the current situation, he said, was an aggressive plan. "If we say that Arabs and Jews will never be able to live in peace, this is a death sentence for Zionism." The party's Center adopted Rosenblueth's position by 25 to 17 (with 2 abstentions).[50]

Now the road was open for unity with the moderate General Zionists. Here again Landauer's camp was, temporarily, a stumbling block, before he finally disappeared from the political scene, embittered and frustrated. The General Zionists supported a settlement with the breakaways (IZL and Lehi), which was too generous according to the party—permitting them to join the Haganah in organized units. An easier issue was the general trend in the party toward a clear Western orientation. Like Ben-Gurion, Rosenblueth (who in October was appointed to the Jewish Agency's advisory delegation to the UN) saw this as a mistake: "We must get used to the fact that we cannot voice publicly everything that we think." The right line would be to seek the support of all states who were willing to assist in the implementation of the UN resolution.[51] In the meantime, the outbreak of Arab-Jewish violence caused great apprehension in Aliyah Hadashah, which had hoped that an international army would come to the Yishuv's rescue. Landauer (whose participation in the Situation Committee—Va'adat Hamatsav—that prepared the governmental apparatus of the Jewish state was described by B. Cohen as self-contradictory) argued that the UN decision on partition could not be implemented without an international army, which would have to remain in the region for years to prevent further clashes. Continuous war with the Arabs, he said, was not a Zionist ideal. Landauer's pessimism was boundless. In his unrelenting search for missed opportunities, he regretted that the Yishuv had not made a concerted effort to eradicate the Jewish terrorist groups—had it done so, Britain might not have withdrawn from Palestine. H. Foerder said the party was living in a "tragic contradiction" and that Landauer's way, if followed, would deprive it of all influence.[52]

Rosenblueth, also speaking at a meeting of the party executive, said that as an opposition group, "We have outlived our usefulness." Not even Weizmann would support the party in its present state. It had become a mere *Landsmanschaft*, and, as such, irrelevant. There was no young generation in the party, and it was crucial to act within the parameters of Jewish government. As for war, it would not topple Zionism's foundations: "We want to implement Zionism peacefully," he said, "but if there is no other way we must fight." Rosenblueth again won a majority and took Landauer's place on the Va'ad Leumi, where he voted for the establishment of the Provisional State Council.[53]

Rosenblueth also carried the day on other issues. His stand in favor of unity with the "progressive" wing of the General Zionists won a two-thirds majority in the party's center.[54] Rosenblueth now supported Ben-Gurion's line on fighting the war as the only choice and was backed by the party.[55] Rosenblueth also pushed through his motion for the party to support the announcement of a provisional government, scheduled to be made in mid-May. Some of the senior figures, such as Landauer, Senator, Y. Lam, and Luft, strongly opposed joining the government, the latter two, for example, fearing that the new state would be perceived as "rebels against the world."[56]

In the provisional government itself, Rosenblueth advanced Aliyah Hadashah's moderate line. When the British government suggested exchanging the Negev for Galilee, the general trend within the party (except for G. Schocken) was to see this as a reasonable compromise. Similarly, the party advocated acceptance of the cease-fire proposed by the UN on 31 May 1948, otherwise the Security Council might impose severe sanctions. Rosenblueth in particular was confident that after the war the Arabs who had fled would return in great numbers and that the government would have to compensate them. He spoke of "concern that the plunder of their property was meant in fact to transfer them forcibly."[57] Rosenblueth supported an internationalized Jerusalem and territorial compromise in the Negev, since the Arabs, in his view, would never give up the idea of territorial contiguity. "It is not true," he declared, "that our fate will be decided by force alone." He was disturbed, therefore, at reports that the Arabs' villages were being burned in order to prevent their return.[58] Bernadotte's proposals underlined Aliyah Hadashah's dilemmas: its sine qua non demands, as expressed in a meeting of the executive, were that western Jerusalem must never be given to the Arabs, independence must be retained at all costs, and immigration was to be controlled by Israel. The rest was open for negotiations, with a compromise solution needed in order to achieve peace.[59] Rosenblueth was certain that the United States and Britain would not permit either side to obtain a decisive victory. As to the future of the party, he insisted that it could not include members who regarded the partition resolution as "a great disaster" and who expressed persistent dissatisfaction with the party's line. He was particularly outraged by the "weeping and wailing" over the war dead in *Mitteilungsblatt*. He justified Ben-Gurion's action on *Altalena*. Increasingly skeptical about the idea of allowing the Arab refugees to return, he said in July 1948 that there was no guarantee they would not "stab us in the back." Certainly there was no question of returning them while the war continued. Still, he was puzzled about Arab "flight" and about the looting psychosis in Israel; he found both inexplicable.[60] Three weeks later he asserted that Arabs of draft age must not be allowed to return. After all, he said, "a terrible war was imposed on us. We made tremendous sacrifices and today we have the right to use our conquests as a trump card. If a transfer of population [to the Arab states] will not be possible, then the Arabs' return will become a bargaining position."[61]

By September 1948, Aliyah Hadashah, after a lengthy process of disintegration, disappeared. It became part of the Progressive Party, which included the moderate General Zionists. In the elections to the First Knesset the new party won five seats and the General Zionists seven. Other former Aliyah Hadashah members, particularly Lam's followers, joined Mapai. Rosenblueth in time became the leader of the General Zionists and Progressives, which in 1961 united as the Liberal Party. In 1965 the Liberal Party joined Herut in an election block (Gahal), but a faction led by Rosenblueth refused and formed the Independent Liberal Party. The General Zionists, by joining Begin, opted for the right after all. Rosenblueth's followers, now no more than a splinter group, joined Labour (the successor to Mapai) in the elections of 1981.

It was, perhaps, Kurt Blumenfeld, the president of the Zionist Organization in Germany (1924–33), who symbolized Aliyah Hadashah's total capitulation. He confessed to his earlier mistake in thinking that Ben-Gurion's policy was destined for failure. "Now I understand the value of the political, military, and spiritual undertaking that is embodied in your work. . . . I am astonished to see that the man who prepared the war is the same man that is educating our people for the enterprise of peace. Max Weber used to say that a statesman must have two traits: the fire of passion and a discerning eye. In the past I saw only the fire of passion in you, now I have become aware that you also possess the second quality in abundance."[62]

IV

The Radical Left

Zionist Strategy and Marxist Tactics?

8

Hashomer Hatza'ir

From Binationalism to Federalism

If Mapai was a social-democratic party of the center, Hashomer Hatza'ir was definitely to Mapai's left. But was it a radical-left party? In the final analysis, it gave priority to Zionism, though it was also a powerful advocate of Marxism and bore unstinting admiration for the Soviet Union. Hashomer Hatza'ir was established in Poland (Galicia) in 1913 as a Scout movement, influenced by the German youth movement Wandervögel. But it was in Mandatory Palestine that it absorbed socialism under the guidance of Meir Yaari, who led it until his death. Initially he was attracted by A. D. Gordon's non-Marxist socialism, but he soon abandoned this in favor of Marxism. The party's attitude toward the Soviet Union was more complicated: the October Revolution was admired, but Soviet bureaucracy was sharply criticized as "decadent." The Ribbentrop-Molotov agreement was justified by Hashomer Hatza'ir by the need for survival, only to be condemned later. Criticism of the Soviet Union tapered off after the Soviet victory at Stalingrad (1942–43). By 1927, Hashomer Hatza'ir was officially established as a kibbutz movement and committed to the "theory of stages," which gave priority to the Zionist revolution over the socialist-Marxist revolution, and to "combined organization" with Arab workers. From the outset it supported binationalism, not as a political regime but as a pure utopia and "prognosis."[1] The stages theory enabled its involvement in Zionist politics; it was part and parcel of the Ichud Olami (World Union) of Poale Zion, associated with Mapai. Increasingly, however, its distinctive ideology required political consolidation beyond a pure kibbutz movement, especially after Mapai announced its "from class to nation" approach (see introduction). Yet, it was not until 1946 that Hashomer Hatza'ir went to the polls as an independent party, after all attempts at unity with Mapai or Le'achdut Ha'avodah had failed. Undoubtedly political ideology revolving around the question of the solution to the Palestine problem was the major stumbling block to unity.

It was the Jewish Agency's Biltmore resolution in 1942 that pushed Hashomer Hatza'ir to adopt an independent policy. It took another four years for an independent party to emerge because, ideology aside, the need for an operative policy arose only after the war, when Britain was about to make a final decision on Palestine's future. Despite its longstanding Soviet orientation, Hashomer Hatza'ir espoused a moderate policy toward Britain. Though condemning British imperialism, the movement saw a "proximity of interests" with Britain, and this had a powerful impact on the movement's Zionist tactics and strategy alike, situating it unequivocally on the side of the moderates in Zionism. (Its unification with Le'achdut Ha'avodah was made possible only after its policy of binationalism collapsed in the wake of UNSCOP's recommendation for partition, which reduced the ideological differences between the two groups. Even then it was only a marriage of convenience, which lasted barely six years; see later discussion.)

The problem with the Biltmore plan was not *aliyah*, which to Hashomer Hatza'ir was as sacred a principle as it was to any other party. It was, rather, the idea of a Jewish state that Hashomer Hatza'ir rejected. The movement put forward an alternative plan calling for "the establishment [in Palestine] of a political regime under international control, under which the Jewish Agency will have the right to manage *aliyah* in accordance with the [country's] full absorption capacity [and] in conjunction with the postwar needs of the Diaspora tragedy." Another article stipulated that the Jewish Agency would be granted the "right to develop the country . . . for the benefit of the two peoples, which will make possible dense Jewish settlement and the development of the Arab *fellaheen* economy." Finally, Hashomer Hatza'ir called for the establishment after the war of "a regime based on political equality for both peoples, which will enable the full and undisturbed implementation of Zionism and move Palestine toward political independence within the framework of a binational regime." The plan noted that while Zionism was the only feasible solution for the Jewish problem, the Zionist movement would assure full civil and economic rights to the Palestine Arabs. Ben-Gurion's plan to bring two million Jews to Palestine within two years was rejected as "imaginary"—if carried out it would cause an "organized catastrophe," turning the Yishuv into "one big Tel Aviv." It was not the immigration of two million Jews that Meir Yaari opposed but the pace—it should be spread over ten years. Since the plan was formulated before the Holocaust became public knowledge (the Yishuv imagined the situation in occupied Poland in terms of pogroms), Yaari also demanded the restoration of Jewish property and the reconstruction of Jewish life in Europe. Only afterward should *aliyah* be implemented. However, this was conditional on an agreement with the Arabs. Hashomer Hatza'ir did not yet dare to ask for a Jewish majority in Palestine itself, preferring the vague formulation of "concentrating the majority of the Jewish people in Palestine and its surroundings." Like Ben-Gurion in the 1930s, Yaari relied on the concept of a federation—now Magnes's grand plan—to sweeten the bitter pill for the Arabs. But in contrast to Magnes (and Ben-Gurion), Yaari held that a socialist regime was a necessity. As for international factors, Yaari did not delude himself that under the "capitalist-imperialist regime" the British imperialist policy of "divide and rule" would disappear. But the hope was that the "best conditions" could be created under this regime to "cross the Rubicon"—meaning to end the period of the Jewish minority in Palestine. America was not to be relied upon, since Roosevelt was still committed to a policy that favored a solution for the Jews outside Palestine. Yaari denied that his party had an irrevocable Soviet orientation, but this was in part implied in his hope that "the victorious powers" would assist the Yishuv on the *aliyah* issue.[2]

After the full horrors of the Holocaust were revealed, Yaari saw no reason to alter his basic tenets, although he no longer sought the reconstruction for the Diaspora first. He was convinced that oil-pipeline interests could preclude a British withdrawal from Palestine but thought that the pressure of five million American Jews combined with "moral" pressure by the USSR would make possible the Yishuv's achievement of numerical parity with the Palestine Arabs. The tragedy would begin, he believed, when Britain objected to further Jewish growth due to fear of an Arab revolt. Ben-Gurion's argument for an "immediate state" was rejected out of hand; only Jewish-Arab equality and fraternity could guarantee mass *aliyah*.[3]

Toward the end of World War II, the debate over the operative meaning of Biltmore sharpened. Yaari explained that he would not mourn if a Jewish state were decided on only after a Jewish majority had been achieved. This was a hint that binationalism was only a ploy to gain a majority by Arab agreement. At this moment, however, immediate Jewish statehood would mean only partition, he said, but the problem was that partition as an instrument for *aliyah* was an illusion. It might actually close the gates of Palestine to eleven million Jews. "Tomorrow there might be a Holocaust in America," he told the Small Zionist Actions Committee. Capitalism could always produce a "Hitler syndrome." A "political agreement" between the two peoples, based on "political equality," was essential in order to reach a "full Zionist solution for the majority of the Jewish people." In full agreement with Aliyah Hadashah, he stated that no one was suggesting a binational state immediately. Nor did he delude himself that an agreement with the Arabs was possible in the near future. Once the Jews numbered 900,000 (to the Arabs' 1.2 million), the Arabs, as "realists," would have to negotiate. Yaari expressed cautious hope for Soviet sympathy with Zionism, as shown concretely in the Soviet delegation's support for the Jewish national home resolution at the World Conference of Trade Unions in London. The historic losses suffered by both the Russian people and the Jewish people in the war further encouraged Yaari to believe that, with socialist faith, Jewish-Soviet understanding would be attained. A new world was in the making, Yaari said, in which the thrust was from capitalism to socialism; Zionism must take account of this development. The example set by the Soviets in Eastern Europe, in installing regimes of national communism, or "people's democracies," was attractive to Hashomer Hatza'ir from the beginning.[4]

On 1 May 1945, Aharon Cohen, the party's Arab expert, noted that although in *The Nationalist Question and Marxism* (1913) Stalin ignored the existence of a Jewish nation, that had been a long time ago, and much had changed since.[5] At the same time, it should be made clear to Arab *fellaheen*, workers, and intelligentsia that all separatist nationalist theories failed. "Look at Tito who is building a state for the Slovenes, Serbs, and Croats."[6]

Mapai's call for unity was rejected, since that "party of reformism" could never find a common language with the "militant left forces." Mapai had not undergone the radicalization that other social-democratic parties had experienced through their involvement in anti-Nazi undergrounds. It was, therefore, preferable to try to unify the true left, meaning a union with Le'achdut Ha'avodah.[7]

Hashomer Hatza'ir was deeply vexed by the Arab question. Another of its Arab experts, Eliezer Bauer, bemoaned the "contempt" toward the Arabs in the Yishuv, though applauding the fact that Jews in general deplored racism. There was no "unbridgeable" antagonism between the two peoples. The benefits the Arabs derived from the Zionist enterprise were not the result of deliberate Zionist intention but a byproduct of the enterprise as such. The Arab Articles added to the Biltmore plan were insufficient, since they did not guarantee the Arabs' equality.[8] Hashomer Hatza'ir tried to give publicity to "progressive" Arabs but also condemned their anti-Zionism when this came the fore. It called on Arab communists to recognize Zionism as a progressive liberation movement and not to be dragged after the reactionaries.[9] At the regional political level, Hashomer Hatza'ir espoused economic federalism, on the model of Switzerland, Belgium, pre-1918 Austria-Hungary, or Tito's Yugoslavia. However, the Arab League's boycott of Zionist goods showed that economic cooperation was still a distant dream.[10]

In Hashomer Hatza'ir's analysis, the Jewish Agency was misreading British policy, believing that only the Jewish factor counted, and forgetting the Arab element. It forgot Palmerston's dictum that "Britain had no eternal enemies or eternal friends, only her interests were eternal."[11] Soviet foreign policy, by contrast, was directed by Marxist-dialectic rules of thought. The Ribbentrop-Molotov agreement was justified by the tactics of the British bourgeoisie aimed at provoking war between Germany and Russia.[12]

Despite its Marxism, Hashomer Hatza'ir was enthusiastic when the anti-Marxist, social-democratic Labour Party won the general election in Britain. It anticipated that the new Labour government would be socialist-revolutionary in internal policy and progressive in foreign policy, particularly toward Zionism and the question of Greece. However, Zionist policy must first show support for Jewish-Arab cooperation.[13] In fact, Hashomer Hatza'ir was hopelessly trapped between its Zionist and its Arab policies. The former rested on the general Yishuv consensus on *aliyah*, while the latter assumed that an agreement could be reached on this issue, notwithstanding the Arabs' total rejection of any immigration beyond the White Paper quotas. The rationale was that in the final analysis there was no contradiction, since a binational political regime would automatically eliminate Arab objections to *aliyah*, which in itself was not negotiable, being an integral part of the Jewish people's rights, now reaffirmed by Holocaust martyrology. Much like Ichud and Aliyah Hadashah, Hashomer Hatza'ir saw as its main task the inculcation of ideology into the Zionist movement and the replacement of Biltmore with a more "realistic" program.[14]

The chief ideologue of binationalism in Hashomer Hatza'ir was Mordechai Bentov. His concern was that the Yishuv was falling into a pattern of matching "national egotism for national egotism, hatred for hatred, force for force" vis-à-vis the Arabs. The history of Poland between the world wars was the best proof that even a morally educated nation could deteriorate. Bentov railed against the "Jewish Jesuits" in the Yishuv emulating the Gentiles who had persecuted Jews. Moreover, "Zionism has no rendezvous with history at a certain date. Its historical actuality will not change whether the gates of Palestine will be opened immediately or we are forced to fight for years."[15]

Weizmann, unlike Ben-Gurion, looked for "every outlet to avoid a final battle." Both, however, were ready to accept partition, the difference lying in the method. Yaari sided with Weizmann, but unlike the other moderate groups—Ichud and Aliyah Hadashah, which were also isolated—he was all too aware of Weizmann's "Achilles' heel": he was a leader without a party, without public support. Ben-Gurion had become a "typical" ally of the radical right. Hence, there was no progressive center that could bridge the gap, no cohesive socialist left to rally the masses. Yaari believed that there was potential for Zionist-Soviet friendship. Zionism in the "people's democracies" could not survive without fully identifying itself with the new regime. If this did not succeed, the result would be stoppage of *aliyah*.[16] Hashomer Hatza'ir, however, rejected a plea from the Palestine Communist Party (PKP) to establish a united front because the latter was still vague on the *aliyah* issue. It now favored Jewish immigration to Palestine but to other countries as well. The PKP was between the hammer and the anvil as it wished to unite with its Arab breakaway, the League for National Freedom.[17]

The founding of the United Resistance Movement, with the revolution it heralded in the basic political concept of the Yishuv, caught Hashomer Hatza'ir unprepared. Ya'akov Riftin, its representative on the X Committee (see chapter 4) and committed to secrecy, even denied that there were negotiations with the breakaways.[18] The movement's paper called for a clear line to be drawn between the Haganah and the "terrorist hoodlum groups" and rejected the notion of the "last battle," which was more suited to Massada and the Warsaw Ghetto. Force must not be the primary means, the paper wrote, urging the adoption of Dunkirk and Stalingrad as the desired symbols.[19] In the meantime, Hashomer Hatza'ir was stunned by Bevin's speech of 13 November 1945, in which he declared the continuation of the White Paper limitations on *aliyah*, Ya'akov Hazan calling it "the great treason." The hope that Britain would pursue a socialist foreign policy was now exposed as an illusion; Britain followed a conscious imperialist, anti-Soviet line, from Greece and Java to Palestine. It was a double betrayal: of Zionism and of the labor movement. Hazan emphasized the movement's readiness to accept loss of life in the Yishuv at this grave hour but insisted on linked struggle, not continuous struggle (see chapter 4). He feared that the leadership would lose control of the Resistance Movement. If its actions were not linked to *aliyah* and settlement, the Haganah would end up like the Austrian Schutzbund (hence the incidents of Kfar Giladi and Atlit were morally justified because they were linked to *aliyah*). Yaari, however, could not abide the thought that the United Resistance involved the "fascists" of the IZL and the Stern Gang. His fear was that even Hashomer Hatza'ir would not resist the temptation to change its traditional line and support the breakaways; his nightmare that cells of the terrorist groups might be established in kibbutzim must be seen, in retrospect, as far-fetched.[20]

At the same time Hashomer Hatza'ir, which was a full member of the Histadrut, the Haganah, and the Va'ad Leumi, could not adopt an opposition line and also continue to help make decisions on resistance in these bodies. Such an extreme attitude would sow confusion in the party. The right approach was to fight within the appropriate bodies for a moderate policy—this was the conclusion reached by the Hashomer Hatza'ir Center, led by Yaari. A majority in the movement always supported this middle course, which promised a maximum of linked struggle and a minimum of collaboration with the Jewish terrorist groups. Still, there was a minority in Hashomer Hatza'ir that wanted a tougher policy, going beyond political struggle and the defense of "essential enterprises." Riftin warned his friends that it would be difficult to draw the line between the two methods of struggle, because the movement was obliged in principle to accept Yishuv discipline.[21] But Riftin himself would not have served on the X Committee if Begin (IZL) or Friedman-Yelin (of Lehi) had also been members. The hatred of Hashomer Hatza'ir for the two offshoots of the Revisionism propounded by the "fascist" Jabotinsky was intense. During the entire period of the United Resistance Movement, the party's organ *Mishmar* constantly warned against the "fascist" groups that might win in the ultimate account. But the paper pledged not to resort to collaboration with the police against the IZL and Lehi.[22]

Hashomer Hatza'ir was clearly in a contradictory situation due to its involvement in the Resistance Movement's decision making. Riftin explained that he had cast the minority vote against the Night of the Railways operation because it was not a military necessity but a "political demonstration." Moreover, such an action would blur the difference between the Haganah and the Revisionist terrorist groups and perhaps lead to unity between them, not only coordination. In retrospect, this fear was not far-fetched but was based on the possibility that the dynamics of the struggle might result in a general uprising. Unfortunately, Riftin said, both the Haganah and the rightist organizations had participated in anti-British operations. A minority, led by Hans Rubin (later a Knesset member), suggested that Hashomer Hatza'ir should split from the Haganah, which was in danger of infiltration by the terrorist groups.[23]

By the time the Anglo-American Committee of Inquiry was about to hold hearings in Palestine, the Hashomer Hatza'ir leadership realized that they could no longer delay formal transformation into a political party. According to one activist, there were three reasons for this: a socialist-Zionist revolutionary party was needed in the Yishuv; the fact that Mapai was basically a reformist-centrist party and therefore could not lead the class struggle of the Yishuv workers; and the absence of leftist unity in the Histadrut.[24] One key cause of the disarray on the left was the growing rift between Hashomer Hatza'ir and Le'achdut Ha'avodah (see also chapter 9). As Yaari saw it, after Bevin's declaration of 13 November Hashomer Hatza'ir followed a "Marxist approach" involving "prolonged struggle, crystallization of power, and utilitarian [activity] linked to the [Zionist] enterprise"; whereas Le'achdut Ha'avodah had adopted an "activist-putschist" approach, which wasted forces, gambled everything on the last card, and led inevitably to a "solid wall."[25]

The creation of the Hashomer Hatza'ir Party presented an opportunity for its leaders to assert their Soviet orientation unambiguously, despite recent disappointments in Moscow. More important, however, was the potential Soviet interest in Palestine and the Middle East. Hence the party's demand to internationalize the Palestine problem. "The Soviet Union has abandoned its traditional inimical position toward Zionism," said one senior member at the party's founding conference. "It does not regard Zionism as a whole as an imperialistic instrument." Admittedly, the USSR had not rid itself of all its prejudices toward Zionism. But if the Yishuv sought a more sympathetic approach from Moscow, the road was not Biltmore but binationalism ("the socialist option").[26]

Inexorably, it seemed, the new party developed a growing sympathy for the USSR, even though the Soviet press failed to recognize the "liberating and progressive" character of the Yishuv and Zionism and objected to the Anglo-American Committee of Inquiry.[27] The new party's program, though remaining within the parameters of the British Mandate, hinged its faith on the "forces of tomorrow" (the USSR).

It would fight to win Soviet sympathy for the Jewish liberation movement. It was not a dog-eat-dog world that was emerging but a new era of socialism and all it stood for.[28]

Hashomer Hatza'ir's major effort to demonstrate the practicability of its binationalist plan came in the form of the memorandum submitted unofficially to the Anglo-American Committee of Inquiry (the newly formed party was not permitted—by the Yishuv leadership—to appear before the committee). The document began by emphasizing the party's full acceptance of the Zionist credo on the inevitability of the Jewish people's return to the Land of Israel and their historical connection with their homeland. The authors of the memorandum declared that "our case morally outweighs the Arab case" on various grounds: Jewish misery in the Diaspora; the international character of the Jewish problem and the need for a "reasonable solution"; Jewish skill at reclaiming barren land; and the "great benefits [accruing] to the Arabs as a result of Jewish activities." Without displacing a "single Arab," the country was sufficient for "many millions of Jews," and within twenty to twenty-five years two to three million Jews could be settled on the land. As for the term "Jewish Commonwealth," this was "as much a misnomer as it would be to call Czechoslovakia a Czech State because the Czechs outnumber the Slovaks." Such an "overstatement" was misleading and only alarmed the Arabs.[29] The party was unrealistic, though, when it claimed that "no deep-rooted racial, religious, or national resentment" existed between Arab and Jew (of course, without this starting point binationalsim would be unfeasible). The present situation was defined as a mere "deadlock"; national aspirations and interests were "compatible," cooperation was "achievable."

Five examples were adduced to demonstrate the feasibility of binationalism even if political hegemony and numerical majority were not identical: South Africa, where the Boers did not dominate the British (the blacks were not mentioned); Yugoslavia, with its Serb majority and Croat minority; Great Britain, where the English did not dominate the Scots or the Welsh; Canada, where French- and English-speaking peoples coexisted in harmony; and Belgium, where the same held true for the Walloons and Flemings. Citing an example closer to home, the memorandum pointed out that in Haifa, where Jews were 55 percent of the population, they did not dominate the Arab residents.[30] On political parity, too, the party pointed to the precedents of the United States, Canada, and Australia. Parity in a legislative council was the best guarantee against eventual domination by either side. There was strong reliance on social-economic solutions, such as occupational intermingling of the two communities, in order to safeguard against racial or national agitation.[31] As for the constitutional aspect, the party cited "communal federalism." Examples given were the "communal voting" in India, the "School Panels" in Quebec, and Palestine itself, where the Religious Communities Ordinance was recommended as a model for organizing autonomous community life. However, the party admitted that the time was not yet ripe to implement this.[32]

The memorandum went into considerable detail about the plan's crucial economic foundation. Instead of competitive economies, which might generate "grave political complications," there should be a merger of the two economies with the aim of raising the Arabs' standard of living as quickly as possible. It was estimated that in twenty years' time the Jewish population would be three million, as compared with two million Arabs (in 1946 the figures were 1.2 million Arabs and 600,000 Jews), producing a total income of 210 million Palestine pounds, as compared with 45 million pounds before the war. Cooperation between Jewish and Arab labor would be "the cornerstone of the whole future of both races in Palestine."[33]

British policy, however, was mistaken and echoed Chamberlain's Munich policy. If continued it would result in Balkanization. It could be avoided by teaching, tolerance, cooperation, and mutual respect. This would eventually bring a Greater Middle Eastern Federation, leaving the Arabs always a majority in the region. The choice was between fascist reaction and democratic progress.[34] The party was careful to omit any reference to its Marxist ideology, fearing that this might prejudice the committee against the memorandum. Richard Crossman, for one, failed to be convinced. Immigration of two million more Jews would bring war with the Arab world and the USSR, he concluded.[35]

The Anglo-American Committee's report was disappointing to the party in the sense that it did not hold out the promise of "great Zionism." Still, there were positive elements, such as the recommendation for 100,000 immigration certificates, the repeal of the Land Laws, nondomination of either people, and rejection of partition. A meeting of the party's Center held immediately after the report's publication, noted, however, that the 100,000 were only a small part of the Jewish refugee problem; that the Jewish Agency was not mentioned as the authoritative body to administer immigration, development, and settlement; that no provision was made for international supervision to guarantee peace; and that there was no elaboration of the phases that would bring about democratization in Palestine. Attlee's demand to dismantle the Jews' "private armies" was rejected out of hand. Like Weizmann, however, the party distinguished between the Haganah and the "fascist terrorist groups," hinting at readiness to consider cooperation with the government to fight them.

A major concern of the party was to avoid the danger that the Jewish community would remain a minority after the achievement of political equality. The country should become independent only after a Jewish majority was achieved; Hazan warned that the half-million Jews in the Yishuv could be slaughtered "like the six million in Europe." On the Arab issue the party was covertly divided between A. Cohen, the Arab affairs expert, who was closer to Magnes's numerical equality concept, and Yaari, the influential party leader, who bitterly opposed the Magnes approach. Yaari, unlike Magnes, was always committed to a Jewish majority, while his binationalism was less urgent, referring to the distant future.[36]

Yaari was convinced that East-West tensions would be exacerbated in the period ahead and was unequivocal about the side to which his party belonged. In historical perspective there is no doubt that Yaari, like many other Western fellow travelers, was naïve about Stalin's motives and goals. "The forces of liberation and progress want to ensure that this period of struggle will endure in order to produce reconstruction, building and peace," he told the first meeting of his party's council in May 1946. Yet, while aware of the danger of a third world war, he also thought that capitalist America and socialist Russia could cooperate on the Palestine question. This incongruous collaboration was necessary, Yaari said, because of the "power" represented by five million American Jews. Nevertheless, the key to the implementation of the Hashomer Hatza'ir plan was the USSR. The latter's victory in the global struggle could help resolve both the Arab-Jewish conflict and the process of Jewish concentration in Palestine, instead of Jewish assimilation in the Diaspora. Soviet lack of support for Zionism was due to Biltmore, hence the urgent need to overthrow that plan and fight for binationalism. But how could this be achieved while Hashomer Hatza'ir remained a minority? The way out of this impasse was to strive for a united workers' front—but not by surrendering to Mapai's demands. Le'achdut Ha'avodah was a greater hope but was not yet ready for unity.[37] Neither did the V League for Friendship with USSR live up to the party's expectations; no breakthrough could be discerned in either Arab-Zionist or Soviet-Zionist relations. The Arab boycott on Zionist goods was played down by the party as being more harmful to Arabs than to Jews.[38]

As has been seen, Bevin's speech at Bournemouth, in which he rejected the Anglo-American Committee's recommendations because they would require of Britain another army division and an increased budget for Palestine, brought about a violent reaction by the Resistance Movement in the form of the Night of the Bridges. The view in Hashomer Hatza'ir was that the perpetrators (Palmach) were not terrorists but "honest working people" and "of the same stock that built the glorious pioneering enterprise." But the part of the operation executed by the "fascist groups" was condemned.[39] The events of the Black Sabbath diminished the party's hope that Britain might sponsor a binational state (with a Jewish majority).[40] After the bombing of British military and civil headquarters at the King David Hotel, *Mishmar* demanded the renewal of the *saison* against the IZL.[41]

Hashomer Hatza'ir was not invited to participate in the plenary session of the enlarged Jewish Agency Executive, held in Paris in August 1946.[42] The party continued to oppose partition vehemently, but did it have a realistic alternative plan? After all, was it not advocating a far-off binational state? Morrison-Grady showed the party that a final political solution could no longer be delayed. Hazan said that the party would have to decide between federalization and partition. He himself preferred federalization because "partition means war preparations by the two peoples," and the party's Center voted for federalization, 14 to 7 (5 abstentions).[43]

The new situation required new allies. *Mishmar* said a "broad front" should be established to ensure "the integrity of the country" in the light of the new British challenge. Yet the only candidate was Le'achdut Ha'avodah. It, too, objected to an immediate solution and emphasized not a state but *aliyah*. Between the White Paper and partition enough of a "political vacuum" existed to be filled with temporary solutions, until "a better political opportunity" could be found. This, however, was impossible under the present Jewish Agency Executive. It is clear in retrospect that Aliyah Hadashah, Hashomer Hatza'ir, and Le'achdut Ha'avodah, with all their fundamental differences, could never have functioned harmoniously in an alternative Jewish Agency Executive. In the event, the latter two parties proposed, at a meeting of the Small Zionist Actions Committee, the boycott of the London Conference if its basis were partition.[44] All these parties gravitated toward the consensus forged by Ben-Gurion rather than building an alternative executive.

Yaari's fear that the party might find itself isolated was materializing, although the League of Jewish-Arab Rapprochement and Cooperation could celebrate its first "victory." On 11 November 1946 a memorandum was signed with Fawzi al-Husseini (and four members of Filastin el-Jadida, "New Palestine") on the basis of a vague version of Hashomer Hatza'ir's binational program, doing away with a Jewish majority or even numerical equality. Instead, immigration commensurate with economic absorption capacity was mentioned as the foundation for later agreement. The whole house of cards collapsed with the assassination of Fawzi on 23 November.[45]

On the eve of the 22nd Zionist Congress, in late 1946, the party's leadership was realistic about its prospects: "We cannot come to power either through revolution or by vote." The possibility of a coalition should, therefore, be considered.[46] The events of 1946 led the party to believe that the Zionist movement was on the verge of collapse. It continued to be "in favor of national political independence, but the question is: in what framework, in what circumstances?" Biltmore was seen as a provocation against the Arab world.[47] On the Arab resolution, however, Hashomer Hatza'ir voted in favor of the first article, which promised "complete" equality, but abstained on the second, which ignored the Palestine Arabs' national aspirations.[48]

The most controversial issue, however, was the degree to which the party contributed to Weizmann's fall from power at the congress. On the question of whether to participate in the London Conference the party insisted on putting forward its own resolution. The vote was rather on whether to attend the London Conference, which was tantamount to voting for Weizmann. There was no question of voting for Silver's resolution, which finally won the day by 171 to 154 (only 25 Hashomer Hatza'ir members voted for their movement's resolution). Had it not adopted an ideological line, political and social, the result would have been to reinforce what the party considered the reactionary Biltmore front. To take a tactical line, like Le'achdut Ha'avodah or the Revisionists, which withdrew their separate motions, might have saved Weizmann, but this, according to Riftin, was seen as a "political ploy, not a serious attitude." In any event, party leaders argued afterward, Ben-Gurion, determined to topple Weizmann, would have done it in another vote.[49]

Hashomer Hatza'ir's inability to find an Arab partner did not prevent it from castigating Le'achdut Ha'avodah for its nonsocialist line on the Arab problem and its disregard of the Arabs' socioeconomic and national aspirations.[50] Yaari pointed out that his party had never promised to find Arabs who would accept an immediate binational state, unlike the "partitionists," who had found an influential Egyptian personality who "agreed" to partition. Morrison-Grady was a warning to the Arabs too that they could never expect independence from imperialist Britain, Yaari wrote.[51] Nonetheless, the party's Arab Department, led by the gullible yet enthusiastic A. Cohen, tirelessly tried to find a replacement for Fawzi al-Husseini's tiny group, claiming that "many" Arabs were "our friends." Cohen welcomed any "progressive factor," not necessarily socialist, be he an intellectual or an Arab businessman, who supported an Arab-Jewish agreement. The Indian Congress Movement was progressive, said Cohen, though not socialist, in the sense that it fought for independence from Britain.[52]

The Bevin-Beeley plan of February 1947, followed by Britain's transfer of the Palestine problem to the UN, accelerated within the party an already existing tendency, which had begun with the Morrison-Grady plan, to abandon the British orientation. As for the USSR, it could be enlisted in favor of a Zionist solution in the UN only on two conditions: if it were to participate in an international trusteeship for Palestine, and if Palestine were recognized as a "combined fatherland" for the two peoples.[53] In any event, the period from February to May 1947 was the nadir for the Zionist parties in the Yishuv. Britain announced its withdrawal, albeit without setting a date, while no other power stepped in to fill the breach. Hashomer Hatza'ir was caught between the wish to see Ben-Gurion's eclipse and a wish for possible unity with a reformed Mapai. Otherwise the "fascists-terrorists" would come to power, Riftin said, "exactly" as their precursors had done in Germany. The party was ready to join the Jewish Agency Executive but only on its own conditions.[54] M. Zippor demanded that the party choose between Moscow and Washington in the ongoing international class war: "There is no third way . . . the Hebrew working class sees itself as the natural ally of the socialist forces in the world."[55] Bentov, however, sought a compromise with Mapai between binationalism and a partitioned, independent state.[56]

Soviet support at the UN for the Jewish Agency as the official representative of the Jewish people, support announced less than two weeks before Gromyko's historic declaration, was interpreted as a cautious change in the Soviet attitude: no more enmity toward Zionism. Nonetheless, Bentov explained that it was better to delay a final decision, including binationalism: it was "better that this battle be conducted by a million Jews in the country, rather than by 600,000." The present leadership, he warned, was leading the Yishuv to catastrophe by refusing to compromise.[57] Weizmann should lead the Zionist camp; though not a socialist, he had the stature of Beneš and Gandhi. As a progressive

Zionist and a nineteenth-century-type liberal, he was better than the "democrats" and the "socialist-humanists" of the twentieth century.[58]

Gromyko's speech of 14 May 1947 was dubbed the "Soviet Balfour Declaration" by *Mishmar,* which also, however, emphasized its significance "for the future." This reservation was added due to the mixed feeling generated in the party by Moscow's failure to give unequivocal support to the binationalist solution. Although Gromyko preferred binationalism to partition, he explained that if both sides were to reject binationalism, then partition would be given priority. This was unacceptable to Hashomer Hatza'ir until the UNSCOP Report recommended partition.[59] Yaari reacted to the declaration with some caution. It would not "bring redemption," he wrote to the later peace activist Simcha Flapan, then the party's delegate in London, but it might "prevent our abandonment." Hoping for a thorough change in Zionism, he was confident that in Britain, too, at least the left would not like to leave the initiative in Soviet hands.[60] Nor would the Americans assist the Soviets to expel the British. Nevertheless, Gromyko had given Zionism "a great chance."[61]

Hashomer Hatza'ir as usual did its best to sharpen its Zionist image without neglecting its Marxist ideology. The Palestine Communist Party was accused of distorting Gromyko's declaration. In the past, the PKP had been an obstacle to Soviet recognition of Zionism. Now, according to Hazan, the PKP still saw Palestine as the home of only those Jews who lived there, whereas Gromyko viewed it as the home of the Jewish people at large.[62] *Mishmar* also took issue with Ben-Gurion's new suggestion: to divide the country into two, part as a Jewish state, the rest a mandate territory; this was "fantastic and provocative" while the Arabs were a majority in most of the country. It was worse than partition because it lacked the element of compromise. In effect Ben-Gurion was proposing a Jewish state in the whole of Palestine, a solution rejected by Gromyko.[63]

By the same token, Hashomer Hatza'ir's plans were, in practice, rejected by the Arabs. The party could find no allies other than the (Arab) League for National Freedom, a small Communist breakaway group based in Palestine. If Aharon Cohen, the Arabist most obsessed with the idea of achieving a peaceful solution between Arab and Jew, was still waiting for more progressive Arab partners to appear on the scene, Yaari thought that it was more important to win over the USSR to the idea of an immediate binational state, conditional on Arab agreement to *aliyah.* However, he believed it would take at least three years to turn the present Jewish minority into a majority. Yaari continued to believe that partition was "an imperialist invention." Convinced that the Soviets supported the "Jewish liberation struggle," he imagined that they had not yet formulated their final position and that they could still be influenced. The greatest danger was that the Soviets might favor an ill-conceived partition.[64] Hashomer Hatza'ir therefore launched a campaign to steer the Soviet Union toward acceptance of its binational plan, and the party could not admit that Gromyko's declaration was a shattering blow to its binational program.[65]

The next test was Hashomer Hatza'ir's decision to appear separately before UNSCOP. Yet the party was concerned that this might make them outcasts from the Zionist viewpoint, like the Revisionists, the communists, and Agudat Israel. For the first time it also considered a joint appearance with Le'achdut Ha'avodah on the basis of opposition to partition, the idea of a transition period under international control, and the principle of nondomination. However, Le'achdut Ha'avodah did not accept the concept of the "common [Arab-Jewish] fatherland" or "equal representation," demanding instead a "democratic basis" after a transition period.[66] But Hashomer Hatza'ir could not resist putting forward another memorandum recommending a binational state, this time after an international trusteeship stage.[67] The party was momentarily encouraged by M. Sneh's proposition to guarantee the continuation of *aliyah* on the basis of nonpartition, and to give Arab and Jew equal representation in a temporary government for a transition period in cooperation with the UN.[68] This proved, however, to be the swan song of Hashomer Hatza'ir binationalism.

The dynamics of history had a greater impact on Hashomer Hatza'ir than did its endless controversies with Zionist parties. The publication of the UNSCOP Majority Report shocked Yaari. It was a shattering blow to the party's basic antipartitionist platform. "We shall have to adapt our binational view to concrete reality," he said, "otherwise we will become a wayward sect."[69] However, the party did not consider the report a final verdict. Bevin, some were certain, would do "every thing in his power" to foil it. Also rejected was the British view that the Mandate was unworkable.[70] Yet, in internal Yishuv politics Hashomer Hatza'ir's ideas were considered unworkable. The party was more isolated than ever, Aliyah Hadashah having abandoned the binational idea in favor of partition. Hazan tried to encourage his colleagues. The Soviets had made it clear that they would support the progressive forces, he noted, and they did not demand that the Jewish Agency adopt a pro-Soviet orientation. What was required now was "an orientation on the forces of progress wherever they may be . . . in the United States or in Britain."[71] To some party members, the complicated borders suggested by UNSCOP justified their foreboding. How could a state twenty kilometers wide survive, particularly one that would be divided into three, with an Arab minority of 460,000, surrounded by Arabs? The immigration article was a mere ploy; partition would cause "tremendous trouble" with the Arabs. The inevitable conclusion remained that an agreement with the Arabs was essential, although Eliezer Bauer was concerned that the Arabs might start anti-Jewish riots.[72]

Internally, the UNSCOP Report had the effect of tightening cooperation between Hashomer Hatza'ir and Le'achdut Ha'avodah; the parties were united in their opposition to both the Majority and Minority reports, and it would not be long before they merged to form Mapam. Both reports conflicted with the programs of the two parties: the Majority Report because it recommended partition, and the Minority Report because it granted the Arabs the upper hand in a federal vote. The two radical-left parties put forward their own joint motion to the Greater Zionist Actions Committee (which adopted the majority report by a vote of 51 to 16). They forsook the term *binational* in their motion, which contained fewer objectionable concepts such as "mutual non-domination" and "equality."[73]

Although Hashomer Hatza'ir voted against the UNSCOP Report, this stand did not reflect the party's internal debate, where its leadership was caught between loyalty to ideology and the perception of a rapidly changing reality. It was clear to Ben-Gurion that the evolving situation would force Hashomer Hatza'ir to abandon binationalism; both the implications of the UNSCOP Report and the common line with Le'achdut Ha'avodah pointed in this direction. A clear indication of this trend was Bentov's agreement to serve on the Jewish Agency Advisory Commission at the UN. Although he would still fight for partition only as a transition phase toward a binational state, the party was at a fateful crossroads: one road led to partition, the other to binationalism; perhaps the solution was partition as a corridor to binationalism. Asked by Ben-Gurion whether, if a situation arose in which it would be essential to establish a government, Hashomer Hatza'ir would join, Yaari replied that under labor hegemony—namely together with Le'achdut Ha'avodah—he would join, provided the Revisionists were excluded. Yaari realized that if a Jewish state were established, the party would have to emulate other revolutionary socialist movements: not abandoning stands but clinging to them tenaciously and trying to exert influence wherever possible. Yaari's nightmare was that America would supplant declining Britain and would view Palestine as a second Greece, and that the Arabs would take the opportunity to accept American loans in return for permitting the establishment of military bases on their territory. Promising that his party would fight this possibility, Yaari reaffirmed its alignment with the USSR, which had sustained Zionism morally when it had been betrayed by British social democracy. The party was in deep perplexity following the announcement of Soviet and American support for partition in mid-October, but the direction was toward coming to terms with this fait accompli. Yaari warned his colleagues in the party's Center that the massacres in the Punjab should serve as a lesson for Palestine that a compromise with the Arabs was a necessity, and Hazan was aware that American Jewry was vital to the Yishuv's survival: "Without that force the Jewish people is no more than a gypsy people."

As the final decision by the UN drew nearer, Hashomer Hatza'ir grew increasingly resigned to the idea that an Arab-Jewish war was inevitable. Nevertheless, none of the party's leaders suggested shelving its binational ideology. They called on both sides to avert bloodshed and to agree to international rule. At the same time, Yaari resorted to an apologetic approach in order to cushion the blow of violence and the radical changes that would occur in the party's structure and ideology alike. Drawing on the old "theory of stages" (1927) that had been the basic program of Hashomer Hatza'ir for the last twenty years, in order to emphasize that in the political struggle no miracles should be relied upon, Yaari asserted that "all our efforts must be directed toward the acceleration of the historical process. . . . This way of thought is characteristic of Marxist policy, or, if you like, of Leninist policy." He was already "bored," he said, with repeating for decades the slogan "To be realistic in judging reality, to be radical in implementing the vision."[74] From such a predicament only unity with Le'achdut Ha'avodah could rescue Hashomer Hatza'ir and imbue it with the new aura to which it aspired after reality had shown that its ideology was too dogmatic. In the past, the leadership had always extricated themselves from such dilemmas. Now, though, the whole binational edifice seemed to have collapsed. Immediately after the publication of the UNSCOP Report, the party began holding intensive talks with Le'achdut Ha'avodah, which was confronted with similar survival problems (see following chapter). Both had long suffered from constant dialectical tensions between their respective ideological visions and the political reality, and after the summer of 1947 their positions became untenable. Two days before the historic UN vote on Palestine, the question of unity with Le'achdut Ha'avodah was the sole item on the agenda of the Hashomer Hatza'ir Center.

In the discussion, Yaari argued that the "determining factor" was that the two parties had resolved their disagreement over the method of struggle. Le'achdut Ha'avodah, Yaari explained, had at long last seen that their differences over this issue were exploited by the "reaction in the Yishuv and the Zionist movement and increased the danger of fascism." Consequently, Le'achdut Ha'avodah, and the Palmach, had accepted linked struggle, realizing that Hashomer Hatza'ir's readiness for a violent struggle over *aliyah* and settlement was not just a passing phenomenon. Second, on the Arab issue Le'achdut Ha'avodah understood that the vision of a nonpartitioned Jewish state must be abandoned, because "socialism means guarding the integrity of the country peacefully, not by conquest." Le'achdut Ha'avodah's declared opposition to irredentism permitted Hashomer Hatza'ir to forsake binationalism. Both parties now abandoned their former radicalism: Hashomer Hatza'ir on the question of the political regime and Le'achdut Ha'avodah on the issue of the integrity of Eretz Israel. However, the question of the future regime, beyond the transition period, which would be characterized by "parity," remained unresolved because of Yaari's wish to save binationalism for the distant future. Yaari believed that partition would not last more than a decade. During that period the Arab state would develop thanks to economic unity with material assistance from the Jewish state. Concurrently, political ties would deepen, resulting in unity on an equal federative basis. Third, in order to achieve better understanding, Hashomer Hatza'ir agreed not to "don the mantle of Communism," Yaari said, because it could have committed the new party, Mapam, to a link with Belgrade (the seat of the Cominform) where international decisions obliged every Communist party to obey the international body's decisions. "We see our road to socialism only through Zionism, the ingathering of the exiles, and the concentration of the Jewish people" in its land, Yaari declared. Fourth, he continued, Le'achdut Ha'avodah had come a long way from the time (in 1945) when the movement believed in incorporating the Arabs into the Jewish state. Similarly, they had once believed in George Nassar, an Arab activist of Left Poale Zion prominent in the Arab list affiliated with Mapam in the elections to the First Knesset (a list that failed to enter the parliament). In contrast, now Le'achdut Ha'avodah understood that the country's integrity could be preserved only by agreement. The unity of the two parties would confront the labor movement with the need to choose between "two fateful alternatives: reformism or revolutionary socialism." Because there was no clear statement concerning the existence of the Palestinian Arab nation—the formulation was the one used by Le'achdut Ha'avodah: "the masses of the Arab people living in the country"—Yaari reintroduced the concept of the "common fatherland" to placate those who objected to unity (including M. Garson, E. Bauer, E. Hacohen, and A. Lipsker).

Though Hashomer Hatza'ir did not recommend following the Soviet version of socialism, or that of the Soviet satellites, this road was left open. One member pointed out that October 1917 could not be emulated because "we did not seize power first and then build the *kolkhozy.*" Lenin had also made compromises, as the treaty of Brest-Litovsk demonstrated. E. Prai adduced the Bolshevik model as well, calling for "avant-gardism and not opportunistic adjustment." Unruffled and self-possessed, Yaari calmed the dissenters at the party's historic convention by asserting that "the best guarantee that unites us is our common vision." Certainly, the vote did not reflect any general dissatisfaction; the Center overwhelmingly supported unification, by 23 to 2.[75] Pragmatism led to unity at a time when ideology, lagging behind historical reality, had become irrelevant in both parties. The unwillingness to leave the labor movement solely in the hands of hated Mapai was another unifying element.

9

Le'achdut Ha'avodah Movement

From the Integrity of "Eretz Israel" to Federalism

The ideological politics of Le'achdut Ha'avodah, which were even less coherent than those of Hashomer Hatza'ir, were soon in the same shambles. Le'achdut Ha'avodah split from Mapai in 1944 following that party's decision to ban factionalism; until then known as Faction B, the radical group ran separately for the fourth Elected Assembly in the summer of 1944, winning 10 percent of the vote, compared to 11.6 percent for Hashomer Hatza'ir and Mapai's 35.9 percent. The nature of its radicalism derived from the idea, propounded by its foremost leader, Yitzhak Tabenkin, of combining activism and class struggle. Social radicalism was central in Hakibbutz Hameuchad ideology, and its resistance to Ben-Gurion's pragmatism ("from class to nation") was adopted by Le'achdut Ha'avodah. Its members did not consider themselves mere settlers but the socialist pioneers of the resurgent Jewish nation.[1] This chapter covers only the radical politics of Le'achdut Ha'avodah in foreign and defense policy. Nothing better illustrates its radicalism than the manifesto of 1 May 1945. Its tone is one of pessimistic nationalism. Although victory over Germany was imminent, the party noted that "Nazi bestiality" was still alive and that fascism was rife everywhere. The fascists placed their hope in the "capitalist regime," and the party hoped that the USSR would be instrumental in bringing about the birth of a new world, classless and free of war.

At the same time, the party claimed to be in the vanguard of the "defeated" Jewish people's struggle against the White Paper in order to open the gates of immigration, maintain the Haganah, and strengthen the settlement movement. The party's slogans, calling for political independence characterized by "solidarity and mutual understanding with the laborers of the neighboring people," were not much different from those of Mapai. Hence also the manifesto's call for unity in the working movement. But it was the party's venerated leader, Tabenkin, who summed up the crisis facing the Jewish people, both in the Yishuv and in liberated Europe, as the party saw it. "We are in a situation of either Jewish independence or Treblinka." Fascism in the Middle East, he said, was still alive in the form of the Arab League, which might perpetrate a massacre of the Yishuv, relegating the Jews to the fate of the Armenians, Kurds, and Assyrians. It was up to the Yishuv to draw the military conclusions.[2]

Although Le'achdut Ha'avodah would eventually find itself in an alignment with Hashomer Hatza'ir, this seemed a remote possibility in 1945. The two differed on the political solution. Hashomer Hatza'ir clung stubbornly to binationalism, whereas Le'achdut Ha'avodah advocated the integrity of "Eretz Israel" under international control, which was not exclusively identified with British interests. The founding conference of the UN in San Francisco, however, at which the Arab states were represented but not the Jewish Agency, confirmed the party's feeling that the world body's initiators "are toying with the hope that Hitler has indeed solved the Jewish question for them as well," as Avraham Tarshish put it at the party's convention in May 1945. The moral failure of the Biltmore plan as a political concept was crystal clear. The San Francisco conference was therefore nothing less than "a second edition of a capitalist Munich without Hitler and Mussolini." But it was also seen as an anti-Soviet conference: capitalism versus the working class. Tarshish argued that "the development of capitalism will lead to fascism, the cause of the Jews' annihilation."[3] Moshe Tabenkin took a middle-of-the-road position, maintaining that the party was campaigning both against the primacy of diplomacy, as reflected in Biltmore, and the Revisionist-IZL view that force alone counted.[4]

Apart from the radical right—the Revisionists, IZL, and Lehi—no party in the Yishuv was more pessimistic about continued British support for the policy of a Jewish national home than Le'achdut Ha'avodah. Yet, Aharon Ziesling (later minister of agriculture), for one, did not think that Jewish and British interests were incompatible. For example, the party was not perturbed by the fact that British oil flowed through a pipeline that terminated in Haifa. Moreover, for Jews to blow it up would be to act "against their own people and interests, while the deed itself would be like the fly striking the elephant. But the reaction could be the elephant trampling the living body of the Jewish nation." Like the USSR, the Yishuv too should recruit all its energy and spirit for the coming struggle.[5] Although the party was hopeful that if Labour came to power in Britain Zionism would benefit, it still preferred an international trusteeship, according to Yehuda Gothelf, who saw British "intrigue" everywhere. It was not only imperialism that was at fault but also socialist Zionism, which had not yet found a balanced approach to the Arab issue. Certainly not Hashomer Hatza'ir, which by preaching binationalism "ignored the great Zionist desire for a fatherland." At the same time, "the defeatist approach" that saw the Arabs as "incorrigibly intolerant" and "hostile to us" must be eradicated. Pointing to Muslim solidarity in the USSR, and in China, Gothelf said it would be wise to convince the Arabs "that we do not intend to form another Christian Lebanon."[6]

The dynamics of the party's increasing sovietization was propelled by the USSR's emergence as a significant actor on the postwar world stage, but in the summer of 1945 the party had high hopes for a Labour victory in Britain. Israel Baer, a member of the party's Center and a senior Haganah officer (in the planning department)—and later convicted of spying for the USSR—wondered whether the British Labour Party, if elected, would have the audacity to implement its radical plans such as nationalizing key industries. Baer believed that only by becoming a Marxist party would Labour be able to implement revolutionary concepts.[7] Indeed, when Labour won, Baer expected the newly formed government to make a series of radical policy reversals in the direction of supporting socialist regimes and "progressive" circles.[8] However, his pro-Soviet orientation was not yet the party's official line, which still claimed not to be adverse to Britain's interests and demanded even-handed international "responsibility."[9] With the benefit of hindsight, it is clear that Baer's Marxist views had little impact on Yishuv policy, but in his party his influence could not be ignored. Though he was an extreme pro-Soviet Marxist, his activist interpretation was not rejected by his party colleagues. On the contrary, it imbued Le'achdut Ha'avodah with a special flavor in the eyes of friends and foes alike. Yet many, like Yitzhak Ben-Aharon (later minister of transport) could not see why the left could not unite, as in France and Italy.[10]

The Labour government's decision to continue the White Paper policy conjured up in Le'achdut Ha'avodah the ominous specter of the Yishuv remaining a permanent minority in an Arab-dominated Palestine. It was, therefore, necessary to take a far-reaching decision to sacrifice, if need be, thousands of Jewish lives to prevent that eventuality. But what the party had in mind was nothing like IZL's "revolt." On the contrary, it remained within the Zionist consensus of *aliyah*, settlement, and *ha'apalah*, but in their most activist sense.[11] This was the meaning of Tabenkin's call for a "Jewish Dunkirk." The Yishuv was not going to miss the boat, like the Jews in the ghettos of Warsaw and Vilna. The only solution, he said, was a Jewish majority in the Jewish homeland.[12] This seemed the right time for Baer to propose that his party toe the Soviet line, but his vision of Soviet support for the Yishuv remained wishful thinking until May 1947.[13] Tabenkin called for caution, knowing that the USSR would not go out of its way to spur *aliyah*—no more than it had fought for the Greek Communists. Nor did he urge a seizure of power, because no one could replace the British, certainly not the Arab rulers. But if oil and airfields were vital, then the British, the Americans, and the Soviets should recognize that they could not have their cake and eat it.[14]

This was not empty talk, for the same tone could be detected in Yitzhak Sadeh's comments. Sadeh, now acting head of the Haganah, hours after giving the orders for the sabotaging of the railways, underlined the Labour government's failure to support liberation movements.[15] Bevin's speech of 13 November added fuel to the fire, though Tabenkin claimed that he was not taken by surprise. He was shocked, though, by the fact that Bevin, who was of proletarian descent, was doing a "service to capitalism." The Yishuv would now have to fight a war for survival, but without identifying either with "anti-British or anti-Soviet [interests]."[16] Looking through a Marxist prism, Baer saw the Jewish-British clash as part of the universal anti-imperialist socialist struggle. Ireland would not be content with home rule, nor India with provincial autonomy. Citing his personal experience, Baer said that the hesitation of the Austrian workers' movement to shed blood in fighting fascism cost it dearly later on. He aroused opposition in the Yishuv, and in his party, when he quoted Marx, in connection with the uprising of the Paris Commune: "There are moments when a war of despair is required, without a chance, in order to educate the masses and prepare them for the next campaign."[17] Baer's influence in Le'achdut Ha'avodah should be neither exaggerated nor ignored. He was counterbalanced by Israel Idelson (later minister of transport and the interior) and Aharon Ziesling. Both were considered responsible leaders whose base was in the Kibbutz Hameuchad movement and who found a common language even with F. Rosenblueth, though not necessarily advocating his Gandhist methods. With all its militancy, the party wished to reflect an image of restraint, to be seen as a body that obeyed national decisions. Both Baer and Idelson stated unequivocally that their party did not question the authority of the Jewish Agency

Executive, in contrast to the IZL and Lehi.[18] The party followed not Baer but rather Tabenkin's more skeptical line on the USSR, which did, however, allow Moscow a share in the search for a Palestine solution.[19] In its political ideology the party emphasized the Yishuv struggle as such, without taking sides in the East-West conflict. Baer's repeated objections to the idea of allowing Britain to establish strategic bases in the Yishuv, which would prevent a Soviet pro-Zionist shift, were not taken seriously before the declarations of Gromyko and Tsarapkin (see chapter 2).[20]

But while rejecting Baer's Marxist-inspired parallels, the party also dissociated itself from those who believed that the "period of crystallization of power" was still under way. That period was perceived to have ended and been superseded by a "period of testing power." Examples of such testing were the arrival of 200 illegal immigrants, the passive resistance in Hefer Valley, and, far more impressive, the Night of the Railways.[21] With this attitude and the constant evocation of images like Treblinka and the Warsaw Ghetto, it is little wonder that Le'achdut Ha'avodah placed no trust in the Anglo-American Committee of Inquiry.[22]

Overall, as befitted its radical orientation, the party's perception was that the committee, and particularly the American representatives, wanted to "annihilate" the Yishuv, either by its own means or through Arab "reactionary forces" equipped with British tanks and guns. In such dire political straits, a Soviet policy shift could be very useful, speakers at the Le'achdut Ha'avodah council meeting said. It was noted that the USSR had recently allowed Jewish immigration from Eastern Europe and that Soviet delegates to the World Conference of Trade Unions in London (which had approved the Jewish national home formulation) had encouraged the movement, even if this was not yet formal recognition of political Zionism. At the same time, the party displayed a siege mentality. The view was that total mobilization was needed to meet a total emergency. The 120 days granted to the Anglo-American Committee represented the time available for the "elimination and extermination" of the Holocaust survivors, who would have to spend the winter in camps after six years of hunger and hard labor under the Nazis, Idelson stated. Not the Jewish Agency's case for a Jewish state but the fate of the DPs should have been the top priority.[23]

With all its militancy, the movement did not feel secure about its independence as a political party, preferring unity. Hence the new argument that the main labor parties differed only in their conception of political timing : Mapai wanted a state even before a Jewish majority was achieved, while Hashomer Hatza'ir believed that it was essential to have a Jewish majority before taking the irrevocable step of establishing a state and deciding on a political regime. But Le'achdut Ha'avodah had to be satisfied with unity on a small scale: with the tiny Left Poale Zion, an old Marxist breakaway from the classic Poale Zion, which in 1944 ran together with Hashomer Hatza'ir for the Elected Assembly.[24]

Le'achdut Ha'avodah's mistrust of the Anglo-American Committee seemed to be vindicated when Prime Minister Attlee rejected the pro-Zionist recommendations, making their implementation conditional on the disarming of the Jewish private armies.[25] Attlee's declaration triggered, as we have seen, more large-scale activism (the Night of the Bridges), as Sadeh intimated publicly.[26] The Black Sabbath seemed to confirm the party's worst fears. And when it accepted the decision to disband the United Resistance Movement and thus terminate its anti-British activities, it did so reluctantly, obeying Yishuv discipline, and not because it accepted Ben-Gurion's strategy. Sadeh, the Haganah's senior military commander, drew "strategic" conclusions far different from Ben-Gurion's. Fully accepting Baer's line, he pointed out that anti-Soviet military bases in the "reactionary" Arab states were vital for Britain. "We must find our allies among those who are against war with the Soviet Union, in Britain, in the Arab states, among the progressive forces in the world," Sadeh said.[27] Thus the Arab League's Bludan conference (June 1946), which was seen by Ben-Gurion as a signal that the Arabs were intent on war, was viewed by Le'achdut Ha'avodah as one more case of British intrigue against the USSR.[28]

Even though it wanted to keep up the anti-British struggle, the party did not endorse the bombing of the King David Hotel, an event it called "the Jerusalem horror." The incident had been morally, politically, and operationally wrong-headed, an unsigned editorial in its *Bulletin* asserted.[29] Baer sought to distinguish between "constructive compromises which *bring it closer* to the final goal, and negative compromises which are nothing but *defeats*." Citing the examples of the Indian and, especially, the Irish (1916) national movements, Baer argued that a resistance movement taking a defensive line had lost even before it began to act. No less important was coordination between military and political tactics. In particular he warned against the assumption that force merely brandished but never used could deter the enemy, as exemplified disastrously in the social democracies of Germany and Austria.[30] Sadeh, who could only endorse such views, reflected popular expectations and thinking not only in Le'achdut Ha'avodah but also in the

Haganah and the Palmach.[31] In the military organizations, and especially in the Palmach, led by Yigal Allon, resentment against Ben-Gurion's consent to disband the United Resistance Movement reached new heights. One day before Ben-Gurion threw to the bewildered Yishuv the slogan "Neither Massada nor Vichy," Sadeh launched a broadside of unprecedented ferocity against the authority of the Yishuv. Three times during the summer and autumn of 1946, Sadeh threatened not to obey the leadership if it refused to continue the struggle. Ben-Gurion, at the beginning of Israel's War of Independence, remembered Sadeh's defiance and refused to appoint him to a key military command. In 1946 he was able to take Sadeh's refusal to obey the political leadership as no more than a rhetorical nuisance.[32] Having no real rivals, thanks to the stable coalition with the General Zionists and the Mizrachi, Mapai was not much impressed by this kind of defiance but at the same time could not ignore it altogether. Sadeh's influence on the youth could not be exaggerated, but Ben-Gurion's charismatic leadership papered it over. Moreover, Mapai knew that Le'achdut Ha'avodah was weak and that one day it would have to unite with another party. Ultimately, this contemptuous attitude cost Mapai dearly, because Mapam constituted a great nuisance to it between 1948 and 1954.

By August 1946, the enlarged Jewish Agency Executive met in Paris and agreed on partition, thus widening the gap between the agency amd Le'achdut Ha'avodah, which was not even invited to the session because it did not belong to the Yishuv coalition. The growing American Zionist influence (through Goldmann's mission) added fuel to the fire and Baer expressed an increasing mistrust of an imperialist America that was preparing for a war against the Soviet Union.[33]

Le'achdut Ha'avodah subscribed to a radical worldview fed by a sense of the imminent "national catastrophe" of the liquidation of the Yishuv. Because the party was not represented on the national decision-making body, the Jewish Agency Executive, and therefore did not take into account pragmatic considerations—such as British reactions, or the limits of the Yishuv's strength, or the potential Arab threat—it was inclined to speak in a hysterical tone, although in the final analysis it accepted Ben-Gurion's national decisions.[34] But what was the party's alternative to the Jewish Agency's policy? Idelson offered a threefold program consisting of incessant struggle, an antipartition stand, and continued settlement. Others, though, were fearful that the party's official line, international control, would turn Palestine under the UN into an arena of international conflicts. In fact, the party refused to elaborate on the substance of the country's political regime. It was adamant, though, on the need for a plan of struggle. The party needed to play a vanguard role, which the IZL did by default. "It seems to me that we are in a situation in which no institution may prohibit us from doing something," claimed Idelson, though "in the arms sphere we must not be independent initiators," as was the IZL. Yet "if, God forbid! the Yishuv should disappoint, we, too, might yield to despondency and turn to special, separate frameworks." Nahum Nir (Rafalkes), formerly of Left Poale Zion (and later a Knesset Speaker) scoffed that if the party's program were to be based on Idelson's three elements, then "we might as well unite with the IZL."[35]

The general feeling in the party was that its organization was loose and its ideology blurred, and that its link with the public was tenuous. Above all, there was disappointment over the recent lack of resistance, especially in connection with *ha'apalah*. In such a state of affairs, the Yishuv was in danger of becoming a new Diaspora, not a spiritual center. Still, Berl Repetur said, it was Mapai that was guilty of "betrayal," not Le'achdut Ha'avodah, which still argued for the integrity of the land.[36] Baer wanted to imbue the party with a clearer leftist image in both internal and external policy. Partition, he said, would serve only anti-Soviet British imperialism. It was the story of the Jewish renegades during Second Temple times all over again, or the Irish tragedy, where Britain had succeeded in splitting the liberation movement, bringing civil war.[37] Despite Baer's efforts, the party, though in despair of both Britain and America, continued to advocate an international trusteeship.[38] Baer's analysis and terminology were accepted but not his conclusions. He also embodied the party's frustration with Ben-Gurion, who was seen to be leading the Yishuv to "suicide and destruction."[39]

The party's platform for the elections to the 22nd Zionist Congress concentrated solely on the anti-British struggle. On international issues it remained vague but did mention the British "conspiracy to turn the country into an anti-Soviet military base" and demanded not only international control but international guarantees as well. On the Arab question, the usual distinction was drawn between the feudal monarchs who collaborated with the "White Paper government" and a possible alliance with the "Arab masses, the workers, and the *fellaheen*" to work together for economic development. Partition was ruled out, and *aliyah* and settlement were urged throughout the country, even if this turned the call for a "Jewish-Arab alliance" into a hollow slogan.[40]

The Soviet Union's suggestion, in November 1946, to refer the Palestine issue to the UN, its advocacy of an international trusteeship, and its criticism of British conduct in Palestine aroused new hope in the party.[41] Baer could not conceive that Britain would evacuate Palestine due to Cold War calculations; Haifa was the only alternative regional naval base to Alexandria.[42] And his Marxist dogmatism led him to ignore entirely Bevin's historic announcement of transferring the Palestine problem to the UN. Socialist revolutionary "consciousness" indicated that no "real and continuous" cooperation was possible between the Zionist "progressive liberation movement" and "exploitative and repressive imperialism" such as that of the British.[43]

Though the party's leadership urged the Elected Assembly of the Yishuv to congratulate Gromyko on his declaration, its dogmatism stood in the way of any programmatic change. The line of international guarantees and control was pursued, despite the intensifying Cold War. It was not Le'achdut Ha'avodah but Aliyah Hadashah that called on the Va'ad Leumi to see Gromyko's speech as a "turning point."[44] Baer, naturally, agreed with this assessment. In view of the fact that he was exposed as a Soviet spy in the early 1960s, it is unclear whether his comments were inspired by his Soviet handlers: would Mapai take up the challenge, fighting together with the Arabs against the British, or would it follow the line of collaborating with the global "reformist social democracy" against the Soviet Union?[45]

Haim Drabkin, a member of the party's Center, countered Marxist ideology within the party by stressing that it was the *national* consciousness of Arabs that was the real cause of their opposition to *aliyah*. He suggested "a federation of two independent republics," though with a central government and one parliament. Independence should not be granted immediately because the Jewish state would then have only a small area, insufficient to absorb immigration by settlement.[46] Drabkin's new formulation reflected the party's attempt to come to terms with Gromyko's declaration, while trying also to influence UNSCOP. Moshe Erem (later a Knesset member) pleaded that Gromyko "was speaking about a biunified [sic] state and not a binational state like that intended by Hashomer Hatza'ir. He [Gromyko] in practice spoke of creating a federal state, which will grant political independence to the two peoples and will not necessitate partition."[47]

Paradoxically, it was UNSCOP's Majority Report that led Hashomer Hatza'ir and Le'achdut Ha'avodah to submit a joint resolution to the Greater Zionist Actions Committee against partition and in favor of establishing "a regime on the basis of mutual nondomination and equality between the Jewish people who have returned to its land and the Arab people living there." Hashomer Hatza'ir forsook binationalism, while Le'achdut Ha'avodah yielded on the "Jewish socialist state."[48] At long last the party accepted Baer's doctrine that "partition in the existing conditions, and a Jewish state against the present international background will be no more than a Morrison-Grady ghetto or another version of the anti-Soviet Transjordan." In other words, the party should not think that the UNSCOP Majority Report was a feasible plan because the world was already irrevocably divided between East and West, and the partitioned Jewish state was destined to be anti-Soviet. Baer's conception was that a Jewish state could be achieved only through a war against imperialism and that only a socialist state could reach an accommodation with the Arabs.[49]

Tsarapkin's declaration in favor of partition generated great pro-Soviet sympathy in the party, particularly because the Soviet representative to the UN had emphasized the special significance of the economic unity principle. At long last the Soviet Union shelved its support for the hated binationalism. The party thought wrongly that partition was bound to evaporate, and that it could implement its plan to open the gates for mass immigration and transfer power to an international body, with the USSR's participation.[50] The changing international circumstances, in which partition was suddenly seen as the only feasible solution, especially after Tsarapkin's declaration, once more brought Hashomer Hatza'ir and Le'achdut Ha'avodah together. Though in public the leaders pretended that their political ideologies remained valid, in fact they lay in ruins. Hence the readiness of both leaderships to press ahead with unity talks. Tabenkin saw the basis for a merger first in the agreement of both parties to the liquidation of the Diaspora by *aliyah*, second in opposition to partition, and third in the importance of unification in the appeal to the communist world.[51]

The meeting of the party's Center held on 30 October 1947 was a turning point in its history. To begin with, understanding was expressed for Hashomer Hatza'ir's fears that a tiny, chauvinistic Jewish state would bring about a thrust toward chauvinistic expansionism among the country's young people. A unified party would create a "political, ideological and educational dam against such a danger," according to Ben-Aharon. Second, in view of the Soviet policy shift, the possibility now emerged for the USSR to find a genuine ally in the form of a large communist-Zionist revolutionary party, which, Ben-Aharon said, would "uphold the ties and bonds with the world Communist movement and the USSR." Nevertheless, he told his colleagues, Hashomer Hatza'ir would ultimately make unity conditional on Le'achdut Ha'avodah's stand on the Arab question. For them, he said, this was an issue of "conscience," the "touchstone" of their political worldview. The two parties were still ideologically apart on the basic question of whether the Arabs should get parity in the government, as Hashomer Hatza'ir urged, or merely national equality as a minority. This ideological bone of contention caused Le'achdut Ha'avodah to suggest unity on the basis of a declaration rather than a program. Baer pointed out that both the idea of a "socialist Jewish state" and the idea of binationalism were vague concepts. Socialist states, he said, had solved the problem of more than one nationality either by granting political equality or by the transfer of the problematic national minority, like the Germans in Poland or Czechoslovakia.

Another obstacle was Hashomer Hatza'ir's opposition to the linked struggle. D. Livshitz (later a member of Knesset) argued that both parties were ripe for unity because their ambitions and dreams had failed, and they had been unable to form a true political force. One speaker likened the two parties to "two camps returning from the battlefield tired and broken." The only opponent of unity was Benny Maharshak, the Palmach's "politruk" (political commissar in charge of communist education and supervisor of loyalty to the regime in the Red Army), who disparaged Hashomer Hatza'ir as a party that never risked anything. It lacked the "ardor to implement things in a brutal way that characterizes our party."[52]

The two parties finally signed a tentative ideological program just as the War of Independence began—an accord that facilitated unity. The two rigid formulations of a binational state and a socialist Jewish state disappeared forever. Instead, a compromise on the crucial question was reached through a much watered-down formula: "Cooperation, mutual aid and equal national and political rights without domination and oppression, between the returning Jewish people and the masses of the Arab people living in the country." But the new party also promised to struggle for the integrity of the land "on the basis of agreement, or international decision." On external affairs it considered itself a partner in the "historical task" of eliminating capitalism, and as "part of the revolutionary workers' movement in its war against manifestations of fascism, racism and anti-Semitism, [and] for stemming the rising reactionary forces and the domination of capitalist-imperialist forces that endanger world peace." The Soviet Union was hailed as "the great socialist construction enterprise that advances the working man, liberates peoples, promotes peace, and implements the historic goals of the October Revolution." The party committed itself to seek "a solid alliance with all the carriers of progress and peace in the UN, and peaceful relations and mutual aid with the Arab states." The Jewish state should be a "people's democracy" allied with the Eastern bloc.[53]

Despite this, Ben-Gurion invited the new party, Mapam (United Workers' Party), to join the provisional government. This was neither surprising nor contradictory, notwithstanding Ben-Gurion's commitment to neutrality, since the USSR was the only great power that actively—militarily and diplomatically—supported the nascent Jewish state. In the case of Mapam, *Innenpolitik* and *Aussenpolitik* converged in the service of Ben-Gurion's conception just as the War of Independence erupted. By the same token, the convergence would fall apart as soon as the war ended.

10

Mapam and the War of Independence

Test Case for an Ideological Party

The outbreak of war in Palestine between Jews and Arabs acted as the final catalyst for the unity of Hashomer Hatza'ir and Le'achdut Ha'avodah. (The former won 12.3 percent of the Yishuv vote in the elections to the Zionist Congress in October 1946, the latter 12.4 percent, but the overall world Zionist vote reduced this to 8.6 for each. In the First Knesset elections the new joint party, Mapam, won 14.7 percent of the popular vote.) As mentioned, the UNSCOP Report dealt a severe blow to both and drove them into each other's political arms at a time of national crisis. The papering over of the ideological differences, which for three years had caused such fierce interparty debate, was the easiest part of the unity argument. The very fact that partition was not implemented peacefully was itself "proof" that an anti-partitionist policy was viable; the war demonstrated that neither Arab nor Jew accepted partition. Such dialectics enabled Mapam to salvage its two-pronged ideology advocating "persistent striving to re-establish the integrity of the country in a constructive way and [to bring about] agreement between the two peoples." But Mapam now had to face reality, in view of the possibility that it might participate in the government. The party feared that Ben-Gurion might prefer a coalition with the right wing, as he had in the Jewish Agency Executive, and Hazan, speaking at the conference that formally united the two parties, argued that one could not simultaneously conduct a "reactionary" internal policy and a "progressive external policy." The main task before the new party was to stand against the "adventurist conquest plans of the Revisionists and the terrorist irredenta groups." However, he was well aware, he said, that everything depended on Mapai. With the Arab-Jewish war already having been raging for nearly two months, Hazan thought it was important to explain that the concept of "heroism" was legitimized by the Marxist left, too, as had been proved by the heroism of the Paris Commune, the Schutzbund in Vienna, and the Spanish Civil War; and Bolshevism harked back to the heroism of Narodnaya Volya and the battleship *Potiemkin* (1905), as much as the image of the Jewish laborer was shaped by the Hashomer defense organization (in the Yishuv before World War I). Moreover, the promise of equal rights to the Arab minority in the Jewish state was not a confession of failure but rather to emphasize the fact that two peoples inhabited the country.[1]

Ideologically, Mapam had no difficulty justifying the Jewish point of view in the war. It was a war of the progressive Yishuv against a "feudal" and "reactionary" leadership operating under cover of British imperialism. But military victory as such was not enough, Meir Yaari told the conference. It was essential as well "to prevent the dominance of imperialism from without and the reaction from within." The latter was perceived as an imminent threat by Mapam in view of the readiness of Yishuv bourgeois circles (such as the owner-publisher of *Ha'aretz*) to grant the breakaways both pardon and legitimacy despite their "unforgivable" split. Yaari, too, saw the danger for Mapam in a possible coalition between Mapai and the bourgeois circles. Despite the intensifying war, Yaari continued to pin his hopes on an Arab-Jewish agreement. Mapam, he said, must be ready to do its part to promote "revolutionary socialism" among the Arab people. As far as the new party was concerned, Yaari admitted that both sides had been forced to compromise, and this inevitably produced disappointments, but what would count, ultimately, was a radical approach and consistency between theory and practice. He was worried that Mapai might follow Léon Blum and Ernest Bevin, who were "subjugated to the dollar," by allying itself with the rightist General Zionists.[2] Tabenkin, in his speech, showed his different background by viewing the problem in socioeconomic terms rather than as a political issue requiring a national solution, which was Yaari's argument. Nothing was said about the need to restore the integrity of the country for the sake of both peoples' national aspirations. Indeed, the Arab question would be the main bone of contention between the two parties when Mapam disintegrated in 1954.[3]

The surprise of the conference was Dr. Moshe Sneh, who joined the new party upon its founding, having resigned only a month earlier, on

21 December 1947, from the Jewish Agency Executive (where he had chaired the illegal immigration department) to protest the stoppage of *ha'apalah* under Anglo-American pressure. Sneh's move from the General Zionists to a pro-Soviet stance is still an unsolved riddle. Undoubtedly, though, it was a gradual process, which began in early 1945, when he refused to view Palestine as a military base. However, it was only after Britain's "treachery" in the form of the Black Sabbath and the Morrison-Grady plan that he broke completely with the Mandate power. Ben-Gurion's refusal to continue the Resistance Movement led him to resign from the Haganah Command (21 September 1946). As yet, though, he had not demonstrated in public a pro-Soviet stand. Even after the Gromyko declaration he was silent (in secret he tried to convince his colleagues in Ha'oved Hatsioni that "salvation" could be achieved only by the Soviet Union), though he did offer a plan for a five-year regime with a council of three Jews, three Arabs, and three UN representatives, under which a million Jews would arrive.[4] A third world war would be nothing less than a "new Treblinka" for the remaining eleven million Jews in the world, including "comfortable" American Jewry. The bastion of the socialist progressive and democratic forces was the USSR, he said. On the Arab issue, Sneh accepted the mixture of Hashomer Hatza'ir and Le'achdut Ha'avodah terminology, referring to a two-states solution promising to turn "economic unity into genuine unity." This, again, depended on choosing the right side in the world confrontation: not "oppressive imperialism" but the "alliance of free peoples liberating themselves from a common foreign yoke."[5]

Another theme at the conference was concern—expressed particularly by the Hashomer Hatza'ir wing—over the "fascist underground" in the Yishuv, in which some elements would be tempted to seize power by "a putsch in the new, weak, and inexperienced state."[6] Mapam, no less than Mapai, was keen to prove that a linkage between *Innenpolitik* and *Aussenpolitik*—in this case, socialist domination internally linked to a Soviet orientation—was vital for national survival.

Initial uncertainty and naïveté as to the kind of war the Yishuv ought to wage gave way to greater realism, following hesitations over the Haganah's methods. Bentov reminded Mapam's political committee that if the Jews failed to agree on a joint program they would not have a majority, since the Arabs constituted 40 percent of the country's population.[7] Livshitz and Sneh believed that a closer association with the Soviet Union would strengthen the Yishuv against the Arabs, while

Yaari and Tabenkin were against foreign intervention, though taking American money was not ruled out. Mapam's official line was not to close any options.[8]

Nor was Sneh enthusiastic about Mapam's joining a Ben-Gurion government. The party, he said, "will be only a fig-leaf." Yaari took the opposite approach, claiming that he had always advocated constructive opposition, like Weimar's leftist parties. His recommendation was unequivocal: "To enter [the government] bravely, not to run away." Similarly, M. Erem scoffed at Sneh's apocalyptic pessimism, and Ziesling too was in favor of participation in the government "until the explosion." The general trend was to assume responsibility because of the grave situation but also because it was imperative to rescue the Palmach, which Ben-Gurion suspected was Mapam's private army. By a 54 to 9 vote the party's Center decided to accept an invitation to join a "progressive" government.[9] Another significant reason to become part of the government was to prevent a possible Revisionist/IZL-Lehi putsch.[10]

Washington's retreat from partition and advocacy of a trusteeship plan in its stead threw Mapam into turmoil. The move was seen as a vindication of the party's basic theory of an international capitalist-imperialist conspiracy against both the USSR and the embryonic Jewish state. The only alternative was to continue *ha'apalah* and settlement on a large scale. Idelson regretted that his party had accepted partition; Ziesling was no less despondent and alarmed that America was about to break the Yishuv. A united workers' front with Mapai was the new panacea. Yaari, as usual, did his best to boost the party's morale, but his optimism was not enough to ease the bitter atmosphere.[11] With the Zionist backlash generated by the American retreat from partition to trusteeship, the prevailing opinion in Mapam was that it would be best to join Ben-Gurion's government and to fight inside for the party's line of trying to get Soviet aid, both diplomatic and economic. With partition virtually a dead letter due to the Communist coup in Prague— which escalated East-West tensions and thus threatened the common front of the two blocs in favor of partition—the only option was to continue the struggle for a state politically and militarily.[12]

This was the propitious moment for those who opposed Yaari's cautious line on a Soviet orientation. Riftin, who on 30 April 1950 would publicly urge Mapam to turn officially Communist, jumped at the opportunity presented by America's change of heart. America, Riftin said, realized that even though the Yishuv was not Marxist, its majority did not wish to be enslaved to imperialism either. Palestine was a link in the imperialist chain of aggression, together with China, Greece, Italy, and Czechoslovakia. The Zionist movement's "social-democratic" leadership had clearly deluded itself as to America's true character. Externally the Yishuv was fighting an "internationale of fascist gangs," according to Riftin, and could only await a Soviet victory: "We shall always direct our historic road according to the northern star, the star of the revolution."

The anti-Western hysteria mounted. Erem unhesitatingly compared George Marshall, the American secretary of state, to Hitler. Sneh declared that the Washington-London Axis was attacking Jews not only in Palestine but also in Britain and Brooklyn. American Jewry must organize against the "psychosis" of anti-Communism. The day the United States retreated from the partition resolution, Jewish equality of rights in America had collapsed. The internal front was equally ominous because of the danger of a possible General Zionist and Mizrachi-IZL agreement. In Riftin's view, a "fascist" putsch was an inevitable element of the emerging Jewish state.[13]

The Deir Yasin massacre was proof, to Mapam, of the breakaway groups' "fascism" and "degenerate" character.[14] At the same time, Mapam disclosed its line on Arab "evacuation" (or "flight"). This was not seen as a moral issue, though the party admitted that many Arabs were "peace lovers"—but they were also seen as "delegates of imperialism." In any event, it denied that any Jewish body had raised, even as "wishful thinking," the idea of an Arab expulsion from the area of the Jewish state. The direct "evacuation" carried out by the Haganah, wrote A. Benshalom, was "minimal" in relation to the Arabs' "headlong" flight. Militarily, the refugees constituted a "great reserve army for our enemies." The issue could become a "poisonous propaganda card" in the hands of Zionism's foes. James Forrestal, the American secretary of defense, was accused of conspiring to arrange an Arab "transfer" in order to reduce Jewish territory.[15] In fact, what perturbed Mapam at this stage was the impact that the IZL's attempt to occupy Jaffa would have on Arab "flight." The urgency felt by Mapam to establish a workers' task force to block a "fascist" attempt at a coup was very real. This was linked to Mapam's failure to muster enough support to outvote the right-wing parties in the Greater Zionist Actions Committee over the agreement between the Haganah and IZL. By a 39 to 32 majority, the latter was allowed to preserve its units' independence in the Haganah. A frightened Nir said that "the entire bourgeoisie, Mizrachi and Hapoel Hamizrachi are at this moment IZL." But 200 Mapam members could have broken the IZL in Tel Aviv, its stronghold, he added.[16]

Mapam's discussions on the Arab refugee question should be considered against the background of the war of survival. At the same time, nothing was more damaging to Mapam's moral code than the fact that the Haganah was involved in what one member called a "carnival of threats," which befitted the IZL. The touchstone was Arab flight. The reckoning was bitter: "Surely the Arabs [had they won] would have dealt with us much worse," said Y. Gelfat, but he readily admitted that this was no argument.[17] A week after the establishment of the state, a gravely anxious Aharon Cohen initiated a discussion on the subject, admonishing his colleagues that the Arabs faced a "human catastrophe" with 400,000 refugees. It was a political issue, too, with ramifications for internal calm and for the fate of Oriental Jewry. Yaari, much disturbed, said that this question would decide the fate of the socialist parties in Israel; a sympathetic attitude toward the USSR could not offset the treatment of the Arabs. Leib Levité, warning about the moral dimension of the problem, asserted that irresponsible acts such as looting must be punished, even by death.[18]

Mapam's Center was shocked by the scale of the Arab tragedy. Hazan, likening the Israeli sweep to a "steamroller" such as not even the Russians, Poles, or Germans had ever driven, declared that "one cannot build a policy on what they would have done to us." It should be "enough to shoot one soldier in order to put a stop" to such incidents, which were "poisonous to our life" and could engender "fascism of the worst kind." Tabenkin did not, however, regard the transfer of Germans by the Czechs and Poles as a "Communist sin." Hazan urged that the Arab worker be treated like his Jewish counterpart, lest a South Africa–like situation be created. L. Cantor, though, said out loud what many were thinking: that Communist Arabs also hated Jews. It was not fascism to uproot an Arab from his village, he explained, citing the Russians' uprooting of the German republic on the Volga. Yaari's "melancholic" rebuttal was that Mapam's program was unsatisfactory on the Arab issue due to the conflicting legacies of its two constituent parties.[19] Mapam considered Arab flight more a moral than a political problem. The party officially condemned their "expulsion" (the term *uprooting* was abandoned) and urged them to stay.

Many in the party, and particularly Sneh, were more concerned about Anglo-American "intrigues" aimed at consolidating two blocs: Western Europe and the Muslim Middle East.[20] Bernadotte's UN-sponsored mediation efforts sharpened Mapam's perspective on the East-West conflict. Sneh complained that Bernadotte's union plan would turn Israel into a Luxembourg within Benelux. The mediator's endeavors reminded him of Lord Runciman's mission to Czechoslovakia on the eve of the Munich Conference of 1938, albeit with three differences: no one could ignore Israel; Israel was winning militarily; and Israel would be assisted by the Soviet Union. Fearful that Israel might be isolated, he lamented that an official representative had been sent to Washington but none to Moscow. Sneh, unaware that Soviet aid had been arriving since April, accused the Israeli leadership of rejecting offers of military aid from Eastern Europe.[21] On 20 May Hazan and Ben-Aharon had begged Ben-Gurion to appeal to the Eastern bloc for assistance, only to find out that he had "no scruples" about doing so and did not need "an alibi vis-à-vis the other powers." Mapam did not know that since January, Ehud Avriel had signed several arms deals with the Czechs. Mapam in fact was largely in the dark about the ultrasensitive arms purchases being negotiated by Ben-Gurion and other Mapai ministers, carefully steering between the two great powers.

Mapam's ineffectuality in the government on Arab and international problems was certainly due in part to the fact that it had only two cabinet ministers out of thirteen. Its political weakness also enabled Ben-Gurion to remove Israel Galili as Haganah commander (3 May) as part of a larger move to keep the actual running of the war in his own hands. At the same time he gradually divested the Palmach of its independent (mostly Mapam) command. Riftin demanded a public campaign to force Ben-Gurion to resign. In the same meeting of the party's Political Committee, Israel Baer blamed Ben-Gurion for the "dilettantish" command of the battle at Latrun, in which the Haganah forces had been defeated by the Arab Legion on 25–26 May. The war, he claimed, was being managed not by GHQ but by "Ben-Gurion's inspirations." Y. Gothelf praised Ben-Gurion and Yaari called for a more balanced perspective: "I do not want to blame Ben-Gurion for every Israeli defeat," he said.[22]

Ben-Gurion's high-handed conduct in the *Altalena* affair, however, delighted Mapam, as it seemed to be the prelude to IZL's disintegration. Mapam's stand, that the special IZL battalions should have been dismantled before, was vindicated. The episode was perceived as the beginning of the struggle for power in Israel, marked by the escalation of the class war (Begin being seen as the protector of the bourgeoisie). Yet, Ben-Gurion had also categorized the Palmach as a private army, and Tabenkin feared that he wanted to foment an armed clash between

Mapam and IZL. Ben-Gurion might punish Mapam for supporting a private army as he had the IZL (by closing down its newspaper). Yaari, aware that the prime minister was commander in chief, opposed calls for his resignation. Mapam's leader feared that his party would be blamed by Ben-Gurion for planning a "political revolt" while the war with the Arabs was going on. He resisted the pressure against Ben-Gurion, and instead the party agreed to call for the formation of a war cabinet.[23]

Mapam now turned back to ideology as a more effective means of influence.[24] Following its revolutionary path, it sought a united front with the Communist Party, rather than an alliance, though Nir warned the Political Committee that the Cominform "did not recognize Zionism" or the right of Jewish immigration, although it did recognize Israel. Mapam, he concluded, would not be able to "digest" the Palestine Communist Party. It would be a subversive element within the party.[25] Sneh, for his part, expressed optimism about cooperation with the people's democracies on *aliyah*.[26]

Yaari, in any event, consistently lauded the Soviet example, likening the Palmach to the Red Army but adding Bar Kochba to the equation in order to maintain a Marxist-Zionist balance. But he knew very well that Mapam's credibility as a leftist party would suffer if the all-important element of the "peoples' fraternity" were belittled. Such an approach—and specifically the party's attitude toward the refugee question—was irreconcilable with its self-image as an anti-imperialist socialist party. Yaari rejected the prevailing notion that the refugees had not been expelled but had fled of their own will and was appalled at talk of wiping out the Palestine Arabs. Anti-imperialism and racial enmity could not coexist, he warned, and moreover the "clever people" who advocated such methods forgot that when it came to the Jews, the world would watch their every move under a magnifying glass. The Americans would not transfer Jewish DPs from Europe only to find "another headache" in the form of hundreds of thousands of Arab refugees. Those who in peacetime advocated "peoples' fraternity" could not, "without lying to themselves," educate for "peoples' hatred" in wartime. "A communist may not be a chauvinist in wartime. A revolutionary in peacetime is not expected to behave like the IZL in wartime."[27]

Similarly, Mapam strongly rejected the public talk about an "exchange of populations" between the Palestinian Arabs and Jews from the Arab states, not only on humane grounds but also for Zionist reasons. First, this would "inevitably" mean the contraction of the 29 November borders; second, it would bury any hope of reintegrating the country; and finally, a transfer of Arabs would mean "persistent, fanatical and vengeful irredentism on Israel's borders. . . . The hope for peace would evaporate. Israel would have to survive as a heavily armed state."[28]

Mapam's public criticism of government policy on such a wide range of issues raised a basic problem: Was the party in the coalition or was it part of the opposition? To be sure, the government had not been established on the basis of a commonly agreed program. Sneh, though, complained that there was an inner coalition within the government from which Mapam was excluded. This group shared an unambiguous Western orientation (and also supported Abdullah). Against this policy of "imperialistic enslavement" Sneh recommended, expectedly, the strengthening of links with the USSR and its satellites. Israel, he said, was developing along the same lines as Western Europe, where the coalitions consisted of bourgeois-religious-socialist-reformist parties, interested only in aid from the "enormously rich Uncle Sam." Another syndrome was the coalition's efforts to create a military force modeled on the British Army, not a "people's army" like the Palmach.[29]

Nonetheless, reality overrode ideology, even in Mapam. Hazan warned that "our dream will either be realized or given a dishonorable burial." It was a choice between dispossession of the Palestine Arabs or development for the benefit of the two peoples. "Everything must be done," he told the Political Committee, to make the government take full responsibility for the development of both the Arab and Jewish sectors. Yaari concurred but stated that Mapam would not be held responsible for "acts of uprooting." Nir, however, like others from Le'achdut Ha'avodah–Poale Zion, was not in principle against transfer. Tabenkin suggested a double standard: to declare that Mapam was against "uprooting" but at the same time to settle the recently occupied Arab village with Jews—otherwise "our survival is at risk."[30] In the Greater Zionist Actions Committee, Hazan demonstrated Mapam's equivocation between its belief in "peoples' fraternity" and the imperatives of the war. Part of the Arabs' flight, he said, had been instigated by Jews, and the matter was far more serious than Shertok pretended. At the same time, he absolved the Israeli government of responsibility for the Arab flight, citing instead British "intrigue," Arab fear of Jewish retaliation, the Mufti's opposition to Arab-Jewish coexistence, and the Deir Yasin massacre, which had panicked the Arabs. Riftin said the government still had the option either to leave the Arab refugees as a "factor of revenge, seeking a war to the death," or employ them as a factor for peace.[31]

Not only did Mapam present an unclear solution on the Arab issue; it was also torn between two loyalties, Zionism and Soviet-style socialism, thus eroding its public standing (Rákosi, the Hungarian prime minister, asked Mordechai Oren when Israel would become an American colony). The party concluded, after heated debate, that it could not appear on a joint list for the forthcoming Knesset elections with the (Arab) Communist League for National Freedom, but given the party's stand on the Arab issue, it was also necessary to find Arabs willing to appear on its list. Mapam linked the Arab refugee issue with the problem of the Jewish DPs. Mapam's favored solution was not partition; the sole solution seemed to be the establishment of an independent Arab state free of foreign bases. The party vaguely hoped for some form of federal solution.[32]

Mapam's participation in the government continued to be extremely problematic. Ben-Gurion and Shertok were (wrongly) suspected of accepting the Bernadotte plan, at least in part. Mapam mistrusted Ben-Gurion because he was perceived to be leading the country into the arms of Begin, as Léon Blum was leading France into the grasp of De Gaulle. The tendency in the party to let Ben-Gurion run the war as he wished was condemned by Bauer and other former Le'achdut Ha'avodah members (like Maharshak, who thought Mapam was not "Bolshevik" enough on the Arab issue), who expressed no sympathy for Arab suffering as long as their friends were being killed in the fighting. Yaari regretted that the Arabs of Ramleh were not treated like the Arabs of Nazareth but would not retreat from what he had learned from Borochov, the greatest Zionist-Marxist theorist: that Zionism should always be given primacy over communism: "Better a coalition with Hapoel Hamizrachi on *aliyah* than a coalition with non-Zionists [i.e., Maki, the Israeli Communist Party]."[33]

Nonetheless, Mapam made it clear, on the thirty-first anniversary of the October Revolution, that it stood unequivocally with the USSR in its fight against the "incitement" of the imperialists toward a third world war. By condemning the "treacherous reformist socialism" of Bevin, Blum, the Italian socialist leader Giuseppe Saragat, and the German socialist leader Kurt Schumacher, Mapam made its position quite clear. Though it failed to create a united front with Maki or the (Arab) League for National Freedom, it tried earnestly to project an image of itself as Israel's true communist party.[34]

Mapam's relationship with Mapai was severely aggravated by the dismantling of the Palmach. The act was done, Mapam believed, in collusion with the right-wing parties, including the Revisionists. Mapai, then, had emerged as a "typical" social-democratic party.[35] Thus, isolated in the Israeli labor movement, caught between Mapai and Maki, Mapam prepared for Israel's first general election. Inevitably, the first item on the party's agenda was the painful transfer question. Yet, this issue was of most concern to former Hashomer Hatza'ir members, who still advocated the idea of "peoples' fraternity" (a phrase which was part of the logo of *Al Hamishmar*, the party's daily). Prai summed up the party's attitude after a bitter discussion in the Political Committee. He condemned the recent "fashion" to support transfer among Israeli public opinion, Mapai's right wing included. Only one transfer had been justified, Prai argued: that of the Germans from Czechoslovakia and Poland—but that was punishment for Nazi crimes. Transfer within the USSR had been implemented only against "remnants" of peoples. Prai argued that the Palestine Arabs are not an "isolated tribe" and were bound to return even if their livelihood had been destroyed, much as the Jews returned to their homes. There would be no choice but to accept them, due to "the threefold pressure of the refugees themselves, of the Arab states, and of world opinion." Prai warned: "Even if we conquer the whole of Eretz Israel, we won't be able to keep it. . . . We will find ourselves in a vicious circle." Invoking the model of Poland's prewar experience with its minorities, he declared: "We are in a much more difficult situation. . . . But no difficulty justifies expulsion of Arabs."[36]

The party's leadership fervently wanted Mapam to appear in the elections as a harmonious body. Mapai was the party of instincts, advocating "expulsion and uprooting" of the Arab population, while Mapam must present itself openly as the upholder of the "peoples' fraternity." Following the Arab question, the two key issues were immigration and the party's "connection" with the USSR.[37] However, the different legacies of the two parties comprising Mapam did not allow for the articulation of a crystallized program. For example, Ziesling, formerly of Le'achdut Ha'avodah, suggested the adoption of land laws linked to development under the auspices of the Jewish National Fund. This notion made little provision for returning Arab refugees. Hazan and Yaari, the leaders of Hashomer Hatza'ir, were afraid that Jewish settlement would cause "uprooting." A partial solution, however, could be Arab urbanization.[38]

While the Arab refugee problem had a centrifugal effect in Mapam, the principle of the "integrity" of the Land of Israel, long since accepted by both sides, acted as a centripetal force. Moreover, the first and foremost article in the party's program was Zionism itself, as Sneh claimed, which in his view could be realized only through an independent state free of Anglo-American imperialism. Israel should be a "people's democracy" with sweeping nationalization, although where land was concerned, only desolate areas should be nationalized. An American loan, though "enslaving" in nature, should not be rejected because Jewish-American private investments would soon be made in Israel. As for the future regime, Sneh knew that a socialist government was an unrealistic goal given that Mapai was a reformist party, apart from the fact that it might prefer the right wing, not Mapam, in the coalition. Yaari, however, was apprehensive that Mapam's wish to restore the "integrity of the country" would entail the "uprooting" of the Arabs from Nablus and elsewhere. On the other hand, Mapam could not confront Mapai without also presenting a full Zionist conception, as Maharshak explained. To support an independent Arab state now, he claimed, would be to make the Mufti its head.[39] Sneh, who not long before had been a hardliner on the Arab issue, was now prepared, like the rest of Mapam, to contemplate an independent Arab state (neither he nor anyone else said anything about borders). But, with the benefit of hindsight, this was no more realistic than Hashomer Hatza'ir's old binational plan. Both were to be regarded as long-range plans, although the former soon collapsed in view of Abdullah's annexation of the West Bank.

Sneh continued to regard identification with the USSR, rather than the Arab question, as the touchstone issue. He had already hailed Stalin's interpretation of proletarian democracy over bourgeois democracy. Now he attacked the newly proposed constitution for Israel, drafted by Dr. L. Kohn, a Foreign Ministry official, as a "bourgeois" document, unsuitable for a proletarian democracy. Stalin's USSR Constitution (1936) was Sneh's preferred example.[40] Nor was Sneh alone in Mapam's slow but steady advance toward the USSR. E. Hacohen, too, after dismissing Plato's and Hegel's idealization of the state, strongly recommended Marx as the sole guide for the state ideal. The public must choose between Mapam's class-war ideology and Mapai's reformist anticlass war.[41] At a more practical level, Mapam had to decide whether to include Arabs on its list of candidates for the Knesset or to create a separate, affiliated list. Bauer and Cohen preferred a joint list, though not Yaari, and the party decided in the latter's favor. Mapam's Arab Department came up with a list called the "Arab Popular Bloc" (headed by George Nassar, the former

Left Poale Zion member—who allegedly spoke fluent Yiddish!); it accused Mapai (which had created two affiliated Arab lists) of being largely responsible for the Arabs' problems in Israel.[42]

One day before the elections, Yaari said he suspected that Ben-Gurion's aim was to keep Mapam far from the decision-making center and to favor the right wing. This was no surprise, he observed, because reformist socialism had always rejected the revolutionary left since the Weimar era, leading to Hitler's rise to power. Mapai's linkage politics system was clear: an alliance with Arab "reactionary" regimes, a Western orientation, and an internal regime with "bourgeois-clerical reactionaries."[43]

Mapam ran well behind Mapai in the elections, which were held on 25 January 1949. Still, it emerged as the second largest party in the Knesset (64,018 votes, or 14.7 percent, and nineteen MKs, soon becoming twenty when the Hebrew Communists leader, E. Preminger, who was elected on Maki's list, defected to Mapam). Although not a victory, it was an "achievement," Yaari said, taking consolation from the results of the armed forces voting, where Mapam won 60 percent. Still, the party's disappointment at the results could not be concealed. It had expected to win at least quarter of the votes, as it had in the Zionist Congress of 1946.[44] Ben-Gurion initiated coalition negotiations with Mapam on the day that the armistice agreement with Egypt was signed. Mapam was skeptical about the prospects. Sneh, for one, believed that Mapai was in collusion with the United States and that the "Marshallization" of the Middle East would subjugate the regional markets to American capital, not to mention the strategic consideration of making the region a linchpin in the West's policy of encirclement against the USSR.[45] Accordingly, Mapam perceived Egyptian rule in the Gaza Strip, stipulated in the armistice agreement, as part of a deliberate plan to turn Gaza into an American base. Generally speaking, the alleged plan to establish a Middle Eastern "annex to NATO" caused great anxiety in the party. Such a fundamental conflict of opinion, *Al Hamishmar* noted, all but ruled out successful negotiations between Mapai and Mapam for a coalition based on the workers' majority.[46]

Mapam encountered an "unfriendly and bad-tempered" Ben-Gurion on their first visit to him. Mapam insisted on retaining the two portfolios it had held in the provisional government (labor and construction, and agriculture) and demanded a third as well; Ben-Gurion said that both labor and defense would go to Mapai. Mapam took umbrage at being offered "second-class" portfolios like housing and health. The feeling was that Ben-Gurion had presented the party with "humiliating conditions,"[47] having repeatedly emphasized its poor showing in the elections.

Mapam decided that it must keep the agriculture portfolio and try to obtain the Interior Ministry (instead of the labor portfolio) as well as a third portfolio. Mapai rejected Mapam's demand for appointments in the Foreign Ministry. Hazan took a staunch stand against entering the government: to do so under these conditions would "degrade our value in the public eye." Ben-Gurion gave priority to an agreement with the religious parties, but socialism could not be implemented with Rabbi Fishman, Hazan said. In general, the party feared that by entering the government, it would diminish its own ideological value. Yaari however was for joining the coalition, explaining: "Better to leave the government over a crucial political issue than not to enter it at all." Former Le'achdut Ha'avodah members, such as Y. Bankuver, less concerned about ideology, were in favor of joining, because in government, they said, the party could at least irritate Mapai: "In this period of struggle and building we must be in the government." Nevertheless, the Political Committee decided by a 14-7 vote (six abstentions) not to enter the government under Ben-Gurion's conditions. The matter now went to the Mapam Council for a final decision.

Underlying the debate on whether to enter the government was a lack of confidence stemming from what was perceived as the party's insufficient ideological cohesion. An ideological party like Mapam, even if unity with Le'achdut Ha'avodah had weakened its internal coherence, could not give up its "positions of principle" or its freedom of speech, and it must have cabinet representation commensurate with its electoral weight, argued Riftin. On all these conditions, the council was told, Ben-Gurion's reply was unsatisfactory. A handful of members warned that if the party remained out of government, it would be isolated and weakened. A battle of historical importance could be fought only inside the government. Besides, it was not "fitting" to sit with Begin in opposition. Sneh, though, argued that before entering the government, Mapam must build a stronger party. The lopsided vote by the council against joining (150 to 33) reflected the feeling that Ben-Gurion had insulted Mapam by offering it disadvantageous terms.[48] Caught, again, between its ideological commitment and its operative political potential, Mapam typically decided not to sacrifice the former on the altar of governmental responsibility.[49]

Still, Mapam was probably better able to deal with its dilemma between Zionism and communism while in the opposition. A case in point was the intensifying anti-Zionism in the people's democracies. A.

Lipsker warned that it was an illusion to believe that a Zionist movement could exist in those countries, especially from the *aliyah* viewpoint. The communist parties considered Mapam a "disloyal ally," he said. Yet, Mapam had all along tried to persuade Ben-Gurion to co-opt Maki to the government in order to obtain legitimation in the eyes of the Cominform, after failing to create a united front with Maki. According to Lipsker, the fundamental Zionist principle of "the ingathering of the exiles" was the stumbling block between Mapam and the Cominform. Hazan was less enthusiastic about the link to communism: "We have ties with both [East and West]," he said. Only 7 percent of the world's Jews lived in Israel, and the other 93 percent "are not necessarily linked with communism." The country's hope lay with the West, Hazan declared, adding that a "united front with Maki will not help us" and urging "the same attitude toward Zionism as toward socialism."[50]

In fact, whether Mapam would ever have joined the government is a moot point in the light of its objections to the armistice agreements that were signed with the Arab states, Jordan in particular. Already during the period of the provisional government, Mapam was divided on the armistice agreements: Bentov was in favor, Ziesling against. Although Ben-Gurion insisted that the agreements were not political or territorial in nature, but purely military accords, Mapam announced that it would not give up the chance to restore the "integrity of the country" by means of an alliance with a "democratic" Arab state. In practice, this was only ideological lip service. Abdullah, though, would "squeeze" more concessions. Similarly, Mapam later opposed the armistice agreements with Egypt and Syria: both were imperialist tools, and a date for a peace treaty should have been fixed.[51] As for the domestic "Arab problem," Mapam pondered whether it should become a Jewish-Arab party or maintain a separate Arab affiliate. The debate was not only ideological but also had practical implications. Few thought that the Arab worker would have an interest in *aliyah;* but Riftin said that Mapam could never be a socialist party if Arabs were excluded. It was decided, by consensus, to establish an Arab "section" in Mapam.[52]

The debate did not, however, die down. Hazan was not disturbed by Arab members who might oppose free immigration, since there were Jewish members who opposed it too. Members of the Le'achdut Ha'avodah faction were naturally more sensitive than those from Hashomer Hatza'ir. The former could not see themselves debating with Arab members "on the foundations of Zionism."[53] Indeed, the party's senior Arab member, R. Bastuni (later a Knesset member) took offense at the very thought of a separate Arab party: "Does Mapam wish to use the Arabs only as a means to achieve a certain goal?" he wondered at a meeting of a party forum. "Are we only a means for propaganda and publicity?" Warning that keeping Israel's Arabs as second-class citizens might ignite the "first spark which would kindle a great fire in all Middle Eastern countries," Bastuni called for "unity in blood." If the gate to full equality should remain closed for the Israeli Arabs, "it will be taken to mean that the party treats us like the British treat the African natives."[54]

Mapam's obsessive fear of a third world war, deriving from its belief that 1949 evoked the "electrifying" atmosphere of 1939, hardly made it a candidate for an outwardly neutral, potentially pro-Western, Israeli government (which Sneh suspected was about to join NATO). This time the danger was perceived to be even greater, Erem detecting an Anglo-German attempt to reorganize the Arab states for a new attack (a "second round") against Israel. It was no coincidence, said an *Al Hamishmar* editorial, that the Arabs had not signed full-fledged peace treaties with Israel.[55] Yigal Allon, still in active command, recommended privately to Ben-Gurion that Israel should conquer the West Bank in order to obtain strategic "depth," in view of the danger that the British might at some future date renew their efforts to "break" Israel. Moreover, the Arab states were building up their armies. But for now, Allon said, the Israeli army was stronger, and "between one session of the Security Council and the next" could reach the Jordan River. As to the argument that the West Bank was heavily populated by Arabs, Allon replied that most of them, especially the refugees, would "retreat" eastward, while the rest would "probably" find a respectable livelihood. In any event, Allon reasoned, it would be best if they were under Israeli control rather than under foreign rule, where they were a source for military recruitment. If this idea were not accepted by Ben-Gurion, Allon said, he should insist that Abdullah fulfill his promise of a partial retreat immediately.[56]

The eve of the First of May 1949 was a time of reckoning for Mapam. May Day was an opportunity to state publicly that the party unambiguously stood by the USSR. George Marshall, the American Secretary of State, would have to cope with Marx, M. Zippor wrote: "We are living at a time when the forces of production sharply contradict the proprietary relations in the capitalist society. The socialist revolution, which is the social revolution in our day, is sweeping the world from Shanghai to Leipzig . . . Our fate, the fate of the Jewish people and of the State of Israel, is linked, for good or ill, with the fate of the great camp struggling for peace, progress and revolution."[57] Mapam's decision to become part of the opposition was not enough to eliminate the conflicting legacies of its factions. Hashomer Hatza'ir took a more revolutionary stand on the Arab question and on the communization and sovietization of the party, while Le'achdut Ha'avodah always lagged behind on these issues. Not surprisingly, already in 1949 there was growing talk of a split along the former lines.[58] Another five years, marked by disappointments on both the Arab and Soviet fronts, were needed, however, before the two camps concluded that their basic contradictions outweighed their shared attitudes. On the other hand, in the dichotomy between Zionism and communism the former won out, but at the price of a split between personalities such as Riftin and Sneh and Yaari and Hazan. Mapam learned through trial and error that it had to choose between implementation of the Zionist and the communist utopia. The two were incompatible.

Overall, both camps could rejoin the government only in 1955 after their final split, and more especially after complete disillusion set in with the Eastern bloc, as a result of the Prague show trials and Mordechai Oren's conviction by the Communist authorities (1952). Mapam in fact failed to offer a socialist alternative to Mapai, but by this very failure it saved its Zionist soul.

IV

The Radical Right

11

The Revisionist Party

A Zionist Sinn Fein?

The Revisionist Party was established in the mid-1920s by Z. Jabotinsky as a result of personal differences with the Zionist leadership headed by Weizmann. All his life Jabotinsky searched for a coherent political-social theory, without success. Undoubtedly, he saw himself as a right-wing leader and ideologue, but his social theory fluctuated from the corporative regime of Italian fascism, J. Popper-Lynkeus's version of the welfare state, the biblical idea of the Jubilee, and Lord Birkenhead's utopia. Though ending up with the idea of a *minimalstaat* (i.e., minimal interference of the state authorities in the life of the individual), Jabotinsky also accepted in his party a self-confessed fascist, Abba Achimeir, who was allowed to stay in the party despite his pro-Nazi tendencies (until April 1933).[1]

A man of paradoxes, Jabotinsky, though a romantic rebel who admired Garibaldi, was surprisingly more pro-British than Weizmann, since he believed that the Balfour Declaration was a moral and judicial treaty between the Jewish people and Britain. Though considering Zionism a national liberation movement, he thought it could be implemented only with Britain's assistance. Very much a dictator in his own party, he led it out of both the Histadrut Federation of Labor (creating his own trade union organization) and the World Zionist Organization (1935), but he failed to form a coherent new organization other than the fiasco of the New Zionist Organization (NZO). Above all, what left him so vividly alive in the collective memory of his party as a charismatic leader was his missed opportunity (1931) to gain the leadership of the WZO, thus leaving the whole movement fixated on an envisioned

seizure of power and constantly harking back to his supposed prophetic qualities as a statesman. His relatively early death at the age of
sixty (1940), and his followers' failure to find a successor, brought the
party to total paralysis. Only the anti-British revolt led by Menachem
Begin (1944) gave the movement a new lease on life, though it also
posed an ideological-operative challenge to Jabotinsky's legacy of a
legal organization. The fact that in his last three years the venerated
leader had also been the IZL's chief commander created confusion in
the party (and in the Betar youth movement, which though legal was
also a recruitment source for the IZL). Begin, who first was Betar commissioner in Palestine, and from late 1943 IZL commander, resolved
the problem by adopting the image of the militant Jabotinsky.

But the story that follows is one of failure, of a rearguard struggle
between the declining Revisionist movement and the rising IZL over
the interpretation of Jabotinsky's credo. In the founding father's view,
the IZL was only a tool in the political struggle. Jabotinsky himself
unequivocally rejected any idea of revolt, which he thought was contradictory to his pro-British ideology and politics. However, he was
unable to control the IZL from his exile in London (he was not permitted to enter Palestine after leaving in 1929 because the British government thought he was enflaming Arab-Jewish relations). From 1940, the
Revisionist leadership tried to establish its control over the IZL, but
with little success. The dead leader left his followers confused as to the
correct operative meaning of his political method: Did he espouse a
fighting liberation movement, in the style of Garibaldi, or a political
movement on the model of Cavour (the Piedmont statesman who unified Italy by diplomatic means)? While Begin initiated a limited revolt
against the British administration, the legal party, the NZO, continued
to believe in Jabotinsky's ideal of the Seventh Dominion, propagated
by Josiah (later Baron) Wedgwood since 1928. Neither international
control, demanded by the left, nor a transition period toward a state,
as advocated by the Jewish Agency, appealed to the NZO. Its leadership could not understand how, in the aftermath of the Holocaust,
"twenty-eight years after the Balfour Declaration, the Eretz Israel affair is a problem between the two parts of the population living in the
country rather than an issue of the remaining eleven million Jews. . . .
We demand the *immediate* foundation of Eretz Israel as a *Jewish state*,
which will join the *British Commonwealth* as an independent dominion." This was the NZO's answer to the Jewish Agency's Biltmore plan,
which was perceived as a calamitous failure.[2] The difference between
the two was that the NZO demanded both sides of the Jordan River,

while the Jewish Agency referred to the west side only. Both, though, relied heavily on the active support of the great powers.

At the end of World War II, the NZO saw no need to go beyond Jabotinsky. Moreover, notwithstanding Begin's contempt for the party, which had rejected his revolt in 1944, the NZO refused to dissociate itself from the IZL. Thus, Achimeir, Begin's chief political mentor, officially remained in the legal party but was a covert IZL sympathizer. Achimeir, having failed to turn the Revisionist party into a fascist movement because of Jabotinsky's realization that there was no alternative to Britain, now concentrated his campaign against communism and social democracy (he did not distinguish much between the two). His main enemy, however, was Jewish socialism, in the form of Mapai, which in 1933 accused him of assassinating Chaim Arlosoroff, the head of the Jewish Agency's Political Department. Socialism endangered Judaism's very existence, according to Achimeir, certainly that of Zionism, while Bolshevism's opposition to Zionism resembled the bitter antagonism to Judaism of Catholicism, Byzantine Orthodoxy, and early Islam.[3] In the 1945 British elections Achimeir supported Churchill, who symbolized the leadership of the "forces that aspire to rescue Western civilization, which is based on private initiative and freedom of the individual from the danger of etatism." He accused the Jewish Agency of running an ideological foreign policy, neglecting the Conservatives in favor of Labour.[4]

Although the NZO was aware of its lack of influence on current events since its departure from the World Zionist Organization, the fact that Weizmann continued to head the WZO engendered tremendous opposition in the NZO against a return to the fold. Weizmann embodied ideological objection to a Jewish state and preference for a gradualist policy. "He is the *symbol* of our defeat and our helplessness and disbelief. He is our Achilles' heel," said *Hamashkif*. Jabotinsky's opposition to his "faltering" leadership was a constant theme; Weizmann was seen as being the very reverse of Jabotinsky's "political activism."[5]

When its disappointment with Britain became clear, after the Labour government announced its policy of continuing the White Paper, all the party could do was to blame Weizmann, whose gradualist policy of "another dunam and another tree . . . was largely responsible for the Jewish disaster in Europe and for our humiliating position in Palestine."[6] The remedy was immediate resignation of the appeaser Weizmann and the establishment of a supreme committee, comprising all sectors of the nation (including the NZO), to direct the Yishuv's struggle in place of the Jewish Agency Executive. Weizmann's resignation would enable the people's vital unity.[7]

Reprinting Jabotinsky's most rebellious articles was the NZO's answer to the general despair it perceived in the Yishuv. None of them called for a united resistance movement, since Jabotinsky (in the 1930s) did not contemplate an anti-British revolt.[8] The *ha'apalah* (illegal immigration) movement was seen by some as an "immoral" act on the part of a leadership not ready to fight for a Jewish state. The NZO's fear was that the Jewish Agency might end up with philanthropic Zionism, not state Zionism.[9] The actions undertaken to acquire power, the raison d'être of the Jewish Agency Executive's policy, were held in contempt by the NZO, which considered them too limited and trivial.[10]

Still, the NZO believed that the actions of the United Resistance Movement were an affirmation of its own policy. A rewriting of history was unavoidable now that the Jewish Agency itself had joined the general struggle. The NZO also ignored the fact that it was the IZL and Lehi that joined the organized Yishuv (accepting strictures on the character of their operations), not vice versa. It is difficult to establish, because of the absence of records of internal discussions, whether the differences between the NZO and the IZL finally disappeared, but they were certainly much diminished. The Jewish Agency's cooperation with the IZL and Lehi led the NZO to believe that the time had come to reshuffle the Yishuv and Zionist movement coalitions. Jabotinsky was invoked, of course, to justify such an audacious step. Since this involved the need to do away with old class conflicts, Y. Bader, a member of the NZO Center and Begin's confidant (and later a member of Knesset), noted that Jabotinsky had always preached the priority of national interests over class interests. He also demanded that the class-war policy of the Yishuv's left wing be shelved.[11] But Bader's optimism was rejected by another NZO leader, Y. Shofman (later a member of Knesset), who argued that the true divide between the NZO and the left was not socialism but the latter's policy of "political compromise." Jósef Pilsudski's socialist party was an example to be emulated, since it gave priority to national liberation over international socialism.[12] A coalition with Mapai was anathema to Achimeir, who, though broken after his imprisonment in the 1930s, still wielded considerable ideological influence in the party and on the IZL. He likened Mapai's "totalitarian" rule in the Yishuv to that of the Bolsheviks. An implacable foe of socialism, he did not conceal his *Schadenfreude* that the two socialists, Bevin and Ben-Gurion, had failed to find a "common language."[13] But overall, the NZO leadership's disappointment was great indeed when they realized that the Jewish Agency did not intend to follow up the agreement with the IZL by entering into an agreement with the NZO as well.

Nor did the NZO welcome the Anglo-American Committee of Inquiry, which Bader saw as a "delaying tactic."[14] The NZO was the only political body to boycott the committee. The organization's leader, Dr. Arye Altman (later a member of Knesset), asserted that giving evidence to the committee was tantamount to surrender, yet he still felt that some attempt should be made to reach an agreement with Britain on the founding of a Jewish state. A world Jewish referendum for a Jewish state was the NZO's panacea in 1945, following Jabotinsky's demand for a state two decades earlier.[15] American participation on the committee was distrusted because Truman's policy was misunderstood by the NZO. Both the U.S. Congress and the administration were seen to be too concerned with Arab susceptibilities and the NZO believed that Zionism and Arabism were incompatible. The most Truman might offer would be moral aid.[16] However, unlike Lehi, its most radical offshoot, the NZO, despite its political despair, was never tempted, in the mounting Cold War, to use the USSR even as a tactical card against Britain. Staunchly anticommunist, the NZO was convinced that the USSR was bound to start a new world war, which might cause the annihilation of another third of the Jewish people.[17]

All in all, no party was more isolated in the Yishuv than the NZO, as it had split from the WZO a decade earlier and then proven itself a sterile opposition. One of its leading ideologues cited three reasons to justify its return to the WZO: first, pressure exerted by soldiers affiliated with the NZO who were serving in the Jewish Brigade and other units; second, the conviction of the Revisionist and Betar members among the Holocaust survivors that this was the right step, including agreeing to a unified Histadrut; and third, Jabotinsky's death, which left the NZO leaderless.[18] In January 1946 the NZO decided to hold an internal referendum on whether to return to the official Zionist fold. The opposition claimed that the reasons for the split a decade earlier were still valid. Weizmann and his cronies, answered those who favored return, should not be permitted to style themselves the sole representatives of the Jewish people's aspirations.[19] The supporters of return cited the new world order; the extermination of East European Jewry, the NZO's main electoral hinterland between the wars; the legitimacy given "now" by the "old" Zionist organization to the "full evacuation" of the Jewish people from Europe to Palestine; and last but not least, the return being tantamount to the reawakening of "Zionist *shechinah* [holy spirit]" against the "defeatists" (namely Weiz-mann).[20]

Achimeir's uncompromising objection to a return could be easily anticipated. This most radical of NZO activists accused the WZO and the Jewish Agency of responsibility for everything from the Holocaust (responsibility shared, in this case, with the democratic world) to the class divisions within the Jewish people. As the debate in the NZO became more heated, he abused the official leadership, Weizmann in particular, as "Vichyites" and "traitors."[21] Yosef Klausner, later the Revisionist/Herut candidate for the presidency of Israel, was in favor of taking the "risk" entailed in rejoining the "old" organization because of the Holocaust and the Arab "chutzpah" in demanding the "land of the prophets" for themselves. Practically speaking, he saw the possibility of a new coalition between the Revisionists and the other right-wing parties, which together might seize power in the Zionist movement.[22]

This was in fact not a tactical but an ideological debate between those who realized that the NZO was on the verge of complete collapse, in view of the new challenges it faced from within and without, and those who did not grasp that Revisionism had reached a dead end. The slogan of the supporters of a return to the WZO was: "Pragmatism is the order of the day." The debate focused not on the "final goal," as before the war, but on whether the state was an immediate target or not, in terms of the time factor and the conditions of the struggle.[23] H. S. Halevy, a veteran member of the movement, bemoaned the loss of Revisionism's own De Gaulle—Jabotinsky.[24] Eliezer Shostak, the leader of the Revisionist "National" Histadrut (and minister of health in the Begin government of 1977) favored rejoining because it meant that the old leadership would have to account for its blunders in the face of Revisionist criticism.[25] The debate forced at least one member to admit that the main idea of the "old" Zionists had triumphed: the crystallization of power in terms of economic, military, and "practical" capacity.[26]

In any event, the NZO referendum in the Yishuv was overwhelmingly in favor of rejoining the Zionist Organization (67.4 percent vs. 29.8 percent). In February 1946, the Revisionist party (Hatsohar) returned to the WZO, and the NZO was dismantled as a separate Zionist organization.[27] No party, including their political enemies, could oppose their return, since they were ready to accept the WZO's discipline. Nonetheless, they remained in opposition outside the Jewish Agency Executive, the Va'ad Leumi, and the Haganah. In view of the growing conflict with Britain, the actions of the Resistance Movement, and the appointment of the Anglo-American Committee, Hatsohar could not lag behind. For the first time, it declared that if Britain concluded that its interests were not "identical" with those of Zionism then the latter was free to seek its future elsewhere.[28]

The ingrained radicalism of its national expectations did not permit Hatsohar to see anything positive in the report of the Anglo-American Committee of Inquiry. Bader was unimpressed by the recommendation that 100,000 Jewish DPs be permitted to immigrate, since this condemned the majority of the European Diaspora, not to mention Oriental Jewry, to eternal exile. He was outraged by the notion of reconstructing European Jewry and even more by the committee's failure to recommend a Jewish state. Nor had anything changed regarding the land problem, in view of the committee's wish to defend the Arab *fellah*.[29]

Like other groups, Hatsohar reacted according to its ideological light (Jabotinsky) to the major events of the period. Unlike Begin, Hatsohar, albeit reluctantly, grasped the significance of *ha'apalah* in the overall Zionist struggle. The improvement of relations with the IZL, however, brought renewed criticism of illegal immigration. The *Exodus* seemed to signify the end of *ha'apalah*, and its final failure, because none of the illegal immigrants had reached the homeland.[30] Hatsohar, in contrast to the official leadership, continued to believe in the British connection even after the Black Sabbath. The only lesson of that traumatic event, the party's ideologues wrote, was that henceforth Britain would concede only to a "collaborationist" Jewish Agency.[31] Though the party condemned the "innocent" blood spilled in the IZL's bombing of the King David Hotel (as was incumbent upon it as a legal party), the only real danger it saw was in Weizmann's role as a "second Pétain."[32]

Despite its continued lack of influence on the decision-making process in the Zionist movement, Hatsohar came out forcefully against the Jewish Agency Executive's Paris resolution in favor of partition. Jabotinsky's opposition to partition was cited, and the party argued that the *effendis* would object as vigorously as they would to a Jewish state on both sides of the Jordan River. Britain would not agree to a small state; small states, which might quarrel with one other, would weaken its position in the region.[33]

Hatsohar envisaged itself playing Sinn Fein's role in the Yishuv. Britain knew very well, Y. Halpern said, that if it wished to negotiate with the Yishuv, it must approach not the free leaders but those in prison, just as Britain had to negotiate with Collins and De Valera.[34]

What type of struggle did Hatsohar advocate? Bader rejected the

"purifying" type of struggle, which he alleged was pursued by the Jewish Agency Executive through "civil disobedience." Nor was Samson's
example—"Let me die with the Philistines"—relevant. Rather, the party
should follow Machiavelli's advice concerning the dual importance of
"fortune" and "virtue." Nonetheless, Hatsohar did not dare to support the IZL openly, fearing it would be outlawed if it did, and preferred instead to emphasize, as did Bader, the role of "moral pressure,"
such as Jabotinsky's criticism of Britain's Zionist policy at the 17th Zionist Congress in 1931.[35] In spite of the temptation to preserve a Sinn
Fein image in its relationship with the IZL, Hatsohar was always guided
by the need to remain a legal party. On the other hand, like Begin in
the underground, Hatsohar, too, though with less frequency, likened
the Jewish Agency—after the collapse of the United Resistance Movement—to the Judenrat.[36]

The party's program for the 22nd Zionist Congress was a typical
right-wing product, both politically and socially, and was faithful to
the founding father, certainly in terms of his lack of direction on socioeconomic questions. There was an unequivocal demand for an immediate Jewish state within the "historical borders of Eretz Israel." Relations with Britain would be established on the basis of equality with
other states, and British interests would be recognized only following
"free negotiations." The mildness of the Arab clause was surprising,
though tactical in nature: "We see the Arabs of Eretz Israel as equal
citizens. This principle must receive expression in the state's constitution." The party did not dare include a transfer clause, as it would do
on the eve of the Knesset elections, when the transfer was a fait accompli. The NZO claimed not to be "shackled" to any sociopolitical theory.
Its only commitment was to the founding of a Jewish state, it proclaimed.

In keeping with their inflated rhetoric, Hatsohar's speakers blatantly
declared that the Jews already constituted a majority in their land. Rejecting official government statistics, Bader claimed that the Jews were
in fact not 30.39 percent of Palestine's general population because, according to the Mandate, millions of Diaspora Jews must also be included. Had it not been for the White Paper policy, "at least a million
Jews would have long since settled in the country." Bader disputed the
"mechanistic and stiff" principle of democratic majority rule, pointing
to the demand of India's Muslims for equality, never condemned by
the Arabs; the minority "proletarian dictatorship rule" in the USSR;
and Britain's minority rule of its empire. If these arguments were not
convincing, he claimed that the Jews constituted 68.5 percent of the

country's taxpayers, their part in public expenses was 80 percent, they were better educated than the Arabs, and they were stronger militarily.[37]

In the elections to the 22nd Zionist Congress, Hatsohar won 10.6 percent of the general vote (71,737), nearly half of it in the Yishuv (29,974, where its 13.7 percent put it second only to Mapai). Though in 1931 it had achieved 21 percent (16.8 percent in the Yishuv), considering that the charismatic leader no longer headed the party, this was a striking electoral achievement: second largest in the Yishuv, third in world Jewry. The explanation for this success should be attributed to Jabotinsky's lasting charisma; though he was dead, his legacy was popular.[38] Hatsohar's pretension to assume the role of Sinn Fein, already fully demonstrated in the congress by the party's pro-IZL speeches, grew as IZL operations intensified and four IZL men were hanged by the British.[39]

Achimeir wanted to see the Yishuv as a whole behind Begin, IRA style. But he could not envisage Hatsohar collaborating with those (Zionists) who were "responsible" for the Holocaust no less than Hitler. The congress elections proved that no radical change had occurred in Zionism, if Hatsohar remained only second. Its rejoining would only strengthen the Jewish Agency and act as "cement" for the three socialist parties. Ben-Gurion was likened to "a wind vane on the roof, spinning whichever way the wind blows." Mapai dreamed of partition only because of "its lust for power." Hatsohar would again be isolated and therefore should fight Zionist "totalitarianism" uncompromisingly on its own.[40]

In the congress, Hatsohar stated officially that the period of cooperation with Britain had come to an end. This did not mean that it had become anti-British, as M. Grossman (cofounder of the Revisionist party with Jabotinsky in the 1920s) explained, but Britain could not be relied upon. The Jewish Agency had finished its task and the congress should initiate a provisional Jewish government. Grossman welcomed resistance by the Yishuv, in whatever form, including *ha'apalah*. Partition was anathema: a "symbolic state" would generate irredentism and a resistance movement against the Jewish Agency.[41] Defending the IZL and Lehi, Altman accused the other parties of having deceived the Yishuv before the elections by pretending to oppose partition (regarded by him as "suicidal").[42]

Grossman recognized that Hatsohar needed to undergo a change in order to become "a fulfillment party," which meant that it must join the Zionist coalition. He denied that they were "a rightist party. . . . We are above class interests; we are a national party."[43] As befitted a radical party, Hatsohar was not impressed by the referral of the Palestine problem to the UN. Rather, the Palestine question should be transferred to the International Court, which would reveal that the conflict was more a Jewish-British problem than a Jewish-Arab one.[44] Bader reflected the party's pessimistic mood regarding the coming UN special session on Palestine when he wrote that repetition of Munich was about to take place at Flushing Meadows. "This time the appeasement will be at expense of the Jews, a people nearly as weak as Czechoslovakia was in 1938."[45] Nor was there much enthusiasm for the Gromyko declaration, as was to be expected given the party's inherent anticommunism. Still, Gromyko's assertion that the Mandate was bankrupt was welcomed. However, the only true test of the Soviet attitude toward Zionism would be the lifting of the prohibition on Zionism in Russia, the release of the "Prisoners of Zion," and permitting Jews in the satellite states to make *aliyah*.[46] Nobody in Hatsohar was more suspicious than Achimeir regarding Gromyko's declaration. Though renewed British and American appeasement toward Germany "poisons our soul," nothing was more sacred than a Western orientation.[47]

With the arrival of the UNSCOP inquiry, Hatsohar, although always first to display its radicalism, was careful not to appear too radical. But Z. Von Weisl, for one, could not resist adducing the transfer idea again, this time less crudely, in the guise of an exchange of population. It was an "utter lie," he claimed, to take the peaceful coexistence between Jews and Arabs in Haifa as an example for the whole country, nor could Iraqi Jewry's precarious position be ignored. Von Weisl suggested the exchange of 550,000 Jews for 300,000 Palestine Arabs, on the Turko-Greek precedent of 1922, thus enabling a small Jewish majority of 50,000 by 1950.[48] In any case, he claimed, only 5 or 6 percent of the Arabs were true Arabs—the Bedouins—and Arabs had ruled Palestine for only 326 years (sporadically between 637 and 1071).[49]

But this kind of radicalism was not enough to characterize Hatsohar as the political wing of the IZL. The ten IZL members who were caught and hanged by the British (there was only one Lehi member among them, Moshe Barazani, who blew himself up in a British prison together with an IZL man, Moshe Feinstein) were praised by Hatsohar as the reincarnation of the "Ten Martyrs" (Rabbi Akiva and his followers) who were slain by the Romans.[50] The Jewish Agency's "fear"—and the Revisionists' greatest hope—was that the British would strike a compromise with the terrorist organizations, as they had done with Smuts, De Valera, and Gandhi. The three latest IZL martyrs (see later discussion) were mourned and glorified, since they fulfilled the same historical mission as the Irish and Boer martyrs. The imprisonment of the party's leadership following the IZL's hanging of the two British sergeants, and the outlawing of Betar, finally brought about Hatsohar's identification with the IZL.[51] At the same time, however, this identifiction isolated Hatsohar in the Yishuv. The IZL was never taken as the Yishuv's national representation. Indeed, there was still the danger that the frequent violent confrontation between the Haganah and the IZL might trigger a civil war.[52]

How did the Revisionists react to the UNSCOP Report? Unlike the radical left, which adjusted itself, after a great dialectical effort, to the dramatic new development, the radical right could not digest it and totally failed to grasp its historic importance. Bader, now in prison, concluded that there was nothing new in the report. The partition and "independence" promised by UNSCOP were mere "fictions" and had only "emotional" value. For the Jewish Agency to accept the report would be "complete surrender." It was nothing more than another attempt to "eliminate Zionism."[53] Achimeir's opposition to the UNSCOP partition plan was based on his historical analysis that partition was always accompanied by "terrible bloodshed." In any event, he noted, Zionism's territorial claims emanated not from a need for settlements but from ancient Jewish history. "We aspire to the historical Eretz Israel of [King] David and Alexander Yanai," he wrote.[54]

It was the radical Achimeir who understood at last that the meaning of A. Creech-Jones's declaration of the British evacuation of Palestine (26 September) was that the Jews would be left to confront the Arabs on the battlefield without "a third force in between." He called for peace with the Arabs but warned that they might try to repeat India's Muslim role in a civil war or Hitler's attempt to annihilate the Yishuv. In the face of this common danger he hoped that the Yishuv would show a united front, but he feared that the dominant "Zionist left" would eliminate its rivals and that this would "constitute a Pyrrhic victory."[55] In short, Hatsohar was completely out of touch with politico-military developments, and was taken by surprise when war broke out after the 29 November 1947 resolution.

Revisionism from War to Dissolution

When hostilities erupted, Hatsohar claimed that the Haganah and the Jewish Agency were not initiating military operations on a scale commensurate with Arab aggression, due to bureaucratic shortcomings.

Ben-Gurion turned down a request by the party's leadership to be included on the Security Committee. "You are an IZL party and you fight the Haganah, to judge by *Hamashkif*," Ben-Gurion rebuked them.[56] Hatsohar was particularly contemptuous of Hashomer Hatza'ir ("deserters from any obligatory national feeling"), who were suspected of not wishing to fight the Arabs because of their faith in the Marxist "peoples' fraternity." Revisionists were also outraged by Hashomer Hatza'ir's pledge to provide education for Arab children and to make medical centers available to the Arab population in the Jewish state, particularly when such assurances were given during a life-and-death war.[57]

What most perturbed the Revisionists was the unification of Le'achdut Ha'avodah and Hashomer Hatza'ir ("the gangrene in the national soul") as the new Mapam party.[58] The Revisionists feared the socialist parties in general, including Mapai, claiming that they had struck a deal with Weizmann: In return for their support of his "defeatist" external policy, he had granted them internal control of finance, *aliyah*, and settlement. Moreover, how could Mapam reconcile its faith in the "dictatorship of the proletariat" with Yishuv democracy and the need for private Jewish capital from abroad to build an economically viable state?

The turning point in Hatsohar's attitude toward the Jewish Agency occurred when it became known that a provisional government and a state council were about to be established. The party Center sought to enter the council only because of Ben-Gurion's announcement about the forthcoming union of the Yishuv's fighting forces. Joining the cabinet, the Center confessed, would mean supporting partition. However, in view of their continued backing of the IZL, they stood no chance of getting in.[59] The party's more extreme members objected to the whole idea, but the majority, relatively more pragmatic, grasped the urgency of the war situation and understood the need to obtain legitimization from the embryonic state.[60] This approach, however, did not signal a modification of the party's opposition line. Like Mapam, the Revisionists, too, albeit from a different perspective, asserted that most Arabs did not want war. But unlike Mapam, they believed that a "large minority [of Arabs] even wishes our good, and gladly would like to live and make a living under Hebrew rule." Like Julius Ceasar in the Gallic Wars, Von Weisl proposed making peace with friendly Arab villages and destroying those that were hostile.[61]

America's retreat from the UN partition resolution and its adoption of the trusteeship plan triggered a sharp reaction by the Revisionists. Von Weisl saw it as an irreversible act: "the last shred of hope for a just world had been destroyed." Envisaging the surrender of the government, he warned that "thousands of Haganah members, who are anyhow imbued with a sense of revolt, because of the weakness of Zionist policy, will stand in one front with IZL and fight the trusteeship government."[62]

The Revisionists took the opportunity of this (temporary) defeat for Zionism to point out that the partition agreed to by the Jewish Agency was a mistake. Zionist policy, Grossman charged, was based solely on improvisation. None of the powers could be relied upon. Even the fulfillment of the Magnes plan, he said, would require a military and political struggle. The immediate establishment of a Jewish government was the order of the day.[63]

It was in the wake of the massacre perpetrated by the IZL and Lehi at Deir Yasin that Hatsohar showed its true colors as a radical-right party. To Von Weisl there had been nothing out of the ordinary in the episode. "Now the Jews have proved," he wrote, "that if the war continues, [they] are able, with only four dead and eight seriously wounded, to defeat 240 Arabs. . . . The Arabs are not geniuses and are unable to manage a proper military attack, or to fight in defense, against an attack which was conducted according to the correct rules of war management, namely *surprise!*" The fighting at the Kastel, at Mishmar Ha'emek, in the Etzion Bloc, and at Deir Yasin was all of the same character, he insisted, and it demonstrated the cowardice of the *fellah*.[64] Nor did Von Weisl stop there. In view of the case of Haifa, where, quoting the Histadrut paper *Davar*, Von Weisl said that a large foreign "rabble" was among the Arab population, the government should immediately announce that "every non-Jew who entered Palestine after 1 April 1920—namely, after the San Remo confirmation of the Mandate on Palestine—must immediately leave the Jewish state area. Only those born to parents who lived here before that date are entitled to be in the Jewish state." To invite those who fled to return, as the provisional government had done, was to invite renewed irredentism.[65] The Revisionists now backed the IZL fully, explaining also its failure to conquer Jaffa as being also due to British intervention. Moreover, it was thought that the recent agreement on unification with the Haganah, by units and not as individuals, would strengthen Hatsohar-IZL in the coming political struggle.[66]

Like IZL, the Revisionist party refused to believe that Ben-Gurion would muster the courage to declare the establishment of a Jewish state. On the very eve of the declaration, Hatsohar and IZL submitted an ultimatum to the People's Administration, warning that if the Jewish

Agency did not proclaim the state and the government immediately, "IZL will head the national revolt."[67] Indeed, it was the leader of the earlier "revolt," Menachem Begin, who headed the Revisionist IZL leadership immediately after Israel's establishment. Begin replaced Altman, whose collaboration with the British at the beginning of Begin's revolt and earlier contradicted the party's heroic self-image. The dubious Sinn Fein role that the party had assumed during the British Mandate period would cost it dearly in the coming Knesset elections. Not foreseeing the coming rift with Begin over the inclusion of Altman and his cronies in the list of candidates to the First Knesset, Kalman Katzenelson (Achimeir's supporter since the late 1920s) greeted Begin's first legal appearance as second only to Herzl and Jabotinsky. "No ordinary speaker delivered a speech, not a military commander, a *leader* spoke."[68] Jabotinsky the gradualist was systematically eliminated and the image of a new founding father was forged, far more militant, to make him compatible with Begin's career. Nothing was said about their famous debate in 1938, in which the topic was Begin's military Zionism vs. Jabotinsky's political Zionism. The party's ideologues now claimed that Jabotinsky had declared that the state would come into being "only if the people were ready to spill their enemies' blood. The commander of IZL was privileged to implement that testament." If the Betar anthem ("To Die or to Conquer the Mountain") was the testament, then the author was right, but to judge by Jabotinsky's last book, which was his true testament—in it the founding father advocated a peaceful political solution rather than a military one—nothing was farther from the truth than the pretense that Begin was Jabotinsky's disciple. The radical Achimeir was his real mentor.[69]

Begin certainly accepted Achimeir's teaching on the Arab question, which should be judged on two levels: the public-tactical one, which emphasized political and cultural values, and the strategic one, which gave priority to militancy. Both approaches relied on free interpretations of Jabotinsky's legacy. Zionism, it was held, had failed, exactly as had Western imperialism, to improve the Arabs' living standards. Any domination of Israel's Arab citizens on the example of the Bolsheviks in Soviet Central Asia, or the Japanese in Korea, was rejected by Achimeir. Nor did he recommend a solution along the lines proposed by Magnes and other "witch doctors" in his group. "They want to destroy the Arab way of life," he argued, adding that it was impossible to eliminate "the division in the Arab society between the *effendi*, the *fellah* and the Bedouin." Urging "respect for the Arab way of life," Achimeir added in the same breath that "Arab society does not live according to the standards of J. S. Mill . . . let us not mix our vintage Israeli wine with the malodorous oriental water."[70]

When it came to contentious issues like transfer, the tactical and the strategic converged. Even the comparatively moderate Hatsohar wing, notwithstanding its support for Israel's joining a neutral regional federation, still favored an "exchange of population," which they said would be far simpler to implement after the departure of 300,000 Arabs.[71] Altman, the party's leader, was unambiguous on the Arab refugee question: "There is no place [here] for Sudeten Arabs," he asserted.[72]

A Revisionist revival under Begin's leadership could be implemented successfully, said K. Katzenelson, only by means of three essentials: ideology, the heroic legendary "epos," and the organizational framework. Ideology tended to be crushed between the epos and the organizational framework (witness what had happened to the Communists' October epos and to Mapai's Kinneret epos). Revisionism's weakness was that it failed to integrate into its epos Trumpeldor the laborer, adopting only his heroic legend. Still, the movement had been saved by the epos of Jabotinsky–S. Ben-Yosef–D. Gruner, the last two being the IZL's most famous martyrs.[73]

Notwithstanding its aggressive criticism, the party wanted to join the government, in order to influence events.[74] But the *Altalena* crisis intervened. As we have seen, the sinking of the IZL's weapons ship *Altalena,* and the clash between government forces and former IZL soldiers (sixteen of whom were killed), brought the new state to the brink of civil war, according to the party's spokesmen. To the party, these events were an integral element of the government's "treasonous" policy in the service of Bernadotte, the UN mediator, who objected to military reinforcements for Israel. The purpose of Bernadotte's conspiracy was to bring Israel under the patronage of Abdullah and J. Glubb, the British commander of the Jordanian Arab Legion. Moreover, the scuttling of the ship "sabotaged" the national military effort, since vital arms were lost. The myth that these arms could have helped the state at a critical time began to be propagated, though in fact the Czech arms had already arrived.[75] Hatsohar called upon the other cabinet members to follow the example of their National Religious colleagues who resigned in protest at the government's brutal treatment of *Altalena.* Nonetheless, the Provisional State Council approved the government's measures by 24 to 4 (5 abstentions).[76]

By mid-August, with the repercussions of *Altalena* slowly fading, Altman again tried his luck with Ben-Gurion, hoping to strengthen his weakening position vis-à-vis Begin by convincing the prime minister that his participation in the government would stem Begin's Herut party. "It is up to you," he told Ben-Gurion, "whether the Revisionists will be a political party or an underground." Ben-Gurion replied that the Revisionist party had not upheld any of the pledges it had made at the last Zionist Congress (not to incite workers, not to support the right wing, loyalty to the WZO, and last but not least, its support for Begin during the *Altalena* crisis). Ben-Gurion warned that if the IZL rebelled again it would be suppressed. The co-option of the Revisionists to the Zionist Executive was marginal compensation.[77] Hatsohar was by now in total disarray. Altman's supporters refused to accept Herut as the successor to the historic Revisionist party. Shocked by its very establishment (in June 1948), they rejected Begin's argument that the "victories" against Britain would attract the masses and bring him to power. Recalling Hatsohar's success in the Zionist Congress elections two years earlier, Altman explained that it was "naïve" to think that the potential voters who condemned the party for supporting the IZL would now vote for Herut. But a good many Revisionists, such as Bader, Begin's loyal "representative" in Hatsohar's Center, reckoned that the IZL's "victories," the confidence it had gained among the people, the dynamism of Herut activists, and Begin's leadership qualities all pointed to the need to replace Altman with Begin.[78] Indeed, Altman's loss was Begin's gain. By a majority of 61 to 32, the party decided to unite with Herut.[79]

But Altman refused to give up. After Bernadotte's assassination by Lehi, the Revisionist representatives in the Provisional State Council, Altman, H. Segal, and B. Weinstein, supported the government in initiating the Command for Prevention of Terror (though they hailed the breakaways' contribution to the "expulsion" of "foreign rule"). This was a surprising, and unforgivable, step from Begin's point of view and finally forced Altman and his colleagues to appear on a different list in the Knesset elections.[80]

In fact, there were no ideological differences between Herut and Hatsohar; it was all at the personal level. Both groups invoked Jabotinsky, leaving the ideological dimension in limbo. Jabotinsky's son, Eri, formerly Betar head in Palestine and later a member of Peter Bergson's (Hillel Kook) Revisionist lobby in the United States, attempted to erase the rightist image of both parties. His father, too, he claimed, had been of the opinion that it was not the social but the political issue that divided Revisionism from the left. Apart from elements of J. Burnham's *The Managerial Revolution* and the Beveridge plan, his basic idea, following the forgotten Austrian Jewish utopian J. Popper-Lynkeus, was to create two economies, one to be financed by the government, the second representing private enterprise. This would involve giving to the poor without taking from the rich and would entail an "immense" expansion of social services while also protecting private initiative.[81]

Eri Jabotinsky, however, wished to reorganize both parties not only around socioeconomic issues; he wanted to reopen the 1930s debate, initiated by E. Gurevitch and Uriel Heilperin, then in the NZO, on whether the classical Jewish identity should be replaced by a new, "Hebrew" Weltanschauung. Indeed, he himself had been expelled from the party in 1946, by Grossman, for pursuing the Hebrew alternative.[82] The concept of Hebrew identity was more than a cultural idea; it was, in this view, linked to the idea of a new regional order of peace, based on a comprehensive revolution in the internal structure of the Middle East. Here, Israel could serve as a bridgehead, in the same way, Jabotinsky said, as the American colonies had after they liberated themselves from British rule, imposing Anglo-Saxon culture on a whole continent. Not only Jews but non-Jews as well would flock to the region, and "we must ensure that the culture that will dominate this continent will be Hebrew."[83]

Needless to say, Revisionist/Herut circles rejected such ideas out of hand. Hebrew regional power was nothing but a figment of Eri's "geopolitical imagination." Why should millions of Jews rush to the Middle East? Moreover, the Arabs, in contrast to the Native Americans, had an "ancient culture." At present they might be "backward," but they would "not for long be ruled by feudals, the slave traders who sell them as 'cannon fodder' to Bevin."[84] Yet Eri Jabotinsky was not a mere visionary. He had clear positions, for example on the issue of Israel's Arab citizens, who should play a "vital" role in the "introduction of culture to the desert," and on the question of separation of state from religion, on which he had also distanced himself from his father.[85]

Nonetheless, Eri Jabotinsky's visions had no impact on classical Revisionism in either Hatsohar or Herut. Hatsohar's platform for the First Knesset elections simply avoided the class war issue, calling vaguely for a "regime of absorption" (of the new immigrants), legislation favoring private initiative, progressive taxes, luxury taxes, and for defending the interests of the workers, small businessmen, and clerks "against the domination of economic monopoly." The principle of compulsory arbitration was dropped, and the party called for a democratic constitution with no class domination. The party claimed to represent "Jabotinsky's doctrine," though in practice little remained of it. On defense and foreign policy, however, the platform was more forthright.

On the eve of the elections Hatsohar reminded Begin that he did not invent the "idea of the revolt," reprimanding him for ignoring the IZL and its "heroic" acts before 1944.[86]

In theory, Hatsohar was more chauvinistic than Herut, because it insisted on an "exchange of population." Israel's remaining Arabs, not only the refugees, should be exchanged for the Jews of Islamic countries. European experience showed that minorities were an "incessant source of intrigues, provocations and foreign interventions." In spite of the advantages of neutrality, an American alliance was unhesitatingly called for in view of both American and Revisionist inherent anticommunism.[87] Altman's list of old Revisionist hands failed disastrously, winning only 2,884 votes, and no member in the Knesset, in comparison to 49,782 for Begin's Herut, and fourteen MKs. Whether this was "complete usurpation" or not, it was certainly not matters of ideology and politics that won the day but Begin's heroic image as Jabotinsky's successor, rather than this being Altman, the uncharismatic politician and sometime collaborator with the British.[88] Little did Begin know that his heroic narrative would not help him reach power. He would need the collapse of the General Zionists (the so-called liberals) and the shock of the Yom Kippur War before he finally jettisoned the ideologically overloaded Revisionist baggage.

12

Menachem Begin, IZL, and Herut

From Underground to Political Legitimacy

By the end of World War II, Menachem Begin had established himself as the leader of the IZL (Irgun Zvai Leumi, or National Military Organization), the larger of the two radical-right underground movements (the other was Lehi). Despite the *saison* (November 1944–March 1945), when some 700 members of IZL were handed over by the Haganah to the British authorities (see chapter 5), Begin managed to keep his organization intact. He was able to do this thanks to IZL's internal cohesion and clandestine methods, as well as its dedication and stamina, typical of most underground movements, but also because the Jewish Agency did not collaborate fully with the police. Moreover, the IZL was not entirely isolated; it was able to draw on the support of propaganda in the United States and on the aid of Polish Military Intelligence in exile, which, albeit for anti-Semitic reasons, wished to "stir up trouble against Great Britain as revenge for Great Britain's attitude toward Poland" (that is, because Britain had not honored its commitment to Poland following Hitler's invasion).[1] Third, IZL did not break up because members had faith in its mission, which enabled it to persevere.

Begin believed in revolt as a raison d'être, contrary to "practical Zionism," though the goal should be adjusted to the means, not the other way around. Political Zionism of the Hatsohar school had failed because it relied on "objective processes" alone, Begin wrote in a situation appraisal in February 1945. Begin, born in 1913 in Russian Poland, rose quickly in the Revisionist and Betar hierarchy. Although defying Jabotinsky's refusal to follow military Zionism, as had been demanded by Abba Achimeir, the true father of Begin's militancy, Begin was able to force upon Jabotinsky a change in Betar's oath from a defensive to an aggressive character. Escaping the Nazi invasion, he fled from Warsaw to Soviet-occupied Poland, only to be arrested by the NKVD. At the end of 1943 he moved from being head of Betar to being IZL commander in Palestine, having arrived as a Polish soldier in April 1942. Declaring revolt in early 1944, he went into hiding, emerging—after being intensively sought by both the CID and the Haganah—only in May 1948.

Besides Jabotinsky, Begin also drew on the Russian Revolution to justify his revolt. Marx had predicted that revolution was bound to erupt first in the industrially developed countries; but the revolution had occurred in backward Russia, Begin explained, fomented by a radical underground that decided the country's fate by organizing a general uprising. Similarly, the Jewish people "will not be able to achieve their goal, whatever the objective conditions may be, if a revolutionary element, a military element, does not emerge from within." Unlike others in Revisionist/IZL circles, Begin did not denigrate the value of land settlement or underrate the significance of diplomacy: "But policy without *force*," he insisted, "is like music without instruments." With the same conviction with which he rejected "practical Zionism," Begin likewise spurned Lehi's individual terrorism. Military uprising was also a way to achieve national liberation: "In Poland and Ireland, in North America and in South Africa, as well as in Greece, both in the nineteenth century and nowadays, we witness the same historical manifestation: military uprising is the way of oppressed peoples to their war of independence."

Begin, however, conceded that international factors must also be reckoned with, as in Greece, where Churchill was forced to negotiate with the rebels. In Palestine, the task would be threefold: capturing the centers of British rule in the big cities, defense on the Stalingrad model, and guerrilla war in the rest of the country. The revolt, Begin calculated, would be partially suppressed, though not fully because the young would continue to fight in different parts of the country. The British would then be forced to negotiate with the rebels and to transfer the country to "its Hebrew owners." Since the IZL, as he admitted, lacked the means to implement its "great plan," it would have to build the army needed for the war of liberation in the course of the fighting, like Garibaldi or ELAS (the Greek communist underground). Three conditions were required for an uprising: the fighting force must "represent and symbolize" the true aspirations of the masses; it must "know its way until the end"; and it must search for an ally, based on the new possibilities arising in the Mediterranean Basin.[2] Following the world war, the IZL renewed its terrorist operations, in the conviction that the Churchill government would not otherwise abolish the White Paper. Begin thought it was essential to renew the "direct war" in the face of the "coming annihilation campaign" by the British, who intended to solve the Palestine question within the context of the Arab world instead of viewing it as part of the world Jewish problem.[3] Now, with the world war at an end, Sneh, who in the autumn of 1944 had warned Begin to stop the revolt, was challenged by the latter to fulfill his promise to launch "war at the end of the war."[4]

But could Begin conduct a serious anti-British struggle without substantial external aid? Though supported by Peter Bergson in America (the Committee for National Liberation), Begin did not yet identify himself as either pro- or anti-American, notwithstanding Truman's announcement that he would not send half a million soldiers to Palestine. Nor was Begin in a rush to depict the IZL as a pro-Soviet force, although he detected signs that the USSR would favor the "evacuation" of Jews from the satellite states, because they were creating unrest there.[5] This should not be wrongly construed as a betrayal of Jabotinsky's beliefs. Begin certainly remained an avowed anticommunist to the end of his life. But he distinguished between basic ideology and pragmatic, or operative, ideology, in foreign policy. Hence, he drew on Jabotinsky's teachings when dealing with sensitive external affairs.

Flexibility in matters of ideology was equally applicable to methods of struggle. To begin with, Jabotinsky had to be "adapted" to the IZL's needs in 1945. First was the case of the "prophecy" that should have led to the "evacuation" of European Jewry in 1936, for fear of massacre ("Bartholomew's Night," the massacre of 5,000 Huguenots—French Protestants—in 1572). But Jabotinsky had been ignored by the official leadership. Jabotinsky's pro-British image had to be changed, and Begin also projected a refurbished picture of Jabotinsky who advocated military conquest. It did not matter to Begin that Jabotinsky was not a militarist. Lacking any original evidence to show that Jabotinsky preached rebellion, Begin quoted an "unpublished" document (ostensibly dated 1939) in which Jabotinsky supposedly said: "The only road leading to the liberation of our country is the sword."[6]

Begin's axiomatic assumption was that the White Paper could not be abolished without the use of force.[7] His propaganda war, reinforced by guerrilla acts, reached new heights in a memorandum he sent in June 1945 to 250 persons in the Yishuv, in which he suggested the establishment of a provisional government and a supreme national council. No one responded, even though he justified the idea by referring to the desperate plight of the survivors in Europe and the Yishuv in Palestine. This step would constitute the first "revolutionary" act to transform the present state of affairs. The new government should begin by declaring a war of liberation against the Mandatory regime, accompanied by a general strike and a refusal to pay taxes. To placate the Arabs, they were promised that their holy places would be extraterritorial, that they would enjoy "full" equality and social progress, and that they could ally themselves in friendship with all the neighboring countries.[8] Despite a momentary halt to the IZL actions, with the possibility of a new Labour government adopting a pro-Zionist line, the IZL on 23 July, together with Lehi, sabotaged a bridge near Yavneh ("one of the vital lifelines of the empire," according to Begin).[9]

The establishment of the United Resistance Movement was not a turning point in the history of the Yishuv or the Zionist struggle for independence, since Ben-Gurion did not surrender to Begin. It was only ad hoc cooperation between adversaries in methods and strategy. Nonetheless, Begin interpreted it as an historic event, notwithstanding the fact that he had to accept, for some nine months, the authority of the hated Jewish Agency. In his view the United Resistance Movement represented an unprecedented victory for the idea of the war of liberation over "defeatists" such as Hashomer Hatza'ir. It was no accident, he said, that the latter (together with Aliyah Hadashah and Ichud) complained that the JAE was emulating Jabotinsky's methods. But he rejected Tabenkin's claim that the IZL was a group of "desperate" people. The Warsaw Ghetto revolt was a desperate war, not that of IZL.[10] Following Bevin's speech of 13 November 1945, which prejudiced the mission of the Anglo-American Committee of Inquiry as far as Begin was concerned, he promised to wage full-scale war.[11]

Yet despite his view of the United Resistance Movement's establishment as a historic event, Begin viewed its initial operations as a tactical rather than strategic change.[12] He was delighted that the movement's leaders on the JAE were branded "terrorists" by the British.[13] Begin was well aware that Hashomer Hatza'ir was against the continuous-struggle policy of the United Resistance Movement. He described as "Jewish self-hatred" Yaari's claim that unity with the breakaways would be justified only in "the final battle," as in the Warsaw and Vilna ghettos. Hashomer Hatza'ir was "the real and classic quisling," Begin said, because it was ready to renew the *saison* and allied itself with bourgeois elements such as Aliyah Hadashah, not with Le'achdut Ha'avodah.[14]

True to his word, Begin deliberately attempted to escalate the United Resistance Movement's activities by independent, if sporadic, operations, such as an attack on CID headquarters in Jerusalem and Jaffa on 27 December 1945. (There were also other attacks, which often failed, aimed at obtaining arms or money). At the strategic level, he was concerned that the Anglo-American Committee would present the struggle on Palestine as a Jewish-Arab conflict, rather than a Jewish-British one. Hence his pressure on the X Committee, the United Resistance Movement's command, to step up the anti-British campaign and show that this was not the case. Following IZL operations against British military aircraft at Kastina and Lydda in February 1946, Begin quoted local Arabs who congratulated IZL's "heroes," and he advised the inquiry committee, and particularly its American members, to come and see "the kind of relations that can be established between the returning Jewish people and the Arab citizens, but for British incitement and grumbling."[15]

IZL could not risk giving evidence to the Anglo-American Committee, lest its witnesses be arrested. Instead, it submitted a memorandum, but only to the American members. Basically, the memorandum said, the British wanted to undermine the Jewish people's unity and thus boost its "defeatist" groups. A second reason for Britain's enthusiasm for the committee was London's desire to show the Americans that the conflict was not between British and Jews but between Jews and Arabs. To Begin this was a typical "divide and rule" policy of the kind that was employed in India, where British policy created a "false impression" of a Hindu-Muslim rift. Begin's constant theme was that there was no Arab-Jewish conflict. It was all "hatched" in the brain of Britain's chief Military Intelligence officer in Cairo (Brigadier I. N. Clayton), who "put in the mouth of the Arabs" that the Jews sought to dominate the Middle East.

Begin denied that the Jews were a minority in Palestine, but even if they were, it was "hypocritical" to argue that it was incommensurate with the democratic principle to transfer power to them, especially if the argument was adduced by the British. "As is well known," Begin wrote to the inquiry committee's American members in heavily sardonic vein: "a vast majority of British rule a negligible minority of Indians in India; and it is well known that in Hong Kong a large majority of British rule a small minority of Chinese, etc." His main argument that the Jews did constitute a majority was based on the *"historical fact"* that Palestine had "always belonged" to the "Jewish people *as a whole;* also, practically speaking we are today an absolute majority in Eretz Israel," most notably with Holocaust survivors about to return to the motherland. He held no fear of a "free plebiscite" among the Jews of Europe, Asia, and Africa to answer one question only: Where do they wish to live? There was room for them in Palestine, as well as for the local Arabs.[16]

Begin was certain that the Anglo-American Committee would not recommend a Zionist solution. On the eve of the publication of the committee's report, the IZL called again for the establishment of a "Hebrew" government. Begin viewed the report's positive recommendations, such as permitting the immigration of 100,000 Jews, as theoretical, particularly in view of Attlee's condition—the dismantling of the Yishuv's private armies. This he likened to the Philistines' demand to the Israelites to hand over Samson.[17] Still, Begin claimed that the recommendation on the 100,000 immigrants was the result of the United Resistance Movement operations.[18] Begin's final conclusion was that the Anglo-American Committee had been a "national catastrophe" and that a "general uprising" was called for.[19] He was prepared for a full-scale clash with Britain, together with the establishment of an emergency government and an army.[20] He described the IZL's bombing of the King David Hotel (killing ninety-one Arabs, Jews, and British) as "one of the greatest attacks ever undertaken by a fighting underground," managing "to infiltrate to the heart of the occupation government."[21]

That operation, although approved by Sneh in the name of the United Resistance Movement command, effectively put an end to the movement. The organized Yishuv could not tolerate what an underground could permit itself. Above all, the bombing did not prevent the British from publishing the Morrison-Grady provincial autonomy plan, which for Begin was nothing more than the recreation of the Warsaw Ghetto, both in size and in spirit. The British were looking only for quislings and for a Judenrat to implement their schemes. To Begin, Weizmann was the appropriate candidate to fill Pétain's role.[22] But there was to be no general uprising. Apart from Lehi, none of the Yishuv parties was prepared to accept Begin's call for a revolt on the model of the Hasmoneans and Zealots (he was careful to dissociate himself from the Massada example).[23] The decision by the enlarged JAE, meeting in Paris, in favor of partition (a "viable state") infuriated him to the point that he denied the existence of national authority, speaking instead of "war authority versus surrender authority."[24] Yet, even at this low ebb of the Zionist struggle, Begin did not seriously challenge Ben-Gurion.

The London Conference on Palestine was condemned as another sellout by the Jewish Agency. In response, on 23 September 1946, IZL attacked an oil-carrying train near Binyamina, to show that British military bases in the country were unsafe.

Begin distinguished three options to obtain victory: (1) with the aid of an ally, as displayed by the Maccabees, the Italians against the Austrians, and the Balkan peoples against the Ottomans; (2) the Irish example, when the "enemy finds himself compelled to *acquiesce* in the abandonment of his rule [and] begin negotiations with a representative body of the fighting people"; or (3) the Polish, Czechoslovak, and Baltic examples: "in the event of war between the occupying power and other power or powers—the enemy's *military might* disintegrates, thus rendering the opportunity for a well poised Liberation Army to 'strike,' to dislodge the foreign rule." What counted in liberation wars, Begin said, was "one factor: the *opportune hour*."[25] Begin hailed the transfer of the Palestine problem to the UN, albeit another "ploy" in the "satanic British maneuvers," as the outcome of IZL's incessant attacks on them, in particular the attack on the Officers' Club in Jerusalem on 1 March 1947. Since Begin was captive to his own theory that only a guerrilla-cum-terrorism struggle would win independence, not the Jewish Agency's political negotiations and illegal-immigration pressure, he saw no reason to change either his strategy or his tactics.[26]

Stepping up the "war of liberation" was therefore all the more necessary, a move that led eight IZL members to the gallows between April and July 1947. Their sacrifice enhanced IZL's self-image and legitimacy as an underground movement, a link in the long chain of Jewish martyrs. To Begin the martyrs represented the zenith of Jewish heroism. Dov Gruner could have saved his life by appealing to the Privy Council, just as Hannah and her Seven Sons, as the Hasmoneans, the Zealots, or the fighters of Massada and Bar Kochba could have lived, but they chose not to surrender to foreign rule. A legend had been created, and it guaranteed eternal freedom for the Jewish people.[27] Afterward some argued that Begin should have instructed Gruner to request a pardon, but Begin was adamant in his belief that national liberation could not be consummated without martyrdom: "So it was throughout history. So it was in Russia. In Poland and in Ireland. In every place where the spirit of freedom triumphed over the instinct of life." Their sacrifice would ensure the IZL its honorable place in history. "They are the symbol of a generation which crossed by means of a 'shortcut' the infinite distance from Treblinka to Acre [where the gallows stood]."[28] Clearly, Begin was determined to write a historic page in Jewish history, rivaling Ben-Gurion.

Though skeptical about Zionism's chances in the UN, Begin submitted his views to UNSCOP in a memorandum, this time displaying greater tactical sophistication than he had vis-à-vis the Anglo-American Committee. Unlike his Revisionist political wing, or Lehi, he was careful not to mention transfer or even exchange of population. Citing Molotov's justification for annexing the eastern parts of Germany to Poland (they were the "cradle" of the Polish state and culture), he emphasized that there would be no "exclusion of the non-Hebrew population which has, in the course of time, taken root in our country. . . . We shall, without exception, regard the Arab population which has established itself in our country as citizens with equal rights in our free State." On the other hand, he declared that the Jews constituted the "clear majority of the population east and west of the Jordan. This majority is composed of those of our people who have already returned to the Homeland . . . and of those of our people, numbering millions, who strive to return to it immediately but are unable to realize their rights because of the British occupation Army."[29]

Begin welcomed Gromyko's declaration as proof that the IZL's unrelenting anti-British war was productive. None of Gromyko's solutions were compatible with Begin's claim for "historical borders," but he correctly evaluated that Soviet recognition was of significance for Jewish historical rights in Palestine, the inevitability of Jewish evacuation from Europe, and the principle of Jewish statehood.[30]

With hindsight, Begin saw UNSCOP as a turning point. Hence his attempt to influence the commission by presenting Zionism's most extreme case (rivaled only by Lehi's memorandum). No Zionist body more sharply indicted British "exploitative" rule in Palestine, beginning with the Cairo Conference of 1921. Among their other "crimes" against the Jewish people, they had falsified the population statistics. But his main argument remained the right of "repatriation" of forcibly expelled peoples, be they Russian, French, Yugoslavs, or Jews, to their homeland. Begin rejected partition because, he said, it would leave a large Arab minority—40 percent in the case of the Morrison-Grady plan, for example. Although he rejected a binational state, he promised to include Arab ministers in the Hebrew provisional government, to be

selected "according to their ability." The new state would bring benefits to the Arabs, and there was no need for transfer, as "there is room
for all."[31]

The Yishuv leadership's agreement to the UNSCOP partition plan
deepened the divisions between the IZL and the Jewish Agency. Nothing was more sacred to Begin than the "integrity" of "Eretz Israel" (both
sides of the Jordan River). In April and May 1947 the verbal war intensified. When *ha'apalah* was temporarily stopped, the IZL castigated the
Haganah as the "Adolph Bevin militia." In fact, as Begin perceived,
the Haganah had been instructed by the JAE to prevent IZL attempts
to escalate anti-British activities, and a Haganah man was killed in one
such incident at police headquarters in Tel Aviv.[32] The IZL could not
grasp why anti-British guerrilla activities had been legitimate during
the period of the United Resistance Movement but were prohibited
afterward.[33] Begin failed to understand that the Resistance Movement
was not an end in itself but a *political* instrument in Ben-Gurion's hands.

Begin saw UNSCOP not as the end of the struggle but rather as the
start of a far more intense confrontation, signified by IZL's hanging of
two British sergeants, in retaliation for Britain's execution of IZL activists. (In his memoirs Begin boasted that he had put an end to the British gallows by IZL's retaliatory act. In fact, if the British did not hang
any more IZL men, it was because of the UNSCOP Report, which was
effectively the coup de grâce to its rule in Palestine.) Begin also diminished the effectiveness of *ha'apalah*, which, he claimed, had hardly increased Jewish immigration beyond the 1,500 legal certificates. However, the expulsion to Germany of "the illegals" aboard the *Exodus*, an
episode which was heavily publicized, threatened to steal the thunder
from IZL's terrorist campaign, which reached its peak in the attack on
Acre prison in May 1947.[34]

Begin rejected the UNSCOP partition out of hand and disbelieved
that Britain would withdraw from Palestine, considering her strategic
interests there. In Begin's mind, Britain's aim was still to "turn western Palestine into a British satellite state with a quisling government."
The IZL reacted with one of its most lethal attacks against the British,
the bombing of police headquarters in Haifa (killing thirteen and
wounding more than fifty).[35]

The growing Arab threats of war following the publication of the
UNSCOP Report, however, brought a change in his policy. For the first
time, he realized that the Arabs might make good on their talk of war,
and he offered IZL participation in the Yishuv's "united front."[36] Al-

though he himself had been oblivious to the Arabs' potential strength, he accused the Jewish Agency of deluding the people that war was far off.[37] But he could not abandon his obsession with the "Nazi-British enemy."[38] Rejecting Von Weisl's call for compromise with Britain, he prevented Hatsohar from fulfilling a dominant Sinn Fein role.[39]

As for an international force to implement the UN partition resolution, this was, correctly, ruled out because America would never agree to Soviet participation in such a force, as this would give the USSR a foothold in the heart of the Middle East.[40] Begin expressed the IZL's confidence in the USSR, in contrast to America's coolness toward the Yishuv. It was inconceivable, he claimed, that the USSR would stand idly by if an attempt were made to annihilate the only democratic element in the Middle East, the Jewish people.[41] Begin would welcome communist Jews no less than any others, whatever Anglo-Saxon provocateurs might say: "Our nation is not communist. But it is not obliged, as a nation, to be anticommunist either."[42]

Unable to implement his vision of cooperating with the Arabs in the fight against Britain, he embraced the Deir Yasin massacre as a more successful policy.[43] The attack was justified by Begin as a heroic deed[44] (even though he probably had no advance knowledge of the operation), proving that the IZL was ready to use extreme measures to implement its war policy, far beyond the Jewish Agency or the provisional government. All in all Begin thought it was too soon to dismantle the IZL, despite the Jewish Agency's policy of "conquest." But he knew that the organization's continued separate existence in wartime was unpopular, hence his public announcement that negotiations for "unity of forces" were underway. Nevertheless, the day before the signing of the "operative agreement" the IZL attacked Jaffa without informing the Haganah (25 April 1948). Begin's excuse was that he was not yet confident that a Jewish state would be established.[45] Indeed, the negotiations were accompanied by Ben-Gurion's unequivocal demand that IZL should dissolve its units. In reply, Begin accused the JAE of wanting to establish a "Judenrat," because it had delayed a proclamation of independence. He now called for a "founding convention" to pursue the "war of redemption." America's trusteeship proposal was an Anglo-American plot for a final Jewish surrender.[46]

On the eve of the proclamation of the State of Israel, Begin summed up with great satisfaction the IZL's contribution. Except for the Magnes "sect," he claimed, everyone acknowledged that "Only Thus!" was the right doctrine; in other words, that force alone had brought about the state's establishment. Nevertheless, the IZL still had to be on guard against the possible emergence of a "Vichy government" in Israel.[47] After more than four years of fighting the British (and the Jewish Agency, verbally), Begin had convinced himself that he was the only true patriot.[48]

From *Altalena* to Legal Opposition

Begin was intent on demonstrating that he was now closing his underground years and moving toward legal party life in the new democracy of Israel (but the underground would continue beyond the official borders, namely in Jerusalem, until the aftermath of Bernadotte's murder in September). Although he did not commit himself to any particular power, he repeated that one principle guided him in foreign policy: mutuality of relations ("hatred for hatred, aid for aid, friendship for friendship"). He mentioned the United States first, distinguishing between the American government and the American people; he noted the USSR second (the order was reversed in his Herut foundation declaration) and France third.[49]

Begin established the Herut movement on 15 June 1948. In its program Begin committed himself to "real" democracy and to social justice along the lines espoused by Jabotinsky. Herut was also established in order to ensure the "continuation of the war of freedom." Begin did his best not to appear as an antisocialist, promising to fight against "all trusts and monopolies . . . for such trusts and monopolies lead inevitably to the exploitation of the working man." Similarly, he demanded nationalization of all "public utility works and basic industries."[50]

The peaceful establishment of Herut was severely imperiled, however, by the *Altalena* affair a week later, when the IZL in Europe forced Begin to accept an arms ship (though not heavy arms), which it claimed, against Begin's judgment, could decide the Arab-Israeli war (see also chapter 4). The incident occurred during the first general cease-fire, which IZL units exploited to desert from the Israel Defense Forces and join the *Altalena* defenders (they had joined the IDF on a unit basis on 1 June), but the armed clash cost the lives of sixteen IZL members and two soldiers. In Ben-Gurion's view, the danger of an armed coup, which he and his cabinet (other than the ministers of the National-Religious Party and the General Zionists) had feared, was averted.[51] It was *Altalena*, and not the founding of Herut as a political party, that put an end to the IZL. In a speech he delivered shortly after the attack on the ship, Begin did not deny that he wanted not only 20 percent of the weapons aboard *Altalena* for the IZL in Jerusalem, where it was still operating as the city's status had not yet been finalized, but also the remaining 80 percent for the six IZL battalions that had joined the IDF. Begin branded Ben-Gurion's order to shell the *Altalena* as "criminal" and "stupid," and threatened that "by lifting one finger," he could have "liquidated your treacherous leaders, if we had wanted."[52] Begin would later order 5,000 former IZL activists who were already in the army not to take the oath of allegiance on the day the IDF was formally established, to protest at Ben-Gurion's attempt to ignore the IZL's "vital role" in gaining independence.[53]

Though he opposed Ben-Gurion's "totalitarian regime," Begin was most concerned about the new state's foreign policy, due mainly to his overbearing hatred for Abdullah, who held what Begin considered the fatherland and was thereby endangering Israel's sovereignty. At the international level, Begin found it difficult to identify with either East or West. Certainly, the blocs were an irrevocable fact, but in terms of Israel's national interests it was "too simplistic" to divide the world into two blocs.[54]

Begin's final reconciliation with the provisional government was effected only after Bernadotte's assassination on 16 September, which forced him to order the IZL in Jerusalem to disperse and join the IDF. The government's ultimatum left him no other choice. The only road was to activate Herut as a legal party; though it had been established in June, its reputation as a democratic party was damaged by the *Altalena* affair. Herut had no detailed program, other than the will to liberate "Greater Israel." Of course it protested at the "totalitarian" emergency laws enacted by the government in the aftermath of the Bernadotte assassination (and at the fact that some IZL men were in prison for the *Altalena* episode), but basically it was a one-issue party demanding the destruction of Jordan. Only two powers, the USSR and France, could be expected to support the aspiration for the liberation of Jewish historical territory. But in any case nothing could be accomplished as long as Ben-Gurion's "dictatorial regime" continued. On crucial issues a referendum was essential, the method to be included in a special extraconstitutional clause. This was Begin's message to his followers in the first Herut Council meeting.[55]

Not surprisingly, the old maximalist circle, led by Achimeir, the poet Uri Zvi Greenberg, and Y. H. Yeivin, sided with Herut rather than with the Revisionist old guard. Yeivin was not happy about the IZL's dissolution. The advent of the messianic process, in which the whole of Israeli youth would adopt the ways of the underground, demanded the liberation of Greater Israel from the Nile to the Euphrates.[56] Deir Yasin had been part and parcel of that process, Yeivin wrote.[57] By the same token, Yeivin objected to the return of any Arab refugees even after the signing of peace.[58] The IDF's withdrawal from es-Suneid in the Gaza Strip, in line with a UN demand, he claimed, was a harbinger of more retreats—from Jaffa, Nazareth, Lydda, Ramleh, Katamon in Jerusalem, and the Kastel hill near that city. "Surrender" was part of the "psychological makeup" of the present government, Yeivin wrote, and consequently "the people must demand the leadership's resignation."[59]

Herut's objection to IDF withdrawals and to negotiations with any Arab state was its main plank in the election campaign for the First Knesset.[60] The official censor had his hands full blue-penciling the statements of party spokesmen. Herut's radical posture was underlined by the fact that its second candidate, after Begin, was the apocalyptic poet Greenberg, who on the eve of the elections predicted that Israel would have to live by the sword "for a very long time" if it did not want to end up like Canaan and the Philistines.[61] Herut's platform warned that Israel had three possibilities to choose from: a "Munich peace," based on invasion and slavery; a permanent state of war "camouflaged by 'cease-fires' and 'armistices'," which would require an enormous standing army; or peace based on freedom and national sovereignty, without invaders or subjugation, to be achieved by the conquest of "historical borders." On the socioeconomic side there was a clear shift to the right in the form of support for private initiative, though also for legislation to prevent the trusts from exploiting the workers.[62]

Throughout the campaign, Herut refrained from criticizing the rival Revisionist list, but on election day it disclosed (in an article in the party's paper) that what had prevented a combined list was Herut's insistence that those Revisionist leaders who had voted in the Provisional State Council for the emergency laws be excluded from the list.[63] Although Herut won only 11.5 percent of the general vote, it pretended to rejoice at its "victory" (actually a setback, as compared with the Revisionists' 13.7 in the Yishuv without the Diaspora, in the 22nd Zionist Congress elections). Ben-Gurion had won temporary popularity by promising peace, wrote Herut, but the end result would be war. In any event, the paper promised that Herut would abide by the decisions of the majority.[64]

Bader—who had defected from Altman's camp earlier and had been appointed by Begin as editor of Herut (and given the number six slot on Herut's Knesset list)—claimed that Herut was in fact the second largest party because Mapam and the religious bloc represented "arrangements" of more than one party, which had fought the election together. Herut rejoiced not only at Mapam's poor showing but also at the divided moderate right (the General Zionists and the Progressive Party together won twelve seats and about 10 percent of the general vote), which had paid the price of its "ideological weakness" and had survived thanks only to its loyalty to Mapai.[65] In 1965 Herut and the General Zionists (by then the Liberals) would agree to unite in order to compete with the united left. In 1949 Begin had no doubt that his party was too isolated to be considered a partner in any coalition, and he accepted the role of a "partner to the fate of the state," but in opposition, where he would remain for nearly three more decades.[66]

Indeed, Herut's uncompromising militaristic outlook necessarily kept it out of the government. The party objected to the armistice agreements with the neighboring Arab states, arguing that rather than acting as a catalyst for peace, they would "push toward war." The party, however, was overwhelmingly defeated (68 to 15) in a vote of no confidence called by Begin over the armistice agreements; only Lehi (now called the Fighters Party because Lehi had become illegal) joined Herut. While Ben-Gurion condemned the Deir Yasin policy, espoused by IZL and Lehi, of "exterminating" the Arab people, *Herut* hailed it as a "blessing" for having signaled the beginning of sweeping conquests and then the "mass migration" of hundreds of thousands of Arabs. Indeed, Yeivin argued, in the final analysis "'operation Deir Yasin' was also very *humanitarian*. It saved a lot of blood, Jewish blood . . . some say Arab blood too."[67]

Although the transfer of Arabs was omitted from its program, Herut spokesmen cited the precedents of Turkey and Greece (1922), Poland and Russia (1945), and India and Pakistan (1947) as "healthy" examples for emulation. The Hitler-Mussolini agreement (1939) on southern Tyrol was cited to show that transfer need not be only a consequence of war but could also result from a friendly agreement. Transfer was mentioned in connection with the debate over the return of the Arab refugees, but implicitly it referred also to the Arabs who had remained in Israel, in the light of Herut's claim for "a strong Hebrew state in its historical borders."[68] Herut's image of the coalition government led by Ben-Gurion was as misplaced as the IZL's perception of the JAE had been before 1948. The party, as Knesset member Shmuel Merlin wrote, believed that the government had a "psychological complex," manifested in its fear of expanding the country's borders, ingathering all the remaining exiles, and creating a strong economic base for industrial independence.[69] Herut would learn by trial and error that governmental responsibility involved the abandonment of radical ideology and the adoption of a different kind of politics. The underground and the opposition were the wrong schools for learning the basic rule expressed in Bismarck's maxim that politics is the art of the possible. Begin in 1949, though, never dreamed of a scenario such as Camp David nearly thirty years later, in which he would agree to sign a peace treaty with Egypt that also recognized the "legitimate rights" of the Palestinian people.

Conclusions

The leadership of David Ben-Gurion is the key to understanding how Zionism triumphed during the period 1936–49, and from 1945 to 1949 in particular. As chairman of the Jewish Agency Executive, Ben-Gurion understood what was necessary to achieve a Zionist breakthrough: relentless consolidation of power founded on demography (i.e., immigration), international sympathy, military preparedness, a solid economic infrastructure, and acquisition of land. The last-named was especially problematic, as in 1948 only 7 percent of the country's land had been purchased by the "national institutions." Consolidation of power was the essential long-term instrument that would provide the firm foundation for a state. At the same time, it was imperative to exploit the consensus, both in the organized Yishuv and outside it. Hence, Ben-Gurion could act as an arbitrator among the four positions that were dominant in Zionist politics: his own partition plan, the intellectuals binationalism, the radical left (split between binationalism and Greater Israel), and the radical right's Greater Israel.

There was nothing inevitable about the success of the thrust for power. Setbacks alternated with progress, and the entire process was fraught with an internal contradiction stemming from British policy. At its peak, in the 1930s, the drive for power became a Zionist response to the mounting distress of the Jews in Eastern and Central Europe, while at the same time constituting a quest to persuade the British authorities to reject the Arabs' national demands. Nevertheless, pragmatic considerations, such as the Yishuv's economic resilience and the high quality of the immigrants in the 1930s (especially from Germany), were no less critical to the consolidation of power than were considerations of Britain's prestige as a global and regional power or British strategy deriving from Palestine's proximity to the Suez Canal, the Empire's lifeline. It was because of this strategic rationale, coupled with concern about being supplanted by another power in the region, that Britain decided against decolonizing Palestine at an early date (1923), not long after it assumed the Mandate. (Zionism was only one tool in British imperial policy, and a temporary one; Britain was as committed to granting self-rule to the local Palestine Arab population as it was to the concept of the Jewish national home.)

Before Ben-Gurion's ascendancy in the Zionist leadership, European Jewry was not yet in dire crisis. It did not yet appear that the Zionist clock was running out due to an evolving dual process: the Arabs' growing influence and threat and Britain's dwindling strength as an imperial power. Seeking to ward off a possible second Arab revolt, the government utilized the White Paper (1939), contrary to its Mandate obligations, to curb Zionist power in critical areas such as immigration and settlement. Although not completely successful, this policy was sufficient to prevent the emergence of a Jewish majority—that is, of critical mass—in Palestine and thus undermined Zionism's ability to accumulate power and wield it in practice.

Following Ben-Gurion's accession to the leadership, rising anti-Semitism in Eastern and Central Europe created the conditions for Jewish immigration. One of Ben-Gurion's fundamental tenets was that power must be pursued in every historical situation but without wasting force in the battle against the authorities. Hence, he induced 30,000 residents of the Yishuv to enlist in the British Army, which was desperate for manpower in the war against Hitler. This tactic created a window of opportunity for Zionism's empowerment, even if the White Paper posed a threat to the long-range prospects. How, then, did Ben-Gurion resolve the contradictions between the positive and negative trends? How was he able to maneuver between domestic and external constraints?

In the first place, there was the precedent of the Peel Commission, which had concluded that the Mandate was a failure and that a Jewish state should be established in part of Palestine. The commission's acknowledgment that already in 1937 the Yishuv possessed the necessary infrastructure to support a state boosted the self-confidence of the leadership, and consequently of the people, in the possibility of an independent state if only the great powers and the Jewish people worked actively to that end. Additionally, Ben-Gurion neutralized the opponents of partition, on both the right and the left, by isolating them. In the background loomed the ominous deteriorating situation of European Jewry, culminating in the Holocaust.

Three entities were crucial for the consolidation of power: the Yishuv, the great powers, and the Jewish people. Concretely, the Yishuv could resort to a variety of means: illegal immigration, aggrandizement of its military capability through mass enlistment in the British Army and Auxiliary Police, mobilization of American Jewry (financially and politically), and diplomatic activity to persuade the great powers that a Jewish state was a vital necessity and could be accomplished with relative ease (via an intensive "information effort" to counter Arab opposition).

In the war's aftermath, the question was how to transform the state-in-the-making into an independent state. It now seemed possible that the 1939 White Paper, which had proposed the establishment of a Palestinian state where the Jews would constitute a one-third minority, might become permanent British policy. Concurrently, the Arab side gained strength through a series of developments: the creation of the Arab League, the Arab states' involvement in the founding of the United Nations, and mounting pressures in Britain and France for decolonization. Whether the new world order would take into account the aspirations of Zionism was a moot point.

In the immediate postwar era, Zionist realpolitik dictated three moves involving high risk. The first was the mobilization of American Jewry in the struggle for a Jewish state, taking advantage of the new presidency to open a new chapter in relations with Washington. The second was to make the Holocaust survivors in Europe an active political factor. The third was the Yishuv's resistance to British government policy. Intensive Zionist propaganda activity persuaded Truman and his representatives on the Anglo-American Committee of Inquiry to accept the slogan urging the immigration of 100,000 Jews to Palestine as a realistic political idea. At the same time, members of the Jewish Agency Executive sought to persuade the traditionally anti-Zionist State Department that the Arabs' sheer negativism was contrary to American interests. The executive's decision to dispatch Goldmann to meet with Acheson, taken at its 1946 meeting in Paris, was a watershed in the history of Zionism. Still, it had taken traumatic events such as the Black Sabbath and the bombing of the King David Hotel to show the Zionist leadership that violence of the sort pursued by the United Resistance Movement was no longer viable and that it was urgent to forge a link between the United States and the Holocaust survivors in the struggle for a Jewish state. The simultaneous realization that it was necessary to adopt realistic considerations over ideological axioms was given expression in the form of the Jewish Agency's public consent to partition (i.e., a viable Jewish state), an implicit acknowledgment of the limits of Zionist power.

This increased American involvement in favor of Zionism. Truman's Yom Kippur announcement in 1946 alluded for the first time to the need for a compromise between British policy and Zionist aspirations. However, this did not yet signify Washington's full support for a Jewish state (that would await the Soviet-American rivalry generated by the Gromyko declaration in 1947). In the meantime, the leadership in Jerusalem walked a thin line between the two rival powers, avoiding excessive anti-Soviet propaganda despite Moscow's ideological opposition to Zionism, while also trying to distance the United States from Britain. Ultimately, Zionism was able to pursue both Soviet and American options, despite the irreconcilable motives of Moscow and Washington for supporting Zionism and despite the U.S. administration's vacillations.

The second window of opportunity, involving the Holocaust survivors, had existed before the war as illegal Jewish immigration to Palestine. However, in the war's immediate aftermath, the campaign to bring the Jewish DPs to Palestine was less a means to consolidate power than it was a political instrument to mobilize the Yishuv and enlist extensive international support. The Zionist leadership hoped that the shock of the Holocaust and the plight of the survivors would transform illegal immigration into a political catalyst on world public opinion and thereby influence the major decision makers.

The struggle for the right of Jewish immigration to Palestine in turn reached its peak concurrent with the work of UNSCOP, the findings of which would affect the decision of the great powers. The favorable UNSCOP decision was achieved by the persuasive powers of Zionist leaders in explaining to the commission members the Palestine Jews' rights under the Mandate, the Yishuv's martyrological struggle, and the seriousness of the quest for a pragmatic solution. Similarly, it was in support of post-Holocaust pragmatism actualized in the Ben-Gurionist partition conception that the national religious parties and the General Zionists, contrary to their position in 1937, repressed their ideologies calling for an undivided Land of Israel.

Illegal immigration thus served a policy of realpolitik and in addition enabled the opening of the final window of opportunity, the activation of the Yishuv itself, by fusing the ambitions and expectations, at least in part, of the advocates of each of the four positions. In fact, the Yishuv had little choice, now that all its previous political options had been frustrated and it found itself pushed into a corner by the British government. Initially, the Yishuv resorted to violence (the United Resistance Movement) in order to demonstrate its destabilizing capability and to ensure that the critical mass of power it had accumulated by the end of the war would remain intact as a lever for the establishment of the state. For a time, then, Weizmann, Aliyah Hadashah, and the intellectuals of Ichud were displaced in favor of the breakaways.

The unprecedented inclusion of the right-wing underground movements, the Irgun and Lehi, in the United Resistance Movement, did not mean the endorsement of their notion of the general revolt. It was, rather, a controlled and basically limited struggle having a dual purpose: to show the British and the world that the Yishuv leadership would resort to all means, even collaboration with its domestic foes, in the pursuit of its goals; and to prepare the Yishuv public for more difficult campaigns to come—against the Arabs. This inclusion provoked a bitter dispute between moderates and extremists. Moderates, such as the internal opposition in Mapai, warned that an unrestrained fight against the British would be ruinous, while at the other pole, groups such as Le'achdut Ha'avodah argued that a suspension of the united struggle with the Irgun and Lehi would be disastrous. Achieving a consensus within the Yishuv was of prime importance to the leadership— but not at the price of forsaking controlled activism.

At this juncture, Ben-Gurion had to wield his charismatic leadership credibly and effectively to bring about joint action based on a minimal program to which the majority of the Yishuv's parties (other than the radical right) could subscribe. Without raising the loaded question of partition, Ben-Gurion took a middle road of dissolving the United Resistance Movement and turning instead to intensified illegal immigration. By this tactic he sought to accomplish several goals: to ensure the broadest possible consensus in the Yishuv and avert the danger of civil war; to enable the continuation of the diplomatic struggle for a state, which emphasized the need to achieve justice for the Jewish people; and to avoid an irreparable break with Britain in the absence of any alternative great power support. In fact, illegal immigration had become the only avenue through which to pursue a struggle both intensive and more cautious, guerrilla warfare (the United Resistance Movement) having exhausted itself. Though illegal, *aliyah*, particularly in the context of Holocaust survivors, assured a broad consensus encompassing even the most moderate elements in the Yishuv. Externally the immigration campaign, signaling a larger number of prospective immigrants, escalated the situation and forced Britain to hasten decolonization. Besides, speed was of the essence: to languish in camps without a binding timetable for immigration to Palestine would erode the survivors' Zionist resolve.

The Yishuv's rapid transition in August 1946 from what was essentially a local struggle to one focused on the survivors' right of immigration was also based on the conception that a confrontation with Britain was both unnecessary and potentially counterproductive in the face of a war looming (since June 1946) with the Arabs. The opposition of the right-wing undergrounds to the illegal immigration campaign—they claimed it exploited the survivors' suffering—and their urging, instead, of war against the British raised a tactical question: Would the state be brought into being by means of the accumulation of power for possible future use against the potential long-term Arab threat or by the use of force in the here and now to evict the colonial power? From the leadership's perspective, the price of dropping the breakaways might be too high in terms of the anti-British struggle, but it was inevitable in view of the mounting Arab danger and the need to preserve the Yishuv's strength for what was perceived as an inevitable showdown on the battlefield.

The radical right denied the existence of a viable Arab factor, claiming that it was an artificial bogeyman created by the British—and why expend force against an illusory threat? To Ben-Gurion and the Yishuv leadership, however, Arab strength was an objective, autonomous fact, which could not be ignored. The British Cabinet's decision of February 1947 to refer the Palestine question to the UN meant that preparation for a war with the Arabs catapulted to the head of the Zionist agenda, relegating the struggle against Britain to second place. Previously, the Arabs had not been considered an intractable enemy against whom preemptive action might be necessary. True, the events of 1936–39 had shown that a military crisis could erupt without warning, but until the middle of 1946, the Yishuv leadership did not contemplate the possibility that the Jewish community in Palestine might have to cope on its own with an all-out attack by the Arab states and therefore did not create a serious deterrent force.

The Haganah's strategic planning had all along been predicated on the assumption of security cooperation with the British. The leadership had begun to realize that holding a dialogue with the Arabs on the basis of the demand for a state was a futile exercise. Though realizing with despair that neither Palestine Arabs (1936) nor the neighboring Arab states (1939) would countenance a Jewish state, Ben-Gurion still hoped for an accommodation with King Abdullah. The terms of the Faisal-Weizmann agreement—a Jewish state within regional Arab unity, guaranteeing Arab rights, but no Palestinian state—remained the constant guideline. Its operative worth, however, was nil; it served only as a propaganda tool to show world opinion and the great powers that some Arabs were supposedly ready to accept a Jewish state in the Middle East.

Ben-Gurion and his colleagues sought to convince the international community and the various commissions of inquiry that the Yishuv's drive to consolidate a power base was valid because Jewish deterrent capability would induce the Arabs to accept the situation on the ground. This line of thought went some way toward strengthening unity within the Yishuv and among the Jewish people; but neither the British nor the Arabs took it seriously. The Yishuv's approach meant that the decision to undertake preparations for a war against the Arabs was made very late, following a learning process that the leadership would afterward admit had been in part naïve. The turning point was the Bludan conference, in June 1946, at which the Arab side treated the Yishuv's call for the immigration of 100,000 Jews as a casus belli. Hence, the Yishuv had to revert to military strength, beginning with an increase in the Jewish Agency's security budget and Ben-Gurion's assumption of the defense portfolio. With this additional concentration of power in his hands, Ben-Gurion became the principal, if not the exclusive, decision maker in the leadership—that is, in the Jewish Agency Executive, Mapai, and the Histadrut.

Indeed, since the Paris conference in the summer of 1946, Ben-Gurion's political decisions had been accepted unquestioningly by the majority, with the exception of the breakaways, who were becoming increasingly isolated. A series of developments—Weizmann's neutralization as a decision maker and his new role as an "explainer" of policy; Shertok's imprisonment and incommunicado status; Sneh's resignations and Galili's dismissal from the Haganah command; and concurrently, the collapse, in the summer of 1947, of the plans adduced by Ben-Gurion's opponents on the right and the left for a political solution to the Palestine crisis—had the result of vesting Ben-Gurion with unprecedented power and enabled him to exercise absolute political control during the War of Independence. At the same time, he intervened ever more directly in the Haganah, having discovered, however late, that its war plans were inadequate and its arms supplies deficient. Nonetheless, the war itself would show that the people of the nascent state were sufficiently motivated and that the minimal infrastructure required to conduct the type of war that developed in 1948 was in place.

Thus we find asymmetry between the Yishuv's lethargic consolidation of power in terms of accumulating the resources needed to wage war and the more rapid pace of the political developments toward an international decision. Ben-Gurion was forced to concede that the Jewish community in Palestine, although far ahead of the local Arab population economically and otherwise, and already bearing the trappings of a progressive Western state, could not win on the battlefield without outside arms and equipment and international political support. Two windows of opportunity thus still had to be opened at the most critical level.

The first came in the form of an intelligence estimate by Yishuv experts, which went unchallenged, holding that the Arab states lacked both the capability and the will for war. Though this appeared to lessen the urgency of Zionist military preparations, externally it proved an effective tool with which to persuade UN member states that the Arabs' war threats were mere rhetoric.

Here, only the second response could prevail: reliance on the Soviet Union. The USSR played a decisive role following several critical months (February–May 1947) when none of the great powers seemed willing to step in and prevent a Yishuv military débâcle. Washington did not support a Jewish state before October 1947 and would impose an embargo that December on arms shipments to the region. Briefly, the Soviet Union saw in the Yishuv a national liberation movement fighting Middle East imperialism and, as such, deserving of military and diplomatic support. Moreover, by proffering such aid, Moscow thought it could obtain the backing of American Jewry in the Cold War. The Yishuv's drive for power, engineered by Ben-Gurion and assuming an anti-British character since the dissolution of the United Resistance Movement and the renewed emphasis on illegal immigration, was the only basis on which Moscow could assist Zionism. Indeed, it is a central thesis of this book that Ben-Gurion would never have dared establish a Jewish state without Soviet support.

What, then, was Ben-Gurion's most important decision in the drive for the Yishuv's empowerment? It was, in fact, a political one: the decision for partition, in 1946. Yet paradoxically, perhaps, it represented tacit acknowledgment of the limits of Zionist power—awareness of which, as we have seen, had begun to take root in 1937, when the Peel Commission recommended partition. Zionism could not gain the whole land, let alone seize it by force. The presence of a massive Arab population in the heart of the country left partition as the only viable option. The lesson was that neither the accumulation of power nor the use of force could assure total success (contrary to the viewpoint, at that time, of Begin and Friedman-Yelin). Ben-Gurion never strayed from his basic doctrine: Zionism could not be realized other than by partition. Diminished territory was preferable to diminished sovereignty. The majority in the Zionist movement and the Yishuv showed that they, too, believed in realpolitik, even if from time to time some indulged in maximalist thinking.

Backing Ben-Gurion was a stable coalition of Mapai, the General Zionists, and Hamizrachi, afterward joined also by the radical left. Until the summer of 1946, however, opposition to Ben-Gurion came from the radical left and the radical right, together constituting perhaps a quarter of the electorate. In any event, neither of the radical extremes threatened to emulate the Irish model (though the right invoked the Irish and other models of "heroic liberation struggles"), with its latent risk of civil war, or the Italian model, which fused armed struggle with external diplomatic support. Ben-Gurion made do with the biblical model of Moses and Joshua, combining spiritual and military leadership, though with a crucial strategic emendation: he affiliated himself with the modern civilized world, thus enabling national existence even in a hostile region until peace could be attained.

Ben-Gurion could not have wished for more pliant partners in the Zionist coalition during this period. The General Zionists, who were constantly splintering and regrouping, were socioeconomically moderate conservatives but politically were centrists (even if one of the party's factions engaged in militant rhetoric). Rosenblueth's coming to terms with Ben-Gurion's outlook in 1947, Gruenbaum's and Bernstein's acceptance of partition, and Sneh's ouster from the General Zionists facilitated Ben-Gurion's efforts to bring to fruition the partitioned state.

Ben-Gurion's second loyal coalition partner consisted of the national religious parties. They too were located in the center of the political map, perhaps even slightly to the left in view of Hapoel Hamizrachi's connection with the Histadrut. Politically, Ben-Gurion had no more faithful ally than these parties, which never asked him to subordinate the process of accumulating power to religious ideology based on the "biblical" Land of Israel.

Outside the Jewish Agency coalition, the radical left, which was a partial ally in the Va'ad Leumi, the Haganah, and the Histadrut, did not represent the same kind of vigorous opposition to Ben-Gurion as did the radical right. The radical left was also first to acknowledge its conceptual failure, following UNSCOP's partition recommendation, and was compelled to accept Ben-Gurion's invitation to join the national emergency coalition if it wished to influence the course of the war. Ironically, though, the radical left was never more neutralized than when it was ostensibly at the core of decision making. Ben-Gurion exploited the left's assumption of full national responsibility to disband the Palmach, the source of the left's pride and strength, as an independent unit while pursuing his "statist" orientation and reinforcing his concentration of authority.

The mainstay of the radical right was the Irgun and afterward the Herut movement, both headed by Menachem Begin. The difference was that Begin, unlike the leaders of the radical left, accepted Ben-Gurion's authority only briefly—as long as the United Resistance Movement existed. Consequently, neither Begin nor the Revisionist mother party (Herut), which supported the Irgun after the dissolution of the United Resistance Movement, was co-opted into the emergency government. Irgun units joined the newly created Israel Defense Forces immediately after the state's establishment. However, Ben-Gurion, who was in the minority as regards his demand that they join on an individual basis and not as complete units, remained deeply mistrustful of them. This had its tragic culmination in the *Altalena* episode. The forcible suppression of what Ben-Gurion feared was an attempted putsch demonstrated potently the metamorphosis of the empowerment process in the era of the state: the necessity now was for a uniform army subject to a single authority, befitting a properly run state. This principle Ben-Gurion applied to both the radical right and the radical left.

In retrospect, though, a fundamental difference marked the opposition mounted by the two extremes. The rivalry with the left was more of a tactical quarrel. Despite political and ideological differences, the left did not challenge Ben-Gurion's basic thesis—the need to accumulate and consolidate power—and collaborated with him in the Haganah, the IDF, and the Histadrut. Later, however, at the height of the Cold War, the left's Marxism, its pro-Soviet stance, and its calls to introduce in Israel a socialist regime modeled on the Eastern bloc type were perceived by Ben-Gurion as a strategic threat to Israel's pro-Western democracy. The left would be deemed qualified to take part in Israel's governance only after it had disavowed the USSR and communism—especially after the mentioned Prague show trial of 1952 in which Mapam member M. Oren was involved and the "Doctors' Plot" of 1953 in the Soviet Union in which Jewish doctors were accused of planning to poison Soviet leaders. The completion of this process, a process the roots of which lay in anti-Semitism, occurred when the Soviet Union shifted its support to the Arab side, and this completion decided the fate of Mapam and ultimately brought about its disintegration. On the other hand, the radical right had to be "punished" and partially delegitimized: it could participate in the general elections but, while Ben-Gurion was prime minister, could not be considered a coalition partner. In the period of the state, then, no less than before, a balance had to be struck between the external and the internal—*Aussenpolitik* intertwined with *Innenpolitik*—in order to ensure a smooth interaction. Ben-Gurion maintained the needed balance masterfully.

Israel's establishment, far from terminating the process of accumulating state power, worked to accelerate it. Ben-Gurion understood immediately that the state would not survive if its power were not enhanced in the short term, by doubling and trebling the population and reinforcing the national infrastructure, military and economic alike. Nevertheless, after 1948 the road to power tended to involve external sources far more than previously. As early as 1949, Israel's exclusive economic dependence on the West, meaning the United States, was a fact of life; indeed, it was a dependence that extended to other realms, cultural and intellectual, ideological and political: plainly Israel was an integral part of the West. Despite this, Ben-Gurion adopted a policy of nonalignment, fearing that any other course would cause the complete severance of the already tenuous lifeline to the huge Jewish population reserves in the Soviet bloc. Ben-Gurion's continuous thrust to augment the power of the state dictated an armistice, however shaky, with the Arab states.

Ben-Gurion's conception of war and peace was shaped on the eve of the 1948 war and evolved during its course. If previously he had secretly prepared for war while speaking in public of peace, in order to enable the Yishuv to consolidate power, in the state era this approach became an operative political formula. The war itself brought home to Ben-Gurion the limits of Israel's power. True, the Jewish state needed victory to survive, but without genuine peace even that victory was only tactical, not strategic. The Jewish state was incapable of defeating its enemies on their home field of battle: victory was possible only in part of the Land of Israel. To forestall an Arab war of revenge, the Jewish state must strive for peace. Ben-Gurion did not seek a final strategic victory, because he based his grand plan not on the concept of an undivided Land of Israel but on the Greco-Turkish model—that is, a tactical approach involving the flight and expulsion of the Arab refugees—rather than annexing the West Bank and Gaza, thus threatening the Jewish majority. His agenda, therefore, was: first, establish a state in part of the country; fight if the Arabs force a war on the state; and seek peace, always remembering that survival is not compatible with the psychology and praxis of a nation that dwells alone.

All three stages entailed the aggrandizement of the state's power. The motivating principles remained constant: ingathering of the exiles in order to revive the once-independent Jewish state, combined with a modern infrastructure able to absorb mass immigration, maintain industry and agriculture, and support an effective army. In Ben-Gurion's perception, modern Israel was the third historic attempt to forge Jewish independence, and he was conscious that the conditions for Jewish survival in the region were no less difficult than in the distant past; however, the certain support of the Jewish Diaspora and the Free World would enhance the prospects of success. Leadership interweaving maximal internal consensus with external support (from the Free World) and grounded in political realism and the consolidation of power: this was the constant code of survival.

Appendix

The Debate on the "New Historians"

In this book I seek to place in new perspective the protracted debate in Israel on the contribution of the "New Historians" to research and specifically to understanding the circumstances of Israel's establishment. The debate revolves around the reliability of the findings and the methodology and parameters of their work. The discussion that follows is focused on three prominent New Historians: Benny Morris, a posivitist historian; Avi Shlaim, a diplomatic historian whose work borders on political science, though his studies on the question of Transjordan and Palestine lack theoretical underpinnings; and Ilan Pappé, an ideologue who purports to espouse a moral approach and should be placed between Postmodernism and Marxism.

To begin with, these New Historians have focused their research excessively on the War of 1948, whereas 1945 is a more felicitous point of departure, marking the reappearance of the Palestine question on the agenda of the Western powers and coinciding with the dawn of a new era following World War II and the Holocaust. Second, while the New Historians address issue-specific questions, such as the Arab refugees and the Zionist movement's relations with King Abdullah of Transjordan (Shlaim's "collusion"), I take the view that in addition to an earlier starting point, a broader discussion is also required, encompassing the entire Zionist perspective. What "myths," then, have the New Historians "shattered"?

1. The Question of the Transfer of the Arab Refugees

Although in *The Birth of the Palestinian Refugee Problem, 1947–1949* (Cambridge, 1989) Benny Morris has uncovered new material, his work does not take into consideration the broad context of Zionist policy at both the tactical and strategic levels. His attempt to equate Zionist policy on the Arab question with the theory and practice of the transfer of the Palestine Arabs is blatantly overstated. Still, he claims correctly that the work of the Peel Commission generated a comprehensive discussion of the transfer question among the Zionist elites, though it soon ended when the program was scotched. David Ben-Gurion, although not rejecting transfer on moral grounds, nevertheless asserted that only Britain could execute it (Morris fails to quote the conclusion of the relevant sentence in his article "Notes on Zionist Historiography and the Transfer Idea, 1937–1944," in *Between Vision and Revision: One Hundred Years of Zionist Historiography,* ed. Y. Weitz [Jerusalem, 1997], 205). Overall, Ben-Gurion's fundamental strategic approach was informed by the awareness that any attempt to place the transfer issue at the top of the Zionist policy agenda would be harmful and wrongheaded.

Morris recently elevated the transfer question another notch by arguing that incipient Zionist thinking on the question originates with Herzl, that is, with the father of Zionism himself (ibid., 195). This is patently incorrect, as the "father" of the transfer idea was the Anglo-Zionist writer Israel Zangwill. In any event, Morris is not the first to claim that Herzl was the progenitor of the transfer idea; the notion was initially propounded by the British writer David Hirst, who is pro-Arab and radically anti-Zionist (David Hirst, *The Gun and the Olive Branch: The Roots of Violence in the Middle East* [London, 1977]; 2d ed., 1984). Shlaim quotes Hirst in the first edition of his book. When Herzl in 1896 raised the idea of moving out the "local residents" (it was not by accident that "Arabs" were not specified), he knew absolutely nothing about the region's Arabs. Herzl became aware of the Arab problem only in the wake of the letter written by Yusuf Zia al-Khalidi, a Jerusalem dignitary, to Rabbi Zadok Kahan of Paris. Indeed, that letter may have been the inspiration for the famous dialogue in Herzl's utopian novel *Altneuland* between Rashid Bey and the Zionists on the benefits that would accrue to the Arabs from Zionist settlement. There is no doubt that Herzl's novel influenced the succeeding generations of Zionist leaders and skewed their view of the natural dimensions of the Arabs' hostility to Zionism. However, not only should we not demand of Herzl recognition of Arab nationalism, which was nonexistent; we must also recall that Herzl entertained no program to expel Arabs and that Zangwill had absolutely no influence on him in this regard. Herzl's remarks on the issue were no more than politically inconsequential ruminations. At all events, he had no intention of breaking the rules of the game of that era, and if he sought a charter for settlement, within the Ottoman Empire or elsewhere, it was a priori only with the consent of the great powers. Morris is equally wrong about context, this time in the sense of the *Zeitgeist*, the spirit of the time. In the late 1890s the Arabs were far from being an autonomous political factor of any weight, and moreover they were loyal Ottoman citizens lacking Arab national consciousness.

Morris ignores the fact that the lexicon of the "Age of Imperialism" was very different indeed from the terminology of the 1930s and 1940s. At the end of the nineteenth century the transfer idea was completely unknown, whereas by the 1930s and 1940s it was brought to life by the transfer of Greeks residing in Turkey to Greece (1922), an operation that was considered to be successful at the time and which the fathers of Zionism considered a model for moving Jews to Palestine. In the wake of the Peel Commission's proposal to transfer Arabs, Zionist public opinion invoked the Greco-Turkish model for the transfer of the Palestine Arabs as well. This approach was retained until late in World War II, when it was supplanted by the model of the Sudeten Germans.

It is noteworthy in this context that, despite the radical nature of his views concerning the centrality of the transfer question in Zionist thought and deed, Morris has not backtracked from his most crucial conclusion: that neither in 1948 nor earlier did Ben-Gurion harbor a master plan to expel or uproot the Arabs, and that the transfer of 1948 was generated by the dynamics of the war itself. Morris should, but does not, explain why the Zionist leadership did not address the transfer question between 1945 and 1948 or, more important, why it was not included in Zionism's programmatic platforms. The naïve expectation after the war (as Ben-Gurion admitted—see chapter 4, this volume) that a Jewish state would come into being in accordance with a formal decision of the great powers meant that priority was given to diplomacy, at least temporarily. Underlying this expectation was the assumption that the Jewish problem could not conceivably be ignored in the immediate aftermath of the Holocaust. As I have explained in this volume, the point of encounter (or convergence) between the interests of the powers and those of Zionism was Ben-Gurion's idea for a political compromise in the form of territorial partition.

Morris wrongly attributes mere tactical significance to Ben-Gurion's consent to partition (B. Morris, *1948 and After* [Oxford, 1994], 9). Although he relies on authentic texts in which Ben-Gurion speaks of territorial expansion beyond the boundaries of the partitioned state as envisaged by the Peel Commission, he does not draw a meaningful distinction between Ben-Gurion's actions as a decision maker and his statements as a maximalist Zionist. The latter were meant for the ears of his maximalist partners in the coalition: the "B" General Zionists (who were hardly "liberal," as Morris asserts) and even some of his colleagues in Mapai (such as the highly influential Berl Katzenelson). Ben-Gurion's letters to his son and his wife, from which Morris quotes extensively, were not meant for their eyes only but in the first place for the elite of Mapai. Hence Ben-Gurion's indulgence in the kind of double game that is characteristic of statesmen and politicians alike, uttering statements simultaneously as a statesman, who accepted partition, and as a tactician, who opposed that solution. This was neither opportunism nor cynicism; Ben-Gurion, rather, was playing by the rules of the game that were forced on him by the political structure of the Yishuv and the Zionist movement, which already in 1937 was threatened by a possible schism over the partition question. In his overall agenda Ben-Gurion was always solely a practitioner of realpolitik. In other words, he always understood the limits of Zionist strength, and therefore, in the decisive, operative sphere—not the ideological one (which as a decision maker he was under no obligation to invoke)—he accepted the partition proposal, both in 1937 and in 1947. Therefore, the transfer of the Arabs as a strategic solution, particularly after the British government had abandoned the idea, was no more than a distant dream for Ben-Gurion; partition was supposed to resolve the problem of the Arab majority and at the same time provide a realistic solution to the Jewish-Arab conflict. Hence also his explanation to the opponents of partition as advocated by the Peel Report, opponents who threatened to bring down his coalition, that this was not the first partition of the country; the first had taken place under Article 22 of the Mandate, which had excluded Tranjordan from the articles on the Jewish national home. He would therefore also support the secret partition plan that was submitted to the Anglo-American Committee of Inquiry in 1946 (involving two-thirds of the territory west of the Jordan River; see chapter 4 and map).

During the period of World War II, if not earlier, Ben-Gurion had come to the realization that the British Cabinet would support only partition, as would the United States and the Soviet Union, which were even less sympathetic to Zionist demands than was Britain. In the last analysis, then, the "myth" that the Yishuv in fact accepted partition "joyfully" was not shattered. The Yishuv as a whole was pleased with the international agreement in principle for the establishment of a state and did not think too much about the implications of this for the country's borders. Ben-Gurion, in contrast, grasped the significance of the revolutionary principle that the very acceptance of partition entailed for Zionist history, but once hostilities erupted he focused his attention on the capability of his armed forces rather than on the political-diplomatic questions relating to the borders.

2. David and Goliath

This refers to the notion that the Jews were supposedly in an extraordinarily weak position militarily in 1948–49 and, pitted against what were considered overwhelmingly superior forces, were nonetheless able to overcome the Arabs. In the wake of the militant decisions adopted by the secret conference convened by the Arab League in June 1946 at Bludan in Lebanon, Ben-Gurion realized that the possibility of establishing a Jewish state purely by political and diplomatic means was no longer viable (see chapter 3). This coincided with the British government's decision to reverse itself and not adopt the conclusions of the Anglo-American Committee. It follows that the shift in Zionism's strategic thought did not occur in the period of Herzl, or in the wake of the Peel Report, but was spurred by an Arab decision to use military force in order to overturn any Zionist solution that the great powers might try to achieve (including Jewish immigration, not only the establishment of a state). The contention of Ilan Pappé (in *The Making of the Arab-Israeli Conflict, 1947–51* [London and New York, 1994], 53) that the shift occurred in the wake of the Haganah's "May 1946 plan" is mistaken, because this was not a plan of conquest (in contrast to Plan D of March 1948) but consisted solely of reprisal raids in response to an Arab offensive initiative. Even if these were to be large-scale reprisals, the plan itself was intended to prevent the Arab masses from becoming involved in the offensive initiative (Slutsky, *History of the Haganah,* 3:1939–43).

In any event, Ben-Gurion moved from diplomacy to the use of force unwillingly, by stages, and only in the face of an existential threat. True, he had already assumed the defense portfolio at the end of 1946 and had sought an increase in the defense budget even earlier. It was, however, only in the wake of the failure of the London Conference on the Palestine question, in February 1947, that Ben-Gurion understood the necessity of operative preparations for war (in a "seminar" he convened that March, he became aware of the Haganah's limited strength in the event of a full-scale military confrontation with the Arabs). Hence the entire question of the myth of David and Goliath that was supposedly shattered by the New Historians needs to be reexamined, since it refers only to the context of the war, even though crucial political decisions regarding the establishment of a state were made beforehand, inspite of the Haganah's military weakness.

In the present work I take account of the strategic gap that existed between the political preparations made by the Zionist elites and the military preparations. Nevertheless, the New Historians are certainly right to emphasize that the key to understanding the Israeli victory lies in the Yishuv's technological and socioeconomic superiority over both the Palestinian Arabs and the Arab states. In contrast, the Arabs' demographic and territorial superiority did not affect the overall balance of forces. The David-Goliath equation would again be put to the test beginning in the mid-1950s; during the War of 1948 itself David would metamorphose into Goliath only gradually. It should be remembered that the New Historians wrote their books when Israel was strong. Hence, Israel's subsequent wars cast doubt on the very relevance of the equation; but on the other hand, the War of 1948 must be examined in the perspective of the developments since 1945—a turning point that ushered in a new period, as Ben-Gurion himself noted. The 1948 conflict created a new regional order in the Middle East, but the UN partition resolution of November 1947 was only the immediate cause of its outbreak. A comprehensive historical explanation must take into account the long-term factors as well. The transfer of power, as noted, was supposed to take place by nonviolent political-diplomatic means. The shift to violence occurred only after all the political and diplomatic options had been exhausted, and thus the David-Goliath equation was also turned on its head.

3. "Collusion" or "Unwritten Agreement"?

A third myth that was purportedly shattered by the New Historians involves a supposed Israeli-Jordanian "collusion" to deprive the Palestinians of their assets and their expectations of independence. As Morris trains an exaggerated searchlight on the refugees, so Shlaim considers Zionism's relations with Abdullah to be the fulcrum of the Israeli-Arab conflict. The convergence of the two—the expulsion of the Palestinians and the collusion—created the Palestinian tragedy, or so Morris and Shlaim would have us believe.

Moreover, whereas Morris plays down the importance of Plan D (March 1948) for the conquest of the Arab villages that lay near Jewish localities and views the war itself as the prime cause of the expulsion, Pappé considers Plan D a kind of master plan for evicting the Arabs (Pappé, *Making of the Arab-Israeli Conflict*, 94, 98). Here Morris's approach is to be preferred, as it attributes greater importance to unfolding events during the war than to plans drawn up in advance. The War of 1948 was no different from other wars in terms of the relevance of the dictum: *à la guerre comme à la guerre*.

This dispute between two of the New Historians, however, does nothing to prevent a basic methodological meeting of minds between Morris and Shlaim, according to which it was not only the Zionists and the Jordanians who deliberately set out to eliminate the Palestinians as a political factor—the British government was also involved. It is instructive that Shlaim initially yielded to the criticism he faced for using the word *collusion* in the title of his book, and in a subsequent abridged version he deleted that giveaway term (A. Shlaim, *Collusion across the Jordan: King Abdullah, the Zionist Movement and the Partition of Palestine, 1921–1951* [Oxford, 1988], and *The Politics of Partition: King Abdullah, the Zionists and Palestine, 1921–1951* [Oxford, 1990]). Surprisingly, Shlaim's last word on the subject was not uttered until five years later, when he said he regretted omitting the word *collusion* from the title (A. Shlaim, "The Debate about 1948," *International Journal of Middle Eastern Studies* 24 [1995]: 287–304).

Naturally, it must be asked what the "collusion" consisted of—if it existed at all. Did the Zionists follow a master plan? Or were they swept up in the dynamics of events, over which the British administration lost control—abandoning the initiatives for a constitutional solution in favor of the United Nations in contrast to British behavior elsewhere, including India? In the end, Shlaim's approach lacks a conceptual overview that would take into account the vacuum left by the British in the region following the failure of their various plans (Morrison-Grady, Bevin-Beeley). The actors on all sides sought to fill that vacuum by means of talks, such as those between Abdullah and the Jewish Agency, though they did not become genuine negotiations until after the armistice agreements. Pappé, more cautious than Shlaim, refers not to collusion but to an "unwritten agreement" (I. Pappé, *Britain and the Arab-Israeli Conflict* [London, 1988], 16).

Despite what the New Historians think, the talks held by Eliahu Sasson and Golda Meir with Abdullah's emissaries were not full-fledged negotiations, certainly not the talks in the summer of 1946, for parallel to them an envoy of the king's proposed to the British foreign

secretary that all of Palestine should be annexed to the Hashemite kingdom, with the Jews to be granted an autonomous status. In this regard, a useful conceptual framework has been adduced, for example,
by the historian of British imperialism John Darwin, who suggested
that in every case of decolonization three elements should be considered: the internal weakness of the imperial power, the dimunition of
its international status, and the resistance of the national movements
in the various imperial territories (J. Darwin, *Britain and Decolonization*
[London, 1988], and *The End of Empire* [London, 1991]).

In the case of Israel (or, earlier, representatives of the Jewish Agency)
and Transjordan, the two political entities involved were relatively
weak—though not in relation to the Palestinians—and did not conduct a proper foreign policy so much as engage in a struggle for survival. As such, they were obligated occasionally, under pressure from
the other Arab states, to seek an existential common denominator, which
finally was found at the expense of the Palestinians. However, the "collusion" itself was not complete, because the two entities fought each
other bitterly on at least two fronts: Jerusalem and Latrun. Moreover,
there were no solid rules of the game between them, since in both cases
their limited strength precluded them from upholding such rules—
their relations had nothing to do with agreements, whether written or
unwritten.

On top of this the Zionists played by different rules of the game
than did Transjordan. It is, after all, no coincidence that Ben-Gurion
never met with Abdullah but instead dispatched bureaucratic diplomats. Therefore, it is wrong to portray the indefatigable Eliahu Sasson
as a decision maker; at best he was the official who floated Ben-Gurion's
trial balloons, at worst the author of inconsequential position papers.
Naturally, in this realpolitik-driven power game the Zionist leadership
endeavored to achieve the maximum in terms of strategic benefits from
the relationship with Transjordan, even if the credibility of the neigh-
bor involved, Abdullah, was questionable.

If there had truly been collusion, Ben-Gurion himself would have
been a major actor, as he was at Sèvres on the eve of the Suez War. In a
situation where the Palestinians perceived the conflict with the Zionists (and to a certain degree with Abdullah also) as a zero-sum game,
no other outcome was feasible. That Israel cast Abdullah as no more
than a supporting player in the effort to break the ring of Arab hostility is attested by the final results (the failure of the peace negotiations),
if the heavy fighting between the sides is not considered sufficient evi-

dence. Besides the fact that the king was under the strict orders of the British government not to cross the partition lines, military weakness prevented his chief of staff, Glubb Pasha, from seizing parts of the territory that had been allocated to the Arab state (such as Lydda and Ramleh). "Bevin's little King," as Shlaim calls him disparagingly, did not fight for British interests, certainly not for Zionist interests, but to further his own cause. Abdullah was in fact too busy fighting for his own political survival to take part in collusions. He was caught in a triple trap: Britain's abrupt backtracking from its original intention of overseeing an orderly transfer of power in Palestine; his inability to obtain the consent of the other Arab states for his expansionist ambitions; and the Zionist aim of achieving political sovereignty at any price. Certainly Ben-Gurion never viewed Abdullah as a partner in any sort of collusion. From the outset he held the king in too little esteem for such a conspiracy to be feasible, either before the state was declared or afterward.

4. The Zionist Movement: Conspiratorial or Pragmatic?

I have shown in this book that the key to success from Ben-Gurion's point of view lay in his ability to bring about an internal consensus by persuading a decisive majority of the Zionist parties to accept a compromise involving the establishment of a Jewish state in part of Palestine. Characteristically, he used the euphemism *viable* because the term *partition* was anathema to many of his political associates. Shlaim, like Walid Khalidi (of whom Pappé is also an ardent follower) and David Hirst (the biased "authorities" whom Shlaim cites in the first edition of his book), is absolutely convinced that the Jewish-Arab conflict began with Herzl and the First Zionist Congress of 1897. The truth is, of course, that the conflict as such did not begin until the period of the British Mandate, when the earlier pledge of a national home for the Jews received official sanction in a legal mandate granted by the world organization of the time, the League of Nations.

The point of departure for understanding the principled approach of the New Historians is their negative attitude toward the goals and tactics of the Zionist movement. Thus, Shlaim gives the Zionist movement poor marks for its activity between 1897 and 1948, arguing that its goal was genuinely conspiratorial: "to project an image of reasonableness and moderation [it] proposed numerous compromise plans for settlement of the dispute with the Palestinian Arabs. The method it employed to achieve its end varied with changing historical circumstances and included not just flexible diplomacy but also bribery, deception, coercion, and physical force . . . the emphasis gradually shifted from persuasion to coercion, from the peaceful to the violent end of the spectrum" (*Collusion*, 10).

In the abridged version Shlaim is less acerbic and strikes a more balanced tone: "In the formative years, the Zionist movement had to compensate for its military impotence by mobilizing all its political and intellectual resources and drawing on traditional Jewish skills in advocacy and persuasion to attain its goals. With the massive increase in military power that accompanied the achievement of independence, these skills were no longer at such a high premium" (*Politics of Partition*, 10–11).

There is no foundation to Shlaim's insinuations that the Zionist movement looks worse than other national movements because it is supposedly more brutal and apparently also completely Machiavellian. Ben-Gurion especially is portrayed as the progenitor of conspiratorial Zionism. Not one of the New Historians has proved that the strategy and methods of the Zionist movement were worse than those of other national movements: neither the European nations that gained liberation in the nineteenth century nor the nations that gained independence through decolonization processes in the twentieth century. Nor have the criteria for Ben-Gurion's demonization been set forth. Was he really worse than Roosevelt, Churchill, and Stalin, when they countenanced the transfer of millions of Germans at the end of World War II, or of Nehru and Jinnah, whose statesmanship involved the transfer and death of millions with the independence of India and Pakistan?

The truth is that Ben-Gurion was not systematic in his strategy and tactics; but from the moment he took his place at the helm of the ship of state, he grasped the limits of Zionist power and steered his methods of operation accordingly. The temporary priority he accorded to diplomacy did not necessarily derive, as Shlaim thinks, from an absence of military means, but arose from his belief that diplomacy could change the destiny of the Jewish people and bring it a homeland without unnecessary sacrifice of life. Ben-Gurion built an infrastructure for the state, but he did not create a full-fledged military force until almost the last minute. Shlaim would have us believe that Zionism and its founders planned every step meticulously from the outset with a specific goal in mind. Under that skewed logic it is "self-evident" that since the last phase of the state-building process involved the use of uncompromising violence, this was "obviously" also the situation from the beginning. History rarely unfolds in this deterministic manner.

To avoid simplistic generalizations, Shlaim, as a historian wishing to elucidate his position on the Zionist approach to the Jewish-Arab conflict, should first have shown the divergent positions that were espoused by the different Zionist parties. But even if his treatment covered only the decision-making elite led by Ben-Gurion, he should have distinguished between the views of its different members. For example, it is essential to differentiate between Ben-Gurion and Shertok; we note that this was not always to Shertok's advantage. Kaplan, Ruppin, and Senator, on the one hand, and Rabbi Fishman, Yitzhak Gruenbaum, and Dov Yosef, on the other, represented contrary approaches to the Arab question. In today's terms, the former were doves and the latter hawks, and not necessarily at the tactical level. Ben-Gurion operated, as I have sought to show, as an arbitrator both within the ruling elite and outside it in an effort to reach a consensus on partition. A discussion that omits completely the debate within and among the various parties (Morris discusses only Mapai and Mapam) on the question of the optimal political-diplomatic solution for Palestine and for the Arab question—and that finds no difference between, for instance, Ben-Gurion and the Revisionists and does not survey systematically the ideological wellsprings of the political developments and the mutual feedback between them—misses the historical truth.

It is not surprising that the New Historians have by and large ignored Anita Shapira's *Land and Power: The Zionist Resort to Force 1881–1948* (New York, 1992), since it deals with the internal background and not with the attitude toward the Arabs. Not only does Morris ignore Shapira's approach to the question of the Arab refugees and to the transfer issue; he and his colleagues have also offered no response to her basic thesis of the "defensive ethos" and its primacy over the "offensive ethos"—a viewpoint that represents a genuine challenge to the New Historians and one that they should have lost no time in refuting. Shapira believes that educational and ideological messages with rhetorical overtones have strategic and operative significance. In the present volume I argue that the defensive ethos did not arise within the Labor movement but from the doctrine of Ahad-Ha'am and his exegesists in Brit Shalom and the Ichud Associations, which supported the idea of a binational state because they believed that partition would induce not compromise but war (see chapter 6).

5. Responsibility for the Failed Peace

The New Historians have not, perhaps, considered that the Israeli victory was achieved with enormous difficulties and at a heavy price. The general feeling was of having nearly lost the war at the beginning. Hence the difficulties of making sacrifices for peace. But have the New Historians been able to disprove, as Morris and Shlaim maintain, the "myth" that "peace was unattainable" in 1949? Was the failure solely the result of "mistaken Israeli judgment"? Again, the root problem is that the *Zeitgeist* is ignored and the present is projected onto the past. The debate is over the essence of the national interest. Is it reasonable to dismiss out of hand as "mistakes" Ben-Gurion's unwillingness to allow a large number of Arab refugees to return to their homes or his refusal to cede a territorial corridor in the Negev to Jordan or to give Syria half of Lake Kinneret? Ben-Gurion's reasoning cannot be understood without a conceptual approach. The fact is that he acted solely on the basis of his interpretation of Israel's national security interest and was broadly backed by Israeli public opinion. In this view the refugees would become a "fifth column," the Negev might be cut off from the rest of the country if Jordan received a corridor, and the implications of giving Syria a crucial water source like the Kinneret (even in return for a "solution" of the refugee problem) were fraught with unacceptable risks. Naturally, in the light of the five costly wars Israel has fought since 1948, it is tempting to argue that an opportunity was missed at the outset. If Ben-Gurion rejected peace, however, it was not from a desire for future expansion but because he viewed the armistice lines as the essential minimum for sheer survival. It is true that priority was accorded to a different agenda—immigration and absorption—but this did not imply a fundamental contempt for peace: it was one element in a constantly shifting order of priorities.

In conclusion, what is needed to effect a balance in Zionist historiography is not proof of the centrality or marginality of the transfer idea in Zionism, or evidence of whether Abdullah and Ben-Gurion hatched a collusion. The need is for a comprehensive study of the tactics and strategy pursued by all parts of the Zionist movement, distinguishing between left and right, conservative right and radical right, social-democratic left and Marxist left. Such an approach will show the Zionist movement to be more pragmatic and less deliberate and planned in its development. It will be seen to be the very opposite of a one-dimensional movement always guided by force. At the same time, it is undeniable that some trends in Zionism were also nourished by Romantic and messianic tendencies and mindsets, though most of the movement (with the exception of the radical right) understood the limits of Zionist strength. Hence the overriding importance of the partition proposal, which was not tactical in character, as Morris claims, but represented a strategic decision. In other words, it was a compromise idea that was intended both to resolve the problem of the great powers' reluctance to grant the Jews sovereignty throughout Palestine and to avert an internal rift. Partition remained the guiding principle: in late 1947, in the prelude to the war, during the war, and afterward in the period of the armistice agreements.

Notes

Introduction

1. Arlosoroff, *Jerusalem Diary*, 333–42.

2. Weizmann was willing to accept "parity," temporary of course, of 60 to 40 in favor of the Arabs in order to avoid Arlosoroff's force-engineered solution; see *Letters and Papers of Chaim Weizmann*, ed. C. Dresener, Series A: *Letters*, 15:350 (28 October 1932).

3. Ben-Gurion, *Memoirs* (1937), 4:60–64.

4. Ben-Gurion, *Memoirs* (1934–35), 2:531; Ben-Gurion Diary, 5 December 1936, Moreshet Ben-Gurion Archives, Sde Boker (hereafter BGA).

5. See Heller, *The Stern Gang*.

6. Cf. Horowitz and Lissak, *The Origins of the Israeli Polity*.

7. Cf. Gorny, "'From Class to Nation': Historical Sources and Ideological Meaning," in *David Ben-Gurion as a Labor Leader*, ed. S. Avineri, 73–91.

8. *Letters and Papers of Chaim Weizmann*, Series A, 18:388–90.

9. Ben-Gurion, *Memoirs* (1937), 4:65.

10. Cf. Ben-Gurion, *Memoirs* (1936), 3:293.

1. Rise of the American Orientation

1. Cohen, *Palestine and the Great Powers, 1945–1948*, 43–55; Brands, *Inside the Cold War*, 168–92.

2. Ben-Gurion, Fourth Mapai Convention, 7 May 1938, in *Bama'arachah*, 2:45–46, 56–59.

3. Ben-Gurion, Letter to Paula, 7 October 1938, *Letters to Paula and the Children*, 242.

4. Ben-Gurion Diary, 22 September 1938, BGA.

5. Ben-Gurion to Mapai Center, 12 September 1939, in Ben-Gurion, *Fighting as a Nation*, 78.

6. "Outlines for Zionist Policy," 15 October 1941, Z4/14.632, Central Zionist Archives, Jerusalem (hereafter CZA).

7. Ben-Gurion in the Jewish Agency Executive (hereafter JAE), 6 October 1942, S25/100, CZA; Ben-Gurion in the Small Zionist Actions Committee, 15 October 1942, where he analyzed his talks with the four main non-Zionist bodies of American Jewry, in *Bama'arachah*, 4:48–56.

8. Ben-Gurion to Fifth Mapai Convention, 25 October 1942, *Bama'arachah*, 4:92.

9. Shertok in Mapai Secretariat (quoting Weizmann), 9 April 1940, Sherrett, *Political Diary* (1940–42), 5:42–44, 252.

10. Shertok in the JAE, 16 December 1944, S/100, CZA.

11. Ben-Gurion in the JAE, 31 December 1944, S/100, CZA; Ben-Gurion to Mapai Center, 15 March 1945, *Bama'arachah*, 3:230.

12. Elath, *The Struggle for Statehood*, and my article "Roosevelt, Stalin and the Palestine Problem at Yalta."

13. S. Meirov to Mapai Political Committee, 29 April 1945, Labor Party Archives, Bet Berl (hereafter LPA).

14. Shertok to the JAE, 15 March 1945, S/100, CZA.

15. Shertok in the Small Zionist Actions Committee, 20 May 1945, S25/1782, CZA.

16. Small Zionist Actions Committee, 31 May 1945, S25/1782, CZA.

17. Weizmann in meeting held at 77 Great Russell Street (Jewish Agency headquarters), London, 13 June 1945, Z4/10.379I, CZA.

18. B. Joseph to Mapai Secretariat, 28 August 1945, and to the Political Committee, 25 September 1945, LPA; Cohen, *Palestine*, 60–61.

19. Kaplan to Mapai Secretariat, 27 September 1945, LPA.

20. Liebenstein in Mapai Secretariat, 27 September 1945, LPA.

21. Ben-Gurion Diary, 24, 29 October 1945, BGA. See I. Alteras, *Eisenhower and Israel*, 29–30.

22. See Chaim Hoffman's report to Mapai Secretariat on 24 July 1946, LPA.

23. Ben-Gurion to Chaim Ben-Asher, 1 November 1945, Ben-Gurion Diary, BGA.

24. Y. Kossoy (Kesseh) to Mapai Center, 14 November 1945, LPA.

25. Mapai Political Committee, 23 February 1946; Mapai Center, 22 November 1945; Mapai Secretariat, 17 December 1945; all in LPA.

26. Mapai Center, 22 November 1945; Mapai Secretariat, 17 December 1945; both in LPA.

27. Ben-Gurion, "Reply to Bevin," *Bama'arachah*, 5:12.

28. Ibid., 5:19.

29. Mapai Council, 30 November 1945–December 1945. Ben-Gurion, *Bama'arachah*, 5:39.

30. Mapai Political Committee, 10 December 1945, LPA.

31. See Heller, "The Anglo-American Committee of Inquiry 1945–46," in *Zionism and Arabism in Palestine and Israel*, ed. Kedourie and Haim, 141.

32. Ben-Gurion and Shertok in meeting at 77 Great Russell Street, London, 29 April 1945 (secret), Z4/10.380, CZA.

33. Ben-Gurion to Paula, 1 May 1946, Ben-Gurion Diary, BGA.

34. Ben-Gurion Diary, 20 May 1946, BGA.

35. Mapai Political Committee, 20 May 1946, LPA.

36. Ben-Gurion Diary, 20 May 1946 and (New York) 1 June 1946, BGA.

37. See Heller, "From the 'Black Sabbath' to Partition," and Cohen, *Palestine*, 116–34.

38. E. Dobkin to Mapai Center, 26 August 1946, LPA. Rabbi Fishman's speech is not available in the original; I rely here on the detailed report by Dobkin, who was present when Fishman spoke.

39. Mapai Political Committee, 31 August 1946, LPA.

40. Ibid.

41. Mapai Sixth Conference, 6 September 1946, LPA; Ganin, *Truman, American Jewry, and Israel, 1945–1948*, 72–73.

42. Mapai Secretariat, 8 October 1946, LPA.

43. Ibid., 15 October 1946; Mapai Council, 16 October 1946, LPA.

44. Shertok to Mapai Secretariat, 25 November 1946, LPA.

45. Silver's speech, 10 December 1946, in *Protocol of the 22nd Zionist Congress*, 45–54. Silver's optimism was emulated in the speeches of Judith Epstein, Hadassah Women's Organization president, on 12 December, and of Goldmann on the same day (in the same *Protocol*, 132–33, 148).

46. G. Meyerson to Mapai Center, 25 February 1947, LPA; cf. *Foreign Relations of the United States*, 1947, 5:1003–4. In fact, Marshall supported the idea of a Jewish national home.

47. Liebenstein in conference with lecturers and active members, 27 February 1947, LPA.

48. Shertok to the JAE, 14 March 1947, S/100, CZA.

49. Shertok to Mapai Secretariat, 19 March 1947, LPA. See also his survey in the JAE the day before, S/100, CZA.

50. Shertok to Mapai Secretariat, 25 March 1947, LPA.

51. Ben-Gurion to Mapai Center, 26 April 1947, LPA.

52. Note on effects of Soviet policy on the Palestine question (n.d.), in Eliahu Epstein to Undersecretary of State Sumner Welles, 29 May 1947, S25/483, CZA. Shertok met with Acheson on 28 May; cf. Shertok to Meyerson, 24 April 1947, S25/3965, CZA.

53. Mapai Secretariat, 11 June 1947, LPA.

54. Shertok to the Small Zionist Actions Committee, 25 August 1947, S5/320, CZA.; Ben-Gurion to Mapai Council, 8 August 1947, *Bama'arachah*, 3:246–47; Dov Shafrir to Mapai Council, 9 August 1947, in *Now or Never*, ed. Avizohar and Bareli, 73 (hereafter *Now or Never*).

55. Mapai Center, 2 September 1947, in *Now or Never*, 85–86.

56. Ben-Gurion to Mapai Center, 3 December 1947, LPA. See also *Bama'-arachah*, 5:271.

57. *Foreign Relations of the United States*, 1948, 5:554–64; see Cohen, *Palestine*, 351–52.

58. Kaplan to Mapai Secretariat, 19 February 1948, LPA.

59. Mapai Secretariat, 20 March 1948, LPA.

60. Ben-Gurion, *Bama'arachah*, 5:287–88.

61. See Forrestal-Byrnes meeting on 3 December 1947, in *The Forrestal Diaries*, ed. Millis, 332, and Meyerson on 20 March and B. Locker on 4 April 1948, in *Now or Never*, 2:357, 359. For a detailed survey of the retreat in America's policy, see Z. Lifshitz memorandum in the compilation from the Israel State Archives and Central Zionist Archives published as *Political and Diplomatic Documents, December 1947–13 May 1948*, ed. Yogev, 339–45 (hereafter PDD).

62. To Mapai Secretariat, 5 April 1948, LPA.

63. Ben-Gurion in the Greater Zionist Actions Committee, 7 April 1948, *Bama'arachah*, 5:304–9.

64. Shertok to Mapai Center, 12 May 1948, LPA. This version should be preferred to the older one in Sharett, *At the Threshold of Statehood, 1946–1949*, 229–38, or in *Now or Never*, 2:501–8. On the meeting of Shertok (and Epstein) with Marshall (and Robert Lovett and Dean Rusk) on 8 May, see PDD, 757–69.

65. Shertok to Mapai Secretariat, 13 June 1948, LPA; Epstein to Shertok, 29 May 1948. *Documents on the Foreign Policy of Israel*, 1:94–96 (hereafter DFPI). The speaker was Loy Henderson, head of the Near East and North Africa desk in the State Department.

66. Shertok to Mapai Secretariat, 13 June 1948, LPA, and DFPI, 1:110.

67. First Mapai Council in the State of Israel, 19 June 1948, LPA.

68. Ibid.

69. Ben-Gurion, *The Restored State of Israel*, 1:200.

70. Shertok to Mapai Center, 24 July 1948, LPA; cf. DFPI, 1:387. On the arms embargo, see Slonim, "The 1948 American Embargo on Arms to Palestine." On Israel's application for a first loan, see DFPI, 1:97, 114–15, 169–70.

71. DFPI, 1:383.

72. Ben-Gurion, *War Diary*, 3:675.

73. Ibid., 3:675–77.

74. Shertok to the State Council, 23 September 1948, in Sharett, *At the Threshold of Statehood*, 290–310. On Bernadotte's mission, see my article, "The Failure of a Mission."

75. Quoted in Ben-Gurion, *Restored State*, 1:292–93.

76. Israel Cabinet Protocols, 26 September 1948, 10:24–25. See also Ben-Gurion, *Restored State*, 1:288, 294.

77. On this see Shlaim, *The Politics of Partition*, 224–26 and note 91.

78. DFPI, 1:604.

79. Ibid., 1:645, 650.

80. Ibid., 2:8.

81. Ibid., 2:45.

82. Ibid., 2:84, 88, 93–4.

83. Ibid., 2:110, 114.

84. Ibid., 2:141, 153, 154.

85. Ibid., 2:171–72; Cohen, *Truman and Israel*, 182.

86. Ibid., 2:182–83.

87. Ibid., 2:312, 395.

88. Ben-Gurion to Mapai Center, 30 November 1948, LPA.

89. DFPI, 2:393; Ben-Gurion, *Restored State*, 5:379–80.

90. DFPI, 2:430–31.

91. Ibid. 2:526, 572.

92. Bialer, *Between East and West*, 71; DFPI, 2:577.

93. DFPI, 2:536–37.

94. Ibid., 2:605; Leffler, *A Preponderance of Power*, 287–88.

95. D. Meron to the foreign minister, Klaus's visit to Israel, 31 January 1949. Chetz/26a/2414, Israel State Archives, Jerusalem (hereafter ISA). According to Meron, State President Chaim Weizmann refused to see Klaus, saying he disliked spies. M. Pragai to the foreign minister, Summary of Klaus visit to Israel, 8 February 1949, ibid. Ben-Gurion, *War Diary*, 3:846, 873, 909.

96. DFPI, 4:45–6.

97. Ibid., 4:66, 69.

98. Ben-Gurion, *War Diary: The War of Independence, Additions and Corrections*, 27 (hereafter Appendix); DFPI, 4:75–77.

99. *Knesset Record*, 1:717–22 (15 June 1949).

100. DFPI, 4:150, 194.

101. Ibid., 4:224–25.

102. Ibid., 4:240.

103. Ibid., 4:248–49, 258.

104. Ibid., 4:283–86. The first request for experts had been made on 2 March 1949; see ibid., 2:523.

105. Ibid., 4:315.

106. R. Shiloah and G. Rafael to Sharett, 15 August 1949, ibid., 4:345–46.

107. Ibid., 4:352–57.

108. Ibid., 4:393–94.

109. Elath (Epstein) to Sharett, 30 August 1949, ibid., 4:408–10.

110. Ibid., 4:466.

111. See NSC 47, Top Secret by Joint Chiefs of Staff, 16 May 1949, *Foreign Relations of the United States*, 1949, 6:1009–12. Cf. also the Report of the NSC from 17 October 1949, ibid., 6:1930–40.

2. Relationship with the Soviet Union

1. Ben-Gurion in debate with Hashomer Hatza'ir representatives, in the 35th session of the Histadrut Council, 8 February 1937, *Bama'arachah*, 1:200–201.

2. Ben-Gurion in a discussion between Mapai representatives and Hashomer Hatza'ir on the issue of unity, 31 March 1937, *Memoirs* (1937), 4:117–18.

3. Ben-Gurion to Fourth Mapai Convention, 7 May 1938, *Bama'arachah*, 2:40; for a fuller version, see *Hapoel Hatza'ir*, 27 May 1938.

4. D. Ben-Gurion, "Outlines for Zionist Policy," 15 October 1941, Z4/14.632, CZA.

5. Ben-Gurion to Fifth Mapai Convention, 30 November 1942, *Bama'arachah*, 4:75.

6. Shertok to Fifth Histadrut Convention, 20 April 1942, in Sharett, *Political Diary*, 5:300–301.

7. E[lieze]r [Liebenstein], "Zionism and Soviet Russia," *Milchamtenu* 9 (August 1943): 3–9 (internal publication).

8. E[lieze]r [Liebenstein], "Zionism and Soviet Russia: The Points of Convergence," *Milchamtenu* 10 (September 1943): 3–6.

9. E. Liebenstein, "A Cable from Moscow," *Hapoel Hatza'ir* 16 (Year 38), no. 1 (29 September 1944): 4–6. Liebenstein appreciated that the cable did not have official Soviet approval and was contrary to Soviet policy at the time. He believed it was a reaction to J. Leshchinsky's book *The Jews in the Soviet Union* (1943), which was critical of Soviet Jewish policy.

10. Y. Schitz, "Left and Right in the Labor Movement in the Yishuv," *Hapoel Hatza'ir* 16 (Year 38), no. 5 (5 November 1944): 3.

11. Shertok to the JAE, 7 May 1944, S/100, CZA.

12. Bohlen, *Witness to History, 1929–1969*, 203; Heller, "Roosevelt, Stalin and the Palestine Problem at Yalta."

13. Friedman (Eliashiv), "What Has Changed in the Soviet Union?" *Milchamtenu* 4, 24 (April 1945): 25–27. Friedman was later head of the East European department in the Israeli Foreign Ministry and served as ambassador to the Soviet Union.

14. Sneh, "Orientation on the World Today," *Ha'aretz*, 2 March 1945; Sneh, "In Defiance of Despair and Complacency," *Ha'aretz*, 20 May 1945; Small Zionist Actions Committee, 20 May 1945, S25/1782, CZA.

15. E. Dobkin to Small Zionist Actions Committee, 31 May 1945, S25/1804, CZA.

16. Mapai Center, 26 June 1945, LPA.

17. Ibid.

18. Reported to the Secretariat of the V League, Protocol 26 September 1945, S25/5717, CZA.

19. Dr. M. Sneh, "The Communists and Zionism," *Ha'aretz*, 14 September 1945.

20. Dr. M. Sneh, "In the Crisis," *Ha'aretz*, 23 November 1945.

21. Mapai Secretariat, 17 December 1945, LPA; Mapai Council, 4 February 1946. On Goldmann's meeting with Beneš (who spoke to Stalin on the Jewish question), see Shertok, 7 May 1944, S/100, CZA. See also Ro'i, *Soviet Decision Making in Practice*, passim.

22. Mapai Political Committee, 23 February 1946, LPA.

23. Ben-Gurion in the JAE, 24 February 1946, S/100, CZA.

24. JAE Session, 1 May 1946, S/100, CZA.

25. Mapai Secretariat, 1 May 1946, LPA.

26. Herzl B[erger], "How to Write on Russia? Is There Any Utility in Hiding the Truth on Russia?" *Beterem*, May 1946, 19–20; for the view of a party member who was also a member of the Jewish Agency's Political Department, A. Levavi, see "Russian Affairs in Our Press: Descriptions of Russia and Zionist Realism," *Beterem*, June 1946, 39–40. Cf. also Y. Schitz, "Thirteen Questions on

the 'Russian Problem' in Our Midst," *Beterem,* September 1946, 22–30. Shitz was apparently influenced by the growing number of anti-Zionist publications in the Soviet Union.

27. Dr. N. Goldmann's speech on 3 August 1946, S/100, CZA. Ben-Gurion's speech of one day earlier could not be found in the archives, but he was quoted at length by Goldmann.

28. A. Levavi, "Monthly Survey of the Development of Russian Policy toward Palestine," no. 1, 4 May 1947, S25/483, CZA. Levavi referred, inter alia, to an anti-Zionist article by the Soviet journalist K. Seriozhin, which appeared in *Novoya Vremya,* no. 15 (1 August 1946): 18–22. A. L[ourie], "Minutes of a Report by Dr. Jacob Robinson: The Press of the USSR and Zionism, July 1945–September 1946," presented at the offices of the American Zionist Emergency Council, 22 October 1946, Z5/470, CZA.

29. Sixth Mapai Convention, 7 September 1946, LPA; Z. Ahronovich, "The Only Criterion," *Davar,* 19 September 1946.

30. Liebenstein's speech, [no place mentioned], 9 October 1946, LPA.

31. Meyerson to Mapai Council, 16 October 1946, LPA.

32. Y. Ben-Aharon to "Dear Friends" (in Le'achdut Ha'avodah), Paris, 22 October 1946, 162/6/4, Hakibbutz Hameuchad Archives, Efal (hereafter KMA).

33. Liebenstein to (Mapai) lecturers and activists, 27 February 1947, LPA.

34. Mapai Secretariat, 25 March 1947, LPA.

35. Ben-Gurion, Sprinzak, Lubianiker, and Grabovsky in Mapai Center, 26 April 1946, LPA. Ben-Gurion's speech was published again (signed G.) under the title "Orientations," in *Ashmoret* 7 (Mapai youth weekly), on 19 June 1947.

36. JAE meeting, 19 March 1946, S/100, CZA.

37. Short minutes of meeting between the Rt. Hon. E. Bevin and Mr. D. Ben-Gurion, FO, 12.2.47, at 9.45 A.M., Mr. H. Beeley also present. Draft. S25/7709, CZA. Cf. the version in Ben-Gurion, *Toward the End of the Mandate,* 354–61.

38. A. Levavi, "Monthly Survey," S25/483, CZA.

39. UN Official Records, Seventy-Seventh Plenary Meeting, 14 May 1947, Discussion of the First Committee on the establishment of special committee on Palestine, 128–35.

40. A. Levavi, "Soviet Policy toward the Palestine Problem," Survey no. 2, May 1947 (internal—for Jewish Agency eyes), S25/6660, CZA. See also the "Observations by Jacob Robinson" on Gromyko's statement, on 15 May 1947, 2268/16, ISA. Robinson noted that Gromyko's demand for the termination of the Mandate was no surprise; what was new was the Soviet motivation. Moreover, Gromyko had been vague about the rights of the Jewish people in Palestine; had left open the question of the DPs' wish to go to Palestine; had made no distinction between the historical ties of Jews and Arabs to Palestine; and had left it to UNSCOP to decide whether binationalism or partition was the preferred solution. Cf. Sharett, *At the Threshold of Statehood,* 73.

41. *Bama'arachah,* 5:175; cf. J1/7223, CZA.

42. Ben-Gurion to the JAE, 22 May 1947, S/100, CZA. For an earlier attempt

to send a delegation to Russia, see Weizmann to Grigg, 25 January 1945, *Letters and Papers of Chaim Weizmann*, Series A, 21:28.

43. G. [Ben-Gurion], "Orientations," *Ashmoret*, 19 June 1946 (see note 35, this chapter). The rest of the article included his neutrality line as stated to Mapai Center, 26 April 1946, LPA (emphasis in the original).

44. E. Epstein to Members of the JAE for Palestine, 31 July 1947 (Confidential), S25/483, CZA.

45. Elath, *The Struggle for Statehood*, 2:175–79.

46. Eliahu Epstein to members of the JAE, 11 September 1947, (Confidential), S25/486, CZA; Elath, *The Struggle for Statehood*, 2:307–9.

47. Mapai Center, 3 December 1947, *Bama'arachah*, 5:267–68.

48. Ibid., 5:304–8 (7 April 1948).

49. Ben-Gurion to Mapai Center, 29 May 1948, LPA.

50. *Protocols of the Provisional State Council*, 17 June 1948, 1:31.

51. Gromyko's speech at the Security Council, 7 July 1948, quoted by Ben-Gurion, *Restored State*, 1:227.

52. DFPI, 1:155–57 (13 June 1948).

53. Ibid., 1:513 (Eban to Shertok, 12 August 1948).

54. Ben-Gurion, *Restored State*, 1:200 (29 June 1948).

55. For a description of interviews with Soviet statesmen and officials, see Namir, *Israeli Mission to Moscow*, 41–42, 52–56.

56. Ibid., 242–50.

57. DFPI, 1:625.

58. Ibid., 1:638.

59. Meeting of the Israeli delegation to the UN General Assembly, Paris, 3 October 1948, ibid., 2:8. On Ratner's discussion (on 5 October) with General Antonov, see Ratner, *My Life and Myself*, 394–401; Namir, *Israeli Mission to Moscow*, 73–75; DFPI, 2:29–30. On the question of Jewish immigration, cf. Bialer, *Between East and West*, 57–77.

60. Meeting in Paris, 12 December 1948, DFPI, 2:286–91. For one example of the increasing difficulties involved in immigration, see 437–40. See also Bialer, *Between East and West*, passim.

61. Bialer, *Between East and West*, 414–16 (1 February 1949).

62. Namir, *Israeli Mission to Moscow*, 109–11; DFPI, 2:440–41 (23 February 1949).

63. DFPI, 2:424–25; Namir, *Israeli Mission to Moscow*, 114.

64. Namir, *Israeli Mission to Moscow*, 114.

65. DFPI, 2:513–16 (18 March 1949).

66. Ibid., 4:27–8.

67. Ibid., 4:54.

68. Ibid., 4:85 (31 May 1949).

69. Ibid., 4:95 (5 June 1949).

70. Ibid., 4:97–98 (6 June 1949).

71. Ibid., 4:269 (Shiloah-Porter conversation).

72. Ibid., 4:224 (13–14 July 1949).

73. Ibid., 4:275 (1 August 1949).

74. Ibid., 4:524 (Sharett to Namir, 4 October 1949).

75. Ibid., 4:551 (15 October 1949); for Meir's report to the cabinet see Cabinet Protocol, 20 February 1949, 18:16; Namir's report is in Cabinet Protocol, 22 November 1949, 5:2–20.

76. DFPI, 4:566–67 (20–21 October 1949).

77. Ibid., 4:625 (15 November 1949).

78. Sharett to M. Eliash, Israeli minister in London, 11 September 1949, ibid., 4:452–53 (emphasis in the original).

79. Ibid., 4:453.

80. Ibid., 4:454–55; on Ben-Gurion's agreement with Sharett's views, see 471.

81. Ibid., 4:718 (14 December 1949).

82. Ibid., 4:728–29. These ideas were presented by Sharett to Justice Felix Frankfurter, U.S. Supreme Court justice, on 15 December 1949, in the hope that they would be transmitted to the secretary of state, Dean Acheson, who was an old friend and former pupil of Frankfurter.

83. Mapai Center, 16 June 1949, LPA.

84. Mapai Secretariat, 28 August 1949, LPA.

85. Ibid. Cf. Ben-Gurion in the Cabinet, 8 November 1949, 15:47.

86. Ben-Gurion, *War Diary*, 3:685.

3. Consolidation of Official Policy

1. Ben-Gurion, *Memoirs*, vol. 4 (1937), and M. Sharett, *Political Diary*, vol. 2 (1937), are indispensable for understanding the perceptions involved in Zionist decision making.

2. Ben-Gurion, *Memoirs* (1938), 5:209–10.

3. Ben-Gurion, *Memoirs* (1937), 4:60–3.

4. Ben-Gurion speech on 29 July 1937, *Bama'arachah*, 1:141–42.

5. Ben-Gurion, *Memoirs* (1938), 5:208. On 12 June, Ben-Gurion told the Jewish Agency Executive that he was in favor of a forcible transfer and saw nothing immoral in it but that only England could implement it. Otherwise, it would pose a "tremendous danger" (216) to the Yishuv and to Jews in general.

6. Protocol of the Committee for Population Transfer, 21 November 1937, second session, S25/247, CZA.

7. Ben Gurion, *Memoirs* (1938), 5:209.

8. Ben-Gurion to JAE, 7 May 1944, S/100, CZA.

9. Sasson to Ben-Gurion, 30 November 1942, in Sasson, *On the Road to Peace*, 260.

10. M.B.-K. [Shertok], "Between Us and the Arabs at This Hour," *Milchamtenu* 2 (January 1943): 15–23 (for internal use only).

11. JAE Session, 12 March 1945, S/100; Small Zionist Actions Committee, 13 March 1945, S25/1787; both in CZA.

12. Small Zionist Actions Committee, 31 May 1945, S25/17787; JAE Session, 12 March 1945, S/100; both in CZA.

13. Full Session of the Va'ad Leumi, 4 June 1945, S25/952, CZA.

14. Mapai Center, 14 November 1945, LPA.

15. Ibid., 26 June 1945.

16. Slutsky, *History of the Haganah*, 3:1898–1901; Shani, "Factors leading to the Disturbance of Defense," *Hachomah* (The Wall), August 1945, 1 (internal; no author); "The Arab League as a Military Factor," *Hachomah*, September 1945, 1, 3.

17. For the original drafts of the speeches of Ben-Gurion and Sneh, see S25/1906, CZA.

18. Joseph, report to Mapai Political Committee, 11 October 1945, LPA; Short Minutes of meeting held at 77 Great Russell Street, London, 8 October 1945, Z4/10.379 II, CZA.

19. Muhammad al-Unsi's talk with Sasson, 18 October 1945, S25/3140 II, CZA; partly in Sasson, *Road to Peace*, 348–49, and partly in B. Joseph, report to JAE, 21 October 1945, no. 9, CZA (secret). Cf. Ben-Gurion Diary, 22 November 1945, BGA.

20. Sasson to Shertok, 21 October 1945, no. 5, and 24 October 1945, both in S25/3140 II, CZA.

21. Ben-Gurion to Bevin, *Bama'arachah*, 5:24–26, 30.

22. For the Arab League reply to Bevin's declaration see Falastin, 7 December 1945, S25/7031, CZA.

23. Sasson to Shertok, 7 December 1945, S25/7690, CZA.

24. Ben-Gurion Diary, 22 November 1945, BGA.

25. Sasson to Shertok, 8 December 1945, S25/2965, CZA.

26. Sasson to Shertok, 24 February 1946, S25/6442, CZA.

27. Ben-Gurion, evidence to the Anglo-American Committee, quoted in *The Jewish Case before the Anglo-American Committee of Inquiry on Palestine as Presented by the Jewish Agency for Palestine*, 55–63 (hereafter *The Jewish Case*).

28. Shertok evidence, ibid., 101–37.

29. See ibid., 80, 94–98.

30. Memorandum of the Jewish Resistance Movement, 25 March 1946, CO/733/75872/138/7, Public Record Office, London; see also "Britain's Middle East Strategy," Memorandum submitted to the Anglo-American Committee, by a Middle Eastern Expert [A. Eban], S25/8065, CZA.

31. Auni conversation with Sasson, Jerusalem, 17 March 1946, in Sasson, *Road to Peace*, 355–58.

32. E. Liebenstein, "Arab Fairy Tales," *Milchamtenu* 9 (33) (September 1945): 3–5; see also his "Arab League—An International Danger," *Davar*, 24 December 1945; Liebenstein and Galili memorandum (March 1939), in Slutsky, *History of the Haganah*, 3:1381–87.

33. E. Liebenstein, "The Arab Factor in Zionist Evidence," *Davar*, 7 April 1946; JAE, 24 March 1946, S/100, CZA.

34. Ben-Gurion in JAE, 24 March 1946, S/100, CZA.

35. For the map, see Heller, "Anglo-American Commission of Inquiry 1945–46," 148–49, and in this book.

36. E. Sasson to Dr. B. Joseph (Shertok's deputy), 12 April 1946, Z5/1083, CZA.

37. Heller, "Anglo-American Commission of Inquiry," 152–53; *Letters and Papers of Chaim Weizmann*, Series A, 22:118–28.

38. Protocol of meeting at 77 Great Russell Street, London, 29 April 1946, Z4/10.380, CZA.

39. JAE, 12 May 1946, S/100, CZA. The treaty with the Maronites was signed on 30 May 1946 by the Maronite patriarch Antoine Pierre Arida, his aide Sheikh Tawfik Awwad, and Bernard Joseph, S25/3269, CZA; see also Arida's letter to Weizmann on 24 May 1946, ibid.

40. Beiruti [?], "Middle Eastern Force," *Ashmoret*, 21 June 1946.

41. Sasson to Epstein, 14 June 1946, in Sasson, *Road to Peace*, 358–62, and Sasson's conversation with Muhammad al-Unsi, 18 June 1946, ibid., 362–64. See also Sasson to Dr. M. Sneh, 18 June 1946, S25/9020, CZA.

42. [No author], "Notes on the Military Strength of the Arab Countries," 11 June 1946, Z6/Packet 17/file 12, CZA (top secret).

43. Apart from the final paragraph, the Hebrew version (signed by Sasson and dated 28 June 1946) and the English one (signed by R[euven Zaslani] and dated 20 June 1946) are identical; S25/485, S25/483, CZA.

44. Ben-Gurion to F. Frankfurter, 17 June 1946, Weizmann Archives, Rehovot (hereafter WA). A special memorandum on this subject, dated 19 July 1946, is in Z5/797, CZA.

45. Cohen, *Palestine*, 195; on Sasson's discussions with Sidky and Abdullah, cf. Sasson, *Road to Peace*, 364–74, and Shlaim, *Politics of Partition*, 69, 76.

46. Ben-Gurion, "Unity and Independence," *Bama'arachah*, 5:102–3; also in LPA, Sixth Mapai Convention file. English translation in Ben-Gurion, *The Rebirth and Destiny of Israel*, 185.

47. A. L[utzky—Alexander Dotan, member of the Political Department], conversation with Auni Abd al-Hadi, 23 August 1946, S25/473, CZA.

48. Sasson to his friends in the Political Department in Jerusalem, 30 September 1946, in Sasson, *Road to Peace*, 375.

49. Short Minutes of a Meeting held at the Dorchester Hotel, London, 30 September 1946, 9 P.M., Z4/10.380, CZA.

50. al-Alami to A. Shukeiry, 20–21 September 1946, private and very secret, London, Dorchester Hotel, in Utz to Giora, 11 August 1948, 105/249, Haganah Archives, Tel Aviv; see also Palestine No. 1 (1947): Proposals for the Future of Palestine, July 1946–February 1947. Cmd. 7044.

51. E. S[asson] and A. S. E[ban], "The Arab Attitude toward Zionism—An Assessment," 6 October 1946, Z4/14.868, CZA (emphasis in the original).

52. Sasson to Shertok, 20 November 1946, S25/2968, CZA. The budget proposed was 200,000 Palestine pounds per year, at least for the following two years, with one-quarter of this allotted to Abdullah's pocket.

53. A meeting with no. 60, 24 November 1946, S25/2966, CZA.

54. Sasson to Shertok, 2 December 1946, S25/63, CZA.

55. *Protocol of 22nd Zionist Congress* (10 December 1946), 59–74.

56. Ibid. (23 December 1946), 480–81.

57. BGA (original in Yiddish); see also Ben-Gurion, *Toward the End of the Mandate* (29 June 1946–March 1947), 266–67.

58. Short minutes of meeting held at the Colonial Office, 6 February 1947, Z4/14.827, CZA (secret; it was attended by top Zionist leaders and officials).

59. Short minutes of meeting between Bevin and Ben-Gurion at the Foreign Office, 12 February 1947, draft, S25/7709, CZA.

60. JAE Session, 14 March 1947, S/100, CZA.

61. Full version in J/7241, CZA.

62. Second Statement by Mr. M. Shertok (16 July 1947), in *The Jewish Plan for Palestine*, 506–15.

63. Danin, *A Zionist without Condition*, 200–203. In an interview with the author (26 April 1994), Yaacov Shimoni spoke about "Danin's theory of the contemptible Arabs." Cf. also Aharon Chaim Cohen, "The Arabs and the Commission of Inquiry," *Davar*, 13 June 1947, in which another thesis was adduced: the "tragic" contradiction between the leadership's repeatedly made threats and the desire of the Palestine Arabs for a normal life after years of strife.

64. [No author], "Are the Arabs a Majority in the Country?" *Beterem*, 15 July 1947, 3–4. Liebenstein is mentioned as the editor.

65. A. S. Eban, "UNSCOP: Situation Report," 4 August 1947, S25/5991, CZA (secret).

66. JAE Sessions, 8, 18 June 1947, CZA.

67. Ben-Gurion, *Restored State*, 1:70–71. Ben-Gurion, *Toward the End of the Mandate* (March–November 1947), 188–89; and see "Agra" [Elazar Galili], "Arab Armies at This Hour: The Egyptian Army," *Ma'arachot* 41 (June 1947): 30, and *Ma'arachot* 42–43 (September 1947): 16–64.

68. In the Security Committee of the Yishuv, 8 June 1947, in Ben-Gurion, *Toward the End of the Mandate* (March–November 1947), 295–96.

69. Mapai Secretariat, 11 June 1947, LPA.

70. Ben-Gurion's statement to UNSCOP in Jerusalem on 4 July 1947, in *The Jewish Plan for Palestine*, 313–30.

71. Ben-Gurion, *Toward the End of the Mandate* (March–November 1947), 303.

72. Mapai Council, 8 August 1947, in Ben-Gurion, ibid., 323–25.

73. Ben-Gurion to the Greater Zionist Actions Committee, 26 August 1947, ibid., 337–38.

74. The conversation is reported in detail by Horowitz, *A State in the Making*, 234–35; see also Caplan, *Futile Diplomacy*, vol. 2: *Arab-Zionist Negotiations and the End of the Mandate*, 274–76. It was mentioned by Ben-Gurion to the Mapai Secretariat, 18 September 1947, in *Toward the End of the Mandate* (March–November 1947), 368.

75. Oral report [to the Political Department] on the political sessions in Sofar, Letter from Egypt, Amram, 26 September 1947, S25/9020, CZA.

76. Summary of a report [to the Political Department] on the deliberations of the Arab League Council at its last session, written by an Arab who attended the meeting, 3 October 1947, S25/9020, CZA; Jamil [Mardam] to Fares [al-Khouri], 13 October 1947, ibid.

77. JAE, 28 September 1947, ibid.

78. Ben-Gurion Diary, 10 October 1947; Ben-Gurion, *Toward the End of the Mandate* (March–November 1947), 393.

79. JAE, 19 October 1947, S/100, CZA.

80. M. S.[?], "Plans for the Occupation of the Country" (conversation with "the vineyardist," Abdel Ghani al-Karmi, Abdullah's secret emissary to the agency, S25/7032, CZA. He was an important source of information, as seen in his reports from 11–19 October 1947, S25/4002, CZA.

81. Ben-Gurion, *Bama'arachah*, 5:245–46 (to the Zionist conference, 29 October 1947).

82. JAE, 16 November 1947, S/100, CZA.

83. Shlaim, *Politics of Partition*, 92–100. The meeting is described in Danin, *A Zionist without Condition*, 185–86.

84. Mapai Center, 3 December 1947, LPA.

85. PDD, 90–91.

86. PDD, 126–29, 143–47, 156–57; Shlaim, *Politics of Partition*, 121–24. In particular David Horowitz, a senior official in the Political Department, was in favor of an arrangement with the king in order to diminish the material damage. For Sasson's peace approach to Azzam on 4 December 1947, see PDD, 27–30.

87. Mapai Center, in *Now or Never*, 293–98, 329. On the limited ability of the Arab states to intervene militarily in Palestine beyond "volunteers," see "Agra" [Elazar Galili], "Arab Armies in Our Generation against the Background of Their Peoples and Their States," *Ma'arachot* 45 (January 1948): 17–144.

88. PDD, 398–402, 1 March 1948.

89. Ben-Gurion, *War Diary*, 224–25 (9 February 1948).

90. PDD, 456–59, 13 March 1948; Shlaim, *Politics of Partition*, 130–31.

91. Greater Zionist Actions Committee, 6 April 1948, S5/322, CZA.

92. See Morris, *The Birth of the Palestinian Refugee Problem, 1947–1949*, 92–96 (Hebrew ed.).

93. Greater Zionist Actions Committee, 6 April 1948, S5/322, CZA.

94. PDD, 625–26, 667–68.

95. Ben-Gurion, *War Diary*, 373.

96. Ibid., 409; *Now or Never*, 496. For the meeting between Golda Meyerson and the king, see Shlaim, *Politics of Partition*, 162–68; Danin, *A Zionist without Condition*, 191–95.

97. PDD, 782.

98. Ben-Gurion, *War Diary*, 487 (5 June 1948). On Weitz, Ben-Gurion, and the transfer question, see Morris, *Palestinian Refugee Problem*, passim.

99. Mapai Secretariat, 13 June 1948, LPA.

100. Ben-Gurion, *Restored State*, 1:163–68; see Cabinet Protocols, 3:19–25; Mapai Council, 19 June 1948, LPA.

101. Ben-Gurion, *Restored State*, 1:167 (Ben-Gurion, *Israel: A Personal History*, 152); Cabinet Protocols, 3:37.

102. Ben-Gurion, *War Diary*, 533 (18 June 1948); Mapai Council, 18 June 1948, LPA.

103. Cabinet Protocols, 2 July 1948, 4:18–41; Ben-Gurion, *Restored State*, 1:215–21.

104. Ben-Gurion, *War Diary*, 582 (11 July 1948); Cabinet Protocols, 4 July 1948, 4:15–16.

105. *Protocols of the Provisional State Council*, 22 July 1948, 1:241–42.

106. Shertok to Mapai Center, 24 July 1948, LPA; DFPI, 1:374; Morris, *Palestinian Refugee Problem*, 197–98. In another speech, however, Shertok stated that the Zionist leadership could never "dream" of a policy leading to the uprooting of any Arab (M. Shertok, "On Israeli Foreign Policy at This Hour," *Davar*, 15 August 1948).

107. M. Assaf, "On the Arab Refugees," *Davar*, 30 July 1948.

108. Cabinet Protocols, 28 July, 6:12–13.

109. E. Liebenstein, "The Arab Refugees," *Davar*, 27 August 1948.

110. Mapai Center, 24 July 1948, LPA; Ben-Gurion, *War Diary*, 605.

111. Cabinet Protocols, 1 August 1948, 6:12–24; Ben-Gurion, *Restored State*, 1:247–51.

112. DFPI, 1:567.

113. Shlaim, *Politics of Partition*, 224–26; Ben-Gurion, *War Diary*, 722; *Restored State*, 1:288, 294; and see Cabinet Protocols, 26 September 1948, 10:24–37, for a fuller report.

114. Secret session of the Provisional State Council, 27 September 1948, in Sharett, *At the Threshold of Statehood*, 290–309.

115. Ben-Gurion, *Restored State*, 1:295–98; Cabinet Protocols, 6 October 1948, 11:28.

116. Cabinet session, 21 October 1948, in *Restored State*, 1:301–4 (where an incorrect date appears).

117. DFPI, 2:126–27 (2 November 1948).

118. Ibid., 2:142–43.

119. Ibid., 2:161–63; Shlaim, *Politics of Partition*, 250–51.

120. DFPI, 2:241–43 (28 November 1948).

121. Ben-Gurion, *Restored State*, 1:320–21.

122. Ben-Gurion, *War Diary*, 853 (27 November 1948). Speaking to the Mapai Center three days later, Ben-Gurion did not mention Mustafa Kemal but repeated that the Arabs would not forget their defeat (LPA).

123. Ibid., 870.

124. DFPI, 2:320–26 (political consultation in the Israeli foreign office on 30 December 1948); ibid., 3:338 (meeting of R. Shiloah and M. Dayan with Major A. Al Tal, the king's confidant, on 30 December 1948).

125. Sharett, *At the Threshold of Statehood*, 337–38; full version in *Protocols of the Provisional State Council*, 11 January 1949, 2:4–11.

126. Cabinet Protocols, 5 January 1949, 16:9, and 11 January 1949, 16:4–7.

127. DFPI, 3:38 (17 January 1949).

128. Ben-Gurion, *War Diary*, 958 (18 January 1949).

129. DFPI, 3:68.

130. Ben-Gurion, *War Diary*, appendix, 23 (speaking to the Knesset's committees on security and foreign affairs and on finance); see also his speech to newly promoted officers in his *Vision and Road*, 1:134–35.

131. DFPI, 2:404–6.

132. See Morris, "Yosef Weitz and the 'Transfer Committees,' 1948–1949," 522–61.

133. M. A[ssaf], "A Suggestion in Damascus for the Settlement of Refugees in Syria," *Davar*, 13 January 1948.

134. DFPI, 3:221–22 (two conversations with the Egyptians on 7 and 8 February 1949 reported by Sasson).

135. Ibid., 3:268 (22 February 1949).

136. Ibid., 3:271–73; Morris, *Palestinian Refugee Problem*, 356.

137. DFPI, 2:458–61.

138. Ibid., 2:502–11 (16 March 1949), drafted by Z. Lifshitz and M. Comay.

139. Ben-Gurion, *War Diary*, 970. Addressing the Mapai Center, he described the armistice as "one of the greatest events and victories of the State of Israel both from the political and the moral point of view," 16 March 1949, LPA.

140. DFPI, 3:270.

141. Ibid., 3:353–55, 377–78.

142. Ibid., 3:464–67 (22 March).

143. Ibid., 2:558.

144. Ibid., 2:571–72.

145. Ibid., 2:589. Cf. Cabinet Protocols, 3 May 1949, 5:6–13; 24 May 1949, 6:9–28; 29 May 1949, 6:4–34.

146. DFPI, 2:592.

147. Ibid., 2:25.

148. Ibid., 4:10, May–December 1949, ed. Y. Rosenthal (Jerusalem 1986); ibid., 3:582; Ben-Gurion, *War Diary*, appendix, 26; DFPI, 3:592 (Document no. 322), note 1. Cf. Rabinovitch, *The Road Not Taken*, chap. 3.

149. DFPI, 4:66 (25 May 1949).

150. Ibid., 4:82–83, 86 (Sasson to Sharett).

151. Ben-Gurion, *War Diary*, appendix, 28–29.

152. *Knesset Record*, 1:717–22.

153. Ibid., 206.

154. Ben-Gurion, *War Diary*, 993 (9 July 1949).

155. Ibid.

156. DFPI, 4:240.

4. David Ben-Gurion, Mapai, and the Victory of Pragmatic Activism

1. Ben-Gurion Diary, 7 May 1945, BGA; Ben-Gurion, *Restored State*, 1:65 (translated in Ben-Gurion, *Israel: A Personal History*, 54–55).

2. JAE, 15 March 1945, S/100, CZA (secret).

3. D. Ben-Gurion, "The Only Solution," *Davar*, 22–24 June 1945.

4. D. Horowitz, "Political Pragmatism," *Davar*, 26 June 1945. Horowitz was criticized by G. Luft (of Aliyah Hadashah) in "Political Pragmatism?" *Davar*, 10 July 1945, and by Hashomer Hatza'ir (see chap. 8).

5. Ben-Gurion, *Restored State*, 1:66–67, where seventeen are mentioned. The diary mentions twenty, including the host.

6. Ben-Gurion Diary, 30 July 1945, BGA.

7. Ben-Gurion, *Bama'arachah*, 4:206–21 (2 August 1945).

8. Mapai Secretariat, 10 August 1945, LPA.

9. For the speeches at the London convention, see S25/1906, CZA; also D. Joseph's summary to Mapai Secretariat, 28 August 1945, LPA. The "first million plan" was raised by Ben-Gurion in 1944 at the JAE in order to change the demographic balance in Palestine, and a special committee ("the planning committee") prepared the economic ground for their absorption.

10. Dr. M. Sneh, "London Station," *Ha'aretz*, 31 August 1945.

11. E. Liebenstein, "Thirteen Principles of Zionist Struggle," *Milchamtenu* 8 (32) (August 1945): 3–18.

12. Mapai Political Committee, 20 September 1945 (reported by D. Joseph) and 25 September 1945, LPA.

13. Histadrut Actions Committee, 26 September 1945, Lavon Institute Archives, Tel Aviv (hereafter LIA).

14. Mapai Secretariat, 27 September 1945, LPA; Ben-Gurion instruction to Sneh: Avi-Amos [Ben-Gurion's son was called Amos], London, 1 October 1945, 183/17, Haganah Archives (hereafter HA).

15. Ben-Gurion to Nahum Goldmann, 27 September 1945, Z6/package 18/file 15, CZA; cf. his order to Sneh on 1 October to begin operations: *Palestine. Statement of Information Relating to Acts of Violence*, Cmd. 6873.

16. Small Zionist Actions Committee, 7 October 1945, S25/1783, CZA.

17. Conversation with Lord Gort, the High Commissioner (Kaplan, Joseph, and Ben-Zvi), JAE, 11 October 1945, S/100, CZA (secret).

18. Sneh, "The Essence of the Struggle," *Ha'aretz*, 26 October 1945.

19. Mapai Secretariat, 19 October 1945, LPA; Mapai Center, 23 October 1945, LPA.

20. Ha'aplah was the underground movement attempting to bring Jews to Palestine in spite of the British policy restricting immigration. It was the brainchild of the Jewish Agency and was organized by Haganah.

21. Ben-Gurion Diary, 25 October–3 November 1945, BGA.

22. Slutsky, *History of the Haganah*, 3:1898–1901. The full text of Plan B is in the History of the Haganah Archives, 7/1, HA.

23. As reported by D. Horowitz, 30 October 1945, in Ben-Gurion Diary, 30 October 1945, BGA.

24. Mapai Political Committee, 6 November 1945, LPA.

25. Ibid.; Ben-Gurion Diary, 8 November 1945, BGA; see the *Hapoel Hatza'ir* leader "On the Events of the Days, a) Two Reactions," *Hapoel Hatza'ir* 17 (Year 39), no. 8 (7 November 1945).

26. Combined session of the JAE and the Va'ad Leumi, 13 November 1945, S/100, CZA. To this special session other representatives of the Yishuv were invited, including non-Zionists like the ultra-orthodox Agudat Israel, or the Industry Association, in order to present a united front.

27. JAE, 14 November 1945, Secret, S/100, CZA.

28. Histadrut Actions Committee, 14–16 November 1945, LIA.

29. JAE Session, 21 November 1945. S/100, CZA; Mapai Center, 22 November 1945, LPA.

30. Allon, *Ma'arachot Palmach*, 129; Sneh, "In the Crisis," *Ha'aretz*, 23 November 1945.

31. Ben-Gurion to the Elected Assembly, Mount Scopus, 28 November 1945, J1/7222, CZA. English version in Ben-Gurion, *Rebirth and Destiny*, 151–75.

32. Ben-Gurion Diary, 29 October 1945 (summarizing Mapai Political Committee session of the same day), BGA.

33. Stenographic Protocol of the full session of the Va'ad Leumi (National Council), 5 December 1945, S25/5931, CZA (secret).

34. Liebenstein's speech to Mapai Council, 1 December 1945, was the only one published in *Davar* ("New Era in Zionism," 9 December 1945); see also his article "The Test," *Beinatayim* (Contemporary anthology), November–December 1945, 3–6. For an analysis of Bevin's policy in November 1945, see Bullock, *Ernest Bevin*, 181–82.

35. Mapai Council, 30 November–1 December 1945, LPA.

36. National Council session (see note 33).

37. Plan for Japheth's Affairs, 17 December 1945, 7/1, HA (secret).

38. Mapai Secretariat meeting as Political Committee, 10 December 1945, LPA.

39. Ibid.

40. Protocol of the Planning Committee, 25 December 1945, 6 January 1946, S53/1776, CZA; JAE, 1 January 1946, S/100, CZA.

41. Dr. M. Sneh, "The Struggle," *Ha'aretz*, 25 January 1946.

42. Mapai Council, 4 February 1946, LPA. Cf. E. Liebenstein, "Zionist Propaganda and its Shortcomings," *Beterem*, February 1946, 5.

43. Fourth Session of Elected Assembly, 12–13 February 1946, J/7223, CZA; full text of Shertok's speech (13 February 1946) is in S25/1547, CZA. For Cunningham's complaint on Shertok see Cohen, *Palestine*, 78–79.

44. Mapai Political Committee, 23 February 1946, LPA.

45. JAE, 24 February 1946, S/100, CZA.

46. JAE, 27 February 1946, ibid.; Small Zionist Actions Committee, 28 February 1946, S5/352, CZA.

47. *The Jewish Case*, 53–100 (11 March 1946).

48. Crossman, *Palestine Mission*, 138–39.

49. Ibid., 164–65.

50. JAE Session, 27 March 1946, S/100, CZA.

51. Mapai Council, 1 April 1946, LPA.

52. Ibid., 2 April 1946.

53. Ibid.; Inter-Party Meeting for Unified List in Elections to the 22nd Zionist Congress, 30 April 1946, LPA. Cf. also meeting of Mapai Secretariat sitting as Political Committee, 1 May 1946, LPA.

54. Cf. B. Joseph words to JAE, 30 April 1946, S/100, CZA.

55. Ben-Gurion to (Mapai) colleagues, Paris, 22 April 1946, in Diary, BGA; Letter to Paula, 1 May 1946, BGA.

56. Short minutes of meeting held at 77 Great Russell Street, London, 30 April 1946, Z4/10.380, CZA.

57. Mapai Secretariat sitting as Political Committee, 1 May 1946 (the morning before Attlee's announcement, and the evening after), LPA.

58. Ben-Gurion to (his son) Amos, 2 May 1946, in Diary, BGA; Ben-Gurion to Paula, 2 May 1946, BGA; JAE, 12 May 1946, S/100, CZA.

59. Ben-Gurion Diary, 5–7 May 1946, BGA.

60. Ibid., 2 May, 1 June 1946, BGA; minutes, National Board of Hadassah, 20 May 1946, Hadassah Archives, New York; David Horowitz to the JAE, 2 June 1946, S/100, CZA.

61. Louis, *The British Empire in the Middle East*, 428.

62. Note of a Meeting between Mr. Ben-Gurion, Mr. Crossman, and Mr. Hall, 20 June 1946, S25/7566, CZA; Note of a Meeting between Mr. Hall and Mr. Ben-Gurion, 19 June 1946, ibid.; JAE Session, 27 June 1946, S/100, CZA.

63. Slutsky, *History of the Haganah*, 3:1253–55, 1939–43.

64. Ben-Gurion, *Bama'arachah*, 5:86–93.

65. Ben-Gurion to F. Frankfurter, 17 July 1946, WA. The plan was also submitted to Harold Laski, the chairman of the British Labour Party, in the hope that he, like Frankfurter, through his connections with the government, would move it forward. I found no trace of the plan in the British archives.

66. Unsigned letter by Shertok from Latrun, 1 August 1946, A245, CZA.

67. Paris JAE Enlarged meeting, 4 August 1946, S/100 CZA; Heller, "From the 'Black Sabbath' to Partition," 344–53.

68. Paris JAE, 4 August 1946, S/100, CZA. The special budget Ben-Gurion had received from the executive and his appointment to head the defense department are mentioned only in Ben-Gurion, *Restored State*, 1:69, 75 (translated in *Israel: A Personal History*, 58, 65).

69. For Ben-Gurion's letter to Mapai Center, see Ben-Gurion, *Rebirth and Destiny*, 176–89; Mapai Center and Political Committee, 3 September 1946, LPA.

70. Mapai Secretariat and Political Committee, 31 August 1946, LPA.

71. Mapai Center and Political Committee, 3 September 1946, LPA.

72. There are two protocols of the conference (5–8 September 1946), one in LPA and the other in Z4/20.277, CZA. The moderates published their speeches at the conference in *Inspecting the Way* (*Levchinat Hederech*) shortly after the conference.

73. Sneh to Ben-Gurion, 21 September 1946, in Slutsky, *History of the Haganah*, 3:1933–34; Ben-Gurion to Sneh and Ben-Gurion to Silver, 1 October 1946, in Ben-Gurion, *Toward the End of the Mandate*, 195–203; Ben-Gurion at a public assembly in Paris, 10 October 1946, *Bama'arachah*, 5:109–11; Ben-Aharon to Le'achdut Ha'avodah party, 22 October 1946, 15/162/4, KMA.

74. *Protocol of the 22nd Zionist Congress* (9–24 December 1946), 59–74, 331–38 (Ben-Gurion), 190–99 (Sneh), 202–8 (Gruenbaum), 311–16 (Liebenstein), 346–62; JAE, 11 December 1946, S/100, CZA; Mapai Secretariat, 1 January 1947, LPA; Fishman in the JAE, 11 December 1946, S/100, CZA.

75. Ben-Gurion, *Toward the End of the Mandate*, 304–9; JAE, 12 January 1947, S/100, CZA; Mapai Secretariat, 1 January 1947; *Protocol of the 22nd Zionist Congress*, 494–98.

76. Mapai Center, 9 January 1947, LPA (by J. Cohen).

77. Mapai Financial Committee, 15 January 1947, LPA.

78. Ben-Gurion to Bevin, 14 February 1947, WA; Meeting between Ben-Gurion and Lord Jowitt, the Lord Chancellor, 13 February 1947, WA. Cf. also Short Minutes of Meeting held at the Colonial Office, 13 February 1947, Z4/14.827, CZA; JAE, 14 March 1947. The Bevin-Beeley new plan (6 February) contained no option for partition after five years, would allow 4,000 immigrants monthly for two years, offered no Negev and Jerusalem cantons, and kept absolute authority in the hands of the high commissioner.

79. Mapai Center, 25 March 1947, LPA.

80. Ben-Gurion to Standing Committee of the 22nd Zionist Congress, 19 December 1946, in *Toward the End of the Mandate*, 286; Ben-Gurion to Histadrut Actions Committee, 26 March 1947, LIA.

81. Shertok to Mapai branches representatives, 27 March 1947, LPA.

82. Mapai Center, 26 April 1947, LPA; E. Liebenstein, "How to Calculate Our Action?" *Beterem*, no. 5 (May 1947): 3–16.

83. Mapai Center, 26 April 1947, LPA.

84. Ben-Gurion, *Chimes of Independence*, 142, 164, 192, 198.

85. JAE, 18 June 1947, S/100, CZA. Ben-Gurion himself did not participate in the voting to protest the "sabotage" of rightist members of the executive who supported the IZL, 15 June 1947, S/100, CZA. See also Ben-Gurion, *Chimes of Independence* (March–November 1947), 216.

86. *The Jewish Plan for Palestine*, 354–55.

87. Histadrut Actions Committee, 6 August 1947, LIA. See Golda Meyerson's interview with the high commissioner, 31 July 1947, S25/5601, CZA; slightly different version in Cunningham Papers, IV/1/72.

88. Mapai Council, 9 August 1947, LPA. Ben-Gurion's pledge to deal mili-

tarily with IZL was made on 30 October 1947, Mapai Secretariat. Cf. *Chimes of Independence*, 445, and compare Lubianiker's anxiety about the ability of the breakaways to undermine the foundations of the state, in *Now or Never*, 221.

89. Greater Zionist Actions Committee, Zurich, 2 September 1947, S25/320, CZA; Ben-Gurion to Paula, 2 September 1947, *Chimes of Independence*, 351. On the considerations that led the majority in UNSCOP to the partition conclusion, see Horowitz, *A State in the Making* (in Hebrew), 190–317; the protocols of UNSCOP internal meeting, 6–13 August 1947, UNSCOP 2 RJB, DAG 13/3.O.1, UN Archives, New York.

90. Diary, 11 October 1947, in Ben-Gurion, *Chimes of Independence*, 393; Mapai Secretariat, ibid., 396.

91. Security Committee Sessions, 19, 23 October 1947, S25/9342, CZA. As to the arms the Haganah possessed as of 20 October 1947, the situation was indeed desperate: 10,749 rifles, 2,709 submachine guns, 736 light machine guns, 166 heavy machine guns, 672 light mortars, and 92 three-inch mortars. See Ben-Gurion, *Chimes of Independence*, 513.

92. Security Committee, 28 October 1947, S25/9342, CZA.

93. Security Committee, 13 November 1947, S25/9343, CZA.

94. Ben-Gurion, *Chimes of Independence*, 494–95.

95. Security Committee, 27 November 1947, S25/9343, CZA; JAE, 30 November 1947, S/100, CZA.

96. On the debate around the *Pan Crescent* and *Pan York*, see Mapai Secretariat, 9 December 1947, quoted in *Now or Never*, 434–44.

97. JAE, 19 January 1948, S/100, CZA; Mapai Council, 6 January 1948, in Ben-Gurion, *War Diary*, 211–12; Security Committee, 3 February 1948, S25/9346, CZA. In fact 2,248 Jews lived in the Negev in 25 settlements (in addition to various nomadic Bedouin tribes).

98. Ben-Gurion, *War Diary*, 63 (the four were Y. Ratner, E. Ben-Arzi, F. Eshet, and Y. Sahar); see 67 for Sasson's view on Plan B.

99. Mapai Secretariat, 8 January 1948, in Ben-Gurion, *Rebirth and Destiny*, 227–33; a fuller version is in LPA and also in *Now or Never*, 286–98.

100. Ben-Gurion, *War Diary*, 127 (9 January 1948).

101. *Now or Never*, 305–7 (16 January 1948).

102. Ben-Gurion, *War Diary*, 172–73 (22 January 1948).

103. Ibid., 160–61 (18 January 1948).

104. Ibid., 266 (Shertok wrote from New York on 18 February 1948; Ben-Gurion replied on 27 February 1948). See also 273–74: M. Stone (Marcus), the American colonel who examined the military status of the Haganah, was skeptical about its ability, given the Arabs' advantage in numbers and arms.

105. Security Committee, 4 April 1948, S25/9348, CZA. Since this committee was only an advisory body, a committee of five would serve as a war cabinet (Ben-Gurion, Kaplan, Shapira, Bernstein, and Remez). On Ben-Gurion's criticism of the Palmach, see *War Diary*, 371–72.

106. Greater Zionist Actions Committee, 6–12 April 1948, S5/322, CZA.

107. Ibid., 6 April 1948.

108. Slutsky, *History of the Haganah*, 3:1955–60.

109. Ben-Gurion, *War Diary*, 136, 350, 404–5 (9 May 1948). In April the two contracts were implemented; they included 14,500 rifles and 1,621 machine guns. By 9 May, six contracts for extensive arms purchases had been signed by Avriel and three by Y. Arazi (ibid., 404–5). See also Bialer, "The Czech-Israeli Arms Deal Revisited."

110. Ben-Gurion, *War Diary*, 353–54 (Yadin's report, 16 April 1948). The Yishuv force numbered 18,900, although M. Avniel, of the Recruitment Center, stated that more than 30,000 could be mobilized. Only a command to recruit married youngsters would raise the number by 15,000. The breakaways numbered 6,000, according to the Security Committee, 18 April 1948, S25/9348, CZA. By 7 May, Ben-Gurion recorded in his *War Diary* that there were 29,900 fighters, including 13,500 "fighter-settlers" (397).

111. *Now or Never*, 462–64, 467–73, 484–89; *Protocols of People's Administration*, 71–76.

112. Ben-Gurion, *War Diary*, 454 (24 May 1948); Mapai Secretariat, 29 May 1948, LPA.

113. Mapai Council, 19 June 1948, LPA.

114. Ben-Gurion, *Restored State*, 1:179–91. Cabinet Protocols, 20 June 1948, 3:51–56; 22 June 1948, 3:22–26; 23 June 1948, 3:4–6; 5 September 1948, 9:75–87. *Protocols of the Provisional State Council*, 23 June 1948, 1:4–46. In the vote over a unified army and a single authority, twenty-two were in favor and four against, while eight abstained; see Ben-Gurion, *War Diary*, 540, and cf. Galili to Ben-Gurion, 20 June 1948, in Galili, *El Veal*, 103–4.

115. Ben-Gurion, *War Diary*, 574 (4 July 1948).

116. Cabinet Protocols, 7 July 1948, 4:12–35, and 11 July 1948, 5:19–20.

117. Ben-Gurion, *Rebirth and Destiny*, 262; Ben-Gurion, *Restored State*, 1:239–40 (Provisional State Council, 22 July 1948).

118. Cabinet Protocols, 1 August 1948, 6:12–24; cf. Ben-Gurion, *Restored State*, 1:247–51.

119. Ben-Gurion, *Restored State*, 1:281–85; Cabinet Protocols, 11 August 1948, 7:19 ff.; 18 August 1948, 7:15; 25 August 1948, 7:9–15; 5 September 1948, 8:61–81.

120. Ben-Gurion, *Restored State*, 1:270–75 (session with Palmach commanders, 14 September 1948), 277–80 (Histadrut Actions Committee, 14–15 October 1948).

121. Ibid., 1:288–98; Ben-Gurion, *War Diary*, 722 (26 September 1948), 733 (6 October 1948). See also Cabinet Protocols, 26 September 1948, 10:24–25; 6 October 1948, 19:28; 10 October 1948, 10:18.

122. See Ben-Gurion, *War Diary*, 771.

123. Ben-Gurion, *Restored State*, 1:301–4.

124. *Protocols of the Provisional State Council*, 28 October 1948, 2:4–8; Ben-Gurion, *Restored State*, 1:311–12 (31 October 1948), and *War Diary*, 789.

125. Ben-Gurion, *Restored State*, 1:324; *War Diary*, 799–800 (6 November 1948).

126. Cabinet Protocols, 18 November 1948, 13:19; *Protocols of the Provisional State Council*, 25 November 1948, 2:4–22.

127. Ben-Gurion, *War Diary*, 848–49 (26 November 1948).

128. Ibid., 901–2 (25 December 1948); see also his *Vision and Road*, 1:45–46 (15 January 1949).

129. Ben-Gurion, *War Diary*, 3:937–38 (8 January 1949), and his *Vision and Road*, 1:9–27.

130. "After the Elections," broadcast 29 January 1949, in Ben-Gurion, *Vision and Road*, 1:49–53.

131. Ben-Gurion, *Vision and Road*, 1:53–60.

132. Bernstein to Persitz, 6 April 1949, A309/20, CZA.

133. *Knesset Record*, 8 March 1949, 1:55–58; 10 March 1949, 1:134–40. See Meeting of Mapai Secretariat and Mapai Members of Knesset (MKs), 1 March 1949, LPA, for a detailed discussion of the portfolios question. See Mapai Secretariat, 28 August 1948, on ideological difficulties with Mapam. See also Cabinet Protocols, 7 March 1949, 1:43.

134. DFPI, 2:570–71 (12 April 1949).

135. Ben-Gurion, *Vision and Road*, 1:267–81 (11 October 1949).

136. Ibid., 1:86–87.

5. Chaim Weizmann and the Collapse of British Orientation

1. Vereté, *From Palmerston to Balfour*, 4.

2. *Letters and Papers of Chaim Weizmann*, Series B: *Papers*, 2: 523–25, 540–43 (hereafter *Papers*).

3. Churchill's warning is in *Hansard*, 5th series, vol. 404, col. 2242; Weizmann, in Small Zionist Actions Committee, 19 November 1944, S25/1804, CZA; *Papers*, 2:553. On Moyne's support for partition, see *Papers*, 2:441–42.

4. *Letters and Papers of Chaim Weizmann*, Series A: *Letters*, 20:17 (hereafter *Letters*).

5. Weizmann at the Zionist Conference in London, 2 August 1945, S25/1906, CZA.

6. *Baffy: The Diaries of Blanche Dugdale, 1936–1947*, 225; *Papers*, 2:66.

7. Shertok to members of the JAE, 2 November 1945, S25/2308, CZA; *Baffy*, 226.

8. *Papers*, 2:72–73.

9. Weizmann meeting with Truman, 4 December 1945 (Halifax present), S25/7497, CZA; *Letters*, 22:88.

10. *Baffy*, 226–27. Cf. R. Crossman's evaluation of Weizmann's evidence as a wonderful mixture of enthusiasm and scientific objectivity (*Palestine Mission*, 133, 8 March).

11. *The Jewish Case*, 3–24.

12. Crossman, *Palestine Mission*, 136; JAE, 7 March 1946, S25/100, CZA.

13. JAE, 10 March 1946, S/100, CZA.

14. *Letters,* ed. Heller, 22:101–2; *The Jewish Case,* 52.

15. *Letters,* 22:115–16, 118–22, 123–28.

16. Ibid., 22:135, 142.

17. Ibid., 22:137–40.

18. Ibid. 22:229–32; Cohen, *Palestine,* 87; Slutsky, *History of the Haganah,* 3:897, 1746; Rose, "Weizmann, Ben-Gurion, and the 1946 Crisis in the Zionist Movement."

19. *Letters,* 22:169–73.

20. Ibid., 22:165, 175–76.

21. *Baffy,* 238; *Letters,* 22:179–80.

22. JAE Protocol, Paris session, 3–4 August 1946, S/100, CZA.

23. *Letters,* 22:185, 187–88.

24. Ibid., 22:191–94, 207–8.

25. This was mentioned only in a draft of his speech prepared for the 22nd Congress; it was omitted from the final version (9 December 1946) and his reply after the discussion (16 December 1946), in *Papers,* 2:629–51. For the (second) draft, dated 18 November 1946, see Z4/15.346, CZA.

26. *Letters,* 22:212–16.

27. Ibid., 22:240.

28. Ibid., 22:249.

29. Ibid., 22:263.

30. Ibid., 22:274–75.

31. Ibid., 22:293–94.

32. Ibid., 22:328–29; remark on Begin, 276.

33. Ibid., 22:336, 345–46.

34. Stein to Weizmann, 8 April 1947, WA (appended are Frankfurter's consent to Stein's plan and two paragraphs from the plan); *Letters,* 22:315–17.

35. The case in point was Syrian Prime Minister Jamil Mardam. See *The Jewish Plan for Palestine,* 538. On Mardam's enmity, see Sasson, *Road to Peace,* 383.

36. *Papers,* 2:690–91.

37. *Letters,* 23:218.

6. The Intellectuals: Ichud and the Politics of Binationalism

1. Goren, ed., *Dissenter in Zion,* 276–77.

2. Ibid., 288–89.

3. Editorial, *She'ifoteinu* 2, no. 2 (April 1931): 41–43. *She'ifoteinu* (Our aspiration) was the monthly journal of Brit Shalom.

4. JAE, 16 January 1938, ibid., 5:42–43.

5. JAE, 24 April 1938, in Ben-Gurion, *Memoirs* (1938), 5:74–88. See also Ben-Gurion, *Meetings with Arab Leaders,* 179–96.

6. Goren, *Dissenter,* 331.

7. E. Simon, "Ichud in the Campaign," *Ba'ayot Hayom* 3, nos. 2–3 (November 1942): 14–15.

8. J. L. Magnes, "Towards Peace in Palestine," *Foreign Affairs,* January 1943, 246–47.

9. M. Smilansky, "Premeditated or Slip of the Tongue?" *Ba'ayot* 1, no. 3 (June 1944): 99–103.

10. M. Buber, "An Additional Clarification: A Reply to Nathan Rothenstreich," *Ba'ayot* 1, no. 5 (August 1944): 229–30. Translated in Mendes-Flohr, *A Land of Two Peoples,* 159.

11. M. Buber, "Dialogue on the Biltmore Program, " *Ba'ayot* 1, no. 6 (October 1944): 242. Translated in Mendes-Flohr, *A Land of Two Peoples,* 163.

12. E. Simon, "The Alternative before the Hebrew Youth," *Ba'ayot* 1, no. 6 (October 1944): 248–51; cf. W. P. Albright, "Only Thus," 286, in the same issue.

13. E. Simon, "On the Cynicism of Our Youth," *Ba'ayot* 2, no. 1 (January 1945): 23–30.

14. Ichud Council Session, 22 April 1945, P3/2547, Central Archives for the History of the Jewish People, Jerusalem (hereafter CAHJP).

15. M. Smilansky, "The Weizmannite Line, " *Ba'ayot* 2, no. 2 (8) (February 1945): 49–56.

16. M. Smilansky, "Lesson," *Ha'aretz,* 10 May 1945.

17. M. Smilansky, "Really?" *Ha'aretz,* 18 October 1945, in which Smilansky expressed his objection to *ha'apalah.* Ichud Council Session, 18 November 1945, P3/2547, CAHJP.

18. Dr. S. Sharshevsky, "Let Us Be Frank and Honest!" *Ba'ayot* 2, no. 2 (February 1945): 67–68 (quoting Ben-Gurion's speech in Kfar Vitkin, 25 October 1942; cf. Ben-Gurion, *Bama'arachah,* 4:96); R. Weltsch, "Declarations and Facts," *Ba'ayot* 2, no. 2 (February 1945): 69–73.

19. J. L. Magnes, "Jews and Arabs—Let Them Meet," *Ba'ayot* 2, no. 3 (9) (March 1945): 97–102; Goren, *Dissenter,* 370. Though admitting that his plan was "maximalist" in view of the "situation," Magnes was confident that the Arabs would accept numerical equality, "especially if we emphasize the humanitarian aspect, but on condition that this would be our last demand." Ichud Council Session, 27 May 1945, P3/2547, CAHJP.

20. J. L. Magnes, "Jewish-Arab Cooperation in Palestine," *Political Quarterly,* October–December 1945, 297–306.

21. G. Stern to Magnes, 14–17 October 1945, P3/2547, CAHJP.

22. J. L. Magnes, "Ways for Cooperation in Palestine, " *Ba'ayot* 3, no. 6 (18) (February 1946): 262–66.

23. D. W. Senator, "Are These Heretic Reflections?" *Ba'ayot* 2, no. 3 (9) (March 1945): 103–9. On his earlier support for transfer see JAE, 7 May 1944, S/100, CZA.

24. M. Buber, "Politics and Morals," in Mendes-Flohr, *Land of Two Peoples,* 170–73; *Ba'ayot* 2, no. 3 (9) (March 1945): 110–13.

25. J. L. Magnes, "Rebellion," in his *In the Perplexity of the Times,* 109–13.

26. S. Zemach, "A Line of Building," *Ha'aretz,* 11 January 1946. Zemach continued officially to be a member of Mapai; see *Hapoel Hatza'ir* 17 (Year 39), no. 4 (8 October 1945): 4–5.

27. G. Baer, "The Question of Cooperation between Jewish and Arab Workers," *Ba'ayot* 2, no. 6 (August 1945): 262–63.

28. E. Simon, "Speak No Ill of the Dead?" *Ba'ayot* 3, no. 2 (October 1945): 71–74.

29. S. Hirsch, "Problems of the Month: Failure and Progress," *Ba'ayot* 3, no. 4 (December 1945): 150–54.

30. E. Simon, "Bundle of Notes: Who Appears?" *Ba'ayot* 3, no. 6 (18) (February 1946): 251–52. In the simulation the participants were E. Simon and S. Hirsch; see Ichud Council Session, 17 February 1947, P3/2502, CAHJP.

31. M. Buber, J. L. Magnes, and M. Smilansky, eds., *Palestine: A Bi-National State,* 7–28. Published version of Ichud's written statement to the Anglo-American Committee of Inquiry, Jerusalem, 5 March 1946 (oral evidence was given on 14 March). Magnes's draft was corrected by a number of colleagues in Ihud in P3/2502, CAHJP.

32. Buber, Magnes, and Smilansky, *Palestine,* 49, 68–70; Crossman, *Palestine Mission,* 142–43.

33. S. Hirsch, "Why Did Ichud Appear before the Committee?" *Ba'ayot* 4, no. 1 (April 1946): 1–4 (emphasis in the original).

34. "Monthly Problems: New Beginning," editorial, *Ba'ayot* 4, no. 3 (May 1946): 105.

35. The more moderate "A" faction split from the "B" faction in 1935, to be reunited in 1946. E. S[imon], "Monthly Problems: In View of the Delays," *Ba'ayot* 4, no. 4 (22) (June 1946): 163–65.

36. "Tragedy," editorial, *Ha'aretz,* 2 November 1945; "Goals and Means," editorial, *Ha'aretz,* 5 April 1946.

37. "The Horror," editorial, *Ha'aretz,* 23 July 1946.

38. M. Buber, "Not Enough," *Ha'aretz,* 26 July 1946; E. Simon, "Our Hands Did Not Spill This Blood?" *Ha'aretz,* 28 July 1946.

39. Senator to Magnes, 30 August 1946, P3/2515, CAHJP (personal and confidential).

40. "Appeal to Dr. C. Weizmann," *Ha'aretz,* 16 August 1946 (date of cable 14 August); M. Smilansky, "At the Time of Crisis," *Ha'aretz,* 15 August 1946.

41. G. Stern, "Federalization and Bi-Nationalism: First Reaction," *Ba'ayot* 4, no. 5 (23) (September 1946): 205–10; M. Smilansky, "The Old-New Problem," *Ha'aretz,* 28 August 1946.

42. E. Simon, "The Roles of the Mandatory Government," *Ba'ayot* 4, no. 5 (23) (September 1946): 210–11.

43. E. Simon, "The Expulsion of the *Olim,*" ibid., 213–17.

44. Rabbi Benyamin, "And Now What?" ibid., 223–24.

45. G. Landauer, "The Roles of Zionist Opposition," *Ba'ayot* 4, no. 6 (November 1946): 267–75.

46. Magnes to A. M. Stroock, 15 January 1947, P3/2557, CAHJP; Magnes to R. Hinden, 11 February 1947, P3/2559, CAHJP.

47. M. Buber, "The Bi-National Approach to Zionism," in *Toward Union in Palestine*, ed. Buber, Magnes, and Simon, 9–13.

48. M. Smilansky, "Without a 'Head'," *Ha'aretz*, 10 January 1947.

49. M. Smilansky, "If You Seek Too Much . . .," *Ha'aretz*, 28 February 1947; and his "Ahad Ha-Am's Truths before the Storm," *Ba'ayot* 5, no. 3 (March 1947): 94–101.

50. W. D. Senator, "In a Misguided Way," *Ba'ayot* 5, no. 1–2 (January–February 1947): 1–10.

51. Y. Luzitanus [Y. R. Molcho], "Fawzi Darwish al-Husseini: Reflections on his Death," ibid., 31–33. See Cohen, *Israel and the Arab World*, 327–32, for a later tribute to the man. Also G. Stern, "Memorandum on the Development of the Husseini Affair," 20 December 1946, P3/2554, CAHJP.

52. S. Hirsch to Magnes, 6 January 1947, and G. Stern to Magnes, n.d., P3/2561, CAHJP.

53. Magnes to L. Crystal, 14 February 1947, P3/2557, CAHJP.

54. E. Simon, "On Those Who Confess Partly," *Ha'aretz*, 28 March 1947; see also N. Rothenstreich's reply, "Assumptions and Conclusions," *Ha'aretz*, 4 April 1947.

55. Ichud Council Session, 11 March 1947, P3/2561, CAHJP.

56. Senator to Buber, 15 June 1947, in N. Glatzer and P. Mendes-Flohr, *The Letters of M. Buber: A Life of Dialogue*, 519–20.

57. Senator to Stein, May 21, 1947, P3/2561, CAHJP; G. Stern, "Gromyko's Alternative," *Ba'ayot* 6, no. 28 (June 1947): 129–35.

58. Oral Evidence before the UNSCOP, 14 July 1947, in Magnes et al., *Palestine—Divided or United?* 31–73. For the public warning by Richard Koebner, who was professor of history at the Hebrew University, see "The Wrong Assumption: England's Interest in Palestine," *Ha'aretz*, 4 April 1947.

59. Quoted from M. Kremer [Keren], "Partition in View of Statistics," *Ha'aretz*, 13 June 1947; Magnes et al., *Palestine—Divided or United?* 74–84. On UNSCOP and Ichud, see Garcia-Granados, *The Birth of Israel*, 147–48.

60. Magnes to Simon, 12 November 1947, in Goren, *Dissenter*, 456–57.

61. *New York Times*, 28 September 1947 (written on 18 September 1947); Simon to Magnes, 7 October 1947, Simon to Hofshi, 26 October 1947, both in P3/2561, CAHJP.

62. S. Sharshevsky to Magnes, 27 November 1947, P3/2560, CAHJP.

63. G. Stern to Magnes, n.d., P3/2561, CAHJP; Hirsch to Magnes, 6 January 1947, P3/2560, CAHJP.

64. Y. Luzitanus [Y. R. Molcho], "New Conditions—New Functions," *Ba'ayot* 6, no. 1–2 (January 1948): 1–3.

65. G. Stern, "In the Bloody Entanglement," ibid., 9–13.

66. Magnes to Buber, 8 February 1948, *Ba'ayot* 6, nos. 3–4 (February 1948): 113–15; Glatzer and Mendes-Flohr, *A Life of Dialogue*, 530–31.

67. Goren, *Dissenter*, 465.

68. Magnes to Hexter, 25 February 1948, P3/2518, CAHJP; "Ichud on the Political Situation" and D. W. Senator, "Time to Make Peace!" both in *Ba'ayot Hazman* 7, no. 1 (1 April 1948): 1.

69. Magnes to Hexter, 25 February 1948, P3/2527, CAHJP; Goren, *Dissenter*, 477–79; see also Magnes to Austin, 25 March 1948, 473–74, and Magnes to T. Wasson, 6 April 1948, 475–77, both in Goren, *Dissenter*.

70. M. Buber, "A Fundamental Error Which Must be Corrected," *Ba'ayot Hazman* 7 (1 April 1948), translated in Mendes-Flohr, *Land of Two Peoples*, 218–19.

71. Rabbi Benyamin, "We Would Not Obscure the 'Deir Yasin' Affair," *Ba'ayot Hazman* 7, no. 5 (29 April 1948).

72. Goren, *Dissenter*, 482–97. Cf. *Foreign Relations of the United States*, 1948, 5:901–904.

73. D. W. Senator, "Even Now a Political Solution Is Required!" *Ba'ayot Hazman* 7, no. 8 (27 May 1948).

74. M. Buber, "Zionism and 'Zionism'," ibid., in Mendes-Flohr, *Land of Two Peoples*, 220–23.

75. D. W. Senator, "Victories Are Not Enough," *Ba'ayot Hazman* 7, no. 6 (6 May 1948): 6.

76. Rabbi Benyamin, "On the 'Bridgehead' Theory," *Ba'ayot Hazman* 7, no. 10 (24 June 1948); G. Luft, "The Mediation Attempt," *Ba'ayot Hazman* 7, no. 11, (2 July 1948).

77. G. Stern, "The Mediator's Suggestions: Negative and Positive," *Ba'ayot Hazman* 7, no. 12 (9 July 1948); D. W. Senator, "Toward Peace?" *Ba'ayot Hazman* 7, no. 13 (16 July 1948); G. Stern, "His Political Testament," *Ba'ayot Hazman* 7, no. 23 (24 September 1948).

78. Dr. H. Strauss, "From Cease-fire to Permanent Peace," *Ba'ayot Hazman* 7, no. 14 (23 July 1948); [unsigned], "Ben-Gurion's Warning," *Ba'ayot Hazman* 7, no. 19 (27 August 1948).

79. G. Stern, "The Touchstone," *Ba'ayot Hazman* 7, no. 16 (6 August 1948).

80. "Ichud Manifesto," 11 August 1948, *Ba'ayot Hazman* 7, no. 17 (13 August 1948), and R. B[enyamin], "Quo Vadis?" ibid.

81. W. Kolarz, "The Truth about the Greek Transfer," ibid., and cf. editorial on Begin's speech, ibid.

82. G. Stern, "The Minority—Vision and Reality," *Ba'ayot Hazman* 7, no. 21 (10 September 1948).

83. "Toward the UN General Assembly Session: Ichud Position," *Ba'ayot Hazman* 7, no. 22 (17 September 1948).

84. Goren, *Dissenter*, 511–18.

85. This was Rabbi Dr. K. D. Willhelm, Ichud's secretary (Ben-Gurion, *War Diary*, 571).

7. Aliyah Hadashah

1. Achdut Ha'am to the Executive of the Jewish Agency, January 9, 1939, signed by E. Auerbach, M. Bielesky, G. Krojanker, S. Moses, and F. Rosenblueth, S25/3114, CZA.

2. "Five Resolutions of Aliyah Hadashah Center," 9 April 1943, in Landauer, *Five Articles on Aliyah Hadashah*, 43.

3. F. Rosenblueth, "Arrogant Criticism (Reply to Ben-Gurion)," *Amudim* (Aliyah Hadashah weekly) 1, no. 1 (21 July 1944): 1–3.

4. G. Krojanker, "'Heroes,'" ibid., 3.

5. G. Landauer, "On Three Things," ibid., 6–7; Kr[ojank]er, "Ideology Is Needed!," *Amudim* 1, no. 9 (15 September 1944): 1–3; Dr. E. Auerbach, "The Future of the 'Citizens' in Eretz Israel," *Amudim* 1, no. 10 (26 September 1944): 1–2.

6. Rosenblueth's keynote speech at Aliyah Hadashah Conference in Ramot Hashavim, *Amudim* 1, no. 24 (12 January 1945): 6–7; and see R. Bachi's lecture, "Natural Growth of the Yishuv," ibid., 5–6.

7. Y. Ben-Tor, "The Country's Consolidation According to the Lowdermilk Plan," *Amudim* 1, no. 38 (13 April 1945): 3, 8.

8. Aliyah Hadashah Executive session, 12 April 1945, J18/73, CZA.

9. Executive session, 24 May 1945, ibid.

10. Protocol of a meeting between Aliyah Hadashah and Ha'oved Hatsioni and General Zionist Association, 12 July 1945, 19 July 1945, J18/102, CZA.

11. F. Rosenblueth, "Clarification," *Amudim* 1, no. 46 (8 June 1945): 1.

12. Executive session, 5 July 1945, J18/102, CZA.

13. R. W[eltsch], "Harbingers of Decision," *Amudim* 1, nos. 56–57 (24 August 1945): 1, and "On the Crossroads of Eras: Reflections for the [Jewish] New Year," *Amudim* 1, nos. 58–59 (7 September 1945): 1.

14. R. W[eltsch], "First Rescue of Refugees," *Amudim* 2, nos. 3–4 (5 October 1945): 1–2.

15. Rosenblueth to the JAE, 14 October 1945, A339/82, CZA.

16. Executive session, 11 October 1945, J18/73, CZA.

17. F. Rosenblueth, "On the Eve of Serious Decisions," *Amudim* 2, nos. 5–6 (19 October 1945): 1–2.

18. F. Rosenblueth, "Only Thus?" *Amudim* 2, no. 9 (9 November 1945): 1–2. Rosenblueth read the censored part in the Va'ad Leumi session on 5 December 1945, S25/5931, CZA; F. Rosenblueth to Y. Ben-Zvi, 8 November 1945, A339/63, CZA.

19. Aliyah Hadashah Center session, 19 November 1945, J18/74, CZA; [unsigned], "After Bevin's Declaration," *Amudim* 2, nos. 10–11 (23 November 1945): 1–2; and see F. R[osenblueth], "First Reading," and H. Foerder, "Disappointing Document," ibid.

20. Executive session, 30 November 1945, J18/73, CZA. On the lack of influence of Aliyah Hadashah in the Va'ad Leumi, see its executive session on 31 May 1945, ibid.

21. Va'ad Leumi Plenary, secret session, 5 December 1945, S25/5931, CZA; Israel Baer, "How Freedom Movements Fight," *Yediot Hatnuah Le'achdut Ha'avodah* (Bulletin of Le'achdut Ha'avodah Movement, hereafter *Bulletin*), no. 70, 28 November 1945.

22. Aliyah Hadashah Situation Committee, 18 December 1945, J18/73, CZA.

23. G. Luft, "After the [Jewish] Agency Session," *Amudim* 2, no. 14 (21 December 1945): 1–2.

24. Executive session, 11 January 1946, J18/75, CZA; Auerbach's detailed plan: "Eine Kantonal-Verfassung fuer Palaestina," (n.d.), in A339/67, CZA.

25. Center session, 12 January 1946, J18/74, CZA.

26. G. L[andauer], "Official Policy Failed: Aliyah Hadashah Demands Ben-Gurion's Resignation," *Amudim* 2, nos. 16–17 (18 January 1946).

27. Executive session, 3 February 1946, J18/73, CZA.

28. Situation Committee, 24 February 1946, ibid. At the same time the party prepared the "Report of the Economic and Planning Commission," which included "Proposals for Consolidation and Immigration in Palestine." Dr. S. Moses acted as the chairman.

29. Dr. E. Simon, "Biltmore Would Lead to War on Two Fronts," *Amudim* 2, no. 20 (1 March 1946): 5–6.

30. "Aliyah Hadashah and Anglo-Jewry: Dr. G. Landauer Speaks in London," *Amudim* 2, no. 21 (15 March 1946): 4.

31. Aliyah Hadashah Manifesto, 7 March 1946, and Dr. E. Auerbach's suggestion, both in *Amudim* 2, no. 22 (22 March 1946): 1–2.

32. Executive session, 25 April 1946, J18/73, CZA; G. Landauer, "Tage der Spannung," *Mitteilungsblatt*, no. 16 (19 April 1946); G. Landauer, "Illegal Aliyah and the Use of Force," *Amudim* 2, no. 25 (3 May 1946): 5–6.

33. Executive session, 2 May 1946, J18/73, CZA.

34. Ibid., 23 May 1946.

35. Ibid., 13 June 1946.

36. F. Rosenblueth, "Our Political Road in the Zionist Movement," *Amudim* 2, no. 28 (14 June 1946): 3–4; G. Landauer, "Bournemouth-Westminster: On Bevin's Speech," *Amudim* 2, no. 29 (28 June 1946): 1–2.

37. Executive sessions, 30 June, 4, 11 July 1946, J18/73, CZA; Rosenblueth to Weizmann, 2 July 1946, A339/68, CZA.

38. Executive sessions, 18, 25 July 1946, J18/73; "Decisions of Aliyah Hadashah Center," *Amudim* 2, no. 32 (9 August 1946).

39. Executive session, 5 August 1946, J18/73, CZA.

40. Executive session, 15 August 1946, ibid.; [unsigned],"Um die Alija," *Mitteilungsblatt*, no. 33 (16 August 1946). The impression was corrected by G. Luft, "Paris, Jerusalem, Haifa, Cyprus," *Amudim* 2, no. 33 (23 August 1946): 3–4.

41. JAE Minutes, 18 August 1946, S/100, CZA.

42. J. V. W. Shaw to Rosenblueth, 6 September 1946, J18/54. CZA; Rosenblueth to Shaw, 8 September 1946, ibid.; U. S. Rapp, "Quislings?" *Amudim* 2, no. 35 (25 September 1946): 6.

43. Executive session, 19 September 1946, J18/73, CZA.

44. E. Simon, "Zionism and the Nations of the World," *Amudim* 3, no. 2 (18 October 1946): 5–6.

45. Rosenblueth to Weizmann, 3 November 1946, WA.

46. Executive sessions, 31 October, 21 November 1946, J18/73, CZA; Center session, 7 November 1946, J18/74, CZA.

47. F. Rosenblueth, "Some Observations on 'Activism': Aliyah Hadashah and Independents," J18/39, CZA, and his "Brief Remarks on Dr. Sneh's Speech," 16 December 1946, ibid.

48. F. Rosenblueth, "Basel," *Amudim* 3, no. 8 (17 January 1947): 1–2; F. Rosenblueth to Weizmann, 30 November 1946, A339/68, CZA.

49. Center session, 27 March 1947, J18/74, CZA.

50. Ibid., 12 June 1947; see also F. Rosenblueth, "Teilung," *Mitteilungsblatt*, no. 25 (20 June 1947); G. Landauer, "Welches is der richtig Weg?" ibid.

51. Executive session, 1 January 1948, J18/76, CZA. On Rosenblueth's failure to make Aliyah Hadashah part of the World Confederation of the General Zionists, as in the past, see the joint meeting of the World Center of General Zionist Federations and Aliyah Hadashah on 15 May 1947, A309/B15, CZA.

52. Executive sessions, 29–30 January 1948, J18/76, CZA; F. Rosenblueth, "Die Grosse Chance," *Mitteilungsblatt*, no. 51 (19 December 1947): 1–2. Rosenblueth updated Ben-Gurion regarding the developments in the future of his party and negotiations toward the foundation of a new party; see Ben-Gurion, *War Diary*, 1:39.

53. Executive session, 30 January 1948, J18/76, CZA. On 19 February 1948 at the party's executive session, Rosenblueth reported that he had voted for the foundation of a government council, ibid.; see also Ben-Gurion, *War Diary*, 1:237.

54. Center session, 13 March 1948, J18/74, CZA. The executive backed him 39 to 24 (with 4 abstentions), 25 March 1948, ibid.

55. Executive session, 5 April 1948, J18/76, CZA.

56. Ibid., 11 April 1948.

57. Ibid., 2 June 1948.

58. Ibid., 18 June 1948.

59. Ibid., 2 July 1948.

60. Ibid., 3 July 1948.

61. Ibid., 23 July 1948.

62. K. Blumenfeld to Ben-Gurion, 6 February 1949, A339/10, CZA.

8. Hashomer Hatza'ir

1. Margalit, *Hashomer Hatza'ir*; Zait, *Pioneers in the Maze of Politics*.

2. Yaari and Hazan, *Against the Current*, 13–26.

3. M. Yaari, "The Account of Our World" (1 May 1944), in *Between War and Peace*, ed. S. Auerbuch et al., 11–14.

4. Small Zionist Actions Committee, 5 March 1945, S25/1787, CZA.

5. This issue of *Mishmar* carried the headline "With the Appearance of Stalin's *Problems of Leninism*," followed by A. Cohen, "Stalin," *Mishmar,* 1 May 1945. See also Yaari in the Small Zionist Actions Committee, 20 May 1945, S25/1782, CZA.

6. Y. Riftin, "On the Day the Enemy Was Defeated," *Mishmar,* 10 May 1945. See also Y. Washitz,"On Our Neighbors," *Mishmar,* 11 May 1945.

7. Editorial, "Unity with Mapai?" *Mishmar,* 16 May 1945.

8. E. Bauer, "Neighborhood and Politics," *Mishmar,* 31 May 1945, and "The Completed 'Biltmore'," *Mishmar,* 20 June 1945.

9. E. Bauer, "Arab Communists and Zionism," *Mishmar,* 17 July 1945.

10. Y. Gelfat, "Chauvinism, Nationality and Economic Federalism," *Mishmar,* 27 July 1945.

11. Editorial, "The Agency Memorandum," *Mishmar,* 9 July 1945.

12. Y. Hurwitz, "Political Pragmatism or Marxist Dialectic," *Mishmar,* 13 July 1945.

13. M. Bentov, "Zionism in View of Labour's Victory," *Mishmar,* 3–5 August 1945.

14. London Zionist [postwar] Convention, 3 August 1945, S25/1906, CZA; editorial, "Truman's Declaration," *Mishmar,* 20 August 1945.

15. M. Bentov, "Catastrophe and Ideology," *Mishmar,* 7 September 1945.

16. M. Yaari, "Conventions Passed, What Then?" *Mishmar,* 28 September 1945. For Liebenstein's view, see his *With the Zionist Debate,* 63.

17. A. Cohen, "Still Tortoise-Like Steps," *Mishmar,* 13 October 1945.

18. Riftin to the Histadrut Actions Committee, 3 October 1945, LIA.

19. Editorial, "Atlit Survivors," *Mishmar,* 12 October 1945; editorial, "Without a Bridge," *Mishmar,* 18 October 1945; Y. Hazan, "For Struggle and Accounting of the Road," *Mishmar,* 30 October 1945.

20. Histadrut Actions Committee, 14–15 November 1945, LIA.

21. Hashomer Hatza'ir Actions Committee and the Socialist League Center, 10 November 1945, (8)5.10.5, Hashomer Hatza'ir Archives, Givat Haviva (hereafter HHA).

22. Editorial, "Up to a Crisis," *Mishmar,* 1 January 1946.

23. Hakibbutz Ha'artzi Actions Committee and the Socialist League Center, 6 November 1945, (7)5.10.5, HHA; Y. Riftin, "Methods and Roads in the Campaign," *Mishmar,* 28 November 1945.

24. Z. Lubliner, "Toward the Establishment of the Workers' Party Hashomer Hatza'ir: From Sympathy to Fighting Membership," *Mishmar,* 8 February 1946.

25. M. Yaari, "Toward the Founding of the Hashomer Hatza'ir Party," *Mishmar,* 15 February 1946.

26. E. Prai, "The Balance of Zionist Policy," in *Hashomer Hatza'ir Workers' Party in Eretz Israel* (Haifa, 22–23 February 1946), 24–31.

27. D. Ben-Nachum, "Investigators, Witnesses and Blunderers," *Mishmar,* 8 March 1946; editorial, "The Soviet Union and Eretz Israel," *Mishmar,* 8 February 1946.

28. Y. Hazan, "True Alliance of a Fighting Political Movement," *Mishmar*, 1 March 1946.

29. *The Case for a Bi-National Palestine*, Memorandum Prepared by the Hashomer Hatza'ir Workers' Party of Palestine, Published by the Executive Committee of the Hashomer Hatza'ir Workers' Party, 11–31 (emphasis in the original). The Hebrew edition notes the authors: M. Bentov, chairman, and Y. Hazan, Z. Lurieh, B. Lin, and A. Prague.

30. Ibid., 32–64.

31. Ibid., 65–75.

32. Ibid., 76–78, 148–62.

33. Ibid., 81–108.

34. Ibid., 129–44.

35. Crossman, *Palestine Mission*, 169.

36. "The Political Resolutions of Hashomer Hatza'ir Party," *Mishmar*, 21 May 1946; Center session, 2 May 1946, (1)A24.90, HHA.

37. First Council of Hashomer Hatza'ir, 17 May 1946, Tel Aviv, (3)24.90. HHA; M. Yaari, "The Inquiry Committee's Conclusions and What Further?" *Mishmar*, 31 May 1946.

38. A. Cohen, "The Arab Boycott in the Political Struggle," *Mishmar*, 3–12 May 1946.

39. See the three editorials in *Mishmar*: "Mistake" and "And Again the Terrorists," 19 June 1946, and "How Should We Defend Ourselves?" 24 June 1946.

40. "Let Us Be an Organized Camp Fighting for Victory, Not a Community of Suicide," Riftin to workers' assembly, *Mishmar*, 14 July 1946.

41. Y. Amit, "In Our Distress," *Mishmar*, 26 July 1946.

42. Yaari to Ben-Gurion, 19 August 1946, S44/731, CZA.

43. Hashomer Hatza'ir Party Center, 15 August 1946, (3)24.90, HHA.

44. Z. Bernard, "Will a New Zionist Leadership Arise?" *Mishmar*, 8 September 1946; Small Zionist Actions Committee, 24 September 1946, S25/1779, CZA.

45. "Internal not for publication": meeting of the Secretariat of the League of Rapprochement and Cooperation at H. M. Kalvarisky's house, 28 August 1946, (3)7.10.95, HHA; Hashomer Hatza'ir Center, 14 November 1946, where Riftin called the signing an "important gain," (1)A24.90, HHA; A. Cohen, "Why Fawzi al-Husseini Was Assassinated," lecture under Hashomer Hatza'ir auspices in Tel Aviv, 24 December 1946, published by Hashomer Hatza'ir (n.d.). The New Palestine group was granted 300 Palestine pounds after Fawzi's assassination, Center session, 30 January 1947, (1)A24.90, HHA.

46. Hashomer Hatza'ir Center, 14 November 1946, (1)A24.90, HHA.

47. *Protocol of the 22nd Zionist Congress*, 11 December 1946, 103–9; on Azzam, see editorial, "The Basis for Agreement," *Mishmar*, 29 September 1946.

48. *Protocol of the 22nd Zionist Congress*, 480–82.

49. Ibid., 491–98; Center session, 30 January 1947, (1)A24.90, HHA.

50. Y. Ronkin, "The Sin of Vagueness and Its Punishment," *Mishmar*, 25 October 1946; editorial, "Fatal Role," *Mishmar*, 2 January 1947.

51. M. Yaari, "Where Is the Way Out?" *Mishmar*, 28 October 1946.

52. Hashomer Hatza'ir Party, Arab Department, Bulletin no. 2, 23 March 1947; Protocol of the Arab Department Session, Hadera, 24–25 January 1947, (1)13.90, HHA.

53. Editorial, "The British Proposals," *Mishmar*, 10 February 1947; editorial, "Two Mistakes," *Mishmar*, 24 February 1947.

54. Center session, 24 April 1947, (1)A24.90, HHA; Riftin to Histadrut Actions Committee, 26 March 1947, LIA.

55. M. Zippor, "World's Peace-Lovers, Unite!" *Mishmar*, 30 April 1947.

56. M. Bentov, "What Else Could be Done? 3. The Political Front," *Mishmar*, 2 May 1947.

57. M. Bentov, "What Else Could Be Done? 3. The Political Front (End)," *Mishmar*, 5 May 1947.

58. Editorial, "Why Weizmann?" *Mishmar*, 9 May 1947.

59. Editorial, "Historical Declaration," *Mishmar*, 15 May 1947; "A Progressive Plan for the Solution of the Palestine Problem," Hashomer Hatza'ir's Memorandum for the World Working Parties, *Mishmar*, 16 May 1947.

60. M. Yaari to S. Flapan, 20 May 1947, (2)55.3 H, HHA.

61. Yaari to L. Greenblatt, 20 May 1947, ibid.

62. Editorial, "Communists from Within," *Mishmar*, 21 May 1947; Hazan in Center meeting, 29 May 1947, (1)A24.90, HHA.

63. Editorial, "Wasted Possibilities," *Mishmar*, 23 May 1947.

64. Center session, 29 May 1947, (1)A24.90, HHA.

65. Y. Hazan, "In View of New Chances," *Mishmar*, 6–8 June 1947; Fourth Session of Hashomer Hatza'ir Council, 27 June 1947, (3)24.90, HHA.

66. Center session, 19 June 1947, (3)24.90, HHA.

67. *The Road to Bi-National Independence for Palestine: Memorandum of the Hashomer Hatza'ir Workers' Party of Palestine*.

68. Editorial, "Dr. Sneh's Proposal," *Mishmar*, 1 July 1947.

69. Yaari to the Secretariat of the Party and of Hakibbutz Ha'artzi, [2 September 1947], (4)17.90, HHA.

70. Hashomer Hatza'ir Fourth Council, 27 June 1947, Tel Aviv, (3)24.90, HHA.

71. Y. Hazan, "Zionist Policy Ought to Change Its Way," *Mishmar*, 8 July 1947.

72. Actions Committee and Center session, 4 September 1947, (A3)19.90, HHA.

73. Israel Idelson (later Bar-Yehuda) in the name of Hashomer Hatza'ir and Le'achdut Ha'avodah, 2 September 1947, S5/320, CZA; Zait, *Zionism and Peace*, 311–12.

74. Center session, 16 October 1947, (A3)19.90, HHA; M. Yaari, "Disillusioned and Loyal to the Idea," *Mishmar*, 24 October 1947.

75. Center session, 27 November 1947, (A3)19.90, HHA. Yaari's speech was published, with important additions, in *Mishmar*, 26 December 1947, titled: "Let Us Build a Road of Fighting Workers' Unity."

9. Le'achdut Ha'avodah Movement

1. Zait, *Pioneers in the Maze of Politics*, 126–43; for general background see Ishai, *Factionalism in the Labor Movement*.

2. Le'achdut Ha'avodah Manifesto, 1 May 1945, *Bulletin*, no. 41, 4 May 1945; Tabenkin at Party Activists Convention, Tel Aviv, 1 May 1945, 13/1/1/2, KMA.

3. Faction B Convention, 26 May 1945, 15/19/6/3, KMA.

4. Ibid.

5. A. Ziesling, "On the Strengthening of the Force," *Bulletin*, no. 46, 7 June 1945.

6. Y. Gothelf, "Vision and Reality in Zionist Policy," *Bulletin*, no. 48, 21 June 1945.

7. I. Baer, "Neither Victory Nor Defeat," *Bulletin*, no. 53, 26 July 1945.

8. I. Baer, "After the Victory—Before the Campaign," *Bulletin*, no. 54, 2 August 1945.

9. A. Ziesling at the Zionist London Convention, 7 August 1945, S25/1906, CZA.

10. Y. Ben-Aharon, "With Our Return," *Davar*, 28 September 1945.

11. [unsigned], "Let's Get Ready," *Bulletin*, no. 63, 4 October 1945.

12. Y. Tabenkin, "Our Force Is Great . . . ," *Bulletin*, no. 65, 18 October 1945.

13. I. Baer, "Eretz Israel—An International Problem," ibid.

14. Y. Tabenkin, "In the Sight of a Turning Point," *Bulletin*, no. 66, 25 October 1945.

15. Y. Noded [Sadeh], "With the Youth: Around the Bonfire," *Bulletin*, no. 67, 1 November 1945.

16. Y. [Tabenkin], "First Reply," *Bulletin*, no. 69, 20 November 1945. The original speech was delivered to the Histadrut Actions Committee, 14 November 1945, LIA.

17. I. Baer, "How Liberation Movements Fight," *Bulletin*, no. 70, 28 November 1945.

18. Va'ad Leumi Plenum, 5 December 1945, S25/5931 (secret); I. Baer, "One Front," *Bulletin*, no. 71, 6 December 1945.

19. I. Baer, "The Soviet Union and the Middle East," *Bulletin*, no. 78, 24 January 1946.

20. I. Baer, "The Soviet Union and the Problem of Eretz Israel," *Bulletin*, no. 82, 28 February 1946.

21. D. Pnimi [?], "On Standpoint and on Resistance," *Bulletin*, no. 72, 13 December 1945.

22. Histadrut Actions Committee, 30 January 1946, LIA.

23. Twelfth Council of Le'achdut Ha'avodah Movement, 4–6 January 1946, 13/5/2, KMA (the speakers were B. Repetor, A. Ziesling, and I. Idelson).

24. A. Z[iesling], "One Workers' Front for the Zionist Congress," *Bulletin*, no. 87, 28 March 1946; A. Tarshish, "On the Margins of a Debate," *Bulletin*, no. 88, 4 April 1946; Conference of Unity, Le'achdut Ha'avodah Party–Poale Zion, "Declaration of Unity," 27 April 1946, *Bulletin*, no. 92, 30 April 1946.

25. A. Tarshish, "False Maneuvers," *Bulletin*, no. 93, 9 May 1946.

26. Y. Sadeh, "With the Youth: Around the Bonfire," *Bulletin*, no. 98, 13 June 1946.

27. Y. Noded [Y. Sadeh], "With the Youth: Around the Bonfire," *Bulletin*, no. 101, 11 July 1946.

28. Z. Abramovitch, "The Twilight of Gods," ibid.

29. L[e'achdut] H[a'avodah], "Not Thus!" *Bulletin*, no. 102, 25 July 1946.

30. I. Baer, "Strategy and Tactics of Liberation Movements," ibid.

31. Y. Sadeh, "With the Youth: Around the Bonfire," ibid.

32. See Y. Sadeh's column "With the Youth: Around the Bonfire," in *Bulletin*, no. 105, 22 August 1946; nos. 109–10, 22 September 1946; and no. 112, 8 October 1946. See also articles in the Mapai youth journal *Mishmeret* by K. K[atz], 16 October 1946; "Turai" [?], 29 November 1946; and Sadeh, 29 November 1946. In his reply Sadeh slightly changed his former style of defiance, arguing that he only expressed "fear and anxiety." On Ben-Gurion and Sadeh see Slutsky, *History of the Haganah*, 3:1496–97.

33. I. Baer, "The United States and the Eretz Israel Problem," *Bulletin*, no. 105, 22 August 1946.

34. I. Idelson, "Motives and Preventives in Our Struggle," *Bulletin*, no. 111, 3 October 1946 (speech to the First Council of the Le'achdut Ha'avodah–Poale Zion Party, 20 September 1946, 15/19/1/1, KMA).

35. First Council of the Le'achdut Ha'avodah–Poale Zion Party, 21 September 1946, 15/19/1/2, KMA; debate, 21 September 1946, in 18/19/1/4, KMA.

36. Debate, 21 September 1946, ibid.

37. I. Baer, "Independence and Partition," *Bulletin*, no. 112, 8 October 1946.

38. L. Cantor, "International Trusteeship and the Problem of Eretz Israel," ibid.

39. D. L. [?], "For a Fighting Leadership," *Bulletin*, no. 114, 23 October 1946.

40. "Le'achdut Ha'avodah–Poale Zion Party Manifesto to the Electors of the 22nd Congress," ibid.

41. Second Council of Le'achdut Ha'avodah–Poale Zion Party, 15–16 November 1946, 15/1/5, KMA; Alexander [D. Loebel], "A Support-Point for Our Policy," *Bulletin*, nos. 118–19, 28 November 1946; *Protocol of the 22nd Zionist Congress*, 12 December 1946, 115, 254 (Tabenkin and Ziesling).

42. I. Baer, "Interim Balance Sheet," *Bulletin*, no. 129, 6 February 1947.

43. I. Baer, "What Further?" *Bulletin*, no. 134, 13 March 1947.

44. "Manifesto of Le'achdut Ha'avodah–Poale Zion Center," *Bulletin*, no. 141, 15 May 1947; "Our Party's Proposals in the Elected Assembly," *Bulletin*, no. 143, 29 May 1947; "From Ziesling's Speech to the Elected Assembly," ibid.

45. I. Baer, "Policy of Sympathy and Hatred," *Bulletin*, no. 142, 22 May 1947; cf. Y. Sadeh, "With the Youth: Around the Bonfire," in the same issue.

46. H. Drabkin, "How Is a Jewish-Arab Settlement to Be Achieved?" *Davar*, 10 June 1947, and "Independence and Federation," *Davar*, 3 July 1947.

47. M. Erem, "Truth Is Needed in Debate Too," *Davar*, 11 June 1947.

48. Joint Motions in the Zionist Actions Committee, of Le'achdut Ha'avodah–

Poale Zion and Hashomer Hatza'ir (2 September 1947), *Bulletin*, nos. 156–57, 11 September 1947; M. Durman, "The Combined Suggestion," *Bulletin*, no. 158, 23 September 1947.

49. I. Baer, "At the Crossroads?" *Bulletin*, no. 158, 23 September 1947.

50. L[e'achdut] H[a'avodah], "On Two Fronts," *Bulletin*, no. 161, 16 October 1947; "Confronting UNSCOP: Summary of the Discussion in Le'achdut Ha'avodah–Poale Zion Center" (4 September 1947), *Bulletin*, nos. 156–57, 11 September 1947.

51. Discussions toward the establishment of Mapam, L. Levité diary, 21 October 1947, meeting with representatives of Hashomer Hatza'ir, 13/8/1/4, KMA.

52. Le'achdut Ha'avodah–Poale Zion Center session, 30 October 1947, 15/3/1, KMA. A recent biography on Idelson claims that he too was against the formation of Mapam; see Goren, *Israel Bar-Yehuda*, 238–42.

53. "Assumptions for Unity" (28 November 1947), *Bulletin*, no. 171, 25 December 1947.

10. Mapam and the War of Independence

1. Y. Hazan, "On Unity," in *The Unity Conference of Hashomer Hatza'ir Party in Eretz Israel and Le'achdut Ha'avodah–Poale Zion Party* (22–23 January 1948), 69–75 (hereafter *Unity Conference*).

2. Yaari, "The Foundations of Our Unity," ibid., 10–21.

3. Tabenkin, "The Substance of Our Unity," ibid., 22–29.

4. See Sneh's letter of resignation to Ben-Gurion in Slutsky, *History of the Haganah*, 3:1933–34; Sneh to Galili, September 1947, Galili files, KMA; Kaplan on Sneh in *Livchinat Haderech*, 31–32; and particularly Ben-Aharon's letters from Paris, October 1946, 162/4, 15/19/6/4, KMA. See also M. Sneh, "All Our Hope—in Ourselves!" *Ha'oved Hatsioni*, nos. 13–14 (167–68), 22 April 1947, 4–5; JAE, 18 June 1947, S/100, CZA; S. Zvuluni, "An Open Letter to Dr. Moshe Sneh," *Ha'oved Hatsioni*, no. 10 (188), 5 February 1948, 3–4.

5. *Unity Conference*, 42–45.

6. Ibid., 55.

7. Bentov in the Political Committee, 29 January 1948, and Livshitz in the Political Committee, 5 February 1948, both in (1)66.90, HHA.

8. Political Committee 2nd session, 5 February 1948, (1)66.90, HHA; M. Sneh, "The Partition in Its First Test," *Al Hamishmar*, 6 February 1948; also in *Al Hamishmar*, see "Factors in the Campaign," 13 February 1948, and M. Sneh, "On the International Force," and Z. Bernard, "The Preparations for a State," both in 20 February 1948.

9. Mapam Center session, 7 March 1948, (1)67.90, HHA.

10. Ibid., 8 March 1948.

11. Ibid., 21–22 March 1948.

12. Ibid., 1 April 1948.

13. Y. Riftin, "After the Turning Point at Lake Success," *Al Hamishmar*, 2 April 1948; Mapam's representatives at the third session of the Zionist Actions Committee, 7–8 April 1948, and resolutions (11 April 1948), S5/322, CZA; editorial, "The Trusteeship Plan," *Al Hamishmar*, 7 April 1948; M. Sneh, "Roadblocks and Ambushes on the Way," *Al Hamishmar*, 9 April 1948.

14. M. Yaari, "The Torturous Road to Freedom," *Al Hamishmar*, 23 April 1948.

15. A. Benshalom, "The Arab Evacuation and Its Conclusions," *Al Hamishmar*, 7 May 1948; see also A. Cohen's apology for Deir Yasin, perpetrated, he said, by Jewish "fascists": "An Open Letter to Dr. Khalidi, Secretary of the Arab Higher Committee," *Al Hamishmar*, 9 May 1948. For a detailed discussion of Mapam's subsequent views, see Morris, *1948 and After*.

16. Center Session, 4 May 1948, (1)67.90, HHA.

17. Center session, 11 May 1948, ibid. The speaker mentioned was S. Kushnir.

18. Political Committee, 21 May 1948, ibid.; Ben-Gurion, *War Diary*, 2:443.

19. Political Committee, 26–27 May 1948, (1)67.90, HHA.

20. M. Sneh, "From the Far to the Near," *Al Hamishmar*, 28 May 1948; Political Committee, 15 June 1948, (1)67.90, HHA; Resolutions of the first session of Mapam Council, 25–26 June 1948, *Al Hamishmar*, 28 June 1948.

21. Political Committee, 1 June 1948, (1)67.90, HHA; M. Sneh, "Rhodes Won't Be Munich," *Al Hamishmar*, 18 June 1948.

22. Political Committee, 15 June 1948, (1)67.90, HHA.

23. Political Committee, 24 June–3 July 1948, ibid.; S. Derech, "The First Crisis in the State of Israel," *Al Hamishmar*, 2 July 1948.

24. M. Bentov, "Fortified and Confident in Victory We Will Continue Our War of Freedom," *Al Hamishmar*, 2 July 1948. See also Riftin in Political Committee, 29 July 1948, (1)67.90, HHA.

25. Political Committee, 20 July 1948, (1)67.90, HHA.

26. Political Committee, 19 August 1948, ibid.

27. M. Yaari, "If You Go to War," *Al Hamishmar*, 30 July 1948.

28. Editorial, "Transfer," *Al Hamishmar*, 3 August 1948; M. Sneh, "On the Principal and the Marginal," *Al Hamishmar*, 6 August 1948.

29. M. Sneh, "In the Government Not in the Coalition," *Al Hamishmar*, 13 August 1948.

30. Political Committee, 19 August 1948, (1)67.90, HHA.

31. Y. Hazan, "Daring War, Bold Policy, Guarantee for Full Victory," *Al Hamishmar*, 27 August 1948; Y. Riftin, "War and Peace in the Arab States," *Al Hamishmar*, 8 September 1948.

32. M. Sneh, "Ostrich Policy," *Al Hamishmar*, 2 September 1948; Political Committee, 2, 14 September, 3 November 1948 (first bad news from Eastern Europe about persecution of Jews), (1)67.90, HHA. Cf. Riftin in the Knesset, 15 June 1949, *Knesset Record*, 1:723–25.

33. Political Committee, 15–16 September 1948, (1)67.90, HHA; see the two replies to Ilya Ehrenburg, by N. Nir and M. Talmy, *Al Hamishmar*, 12 October 1948.

34. Mapam Center, "To the Workers of Eretz Israel," *Al Hamishmar*, 5 November 1948. Soviet diplomatic representatives in Israel contributed special articles to *Al Hamishmar* on 2 November 1948. On the rift with Maki over a united front, see their exchange of letters in *Al Hamishmar*, 12 November 1948.

35. Editorial, "The Dismantling of Cooperation," *Al Hamishmar*, 2 November 1948.

36. E. Prai, "Really Transfer?" *Al Hamishmar*, 19 November 1948.

37. Political Committee, 18 November 1948, (1)67.90, HHA.

38. Ibid., 25 November 1948.

39. Ibid., 15 December 1948.

40. M. Sneh, "The Working Class and the State Constitution," *Al Hamishmar*, 31 December 1948.

41. E. Hacohen, "The State of Israel in a Marxist Perspective," *Al Hamishmar*, 7 January 1949, and "The Goal of the Workers' Movement," *Al Hamishmar*, 10 January 1949.

42. Political Committee, 23–30 December 1948, (1)67.90, HHA; Mapam Arab Department, "Mapam and the Arab People," January 1949, (2)31.90, HHA. This pamphlet, with its upbeat picture of the party's attitude toward the Arabs, hardly reflected the internal debate in Mapam. The Popular Arab Bloc failed to get a seat in the Knesset, obtaining only 2,812 votes. Mapai's Nazareth Democratic List returned two MKs. See Mapam Arab Department, Bulletin no. 5, "The Arabs in the Elections to the First Knesset," 20 February 1949, (2)21.90, HHA.

43. M. Yaari, "For Workers' Hegemony in a Progressive Government," *Al Hamishmar*, 24 January 1949.

44. Political Committee, 30 January–1 February 1949, (1)67.90, HHA.

45. M. Sneh, "Anti-Harriman," *Al Hamishmar*, 11 February 1949.

46. Editorial, "In Rhodes and Around It," *Al Hamishmar*, 21 February 1949.

47. Y. Riftin and Y. Ben-Aharon meeting with Ben-Gurion, 24 February 1949, (4)41.90, HHA; Political Committee, 28 February 1949, (1)67.90, HHA.

48. Political Committee, 1–2 March 1949, (1)67.90, HHA; Mapam Council, 2 March 1949, ibid.

49. On the American loan issue the vote was 15 to 3 with 15 abstentions for Hazan's suggestion to abstain in the Knesset; see Political Committee, 11–17 March 1949, (1)67.90, HHA; Z. Abramovitch, "The Loan and its Conditions," *Al Hamishmar*, 18 March 1949.

50. Political Committee, 16 March 1949, (1)67.90, HHA. See also M. Talmi, "Let Us Examine Our Road in the Lands of the People's Democracies," *Al Hamishmar*, 18 March 1949.

51. *Knesset Record*, 4 April 1949, 2:287–89, and 15 June 1949, 1:723–25, 749–51; editorial, "The Controversy Over the Rhodes Treaties," *Al Hamishmar*, 6 April 1949.

52. Political Committee, 26–30 March 1949, (1)67.90, HHA.

53. Ibid., 18 May 1949.

54. Mapam Secretariat of the Center, 14 June 1949, Tel Aviv, 28 June 1949, (1)13.90, HHA.

55. Editorial, "We and the Congress of Peace," *Al Hamishmar*, 21 April 1949; M. Sneh, "The Shadow of the Atlantic Treaty," *Al Hamishmar*, 25 March 1949; M. Erem, "Nazi Army in the Labour Party's Service," *Al Hamishmar*, 18 April 1949.

56. Y. Allon to the prime minister, 24 March 1949, "Private and Top Secret," 15/4/1, KMA.

57. M. Zippor, "Peace-lovers—Unite!" *Al Hamishmar*, 30 April 1949.

58. See, for example, the meeting in Shaar Ha'amakim, 17 September 1949, (13) 5.10.5, HHA.

11. The Revisionist Party

1. Heller, "The Failure of Fascism in Jewish Palestine."

2. Editorial, "On the Road of the Blurring and Fog," *Hamashkif*, 29 April 1945. See also N. A. Rose, "The Seventh Dominion."

3. A. Sikra [Achimeir], "Reflections on May Day 'Festival'," *Hamashkif*, 1 May 1945.

4. Avishai [Achimeir], "Anti-Ma[rxism] Articles," *Hamashkif*, 14 June 1945, and "A Few Loud Reflections," *Hamashkif*, 22 June 1945.

5. Editorial, "NZO and the Agency," *Hamashkif*, 15 August 1945; Dr. Y. Bader, "Weizmann—The Main Obstacle," *Hamashkif* 17 August 1945.

6. Editorial, "Each New Dunam," *Hamashkif*, 21 September 1945.

7. Editorial, "What Should Be the First Retaliation Act?" *Hamashkif*, 25 September 1945.

8. Jabotinsky, "Vanity of Vanities," *Jewish Herald*, 17 January 1939, reprinted in *Hamashkif*, 19 October 1945; his "The Escalation of the Conflict," *Rassvet*, 21 April 1932, reprinted in *Hamashkif*, 26 October 1945; and his "National Sport," *Moment*, 28 April 1939, reprinted in *Hamashkif*, 26 April 1946.

9. Y. Shofman, "The Victorious Distortion," *Hamashkif*, 26 October 1945.

10. Dr. Y. Bader, "The Old Poem," *Hamashkif*, 11 January 1946.

11. Dr. Y. Bader, "Coalition with Whom and for What?" *Hamashkif*, 9 November 1945.

12. Y. Shofman, "What Changed?" *Hamashkif*, 16 November 1945.

13. A. Achimeir, "Ben-Gurion's Speech without Cosmetics," *Hamashkif*, 7 December 1945.

14. Dr. Y. Bader, "Do Not Exaggerate and Do Not Obfuscate," *Hamashkif*, 23 November 1945. Bader compared the need to evacuate the Jewish Diaspora to the abolition of slavery by W. Wilberforce.

15. "The National Movement Replies Proudly to Bevin's Announcement: Let Us Have the Inquiry Committee Boycotted by Every Jewish Body!" *Hamashkif*, 5 December 1945; Dr. Y. Bader, "Jabotinsky's Plan before the Committee of Inquiry," *Hamashkif*, 15 January 1946.

16. Dr. Y. Bader, "Azzam Bey Is Right," *Hamashkif,* 28 December 1945; his "What Will America Say?" *Hamashkif,* 14 May 1946; and his "Christian Diaspora," *Hamashkif,* 7 December 1945.

17. Dr. Z. Von Weisl, "1946—On the Verge of a New World War," *Hamashkif,* 4 January 1946. Cf. A. Weinshall, "Our Foreign Policy," *Hahevrah,* year 5, no. 70 (January 1946): 959–60. Weinshall did not mention the USSR but called for new allies, even "the devil himself."

18. A. Remba, "Will the NZO Attend the Next [Zionist] Congress?" *Hamashkif,* 21 December 1945. Cf. A. Weinshall, "Will the Revisionists Return?" *Hahevrah,* year 5, no. 68 (October 1945): 925–27. Weinshall, a former Revisionist leader, thought a return to the old Zionist movement would not constitute a real change but would only create a new "public face" with a "national conscience" and "public responsibility."

19. A. Remba, "Will the NZO Attend the Next Congress?" *Hamashkif,* 21 December 1945.

20. A. Remba, "Yes!" *Hamashkif,* 11 January 1946.

21. A. Sikra [Achimeir], "No!" ibid., and "'Vichy'," *Hamashkif,* 25 January 1946; A. Shamai [Achimeir], "In the Fortune of Mars: Lie and Bad Luck Combined," *Hamashkif,* 2 May 1946.

22. Prof. Y. Klausner, "If Not Now—When?" *Hamashkif,* 18 January 1946.

23. Y. Odem [Rubin], "Tempo, Principles and Framework," *Hamashkif,* 25 January 1946.

24. H. S. Halevy, "From Coldness and Fastness," *Hamashkif,* 31 January 1946.

25. E. Shostak, "We Will Go, We Will Fight and Succeed," *Hamashkif,* 1 February 1946.

26. Y. Odem, "We Do Not Have Either Eternal Enemies or Eternal Friends—We Have Eternal Interests!" ibid.

27. "Final Summation of the NZO Referendum," *Hamashkif,* 8 February 1946.

28. Dr. Y. Bader, "The Policy of Alliances," *Hamashkif,* 20 March 1946.

29. Dr. Y. Bader, "0.0," *Hamashkif,* 3 May 1946.

30. Y. Shofman, "Our Anxiety," *Hamashkif,* 17 May 1946; K. K[atzenelson], "The End of *Ha'apalah:* The Continuation of Surrender," *Hamashkif,* 25 July 1947.

31. L. Avshalom, "The Seventh Dominion," *Hamashkif,* 5 July 1946; Dr. Y. Bader, "The Truth Comes with Tanks," ibid.

32. Editorials, "In Front of the Victims" and "Until When?" *Hamashkif,* 23 July 1946.

33. Dr. Y. Bader, "Let's Not Fight against Partition," *Hamashkif,* 23 August 1946.

34. Captain Y. Halpern, "Leader or Quisling?" *Hamashkif,* 30 August 1946.

35. Dr. Y. Bader, "I Too Believe," *Hamashkif,* 25 September 1946.

36. Dr. Y. Bader, "Then—Inform on Me!" *Hamashkif,* 18 October 1946; S. Rosenfeld, "Day and Night with the Palmach *Ma'apilim,*" *Hamashkif,* 1–2 October 1946.

37. Dr. Y. Bader, "The Jewish Majority in Eretz Israel—A Fact!" *Hamashkif,* 1

October 1946. In "On Congress and 15 Parties" in the same issue, Dr. Z. Von Weisl added that Jews constituted 80 to 95 percent of the intellectuals and 90 to 100 percent of the musicians and artists. See also A. Weinshall, "For the Attention of the 'Interrogated'," *Hahevrah*, year 6, no. 73 (March 1946): 1004–5.

38. Dr. Y. Bader, "'Declaration'," *Hamashkif*, 1 November 1946.

39. Dr. Y. Bader, "I—Against Terror," *Hamashkif*, 22 November 1946; see also his "Defense on Dissent," ibid., 10 April 1947, and "Operation Acre," ibid., 18 April 1947. On the Revisionist pretension to play the Sinn Fein role, see J. B. Schechtman's counterproposal for the congress's antiterrorist resolution, *Protocol of the 22nd Zionist Congress*, 487–88.

40. A. Sikra, "Reflections of an Intellectual," *Hamashkif*, 15 November 1946. Achimeir's status as an ideologue should not be underrated. See, for example, the praises heaped on him on the occasion of his fiftieth birthday, in *Hamashkif*, 1 November 1946.

41. *Protocol of the 22nd Zionist Congress*, 11 December 1946, 97–103.

42. Ibid., 13 December 1946, 174–79.

43. M. Grossman, "Unity, Concentration, Reorientation," *Hamashkif*, 14 February 1947.

44. Dr. Y. Bader, "If to the UN—Then to the International Court," *Hamashkif*, 28 February 1947; "World Hatsohar on the Ways to Implement Zionism," *Hamashkif*, 28 March 1947.

45. Dr. Y. Bader, "A Ghost Rising from Munich," *Hamashkif*, 2 May 1947.

46. A. R. [?], "The Surprise—Gromyko," *Hamashkif*, 16 May 1947, and S. Rosenfeld, "After the Soviet 'Balfour Declaration'," ibid.

47. A. Shamai, "'Nations Fraternity': 'Gromyko's Declaration'," *Hamashkif*, 22 May 1947.

48. Dr. Z. Von Weisl, "Proposition for the Inquiry Committee," *Hamashkif*, 27 June 1947.

49. Z. Von Weisl, "Eretz Israel and the Arabs," *Hamashkif*, 11 July 1947.

50. Headline, "The Ten Martyrs," *Hamashkif*, 30 July 1947.

51. Dr. Y. Bader, "In the Shadow of the Gallows," *Hamashkif*, 1 August 1947; K. K[atzenelson], "The Revisionist Spiritual Reckoning," *Hamashkif*, 8 August 1947; Editorial, "From Coldness and Steadfastness," *Hamashkif*, 6 August 1947.

52. B. S. [?], "In Days of Anxiety," *Hamashkif*, 15 August 1947.

53. Dr. Y. Bader, "Plan No. 2 of the Anonymous Clerk," *Hamashkif*, 18 September 1947.

54. A. Sikra, "Partition as a Ban," *Hamashkif*, 19 September 1947.

55. A. Sikra, "The Creech-Jones Declaration," *Hamashkif*, 5 October 1947.

56. Dr. Z. Von Weisl, "Enemy No. 3," *Hamashkif*, 9 January 1948, and "The Only Road to Victory," *Hamashkif*, 7 March 1948; Ben-Gurion, *War Diary*, 1:18.

57. Dr. Y. Yanay, "The Wickedness of Pseudo-Revolutionary Gentlemen," *Hamashkif*, 30 January 1948.

58. Y. Shofman, "Between Verbosity and Fervor," ibid.; A. Shamai, "Rottenness in the House of Jacob: The Anti-Semitic Conference," *Hamashkif*, 1 February 1948.

59. "Hatsohar Center Decides to Join the State Council, Not Cabinet," *Hamashkif,* 8 March 1948.

60. Z. Loewenberg, "Mistake!" *Hamashkif,* 9 March 1948; A. Babkov, "The Right Step," *Hamashkif,* 11 March 1948.

61. Dr. Z. Von Weisl, "Our Strategy Regarding the Arabs," *Hamashkif,* 12 March 1948.

62. Dr. Z. Von Weisl, "It Never Happened," *Hamashkif,* 22 March 1948.

63. Grossman to the Zionist Actions Committee, 7 April 1948, S/322, CZA.

64. Dr. Z. Von Weisl, "The Military Situation after Deir Yasin and before Lake Success," *Hamashkif,* 16 April 1948.

65. Dr. Z. Von Weisl, "Our Mistake vis-à-vis the Arabs," *Hamashkif,* 12 May 1948.

66. K. Katzenelson, "On This Day," *Hamashkif,* 27 April 1948; Y. Shofman, "Peace in Israel,"*Hamashkif,* 29 April 1948; A. Remba, "The Agreement: What It Includes and Excludes," ibid.

67. Y. Shofman, "Between Fear and Fear," *Hamashkif,* 14 May 1948; see also Dr. Y. Bader, "The Choice," ibid.

68. K. Katzenelson, "A Leader Spoke," *Hamashkif,* 18 May 1948.

69. Y. Shofman, "Three Generations," *Hamashkif,* 21 May 1948; see the selective quotations reprinted from Jabotinsky's writings in the article bylined Z. Jabotinsky, "The Order Which Expelled the Foreign Rule," *Hamashkif,* 14 May 1948; Sofer, *Begin,* 22–23; Heller, *The Stern Gang,* 11–64.

70. A. Sikra, "Our Relations with the Arabs," *Hamashkif,* 4 June 1948. The epigraph for this article is Kipling's "West Is West and East Is East."

71. M. Grossman, "How to Achieve Agreement with the Arab World," *Hamashkif,* 30 July 1948.

72. Dr. A. Altman, "Let Us Flood the Country with One Million Olim Immediately. A Speech to the Greater Zionist Actions Committee," *Hamashkif,* 29 August 1948.

73. K. Katzenelson, "The Revisionist Movement: Where To?" *Hamashkif,* 11 June 1948.

74. M. Grossman, "Hatsohar and the State of Israel," *Hamashkif,* 21 June 1948 (speech delivered on 16 June 1948).

75. Editorials in *Hamashkif:* "The Government Stained Its Hands with Jewish Blood," 22 June 1948, and "The Provisional Government Sabotaged the Military Effort," 23 June 1948; Dr. Alef [Achimeir], "The Fire Ignited by Ben-Gurion," *Hamashkif,* 24 June 1948.

76. *Protocols of the Provisional State Council,* 23 June 1948, 1:4–41; editorial, "Our New State Is Led to the Abyss," *Hamashkif,* 24 June 1948; Dr. Y. Bader, "They Broke the Restraints," *Hamashkif,* 25 June 1948.

77. Ben-Gurion, *War Diary,* 3:648–49; editorial, "Hatsohar in the Zionist Executive," *Hamashkif,* 5 September 1948.

78. "Hatsohar at a Crossroads: Before the [Party] Conference," *Hamashkif,* 20 August 1948; see also Y. Yelin, "Inevitable Debate," and Dr. Y. Bader, "To-

ward Unity," ibid.; Yelin's article emphasized the personal aspect of the rift. See also Group of Members, "Only for Hatsohar Members! Notes on the Internal Debate in Hatsohar," 12 August 1948, A232/68, CZA.

79. "Hatsohar Conference Decides to Join Herut," *Hamashkif*, 11 September 1948. Hatsohar demanded that Herut remove the "Only Thus!" symbol and the words "founded by the IZL" from the Herut name. See Ben-Gurion, *War Diary*, 3:695.

80. *Protocols of Provisional State Council*, 23 September 1948, 1:9–34; *Ha'aretz*, 4 January 1948, reported that the Herut Actions Committee voted 38 to 1 (with 1 abstention) against Altman and associates on a joint list. See also A. Remba, "The Government and the Opposition," *Hamashkif*, 1 October 1948, and Y. Klarman to M. Grossman, 10 February 1949, A232/68, CZA.

81. E. Jabotinsky, "Our Movements and the Social Program," *Hamashkif*, 15 October 1948.

82. E. Jabotinsky, "On Free Debate," *Hamashkif*, 22 October 1948.

83. E. Jabotinsky, "The Second Phase," *Hamashkif*, 29 October 1948.

84. Ben-Tabaria, "A Letter to Eri Jabotinsky (On the Basis Free Debate)" *Hamashkif*, 19 November 1948.

85. E. Jabotinsky, "My Arab State Citizens," ibid., and his "Religion and the State," *Hamashkif*, 26 November 1948.

86. "Program of the Revisionist Zionist Alliance for the First Knesset," *Hamashkif*, 7 January 1949; A. Remba, "In the Full Name: Hatsohar, Jabotinsky Movement," ibid. Ben-Gurion rejected out of hand Altman's last-minute maneuvers against Herut; see Ben-Gurion, *War Diary*, 3:868, 899; "Reply to M. Begin," *Hamashkif*, 24 January 1949.

87. Dr. A. Altman, "We Are the Only Party Which Is Permitted to Ask the People's Confidence," *Hamashkif*, 25 January 1949. Cf. also his speech at a public rally, *Hamashkif*, 23 January 1949.

88. Cf. Sofer, *Begin*, 51–56.

12. Menachem Begin, IZL, and Herut

1. T. Kollek to R. Moore, Jewish Terrorist Gangs in Palestine, 26 January 1945, RG 226, Records of the Office of Strategic Services, Entry 190—Box 73. Cairo-SI-OP-7 (Operations—Jewish Agency), 15 January 1945, National Archives, Washington, D.C.

2. [M. Begin], Survey, February 1945, "Top Secret," K4/12/2/2, Jabotinsky Institute Archives, Tel Aviv (hereafter JIA).

3. Begin, *In the Underground*, 1:228–31.

4. Ibid., 1:241.

5. Ibid., 1:245, 281.

6. Ibid., 1:250.

7. Ibid., 1:257–60.

8. Ibid., 1:263–68.

9. Ibid., 1:275–77; [M. Begin], Survey, Internal, September 1945, JIA.

10. Begin, *Underground*, 1:9–12; Survey, December 1945–January 1946, JIA.

11. Begin, *Underground*, 2:20–21.

12. Ibid., 2:22–26.

13. Ibid., 2:29–32.

14. Ibid., 2:44–46; see also Begin, "The Defeatist Alliance of the Rich," *Herut*, no. 53, December 1945, and "Definitions Must Be Precise," *Herut*, no. 58, May 1946.

15. Begin, *Underground*, 2:83–84.

16. IZL to the *American* Members of the Inquiry Committee, n.d. [March 1946], K4/15/1, JIA (emphasis in the original).

17. Begin, *Underground*, 2:121–22, 132–33.

18. Ibid., 2:137.

19. Ibid., 2:145–46.

20. Ibid., 2:174–75. Translated in *Psychological Warfare and Propaganda*, ed. Tavin and Alexander, 61–62. This selection is unrepresentative of IZL source material and accompanied by tendentious introductions.

21. Begin, *Underground*, 2:201, and *The Revolt*, 278.

22. Begin, *Underground*, 2:213; [Begin], "Jews, Pay Attention!" *Herut*, no. 61.

23. Begin, *Underground*, 2:231–34, 244–45.

24. Ibid., 2:237–38.

25. IZL [to the Zionist Congress Members], n.d., LK 11/Box 10, CZA; Begin, *Underground*, 3:27–29.

26. Begin, *Revolt*, 322. Begin claimed (*Underground*, 3:353–55) that this attack brought about the UN special General Assembly session in April. This is not substantiated by archival sources.

27. Begin, *Underground*, 3:66–67. Begin was following Jabotinsky's apotheosis for Shlomo Ben-Yosef's execution in 1938, with one difference: the latter had done his utmost to save Ben-Yosef from the gallows.

28. Begin, *Underground*, 3:295–96.

29. *Psychological Warfare*, ed. Tavin and Alexander, 177; Begin, *Underground*, 3:114–15.

30. Begin, *Underground*, 3:98–99; IZL, Survey, June 1946, K4/12/2/2, JIA. Begin likened the IZL's attack on the Acre prison on 13 May to the storming of the Bastille in the French Revolution (*Revolt*, 298).

31. Notes on Conversation with M. Begin of IZL [24 June 1947], 4 August 1947, UNSCOP 2 RJB Series 1–9, DAG 13/3.0.1, UN Archives, New York.

32. Begin, *Underground*, 3:123–24, 126–27.

33. Ibid., 3:130.

34. Ibid., 3:224–26.

35. Ibid., 4:10–12; Niv, *History of the Irgun Zvai Leumi* 5:330–31, 338; Begin, *Revolt*, 310.

36. Begin, *Underground*, 4:21–27, 42–44.

37. Ibid., 4:63–65.

38. Ibid., 4:95–97, 103 (reprint from *Herut*, no. 82–83).

39. Begin, *Underground*, 4:130, 209–10.

40. Ibid., 4:167–69.

41. [M. Begin], "Relations with the Soviet Union," *Herut*, no. 85, January 1948. Begin later eliminated this article from his collected writings, in view of Israel's deteriorating relations with the USSR. It did not fit his self-image as a prophet and liberator.

42. Begin, *Underground*, 4:181.

43. [Begin], "The Semi-Fertile Crescent," *Herut*, no. 90 (February 1948).

44. Begin, *Underground*, 4:282–85; Begin, *Revolt*, 221–23.

45. Begin, *Underground*, 4:136–38; "'How Dissidence Could be Justified,'" *Herut*, no. 87. On Begin's excuse see *Underground*, 4:292, and *Revolt*, 424. On the "operative agreement" see *Underground*, 4:308–9.

46. Begin, *Underground*, 4:245–47, 248–49, 263–68.

47. Ibid., 4:289–93.

48. Ibid., 4:325–26.

49. Ibid., 4:326–33.

50. *Herut*, no. 99, [15] June 1948, in *Psychological Warfare*, ed. Tavin and Alexander, 251–57.

51. Begin, *Revolt*, 242–51. Begin's version must be compared with Ben-Gurion's diary and the cabinet protocol, which make it clear that on 20 June the cabinet was unanimously behind Ben-Gurion (Cabinet Protocols, 2:51–56). Out of the ten present, nine voted in favor of use of force (Levin, Remez, and Shapira were absent).

52. M. Begin, "The Truth about Altalena," 22 June 1948, IZL broadcast, 20/75, HA.

53. The Voice of Herut (Herut Independent Radio Station), "The Day of Oath," 26 August 1948, 20/75, HA.

54. M. Begin, "Five Principles," *Hamashkif*, 27 August 1948.

55. See Begin's speech in *Herut*, 20 October 1948; M. Begin, "Freedom, Abundance and True-Peace [Shlom-Emet]," *Herut*, 14 November 1948. Here Begin admitted that on socioeconomic issues he had only "headlines" to offer.

56. Dr. Y. H. Yeivin, "The Torturous Crystallization of a Liberation Movement," *Herut*, 3 October 1948.

57. Dr. Y. H. Yeivin, "The Conservatism of Regime and the Process of the Hebrew Revolution," *Herut*, 8 October 1948.

58. Dr. Y. H. Yeivin, "Yosi Ben-Yosi's 'Declaration' and the Announcement of Mapai's Foreign Minister," *Herut*, 19 November 1948.

59. Dr. Y. H. Yeivin, "The Surrender of the Provisional Government," *Herut*, 26 November 1948.

60. Y. Odem, "Peace? Yes, but True-Peace," *Herut*, 14 January 1949.

61. U.-Z. Greenberg, "Chapters in the Theory of the State," *Herut*, 21 January 1949.

62. "Herut Program for the Founding Assembly," ibid.

63. [Unsigned], "Jabotinsky's Loyalists—Be Faithful to His Doctrine," *Herut*, 25 January 1949.

64. Editorial, "How They Gained the Majority," *Herut*, 27 January 1949.

65. Dr. Y. Bader, "And Therefore We Will Go On!" *Herut*, 28 January 1949.

66. M. Begin, "Government and Opposition," *Herut*, 4 February 1949.

67. Dr. Y. H. Yeivin, "A Year for Operation Deir Yasin," *Herut*, 25 March 1949 (emphasis in the original).

68. Y. Odem, "For the Information of the Arab Members of Knesset," *Herut*, 24 June 1949; E. Jabotinsky, "Open Talk to the Arabs," *Herut*, 5 August 1949. Jabotinsky's son, now an MK, did not mention transfer but recalled his father's promise (1940) of an Arab president in a Jewish state. But unlike his father he hinted at a new Hebrew ("Canaanite") culture, which the Arabs of Israel would help spread through the region (see chapter 11, this volume).

69. S. Merlin, "The Mania for Fiasco," *Herut*, 26 August 1949.

Bibliography

Manuscript Sources

Central Zionist Archives, Jerusalem

Protocols of the Jewish Agency Executive S/100
Protocols of the Small Zionist Actions Committee S5
Va'ad Leumi Executive and Full Session J1
Political Department S25
London Jewish Agency and Zionist Office Z4
Jewish Agency Office, New York Z5
Nachum Goldman Bureau, Geneva Z6
Aliyah Hadashah files J18
Private archives: F. Rosenblueth, M. Grossman

Labor Party Archives, Bet Berl

Mapai Convention, Mapai Council, Mapai Center, Mapai Political Committee,
Mapai Secretariat

Moreshet Ben-Gurion Archives, Sde Boker

Ben-Gurion diary
Ben-Gurion private correspondence

Weizmann Archives, Rehovot

Hakibbutz Hameuchad Archives, Efal

Hatnua Le'achdut Ha'avodah, Council and Center, correspondence, Galili files

Haganah Archives, Tel Aviv

Hashomer Hatza'ir Archives, Givat Haviva

Protocols of Hakibbutz Ha'artzi Council, Mapam Center, Secretariat, and Political Committee

Israel State Archives

Cabinet Protocols
Foreign Office files

Jabotinsky Institute

Irgun Zvai Leumi files

Lavon Institute Archives: Histadrut Archives

Actions Committee files

Central Archives for the History of the Jewish People

Magnes files

St. Antony's College, Oxford

Cunningham Papers

Hadassah Archives, New York

Executive and correspondence

United Nations Archives, New York

United Nations Special Committee on Palestine files

Published Documents

The Case for a Bi-National State Palestine. Memorandum Prepared by Hashomer Hatza'ir Workers' Party of Palestine. Tel Aviv: Hashomer Hatza'ir Center, March 1946.

Documents on the Foreign Policy of Israel. Israel State Archives. 1981–. Ed. Y. Freundlich et al. Vols. 1–4 (14 May 1948–December 1949). Jerusalem, 1981–84. Vol. 1: May–September 1948 (ed. Y. Freundlich, Jerusalem, 1981). Vol. 2: October 1948–April 1949 (ed. Y. Freundlich, Jerusalem, 1984). Vol. 3: Armistice Negotiations with the Arab State, December 1948–July 1949 (ed. Y. Rosenthal, Jerusalem, 1983). Vol. 4: May–December 1949 (ed. Y. Rosenthal, Jerusalem, 1986).

Foreign Relations of the United States. 1947: vol. V, *The Near East and Africa* (Washington, 1971); 1948: vol. V, part 2, *The Near East, South Asia, and Africa* (Washington, 1976); 1949: vol. VI, *The Near East, South Asia, and Africa* (Washington, 1977). Published by the Government Printing Office.

Hashomer Hatza'ir Workers' Party in Eretz Israel: Founding Conference. Tel Aviv: Hashomer Hatza'ir Center, June 1946.

The Jewish Case before the Anglo-American Committee of Inquiry on Palestine as Presented by the Jewish Agency for Palestine: Statements and Memoranda. Jerusalem, 1946.

The Jewish Plan for Palestine: Memoranda and Statements. Presented by the Jewish Agency for Palestine to the United Nations Special Committee for Palestine. Jerusalem: The Jewish Agency for Palestine, 1947.

Knesset Record (Divrei Haknesset)

The Letters and Papers of Chaim Weizmann. Series A: *Letters,* 23 vols., ed. L. Stein et al., 1968–80. Vols. 1–3: Oxford, Oxford University Press. Vols. 4–5: Jerusalem, Israel University Press. Vol. 6: Oxford: Oxford University Press; Jerusalem: Israel University Press. Vol. 7: Jerusalem, Israel University Press. Vols. 8–23: Jerusalem, Israel University Press; New Brunswick, N.J.: Transactions/Rutgers University Press. Series B: *Papers,* 2 vols., ed. B. Litvinoff. New Brunswick, N.J.: Rutgers University Press; Jerusalem: Israel University Press, 1979–83.

Levchinat Hederech (Inspecting the way), published by a group of Mapai members. Tel Aviv, 1947.

Now or Never: Proceedings of the Mapai Center in the Closing Year of the British Mandate. 2 vols. Ed. M. Avizohar and M. Bareli. Bet Berl: Ayanot, 1989. In Hebrew.

Palestine. Statement of Information Relating to Acts of Violence. Presented to Parliament by the Secretary of State for the Colonies, July 1946. Cmd. 6873.

Palestine. No. 1 (1947) Proposals for the Future of Palestine, July 1946–February 1947. Presented to Parliament by the Secretary of State for the Colonies and the Secretary of State for Foreign Affairs. Cmd. 7044.

Political and Diplomatic Documents, December 1947–13 May 1948. Ed. G. Yogev. Jerusalem: Central Zionist Archives and Israel State Archives, 1979.

Protocol of the 22nd Zionist Congress, Basel, 9–24 December 1946. Jerusalem: The Jewish Agency for Palestine, n.d. [1947]. In Hebrew.

Protocols of the People's Administration, 18 April–13 May 1948. Jerusalem, 1978. In Hebrew.

Protocols of the Provisional State Council, 1948–1949. 2 vols. Tel Aviv, n.d. [1949].

Psychological Warfare and Propaganda: Irgun Documentation. Ed. E. Tavin and Y. Alexander. Wilmington, Del.: Scholarly Resources, 1982.

The Road to Bi-National Independence for Palestine: Memorandum of the Hashomer Hatza'ir Workers' Party of Palestine. Tel Aviv: Executive Committee of the Hashomer Hatza'ir Workers' Party, August 1947.

United Nations. *Official Records of the First Special Session of the General Assembly.* Vol. 1: *Plenary Meetings, Verbatim Record, 28 April–15 May 1947.* Lake Success, N.Y.

The Unity Conference of Hashomer Hatza'ir Party in Eretz Israel and Le'achdut Ha'avodah–Poale Zion Party. Tel Aviv, n.d. [23–24 January 1948].

Newspapers

Al Hamishmar
Amudim
Ashmoret
Ba'ayot
Ba'ayot Hayom
Ba'ayot Hazman
Beterem
Davar
Ha'aretz
Hachomah
Hahevrah
Hamashkif
Ha'oved Hatsioni
Hapoel Hatza'ir
Herut
Ma'arachot
Milchamtenu
Mishmar
Mishmeret
Mitteilungsblatt
She'ifoteinu
Yediot [Bulletin] *Hatnuah Le'achdut Ha'avodah*

Books and Articles

Allon, Y. *Ma'arachot Palmach.* Tel Aviv: HaKibbutz HaMeuchad, 1965. In Hebrew.

Alteras, I. *Eisenhower and Israel: U.S.-Israeli Relations, 1953–1960.* Gainesville: University Press of Florida, 1993.

Arlosoroff, C. *Jerusalem Diary.* Tel Aviv: Mapai, 1949. In Hebrew.

Auerbach, S., et al., eds. *Between War and Peace.* Merchavia: Hashomer Hazai'r, 1943. In Hebrew.

Avineri, S., ed. *David Ben-Gurion as a Labor Leader.* Tel Aviv: Am Oved, 1988.

Baffy: The Diaries of Blanche Dugdale, 1936–1947. Ed. N. A. Rose. London: Vallentine, Mitchell, 1973.

Begin, M. *In the Underground.* 4 vols. Tel Aviv: Hadar, 1959; rpt. 1978. In Hebrew.

———. *The Revolt.* London: W. H. Allen, 1950.

———. *The Revolt: The Memoirs of the Commander of the Irgun Zvai Leumi.* Tel Aviv: Achiasaf, 1950; 5th ed., 1962. In Hebrew.

Ben-Gurion, D. *Bama'arachah.* 5 vols. Tel Aviv: Mapai, 1957 (1st ed., 1947–49). In Hebrew.

———. *Fighting Israel.* 5 vols. Tel Aviv: Mapai, 1959. In Hebrew.

———. *Israel: A Personal History.* New York: Funk and Wagnalls; Tel Aviv: Sabra, 1971.

———. *Letters to Paula.* London: Vallentine, Mitchell, 1971.

———. *Letters to Paula and the Children.* Tel Aviv: Am Oved, 1968. In Hebrew.

———. *Meetings with Arab Leaders.* Tel Aviv: Am Oved, 1968. In Hebrew. (*My Talks with Arab Leaders.* Jerusalem: Keter Books, 1972. In English.)

———. *Memoirs.* Vol. 2: *1934–1935.* Tel Aviv: Am Oved, 1972. In Hebrew.

———. *Memoirs.* Vol. 3: *1936.* Tel Aviv: Am Oved, 1973. In Hebrew.

———. *Memoirs.* Vol. 4: *1937.* Tel Aviv: Am Oved, 1976. In Hebrew.

———. *Memoirs.* Vol. 5: *1938.* Tel Aviv: Am Oved, 1982. In Hebrew.

———. *Memoirs (January–August 1939).* Tel Aviv: Am Oved, 1987. In Hebrew.

———. *Memoirs (September 1939–April 1940): Fighting as a Nation.* Ed. M. Avizohar. Tel Aviv: Am Oved, 1997. In Hebrew.

———. *Memoirs (June 1946–March 1947): Toward the End of the Mandate.* Ed. M. Avizohar. Tel Aviv: Am Oved, 1993. In Hebrew.

———. *Memoirs (March–November 1947): Chimes of Independence.* Ed. M. Avizohar. Tel Aviv: Am Oved, 1993. In Hebrew.

———. *The Restored State of Israel.* 2 vols. Tel Aviv: Am Oved, 1969. In Hebrew. (See English version, *Israel: A Personal History.*)

———. *Rebirth and Destiny of Israel.* New York: Philosophical Library, 1956.

———. *Vision and Road.* 5 vols. Tel Aviv: Mapai, 1951. In Hebrew.

———. *War Diary.* 3 vols. Ed. G. Rivlin and E. Orren. 1st ed., Tel Aviv: Ministry of Defense, 1982; 3d ed., Tel Aviv: Ministry of Defense, 1984. In Hebrew.

Bialer, U. *Between East and West: Israel's Foreign Policy Orientation, 1948–1956.* Cambridge: Cambridge University Press, 1990.

———. "The Czech-Israeli Arms Deal Revisited." *Journal of Strategic Studies* 8, no. 2 (1987): 307–15.

Bohlen, C. E. *Witness to History, 1929–1969.* New York: W. W. Norton, 1973.

Brands, H. W. *Inside the Cold War: Loy Henderson and the Rise of the American Empire.* New York and Oxford: Oxford University Press, 1991.

Buber, M., J. L. Magnes, and E. Simon, eds. *Toward Union in Palestine: Essays on Zionism and Jewish-Arab Cooperation.* Jerusalem: Ihud (Union) Association, 1947.

Buber, M., J. L. Magnes, and M. Smilansky, eds. *Palestine: A Bi-National State.* New York: Ihud (Union) Association of Palestine, August 1946.

Bullock, A. *Ernest Bevin: Foreign Secretary, 1945–1951.* London: Heinemann, 1983.

Caplan, N. *Futile Diplomacy.* Vol. 2: *Arab-Zionist Negotiations and the End of the Mandate.* London: Frank Cass, 1986.

Cohen, A. *Israel and the Arab World.* Merchavia: Sifriat Poalim, 1964 (in Hebrew); New York: Funk and Wagnalls, and London: W. H. Allen, 1970.

Cohen, M. J. *Palestine and the Great Powers, 1945–1948*. Princeton, N.J.: Princeton University Press, 1982.

———. *Truman and Israel*. Berkeley: University of California Press, 1990.

Crossman, R. *Palestine Mission: A Personal Record*. London: Hamish Hamilton, 1946.

Danin, E. *A Zionist without Condition*. Ed. G. Rivlin. Tel Aviv: Kidum, 1987. In Hebrew.

Darwin, J. *Britain and Decolonization*. London: Macmillan, 1988.

———. *The End of Empire*. Oxford: Basil Blackwell, 1991.

Elath, E. *The Struggle for Statehood: Washington, 1945–1948*. 3 vols. Tel Aviv: Am Oved, 1979. In Hebrew.

The Forrestal Diaries. Ed. W. Millis. London: Cassell, 1952.

Galili, I. *El Veal. Letters and Personalities*, Ed. A. Azariahu and D. Eshkol. Efal: Yad Tabenkin, 1990. In Hebrew.

Ganin, Z. *Truman, American Jewry, and Israel, 1945–1948*. New York: Holmes and Meier, 1979.

Garcia-Granados, J. *The Birth of Israel: The Drama as I Saw It*. New York: A. Knopf, 1949; Tel Aviv: Achiasaf, 1950 (in Hebrew).

Glatzer, N. N., and P. R. Mendes-Flohr, eds. *The Letters of Martin Buber: A Life of Dialogue*. New York: Schocken Books, 1991.

Goren, A. A., ed. *Dissenter in Zion: From the Writings of Judah L. Magnes*. Cambridge and London: Harvard University Press,1982.

Goren, Y. *Israel Bar-Yehuda: Emissary of the Movement*. Efal: Yad Tabenkin, 1992. In Hebrew.

Gorny, Y. "'From Class to Nation': Historical Sources and Ideological Meaning." In *David Ben-Gurion as a Labor Leader*, ed. S. Avineri, 73–91. Tel Aviv: Am Oved, 1988. In Hebrew.

Heller, J. "The Anglo-American Commission of Inquiry, 1945–46: The Zionist Reaction Reconsidered." In *Zionism and Arabism in Palestine and Israel*, ed. E. Kedourie and S. G. Haim, 137–70. London, 1982. Reprinted in J. Reinharz and A. Shapira, eds., *Essential Papers on Zionism*, 689–723. New York and London: New York University Press, 1996.

———. "The Failure of Fascism in Jewish Palestine." In *Fascism Outside Europe*, ed. T. U. Larsen. New York: Columbia University Press, forthcoming.

———. "The Failure of a Mission: Bernadotte and Palestine 1948." *Journal of Contemporary History* 14, no. 3 (1979): 513–34.

———. "From the `Black Sabbath' to Partition: Summer 1946 as a Turning Point in the History of Zionist Policy." *Zion* 43 (1978): 314–61. In Hebrew.

———. "Roosevelt, Stalin and the Palestine Problem at Yalta." *Wiener Library Bulletin* 30, no. 41–42 (1977): 25–35.

———. *Lehi: Ideology and Politics, 1940–1949*. 2 vols. Jerusalem: Keter and Shazar Center, 1989. In Hebrew.

———. *The Stern Gang: Ideology, Politics and Terror, 1940–1949*. London: Frank Cass, 1995.

Hirst, D. *The Gun and the Olive Branch: The Roots of Violence in the Middle East.* New York: Harcourt Brace Jovanovich, 1977; 2d ed., London: Faber and Faber, 1984.

Horowitz, D. *A State in the Making.* Tel Aviv: Schocken Books, 1951; New York: A. A. Knopf, 1953.

Horowitz, D., and M. Lissak. *The Origins of the Israeli Polity: Palestine under the Mandate.* Tel Aviv: Am Oved, 1977 (in Hebrew); Chicago: University of Chicago Press, 1978.

Ishai, Y. *Factionalism in the Labor Movement: Faction B in Mapai.* Tel Aviv: Am Oved, 1978. In Hebrew.

Kaplansky, S. *Vision and Fulfillment.* Merchavia: Sifriat Poalim, 1950. In Hebrew.

Khalidi, W., ed. *From Haven to Conquest: Readings in Zionism and the Palestine Problem until 1948.* Beirut: Institute of Palestine Studies, 1971.

Landauer, G. *Five Essays on Aliyah Hadashah.* Jerusalem: Aliyah Hadasha Publication, 1944. In Hebrew.

Leffler, M. *Preponderance of Power: National Security, the Truman Administration and the Cold War.* Stanford, Calif.: Stanford University Press, 1992.

Liebenstein, E. *With the Zionist Debate.* Tel Aviv: Am Oved, 1944. In Hebrew.

Louis, William Roger, *The British Empire in the Middle East, 1945–1951: Arab Nationalism, the United States and Post-War Imperialism.* Oxford: Oxford University Press, 1984.

Magnes, J. L. *In the Perplexity of the Times.* Jerusalem: The Hebrew University, 1946. In Hebrew.

Magnes, J. L., M. Reiner, Lord Samuel, E. Simon, and M. Smilansky, eds. *Palestine—Divided or United? The Case for a Bi-National Palestine before the United Nations.* Jerusalem: Ihud (Union) Association, 1947.

Margalit, E. *Hashomer Hatza'ir: From Youth Commune to Revolutionary Marxism, 1913–1936.* Tel Aviv: Tel Aviv University, 1971. In Hebrew.

Mendes-Flohr, P. R., ed. *A Land of Two Peoples: Martin Buber on Jews and Arabs.* New York: Oxford University Press, 1983; Tel Aviv: Schocken, 1988 (in Hebrew).

Morris, B. *The Birth of the Palestinian Refugee Problem, 1947–1949.* Cambridge: Cambridge University Press, 1989; Tel Aviv: Am Oved, 1991 (in Hebrew).

———. *1948 and After.* Oxford: Oxford University Press, 1994.

———. "Notes on Zionist Historiography and the Transfer Idea, 1937–1944." In *Between Vision and Revision: One Hundred Years of Zionist Historiography,* ed. Y. Weitz. Jerusalem: Shazar Center, 1997. In Hebrew.

———. "Yosef Weitz and the 'Transfer Committee,' 1948–1949." *Middle Eastern Studies* 22, no. 4 (October 1986):522–61.

Namir, M. *Israeli Mission to Moscow.* Tel Aviv: Am Oved, 1971. In Hebrew.

Niv, D. *History of the Irgun Zvai Leumi.* 6 vols. Tel Aviv: Hadar, 1965–80. In Hebrew.

Pappé, I. *Britain and the Arab-Israeli Conflict, 1948–1951.* London: Macmillan in association with St. Antony's College, Oxford, 1988.

————. *The Making of the Arab-Israeli Conflict, 1947–51*. London: I. B. Tauris, 1992.

Rabinovich, I. *The Road Not Taken: Early Arab-Israeli Negotiations*. New York: Oxford University Press, 1991.

Ratner, Y. *My Life and Myself*. Tel Aviv: Schocken, 1978. In Hebrew.

Ro'i, Y. *Soviet Decision Making in Practice: The USSR and Israel, 1947–1954*. New Brunswick, N.J., and London: Transactions Books, 1980.

Rose, N. A. *Chaim Weizmann: A Biography*. London: Weidenfeld and Nicolson, 1986.

————."The Seventh Dominion." *Historical Journal* 14, no. 4 (1971): 397–416

————. "Weizmann, Ben-Gurion, and the 1946 Crisis in the Zionist Movement." In *Power, Personalities and Politics: Essays in Honour of Donald Cameron Watt*, ed. M. G. Fry, 258–77. London: Frank Cass, 1992.

Sasson, E. *On the Road to Peace: Letters and Conversations*. Tel Aviv: Am Oved, 1978. In Hebrew.

Shapira, A. *The Army Controversy, 1948: Ben-Gurion's Struggle for Control*. Tel Aviv: HaKibbutz HaMeuchad, 1985. In Hebrew.

————. *Land and Power: The Zionist Resort to Force, 1881–1948*. New York: Oxford University Press, 1992.

Sharett, M. *At the Threshold of Statehood, 1946–1949*. Tel Aviv: Am Oved, 1966. In Hebrew.

————. *Political Diary*. 5 vols. Tel Aviv: Am Oved, 1968–79. In Hebrew.

Shlaim, A. *Collusion across the Jordan: King Abdullah, the Zionist Movement, and the Partition of Palestine, 1921–1951*. Oxford: Clarendon Press, 1988.

————. *The Politics of Partition: King Abdullah, the Zionists and Palestine, 1921–1951*. Oxford: Oxford University Press, 1990.

Slonim, S. "The 1948 American Embargo on Arms to Palestine." *Political Science Quarterly* 94, no. 3 (Fall 1979):495–514.

Slutsky, Y. *History of the Haganah*. 3 vols. Tel Aviv: Ma'arachot and Am Oved, 1963–72.

Sofer, S. *Begin: An Anatomy of Leadership*. Oxford: Basil Blackwell, 1988.

Vereté, M. *From Palmerston to Balfour: Collected Essays*. Ed. N. A. Rose. London: Frank Cass, 1992.

Yaari, M., and Y. Hazan. *Against the Current*. Merchavia: Hakibbutz Haarzi, 1943. In Hebrew.

Zait, D. *Pioneers in the Maze of Politics: The Kibbutz Movement, 1927–1948*. Jerusalem: Yad Izhak Ben-Zvi, 1993. In Hebrew.

————. *Zionism and Peace*. Givat Haviva: Sifriat Poalim, 1985. In Hebrew.

Index

Joseph Heller is associate professor of international relations at the Hebrew University of Jerusalem. He is the author of *The Stern Gang: Ideology, Politics, and Terror, 1940–1948*, and editor of *Zionist Politics, 1936–1948: A Documentary Record*.